TExES
The Texas Examination of Educator Standards
Second Edition

TExES

The Texas Examination of Educator Standards

Second Edition

Ann Hall, Carolyn McCall,
and Linda Burkhardt

KAPLAN
PUBLISHING

New York • Chicago

TExES™ is a registered trademark of National Evaluation Systems, Inc.™ (NES®).

This publication is designed to provide accurate and authoritative information in regard to the subject matter covered. It is sold with the understanding that the publisher is not engaged in rendering legal, accounting, or other professional service. If legal advice or other expert assistance is required, the services of a competent professional should be sought.

Editorial Director: Jennifer Farthing
Senior Editor: Ruth Baygell
Production Editor: Caitlin Ostrow
Production Artist: John Christensen
Cover Designer: Carly Schnur

© 2006 by Kaplan, Inc.

Published by Kaplan Publishing, a division of Kaplan, Inc.
888 Seventh Ave.
New York, NY 10106

All rights reserved. The text of this publication, or any part thereof, may not be reproduced in any manner whatsoever without written permission from the publisher.

Printed in the United States of America

November 2006
10 9 8 7 6 5 4 3 2 1

ISBN-13: 978-1-4195-4222-0
ISBN-10: 1-4195-4222-2

Kaplan Publishing books are available at special quantity discounts to use for sales promotions, employee premiums, or educational purposes. Please call our Special Sales Department to order or for more information at 800-621-9621, ext. 4444, e-mail kaplanpubsales@kaplan.com, or write to Kaplan Publishing, 30 South Wacker Drive, Suite 2500, Chicago, IL 60606-7481.

TABLE OF CONTENTS

About the Authors vii

SECTION ONE: **Preparing for the TExES**

Chapter 1: Introducing the Texas Examination of Educator Standards (TExES)....... 3

Chapter 2: TExES Test-Taking Strategies 11

Chapter 3: How to Use the Tests in This Book 61

SECTION TWO: **TExES Domains**

Chapter 4: Domain I: Designing Instruction and Assessment to Promote Student Learning (Includes Competencies 001-004) 65

Chapter 5: Domain II: Creating a Positive Productive Classroom Environment (Includes Competencies 005-006) 77

Chapter 6: Domain III: Implementing Effective, Responsive Instruction and Assessment (Includes Competencies 007-010) 85

Chapter 7: Domain IV: Fulfilling Professional Roles and Responsibilities (Includes Competencies 011-013) 93

SECTION THREE: **Diagnostic and Practice Tests and Answers**

Chapter 8: Diagnostic All-level Pedagogy and Professional Responsibilities Test 103

Chapter 9: Diagnostic All-level Pedagogy and Professional Responsibilities Test Answers and Explanations 119

Chapter 10: Practice EC-4 Pedagogy and Professional Responsibilities Test I 139

Chapter 11: Practice EC-4 Pedagogy and Professional Responsibilities Test I Answers and Explanations 169

Chapter 12: Practice EC-4 Pedagogy and Professional Responsibilities Test II....... 207

Chapter 13: Practice EC-4 Pedagogy and Professional Responsibilities Test II Answers and Explanations 233

Chapter 14: Practice 4-8 Pedagogy and Professional Responsibilities Test III 267

Chapter 15: Practice 4-8 Pedagogy and Professional Responsibilities Test III

    Answers and Explanations 299

Chapter 16: Practice 8-12 Pedagogy and Professional Responsibilities Test IV 331

Chapter 17: Practice 8-12 Pedagogy and Professional Responsibilities Test IV

    Answers and Explanations 363

Getting Started: Advice for New Teachers 395

APPENDICES

    Appendix A: Glossary of Important TExES Terms 407

    Appendix B: Code of Ethics and Standard Practices for Texas Educators 431

    Appendix C: TExES Competencies 435

    Appendix D: List of TExES Exams Currently Available 437

About the Authors

Ann Hall received her Ph.D. from the University of Texas at Austin in Curriculum and Instruction with a specialization in Reading Education. Her 14 years at Texas State University in San Marcos, TX have included teaching courses in Reading Education, Curriculum and Instruction, and aligning the elementary teacher education curriculum to the TExES exam.

Carolyn McCall received her M.Ed. in Speech-Language Pathology and Audiology from Texas State University. She is the TExES Coordinator for Texas State University in San Marcos, TX and has extensive experience conducting training workshops and reviews for the ExCET and TExES exams. Ms. McCall's 30 years of teaching experience includes teaching classes in Special Education and serving as Director of the Academic Learning Clinic.

Linda Burkhardt received her M.Ed. in Reading Education from Texas Tech University in Lubbock, TX. Her 12 years of teaching at Texas State University have included student teacher supervisor, reading education classes, certification and placement officer, and coordinator for the ExCET Exam. She has extensive experience conducting training workshops and reviews for the ExCET and TExES exams.

www.kaptest.com/publishing

The material in this book is up-to-date at the time of publication. However, the Texas State Board for Educator Certfication and National Evaluation Systems, Inc. may have instituted changes in the test or test registration process after this book was published. Be sure to carefully read the materials you receive when you register for the test.

If there are any important late-breaking developments—or any changes or corrections to the Kaplan test preparation materials in this book—we will post that information online at www.kaptest.com/publishing. Check to see if there is any information posted there for readers of this book.

Section One

PREPARING FOR THE TExES

CHAPTER ONE

Introducing the Texas Examination of Educator Standards (TExES)

HOW TO PASS THE TEXES PEDAGOGY AND PROFESSIONAL RESPONSIBILITIES EXAM

As you begin this book, we recognize that you want to pass this exam and expect this book to help you with that task. You will undoubtedly turn to the practice exams and think to yourself, "The heck with reading this entire book. I'll just take these practice tests and then I'll pass the real exam." After talking to many students, we recognize that is the way most students think. However, we strongly encourage you to read each chapter and try to get an overview of the TExES exam. By doing that you will build a strong foundation for understanding why the TExES is important, its history, and its components.

State law passed by the Texas 78th legislature in 2003, H.B. 1002, states that failure *to acquire full certification voids the educator's employment contract without any need for a termination or non-renewal hearing.* The test is required for certification and if you don't pass the exam, the school district where you have a contract may legally void your teaching contract.

The fees for this exam are as follows: one test costs $82, two tests cost $164. In addition, as of October 1, 2003, all first-time applicants for an initial credential must be fingerprinted for a national criminal background check for $45. If you are already certified from another state or country and are seeking Texas certification, there are additional fees.

A Brief History of Recent Texas Teacher Examinations

When did all of this begin? In 1981 the Texas Legislature approved legislation to test Texas teachers. The examination used was the Examination for the Certification of Educators in Texas (ExCET). It included over 60 different tests for different certifications. Although several of these ExCET exams were discontinued in June 2003, others will be phased out between now and 2006. As the ExCETs are phased out, they are replaced by the Texas Examination of Educator Standards (TExES). How did the TExES come to be?

In 1993, ten thousand Texas educators were surveyed to determine the important proficiencies for all educators to possess for the 21st century. Public school teachers and administrators, as well as university teacher-educators participated in the survey. Almost 95% of the proficiencies on the survey were rated by the participants as of "great importance" or "very great importance." In 1994 the Texas State Board of Education adopted these teacher proficiencies as the foundation for the preparation of all teachers.

The State Board for Educator Certification (SBEC) was created in 1995 by the 74th Legislature to govern the standards of the education profession in Texas. SBEC approved and adopted proficiencies for teachers, administrators and counselors in 1997. These proficiencies, Learner-Centered Proficiencies for Teachers, are integrated into the educator preparation program approval process. (Source: *Learner-Centered Schools for Texas, A Vision of Texas Educators,* State Board of Educators Certification, Austin, TX, 1997.) Complete, approved standards are available at: http://www.sbec.state.tx.us.

Learner-Centered Proficiencies for Teachers

These proficiencies, which teachers should know and be able to do, are the foundation for Texas teachers. From them, the state has created the standards for new educators, and the TExES (Texas Examination of Educator Standards) tests new teachers on these standards.

1. **Learner-Centered Knowledge: The teacher possesses and draws on a rich knowledge of content, pedagogy, and technology to provide relevant and meaningful learning experiences for all students.**

The state of Texas is saying that in order to be certified in Texas, teachers must focus on the learner, not on the content. Teachers should be well-versed in the subject matter, how to teach (pedagogy), and technology in order to deliver meaningful instruction to each learner at the appropriate instructional level.

2. **Learner-Centered Instruction: To create a learner-centered community, the teacher collaboratively identifies needs and plans, implements and assesses instruction using technology and other resources.**

Teachers in Texas are expected to collaborate with other professionals and use technology and other resources to create an environment that is focused on each learner. Assessment is necessary in order to plan appropriate instruction for each learner. Once the appropriate level of instruction is determined, teachers in Texas must know how to deliver meaningful instruction in ways other than "stand and deliver." The state wants classrooms to use methods of learning, such as cooperative and inquiry learning, as well as direct instruction, to actively involved students in constructing new knowledge.

3. **Equity in Excellence for All Learners: The teacher responds appropriately to diverse groups of learners.**

As the demographics of Texas change, so do the demographics of the school. Teachers must learn about all students and strive to provide a quality education to all, regardless of the differences. These differences include, but are not limited to, language, ethnicity, learning ability, and gender.

4. **Learner-Centered Communication: While acting as an advocate for all students and the school, the teacher demonstrates effective professional and interpersonal communication skills.**

The teacher communicates well when speaking and writing. The teacher is aware of verbal and non-verbal forms of communication. Teachers are expected to communicate clearly when teaching students, working with the school districts, and interacting with families of students.

5. **Learner-Centered Professional Development: The teacher, as a reflective practitioner dedicated to all students' success, demonstrates a commitment to learn, to improve the profession, and to maintain professional ethics and personal integrity.**

Texas teachers are expected to continue to learn after graduation from college. In addition to professional development provided by the school district, teachers should reflect on their teaching and strive to find ways to become a better teacher and improve the teaching profession in general. At all times, teachers are bound by the *Code of Ethics and Standard Practices for Texas Educators* [see Appendix B] which includes professional ethical conduct, practices and performance, ethical conduct toward professional colleagues, and ethical conduct toward students.

What is the TExES (Texas Examination of Educator Standards)?

The Texas Education Code 21.048 requires successful performance on educator certification examinations in order to become a certified teacher in Texas. Since 1997, SBEC has developed specific standards that specify what educators should know and be able to do. These standards are based on the state-required curriculum, the Texas Essential Knowledge and Skills (TEKS), for kindergarten through grade 12. The TEKS for all grade levels are available at http://www.tea.state.tx.us/teks/. If you are not familiar with the Texas Essential Knowledge and Skills (TEKS), we suggest that you go the website above and learn about the state curriculum.

The content of the TExES Examinations is based on the TEKS. This state-required curriculum and the related standards for new educators provide vertical alignment for kindergarten through college. This alignment of kindergarten through grade 16 is an effort to provide newly certified teachers with the essential knowledge and skills to teach the appropriate TEKS for their assigned classrooms. See the appendix for a listing of all the TExES exams that are currently offered in Texas and the dates for future tests that are being developed.

All the TExES Exams are organized the same way. The framework of each exam is organized around the broad areas of content covered called domains. Each domain contains competencies that define the domain in more detail. Each competency is composed of two parts. First, the competency statement broadly explains what an entry-level educator should know and be able to do. Following the competency statement are the descriptive statements explaining in greater detail the knowledge and skills that may be tested. Specific domains, competencies, and descriptive statements will be discussed in detail in later chapters.

This particular study guide is limited to the TExES exam that measures educators' entry-level knowledge and skills about how to teach—the Pedagogy and Professional Responsibilities (PPR) exam. Other TExES exams cover specific subject matter content.

Kaplan Tip: This test does not test your knowledge of content or subject matter. It covers only pedagogy, classroom management, the role of assessment, diversity, working with families, and professional development. For this reason, by taking any of the four practice tests you will be practicing pedagogical concepts that are the same at all teaching levels.

Who takes the Pedagogy and Professional Responsibilities (PPR)?

Everyone seeking an initial certificate in Texas must pass a pedagogy test (PPR) and content-area requirements. There are four different pedagogy tests in the new TExES. The grade level of pedagogy must correspond to the grade level of the initial content-area certificate sought. The content-area test, not the pedagogy test, determines the certificate and its levels. See the table below.

Initial Certificate Being Sought	Acceptable TExES Pedagogy Tests (PPR)
Early Childhood–Grade 4 (EC-4)	PPR EC-4 or PPR EC-12
Grade 4–Grade 8 (4-8)	PPR 4-8 or PPR EC-12
Grade 8–Grade 12 (8-12)	PPR 8-12 or PPR EC-12
Early Childhood–Grade 12 (EC-12)	PPR EC-12

What is a passing score and what happens if I fail?

For all TExES tests, the scaled score range is 100–300. The minimum passing scaled score is 240. Students not passing a test may retake the test at any subsequent test administration date.

When are the tests given?

The TExES is typically given multiple times each year. The TExES tests are given each month in the calendar year. The registration brochure will provide you with specific dates, registration deadlines, and test locations. Additionally, the EC-4 PPR and the Generalist EC-4 may be taken on computers at specially equipped computer test centers across the state. These computer administered tests are appropriately named TExES Computer-Administered Tests (TExES CAT). The TExES CAT costs $82 for each test.

Where can I find information about registering for the TExES?

Current registration information is available at http://www.texes.nesinc.com or by calling 1-800-523-7088.

Why is it important to study for the TExES?

Teacher assessments must ensure that teachers can demonstrate higher-order thinking; that the purposes of instruction relate to real-world outcomes; and that the interdisciplinary nature of the curriculum, rather than isolated skills and knowledge, is the focus of instruction. Teachers must be prepared to use new technologies so that students will be prepared to enter a high-tech world as they leave the school system. Today's teachers must demonstrate flexibility and creativity in solving the problems they face in their classrooms. The teaching role has expanded to communicating within the larger school organization and local community. To this end, the TExES tests measure an individual's preparedness to deal with changing roles and expectations that teachers face in Texas public schools.

As previously discussed, the TExES tests are based on broad domains and specific competencies that are tied to the TEKS and current standards. The state is interested in determining if entry-level teachers know how to teach and know subject matter content. For this reason, it is important to realize that the test is biased. The state is saying, "If you remove all obstacles and excuses, will this teacher know best practice?" This means that you must not let prior experiences or current opinions interfere with knowing what is "best practice." Your teacher training may have covered all the domains and competencies; however, our experience from previous test-takers indicates that reviewing the domains and important concepts improve test scores. For example, many of the test questions have two answers that seem correct. Those students who study for the test are better informed of what competencies the state values and which "buzz word" will assist you in finding the correct response. Chapter 2 will provide you with specific strategies for choosing that correct response.

How will I find out how I did on the TExES?

You will receive your official test results by mail approximately four weeks after taking the exam. Unofficial scores are reported on the Internet by 5:00 PM Central Standard Time on the day official scores are mailed.

About the Pedagogy and Professional Responsibilities (PPR) Tests

There are four PPR tests offered in the TExES. They are EC- 4 (Early Childhood through 4th grade), EC 4-8 (4th grade through 8th grade), EC 8-12 (8th grade through 12th grade), and EC-12 (Early Childhood through 12th grade). Each test covers the same domains and competencies. Each test is composed of 80 multiple-choice questions and about 10 questions that are on the test for field-testing to use on future exams. Our practice tests in this book contain 80 multiple-choice questions that reflect the balance of the domains as they would appear on the real test.

Introducing the Texas Examination of Educator Standards (TExES)

Each test is a criterion-referenced test, which means that the test measures your performance against specific criteria rather than comparing your score to others taking the test. For example, your score report will indicate your performance in each domain as well as your proficiency in answering each question based on the competencies. It should be noted that Domain I and Domain III each comprise 31% of the exam for all four tests. Domain IV is 23% of the test and Domain II is 15%. These percentages will not change from test to test, but the weight of each competency within the domains will. For example, the 4-8 test may have 9 questions about a particular competency while the 8-12 test may have only 5 questions about the same compentency.

How the PPR is scored

There is not a penalty for guessing on the TExES exams. You should answer every question.

How Do I Register?

Be sure to refer to the appropriate text or web site to find current information about the TExES dates, times and deadlines. Here is a list of web sites that you will find helpful:

State Board of Educator Certification
http://www.sbec.state.tx.us/

Registration Bulletin for the TExES
http://www.texes.nesinc.com

Educator Standards
http://www.sbec.state.tx.us/SBECOnline/standtest/educstan.asp

Test Frameworks
http://www.sbec.state.tx.us/SBECOnline/standtest/testfram.asp

Test Dates
http://www.sbec.state.tx.us

Study Guides and Preparation Manuals
http://www.sbec.state.tx.us/SBECOnline/standtest/guidprepman.asp

Test Scores and Reports
http://www.sbec.state.tx.us/SBECOnline/standtest/scorrept.asp

CHAPTER TWO

TExES Test-Taking Strategies

This chapter provides information that will allow you to apply a strategy to every question you encounter on the TExES. The suggestions, strategies, and test-taking tips offered in this chapter are the result of our experience over the past five years of providing reviews to students taking the exam that focuses on teaching and professionalism. Feedback from former students who had been unsuccessful on the test has taught us how best to prepare students to take the exam. Many of these students returned to us after having taken the test numerous times and told us how the strategies had or had not helped them. From this feedback, we have developed these new strategies. We encourage you to study the examples provided, utilize the strategies as you work on practice items, and apply them consistently so they will become second nature to you. We believe the use of these strategies will make the difference for YOU!

The State of Texas is known for cowboys, rodeos, hot peppers, and roping events. To keep this study guide within that genre, you will see analogies to these and other Texas symbols. As we describe the strategies to you, we will use terms such as "cowboy whispers" to remind you to use self-talk, or whispers, as you analyze each question. We will ask you to watch out for lariat words. These are words that may clue you to a correct answer. Because a lariat is used to capture something, we want you to capture the concepts with the lariat words we identify for you. You will also be reminded to be alert to the "red pepper words." These are words that should be a clue to you that you may want to avoid the selection of a particular answer that contains one of these words. But check out the "green pepper words" and consider these closely as possible clues for narrowing your answer choices.

So let's "giddy-up" and head to the corral to prepare for the test.

As we round the bend to get to the corral, we see a line of stars containing important information about the TExES... we'll call these the **13 Stars of TExES**. They are:

1. Human development
2. Diversity
3. Designing effective instruction and assessment
4. Learning theory; factors impacting learning; planning instruction and assessment
5. Classroom climate and environment
6. Classroom organization and management
7. Communication
8. Student engagement
9. Technology
10. Assessment and feedback
11. Family involvement and communication with families
12. Professional growth and interactions
13. Legal and ethical requirements of education in Texas

These 13 stars are quick ways to familiarize yourself with the 13 TExES competencies and are described in detail in Chapters 4–7.

As you approach each question, help yourself understand what you are being asked by using "cowboy whispers" or "private speech." We tend to think that as adults we should read only silently, but we would like to share with you a tool that will be very useful when you are taking the TExES examination. We call it "private speech." We have been taught since our youth that moving our lips or reading aloud is inappropriate. We would like to change that perception by telling you that in moving your lips while you read, you are discovering a way to absorb concepts. To answer the TExES questions correctly, it is important that you internalize the information conveyed in the scenarios and questions. As you move your lips, you are engaging your brain at a different level and are acquiring a new study skill.

As you analyze each question, you will begin to see words and phrases that are related to the competencies in that they reflect important ideas and concepts that the State of Texas wants you to utilize in teaching. We call these your **"Lariat Words and Phrases."** Get your lariat around these ideas and make them meaningful by thinking of how they fit within the context of your teaching and your students' learning. These **Lariat Words and Phrases** are listed as follows:

TExES Test-Taking Strategies

Lariat Words and Phrases	Competency Source
Lifelong learning	001
Positive environment	001
Developmentally appropriate	001
Self–esteem	001
Diversity	002
Appropriate accommodations	002
Integrated learning	003
Texas Essential Knowledge and Skills (TEKS)	003
Age appropriate	003
Student reflection and self-assessment	003
Active learning	004
Instructional planning	004
Approaches to learning (auditory, visual, tactile, kinesthetic)	004
Cooperative learning	004
Prior knowledge	004
Teacher as facilitator	004
Student as active learner	004
Modeling	004 & 006
Higher-order thinking skills (HOTS)	004 & 007
High academic expectations	005
Equity in learning	005
Productive classroom environment	005
Collaboration	005
Teacher enthusiasm	005
Safe, nurturing environment	005
Classroom arrangement	005
Active student engagement	005
Organizational skills	006
Routines and procedures	006
Managing student behavior	006
Inquiry	007
Critical thinking	007
Discovery and exploration	007
Problem–solving	007
Open-ended questioning	007

TExES

Appropriate and effective communication	007
Skilled questioning	007
Motivational strategies	008
Appropriate use of technology	009
Ongoing assessment and feedback	010
Involvement with families	011
Professional development	012
Professional relationships	012
Teacher reflection and self-assessment	012
State code of ethics	013

As you go through the test (and throughout your studying), you may notice some words that often indicate a wrong answer. Although this may not ALWAYS be the case, watch out for these **"red pepper words."** Don't let them burn you!

List
Handout
All students
Predetermined
Precisely
Concrete (this could be ok, but may not be)
Worksheets
Lecture
Confront

The list of words on the previous page is intended to give you some "warnings" along the way that these may not be your best choices; however, you will often find some words that will assist you in focusing on the correct answer! We call these words **"green pepper words."** Like the previous list, these "green pepper words" may not ALWAYS indicate a correct response, but we believe that they will OFTEN serve as an indicator to point you to the correct choice. Some of these words and phrases include:

- **Most likely**
- **Most appropriate**
- **Except**
- **Best illustrates**
- **Best describes**
- **First step**
- **Primary purpose**
- **Not**
- **Higher-order thinking**
- **Model**
- **Foster**
- **Compare-contrast**

Now you have some ideas to help you as you get ready to take the actual test. Before moving on with a "tried and true" strategy, let's sum up the things you need to do as you approach the test.

1. Use your "cowboy whispers" as you quietly move your lips while reading each scenario and question.
2. Familiarize yourself with the lariat words and phrases as a method for keeping the main idea of each competency in mind.
3. Remember to think about the red and green pepper words to help you know what may or may not be an appropriate choice.

With all this in mind, we now give you a strategy to apply as you approach each test item. We call it the **TEXAS procedure** and here is how it works. Read each question and think through it using this format:

T – Take control. In this step, you should formulate a picture in your mind of exactly what is happening in the information presented. Is there a teacher? Who is it? What is the teacher doing? What is happening in the classroom? Who are the students? You may want to actually DRAW what is happening!

REMEMBER: Taking control does NOT mean that you are the sheriff wearing the star! Instead, you are the teacher creating the stars. Best practice for teachers in Texas includes **guiding** students, not directing them; **enabling** students, not forcing them to do things "your" way; **facilitating** their learning, not forcing it.

As you quietly move your lips while reading the information provided in the test, visualize what you have just read. Then ask yourself the following questions:

- What grade level is it?
- What is the subject matter being presented?
- What is the teacher doing?
- What are the children doing?
- Is there someone else in the classroom? If so, who is it? Is it someone from the school? Is it someone from the community? In what way might that person affect the dynamics of the classroom situation?
- Is it a diverse classroom?
- Are the students behaving (according to the test information presented)?
- What time of day is it or do you know?

Good... now you have immersed yourself in the classroom and you are ready to move on to the next step:

E – Examine the question. Put the question in your own words. Be sure you know what is being asked. Is it asking about the teacher? Is it asking about classroom management? Is it asking about the students?

X – X-ray the choices. Which choice really answers the question? Do any of the lariat words help you narrow down your choices? Delete those responses that you know are <u>wrong</u>. If the question asks about the teacher, make sure the answer relates to the teacher.

You may think you have found the answer immediately, and you may have, but rather than make your choice at this point, choose instead to delete choices that you know are not the correct ones. Most of the time, you will be able to narrow your choices down to two.

A – Assimilate knowledge. Ask yourself, "Am I selecting this answer choice based on knowledge gained from classes I have taken, from the lariat words and phrases, and from the competencies?" Then remind yourself, "I should NOT visualize the classroom where I teach or observe."

REMEMBER: In the case of the TExES, experience is not always the best teacher.

S – Scrutinize your decision. Look closely at your answer choice. Does it really answer the question? Is it consistent with what you know from the lariat words and phrases and from the competencies? When it is, grab your branding iron and mark it!

Kaplan Tip: Even though you will take only one PPR test that matches your chosen certification level, studying questions from all test levels will help establish what the State of Texas considers "best practice."

Before practicing the TEXAS strategy, here are a few reminders about the test itself.

- Each PPR test will include 80 scorable multiple-choice items and approximately 10 nonscorable items. These 10 items are typically items that the state test writers are "field testing." You will not know which items these are as you take the test; however, if you find questions that seem to cover an area that is very different from the competencies you have studied, these may be the "field test" items. In the practice tests included in this study guide, you will find only 80 items which are all focused on the TExES competencies.
- Three types of multiple-choice questions will be included on each PPR test:
    - **Single Item.** In these questions, there will be a short question stem with four possible choices. You should apply the TEXAS strategy to select the best choice.
    - **Clustered Items.** In these questions, you will find the question preceded by stimulus material that relates to the question. This stimulus material may include examples of teacher notes, student work, or descriptions of classroom situations. In these cases, you will typically be given information followed by an event to analyze, a problem to solve, or a decision to make.
    - **Teacher Decision Sets.** In these questions, you will start with a stimulus regarding situations such as a classroom occurrence, a field trip, or a parent-teacher conference. There will be one or more questions related to that stimulus, then additional stimuli will be added that lead to additional questions. A typical Teacher Decision Set includes two or more stimuli and 3–12 questions that may represent competencies from all four domains of the test.

PRACTICE OF THE TEXAS PROCEDURE

Now that you have familiarized yourself with the TEXAS procedure, you will find practice exercises for grade levels EC-4, 4-8, and 8-12 that reflect the types of questions you will encounter on the actual TExES PPR tests. Notice the single-item, clustered items, and decision set types of questions as you work through these exercises.

EC–4 Questions

Single Item

1. It was the third day of school and five-year-old Kolby sat in the corner crying. When his teacher asked him what was wrong, he said, "I don't understand you." As she questioned him about what he meant, she realized he was talking about the directions she had just given the class about changing to a different activity. What is the primary consideration a kindergarten teacher should keep in mind when presenting information to the students?

    A. As the children sit in the circle first thing in the morning, review the day's activities so the teacher does not have to interrupt the students when they are changing from one activity to another.
    B. Focus on one thing at a time and keep instructions and expectations clear and simple when talking about directions, procedures, and routines.
    C. Provide a nurturing environment by asking the students to learn the routine and then tell each other the assignments for the day because children love to learn from their peers.
    D. Using a flannel board or similar device, have pictures of what the students are to do and then remind them of the procedures and routines.

T–Take control:

Remember to say to yourself, "What is this question asking me, and what should I be thinking?" Let's mentally picture what is happening. We have a five-year-old boy sitting in the corner crying. The teacher recognizes Kolby is having a problem and discovers that he didn't understand her. She is able to get him to verbalize his concerns. We do know the teacher has just given instructions or directions so it might have something to do with that.

E—Examine the question:

Remember to put the question in your own words. So in your own words, the question, "What is the *primary* consideration a kindergarten teacher should keep in mind when presenting information to the students?" is asking about a kindergarten teacher and the primary thing the teacher has to keep in mind when explaining, instructing, or guiding students at this age level. Does that mean the question is going to be about the teacher or about the students? In this case, the teacher is presenting information to the students, so you need to know something about this age level.

X—X-ray the choices:

Remember to look at each choice before deciding on an answer and delete the choices that you know are <u>wrong</u>. The choices for this question are:

A. *As the children sit in the circle first thing in the morning, review the day's activities so the teacher does not have to interrupt the students when they are changing from one activity to another.* Well, this sounds good, but if you remember correctly from the study of human growth and development, do you think students at this age could remember all the details if everything were mentioned at one time? In fact, as adults we can't remember everything so why would we expect a kindergarten student to be able to? We'll go on to the next choice.

B. *Focus on one thing at a time and keep instructions and expectations clear and simple when talking about directions, procedures, and routines.* This sounds pretty good because children at this age level do have to focus on one thing and the teacher would want to make the instructions clear and precise.

C. *Provide a nurturing environment by asking the students to learn the routine and then tell each other the assignments for the day because children love to learn from their peers.* Wait a minute! Here we are now reading about a nurturing environment so we'd better not be too hasty in thinking that B is the choice. Whoops, now the choice is talking about having students tell each other something about the assignment and we thought the question was asking about the teacher. We'd better move on.

D. *Using a flannel board or similar device, have pictures of what the students are to do and then remind them of the procedures and routines.* The flannel board idea sounds great, but what if children are easily distracted and need verbal reinforcement?

A—Assimilate knowledge:

We know we are to use the Lariat Words when we assimilate knowledge, so *developmentally appropriate* comes to mind along with *positive environment*.

S—Scrutinize your decision:

Let's see how we did: In this particular case, Kolby is upset and his teacher questions him to find out what the problem might be. She is able to determine that he didn't understand her. Children at this age need clear, precise instructions that focus on one thing at a time. If the teacher were to do as (A) suggests, some of the more advanced students might be able to remember the day's requirements, but the majority of children would get lost trying to focus on so many things at one time. Once the instructions have been given in a clear manner, it is perfectly appropriate for the teacher to ask a student what she just said to clarify if her instructions were clear, but not to rely on the students to teach their peers about routine as (C) suggests. Using a flannel board, as in (D), is also a permissible idea once the routines are established, but it should not be used until these procedures are well in mind and even then, the daily activities will need explicit instructions. Answer (B) looks the best because it does answer the question and it is consistent with what we have been taught.

The answer to the question is (B) and addresses information from PPR Competency 001. The teacher understands human development processes and applies this knowledge to plan instruction and ongoing assessment that motivate students and are responsive to their developmental characteristics and needs.

Good job!

You are now ready for the next group of questions. Just in case you need help, look back at the strategies provided, the lariat words, and the competencies. Note that "Clustered Items" appear before the questions, which means that all of the questions will be pertaining to the same scenario and you must be aware that there will be additional information you may need to use to answer them.

TExES Test-Taking Strategies

Clustered Items

1. Mr. Hammes learns that a student who is hearing-impaired, Megan, will be joining his fourth-grade English class. After attending an Individual Education Plan (IEP) meeting he realizes there are many modifications he should make. All of the following *except* one are practices he should incorporate either before instruction or during the delivery of the lesson.

   A. Provide small-group interaction to help Megan's involvement with students who have no difficulty hearing.
   B. Arrange to have Megan always seated in the front of the room.
   C. Present lessons using a variety of instructional formats to make sure Megan has every opportunity to learn.
   D. Speak distinctly and clearly using a normal voice.

T—Take control:

You must remember to say to yourself, "What is this question asking me, and what should I be thinking?" You are supposed to get a picture in your mind as to what is happening. You have a fourth-grade classroom and a new student who is hearing-impaired. You know there has been an IEP meeting and modifications have been made. You also realize that you have a situation here that is talking about "exceptionality" so it must have something to so with diversity (Competency 002).

E—Examine the question:

You next need to put the question in your own words. The question, "All of the following *except* one are practices he should incorporate either before instruction or during the deliver of the lesson," is asking you to look for the one thing the teacher would not consider as best practice when teaching or giving instructions.

X—X-ray the choices:

Look at each choice before deciding on an answer and delete the choices that you know are <u>wrong</u> or in this case that are <u>right</u>. The choices for this question are:

A. *Provide small-group interaction to help Megan's involvement with students who have no difficulty hearing.* You know that cooperative learning is an excellent choice when working with students in diverse situations, so keep this choice for now.

B. *Arrange to have Megan always seated in the front of the room.* You know a student who is hearing-impaired should be close to everything that is going on. What if teaching occurs in the back of the room, or the side of the room? This choice may have to wait until you look at the rest; besides, you saw the red-pepper word, "always."

C. *Present lessons using a variety of instructional formats to make sure Megan has every opportunity to learn.* This one looks good too, because teachers should provide as many formats as possible to help a diverse student group. For now, keep this choice.

D. *Speak distinctly and clearly using a normal voice.* Keep this choice as well because all teachers are encouraged to speak distinctly and in a normal voice when addressing their students in a classroom. In addition, by using the term "normal voice," it means that teachers should not elevate their voices.

A—Assimilate knowledge:

The Lariat Words to note here are cooperative learning and a variety of formats. The question on diversity talks about accepting students with diverse needs and planning learning experiences, and the Lariat Words also mention appropriate accommodations.

S—Scrutinize your decision:

Choice (A) was definitely plausible because of the cooperative learning, and (C) talked about variety so this is one you want to keep. Choice (D) also makes perfect sense for a person who is hearing-impaired. The answer to the question is (B) and addresses information from PPR Competency 002. The teacher understands student diversity and knows how to plan learning experiences and design assessments that are responsive to differences among students and that promote all students' learning.

2. Megan's parents made an appointment with Mr. Hammes to voice their concerns about recent incidents that occurred at school. It seems as though several students in the room were making fun of Megan by pretending to use sign language. How should Mr. Hammes respond to the concerns of Megan's parents?

   A. Mr. Hammes can invite Megan's parents to observe the class so they can see that the students are a nice group of boys and girls and meant no harm to Megan.
   B. Mr. Hammes should have the students send a letter of apology to the parents telling them they were only trying to get Megan to feel like a member of the class.
   C. Mr. Hammes should talk to Megan and her parents and see if she would agree to share some basic sign language gestures with the class.
   D. Mr. Hammes can send a letter home to all the other parents explaining there is a new student who is hearing-impaired in the class in hopes the parents will instruct their own children on how to accept children who are different.

TExES Test-Taking Strategies

T—Take control:

Say to yourself, "What is this question asking me, and what should I be thinking?" Students in Mr. Hammes's class are making fun of Megan by pretending to use sign language and Megan's parents are obviously upset over the incidents.

E—Examine the question:

Next put the question in your own words. The question, "How should Mr. Hammes respond to the concerns of Megan's parents?" is asking what Mr. Hammes, as a teacher, should do to let the parents know he understands the seriousness of the situation.

X—X-ray the choices:

Remember to look at each choice before deciding on an answer and delete the choices that you know are wrong. The choices for this question are:

A. *Mr. Hammes can invite Megan's parents to observe the class so they can see that the students are a nice group of boys and girls and meant no harm to Megan.* It certainly is permissible to invite Megan's parents to class, but he can't think that just having the parents in the class will rectify the situation.

B. *Mr. Hammes should have the students send a letter of apology to the parents telling them they were only trying to get Megan to feel like a member of the class.* At this point, don't completely rule out this answer choice, although it doesn't seem like something a teacher would do.

C. *Mr. Hammes should talk to Megan and her parents and see if she would agree to share some basic sign language gestures with the class.* This is a good solution, because instead of making fun of Megan, the students would learn to communicate with her and she would feel more involved in the school community.

D. *Mr. Hammes can send a letter home to all the other parents explaining there is a new student who is hearing-impaired in the class in hopes the parents will instruct their own children on how to accept children who are different.* This choice isn't as good as the others because sending a letter home doesn't solve the problem for several reasons. The teacher does not have a guarantee that the letter will make it home, it may never be addressed, it singles out a particular student, and it leaves the instructing and problem solving with the other children's parents.

A—Assimilate knowledge:

The Lariat Words to note here are involvement with families. In addition, teachers should make an effort to educate the students who do not have a hearing problem, and understand and assist the student who is hearing-impaired.

S—Scrutinize your decision:

Choice (A) doesn't seem appropriate because Megan would feel very uncomfortable having her parents visit the class. It would be as if they were waiting to "catch" the other students in the act of humiliating her. (B) is also putting Megan on the spot. Choice (D) is incorrect because the question asks how the teacher will respond to Megan's parents. If her parents are willing to come to the class and teach basic sign language, then the teacher needs to notify the parents of this occurrence, but just sending a letter to parents and hoping the parents will talk to their children is not the best choice.

Mr. Hammes can visit with Megan and her parents and explain how he would like Megan to get more involved in the class and in small group activities. If students in the class were taught some familiar American Sign Language (ASL) signs or were able to fingerspell letters, then the hearing-impaired student would be able to convert the disability into a positive experience. In using basic sign language, the students in the class would be better able to communicate with Megan and help create a more positive classroom environment. This, in turn, would help alleviate the parents' concerns.

The answer to the question is (C) and addresses information from PPR Competency 011. The teacher understands the importance of family involvement in children's education and knows how to interact and communicate effectively with families.

Note that the next group of questions is a decision set. That means the questions will all pertain to the same information.

Decision Set

Mr. Beck and the first-grade-level team began organizing an interdisciplinary unit focusing on the Texas Essential Knowledge and Skills (TEKS) science concepts in which students are expected to observe and record changes in the life cycle of an organism. The team selected frogs as a means of meeting this goal and prepared to discuss the unit and the process of metamorphosis. The teachers wrote age-appropriate goals and objectives. They also made decisions on the unit time frame and student-center activities such as appropriate books, projects, Internet sites, and unit extensions.

Mr. Beck delighted in teaching the class, and the students could sense his enthusiasm. He began the unit relating the concept of change to prior lessons in which the students learned about changes that occurred in weather. He then presented a video on the metamorphosis of a tadpole as well as the following chart.

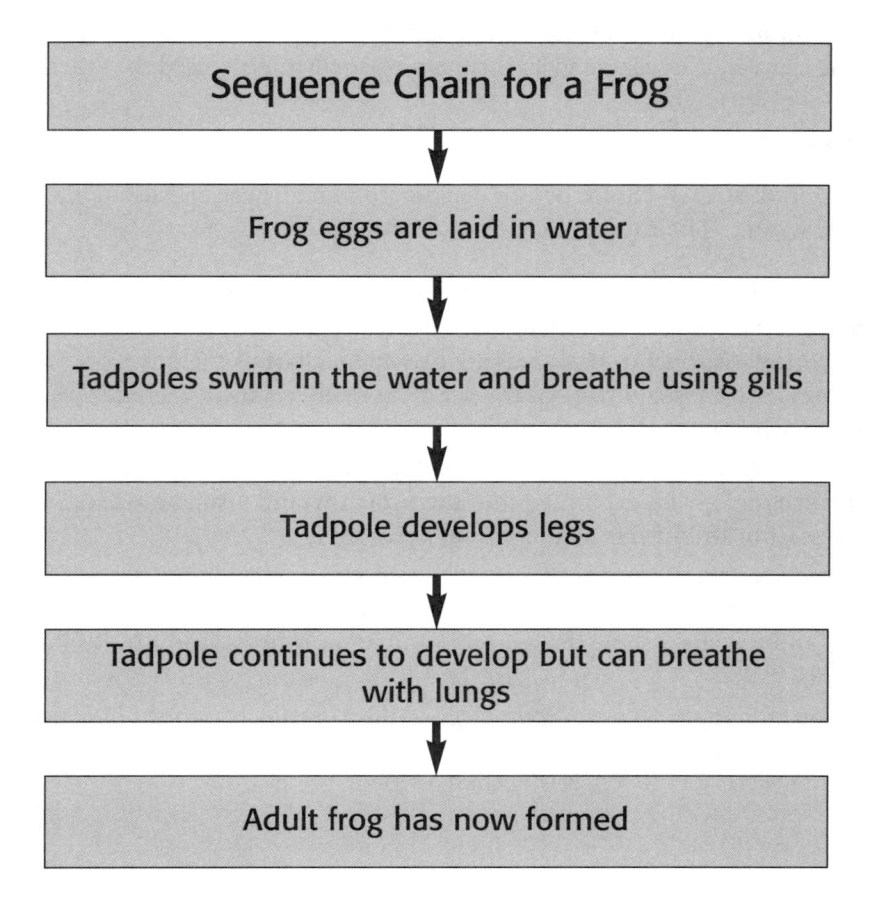

Sequence Chain for a Frog

↓

Frog eggs are laid in water

↓

Tadpoles swim in the water and breathe using gills

↓

Tadpole develops legs

↓

Tadpole continues to develop but can breathe with lungs

↓

Adult frog has now formed

1. Mr. Beck's primary reason for using a video and the chart is that:

    A. He wanted to make sure those students who have never seen frogs will now have been exposed to the chance to see what one looks like.
    B. He wanted to meet the district's objectives of using charts and visuals.
    C. He wanted to effectively communicate the concepts of change and provide varied formats in which to do so.
    D. He wanted to show his use of technology in the everyday planning of units and lessons.

T—Take control:

We have a first-grade-level team organizing an interdisciplinary activity in which students are expected to observe and record changes in the life cycle of an organism during the process of metamorphosis. The teachers made decisions and explored activities. Mr. Beck began the unit by relating the concept of change to changes that occur in weather and presented a video and chart on the metamorphosis of a tadpole.

E—Examine the question:

Put the question in your own words. The question, "Mr. Beck's *primary* reason for using a video and the chart is…" is asking what the main reason Mr. Beck used the video and chart is.

X—X-ray the choices:

Remember to look at each choice before deciding on an answer and delete the choices that you know are <u>wrong</u>. The choices for this question are:

  A. *He wanted to make sure those students who have never seen frogs will now have been exposed to the chance to see what one looks like.* This choice is acceptable but it isn't the primary reason Mr. Beck uses a video and a chart as the question mentions. It will reinforce a visual image of frogs, but he really wants to include a variety of formats when he teaches.
  B. *He wanted to meet the district's objectives of using charts and visuals.* Well, the state wants technology incorporated into the program, and visuals are excellent for all students, but would this be the primary reason?
  C. *He wanted to effectively communicate the concepts of change and provide varied formats in which to do so.* This choice sounds much more plausible because both the video and the chart show the concept of metamorphosis, and Mr. Beck used various formats.
  D. *He wanted to show his use of technology in the everyday planning of units and lessons.* If Mr. Beck really wanted to demonstrate the use of technology, he'd probably use the internet or CD-ROM, rather than a video.

A—Assimilate knowledge:

The Lariat Words to note here are variety of contexts and effective communication. In addition, because children respond to learning in different ways, remember to present information in a variety of formats.

S—Scrutinize your decision:

Choice (A) will help reinforce what frogs and tadpoles look like and the process of metamorphosis, but it isn't a strong enough reason. Choices (B) and (D) talked about satisfying school and district goals, and even though those are important reasons for goal setting, this probably wasn't his primary reason. Choice (C) addresses effective communication and differentiating instruction in a regular classroom as well as providing a wide variety of learning strategies. Because Mr. Beck wanted to communicate the concepts of change effectively and provide varied formats, he found the video that would address the visual as well as the auditory learner, and the chart would help students who needed organization for the new information they were receiving.

The answer to the question is (C) and addresses information from PPR Competency 007. The teacher understands and applies principles and strategies for communicating effectively in varied teaching and learning contexts.

2. Using a long strip of paper for an art activity, Mr. Beck next divided the students into teams of two for a mural project. Each team was given colored markers and assigned an area on which to work. He allowed the students to move around in the classroom and to look at books and magazines as they researched ideas. In addition, he accepted a productive level of noise and activity as they designed their portion of the mural. By allowing students a certain freedom of movement while they worked, Mr. Beck understood that:

   A. children need a time to bond, and working on a mural and in teams provides a perfect opportunity to meet this important objective.
   B. parents will accept the fact that the students used markers if they find less evidence on the students' clothing.
   C. a mural of this size and caliber would never fit on the students' desks even if they moved several together.
   D. first-grade students' need for physical activity ultimately affects how Mr. Beck instructs and how the students learn.

T—Take control:

Students are working on a mural and have been divided into teams of two, and there is movement and activity as the students create.

E—Examine the question:

The question, "By allowing students a certain freedom of movement while they work, Mr. Beck understood that…" is asking you to put yourself in Mr. Beck's place and to discern why he is giving students the latitude of being so mobile in the room.

X—X-ray the choices:

Look at each choice before deciding on an answer and delete the choices that you know are <u>wrong</u>. The choices for this question are:

A. *Children need a time to bond, and working on a mural and in teams provides a perfect opportunity to meet this important objective.* Well, this choice makes a point of building community among students, but is this why Mr. Beck has chosen this activity and format for students to express themselves?

B. *Parents will accept the fact that the students used markers if they find less evidence on the students' clothing.* Now this makes sense, but doesn't have much to do with the question.

C. *A mural of this size and caliber would never fit on the students' desks even if he moved several together.* This one makes some sense as well, but doesn't have much to do with the question.

D. *First-grade students' need for physical activity ultimately affects how Mr. Beck instructs and how the students learn.* Mr. Beck is taking the characteristics of the students into account.

A—Assimilate knowledge:

Lariat Words to focus on here are active learning, appropriate learning, and cooperative learning. In addition, children in early childhood, kindergarten, and first grade have short attention spans and require activities that address their needs for physical activity.

S—Scrutinize your decision:

Choice (A) talks about bonding but is this why Mr. Beck has allowed the movement during a learning activity? Choice (B) sounds like a parent would think this is agreeable but again, it doesn't address teaming and working together. Choice (C) doesn't address the research the students are conducting or the productive noise level. Choice (D), however, does address learning processes and factors that affect learning. Children have been given an opportunity to quietly, yet productively, look for information and transfer that information to a mural. They are active learners in the classroom working in a cooperative learning format, and research tell us that cognitive development is connected to physical development because movement provides a way for children to learn about themselves and what is going on in the classroom.

The answer to the question is (D) and addresses information from PPR Competency 004. The teacher understands learning processes and factors that impact student learning and demonstrates this knowledge by planning effective, engaging instruction and appropriate assessments.

3. At the beginning of the year, Mr. Beck contacted the biology department at the local university for assistance in developing an observational outdoor center that, when finished, would include a large pond. University students designed the center so that plants and fish could live in the pond, which would allow children to study an ecosystem. Mr. Beck worked with the local fish hatchery as well as the university biology department to obtain appropriate pond plants. The university students made sure the plants were well established before frogs arrived to lay spawn. Mr. Beck's *main* reason in contacting the local university and community resources was to:

   A. take the initiative in the development of the outdoor learning project as he wanted to receive an excellent evaluation and knew it would require going above and beyond the usual lesson format.
   B. be an advocate for his students and school by interacting with the university and community.
   C. show he understands diversity in the community and effectively wants to show knowledge and support.
   D. interact appropriately with support systems to address students' needs to enhance involvement in student learning.

Take control:

Picture what is happening. Mr. Beck contacted the local university and fish hatchery for assistance in developing an outdoor center.

E–Examine the question:

The question, "Mr. Beck's *main* reason in contacting the local university and community resources was to…" is asking you the reason that Mr. Beck contacted the local community resources.

X—X-ray the choices:

Look at each choice before deciding on an answer and delete the choices that you know are wrong. The choices for this question are:

A. *Take the initiative in the development of the outdoor learning project as he wanted to receive an excellent evaluation and knew it would require going above and beyond the usual lesson format.* This might give him a few extra points on his evaluation, and it shows initiative on his part, but would this be his main reason?

B. *Be an advocate for his students and school by interacting with the university and community.* By making contacts with the community, Mr. Beck would certainly be building a relationship for future transactions.

C. *Show he understands diversity in the community and effectively wants to show knowledge and support.* Although there is most likely a representative diverse culture in the classroom, does this choice show diversity?

D. *Interact appropriately with support systems to address students' needs to enhance involvement in student learning.* Now this choice sounds more like it.

A—Assimilate knowledge:

Support systems are Lariat Words. In addition, in utilizing the support of local resources, Mr. Beck was building a sense of trust. It is important to develop a partnership that reaches out beyond the public schools and in turn produces the shared responsibility of educating our children as a common goal.

S—Scrutinize your decision:

Choice (A) talks about the teacher's evaluation and the question is discussing community building. Choice (B) suggests Mr. Beck is advocating for the students. He is building a relationship. Choice (C) talks about support and knowledge, but is he really understanding diversity in the community because he contacts the local resources? Choice (D) has Mr. Beck interacting with support systems, involving the community, and enhancing student learning. This choice says it all, because the schools cannot act entirely alone in educating the children. Everyone must share in the responsibility and take pride in the accomplishments of the students.

The answer to the question is (D) and addresses information from PPR Competency 012. The teacher enhances professional knowledge and skills by effectively interacting with other members of the educational community and participating in various types of professional activities.

4. During the unit, Mr. Beck arranged to have the students in his class visit the pond at different intervals so they could witness first hand the stages of frog development. In math class, students predicted how long it would take for the tadpoles to develop into adult frogs and charted their growth. Mr. Beck combined music and dance to further extend the unit on frogs and let students move to a song he developed. Students discussed different types of frogs and where many of the frogs were found in the United States. He provided a tape recording of frogs and asked the students to identify different frogs based on their "croak." In addition to the above activities, which of the following would show Mr. Beck realizes the importance of providing students with effective and appropriate opportunities to explore content?

   A. Mr. Beck shows the class a video of a frog being dissected and discusses the important contributions frogs have made to the field of science.
   B. Mr. Beck guides the writing of a class book titled, "The Little Frog That Couldn't Hop."
   C. Mr. Beck asks the students to draft a letter to the National Wildlife Federation asking the organization for additional information on ecosystems.
   D. Mr. Beck provides the students with an activity that requires coloring a picture of a tadpole and a frog in their natural environment.

T—Take control:

Note that during the course of the unit, Mr. Beck has arranged for a variety of activities to actively engage the students in learning.

E—Examine the question:

The question, "In addition to the above activities, which of the following would show Mr. Beck realizes the importance of providing students with effective and appropriate opportunities to explore content?" is asking you to select one of the choices that will indicate Mr. Beck realizes the importance of having his students use inquiry learning to increase their knowledge about frogs and metamorphosis.

X—X-ray the choices:

Look at each choice before deciding on an answer and delete the choices that you know are wrong. The choices for this question are:

A. *Mr. Beck shows the class a video of a frog being dissected and discusses the important contributions frogs have made to the field of science.* The question specifically mentions an activity that is age appropriate, and watching a frog dissection probably wouldn't be considered suitable for this age group.

B. *Mr. Beck guides the writing of a class book titled, "The Little Frog That Couldn't Hop."* This choice seems more congruent with what first-grade students would be able to accomplish.

C. *Mr. Beck asks the students to draft a letter to the National Wildlife Federation asking the organization for additional information on ecosystems.* The teacher could draft the letter with the students' help, but the choice doesn't indicate this to be the case—the students are to write it themselves.

D. *Mr. Beck provides the students with an activity that requires coloring a picture of a tadpole and a frog in their natural environment.* Coloring is not considered higher-ordered thinking.

A—Assimilate knowledge:

Age appropriate and integrated learning are Lariat Words in this question. In addition, up to this point, all the descriptions of Mr. Beck's involvement, students, and classroom have focused on providing an integrated curriculum, involving students working on projects, and providing students with opportunities to explore nature.

S—Scrutinize your decision:

Choice (A) talks about dissection and even though students are encouraged to reflect on other points of view and engage in the learning process, there would probably be students, administration, and parents who would consider the strategy inappropriate for the age group. Choice (C) is a good idea, but the activity would be designed to meet the needs of older students. Choice (D) discourages inquiry learning and students being actively engaged. Choice (B) has the students involved and engaged in the learning experience by putting together a class book. If the students are going to write something about frogs, then they will need to use the knowledge they have gained through their field trip, charts, videos, and other integrated resources to adequately portray a frog.

The answer to the question is (B) and this question addresses information from PPR Competency 003. The teacher understands procedures for designing effective and coherent instruction and assessment based on appropriate learning goals and objectives.

5. Mr. Beck extended the unit by incorporating technology whereby students would learn to appreciate the ways frogs contribute to the environment. A resource he found most helpful with this endeavor was the National Wildlife Federation website, http://www.nwf.org. In addition, he discovered educational software the students could use in conjunction with the other activities in the unit. When selecting technology that will enhance a lesson or support instructional strategies, which of the following would NOT be one of Mr. Beck's primary considerations?

   A. Mr. Beck should carefully select technology that is designed to meet the state goals and objectives and meet the needs of the students.
   B. Mr. Beck should carefully select technology that is fun and attractive so the students will want to be actively engaged in learning.
   C. Mr. Beck should carefully select technology that is consistent with the goals and objectives he is using and is in tune with the way he teaches and presents information.
   D. Mr. Beck should carefully examine the technology to make sure the information presented is accurate, involves the learner, and is of high educational value.

T—Take control:

Note that Mr. Beck has explored Internet possibilities and discovered useful websites. He has also looked for appropriate software for his students.

E—Examine the question:

The question, "When selecting technology that will enhance a lesson or support instructional strategies, which of the following would NOT be one of Mr. Beck's primary considerations?" is asking you to decide which of the choices should Mr. Beck NOT consider.

X—X-ray the choices:

Look at each choice before deciding on an answer and delete the choices that you know are wrong, in this case that are right. The choices for this question are:

- A. *Mr. Beck should carefully select technology that is designed to meet the state goals and objectives and meet the needs of the students.* This is a good choice because as a teacher, Mr. Beck should incorporate technology when he plans lessons, teaches, or evaluates his instruction.
- B. *Mr. Beck should carefully select technology that is fun and attractive so the students will want to be actively engaged in learning.* Even though Mr. Beck wants his students to enjoy learning, selecting technology that is fun and attractive shouldn't be the primary consideration. The words "fun" and "attractive" are distractors.
- C. *Mr. Beck should carefully select technology that is consistent with the goals and objectives he is using and is in tune with the way he teaches and presents information.* Mr. Beck has taken into consideration his own objectives for the lessons as well as the state's goals and objectives. Sounds like a good choice.
- D. *Mr. Beck should carefully examine the technology to make sure the information presented is accurate, involves the learner, and is of high educational value.* This choice is good because it suggests that Mr. Beck has examined the selected technology to make sure it is accurate and appropriate for the students.

A—Assimilate knowledge:

In this secenario, appropriate use of technology is a Lariat Phrase. In addition, children in early childhood, kindergarten, and first grade have short attention spans and require activities that address their needs for physical activity. Research tells us that cognitive development is connected to physical development because movement provides a way for children to learn about themselves and activities that occur in the classroom.

S—Scrutinize your decision:

Choice (A) talks about selecting software that meets the needs of the students, and a teacher knows this is not a matter of choice but sound educational principles. Choice (C) mentions selecting software that provides information that is congruent with the way Mr. Beck teaches. This seems to be important because the information, the vocabulary, and the content would coincide with what Mr. Beck is already teaching. Choice (D) also suggests the student needs to be involved and that the information is correct, which is something every teacher should consider when selecting software. Choice (B) describes a situation in which the students require software to be fun and attractive, but this should not be a major consideration.

The answer to this question is choice (B) and addresses information from PPR Competency 009. The teacher incorporates the effective use of technology to plan, organize, deliver, and evaluate instruction for all students.

4–8 TEST QUESTIONS

Single Item

1. At the back-to-school parent night, the seventh-grade teacher is explaining to parents that he plans for the classroom to be a "community of learners." One parent asked, "I'm not sure I understand what you mean by that term. Can you define it or provide some examples?" The teacher did NOT include which of the following:

   A. Students make positive contributions to the class discussions and do not take away from the instruction through their actions or words.
   B. Students effectively communicate ideas so that others can understand.
   C. Students work independently on projects and learn to be self-disciplined.
   D. Students are respectful of one another and the teacher in the ways that they exchange ideas.

T—Take control:

Picture what is happening: At the back-to-school parent night, the seventh-grade teacher talks to parents about the classroom becoming a "community of learners." Parents are not sure what he means by that term.

E—Examine the question:

The question, "Can you give me some examples of what that means?" is asking you to provide examples of what "community of learners" means.

X—X-ray the choices:

Look at each choice before deciding on an answer and delete the choices that you know are <u>wrong</u>. The choices for this question are:

   A. *Students make positive contributions to the class discussions and do not take away from the instruction through their actions or words.* This choice promotes community in the classroom. Sounds like a good choice to keep.
   B. *Students effectively communicate ideas so that others can understand.* This choice suggests that students communicate in a positive way. This also appears to be a good option.
   C. *Students work independently on projects and learn to be self-disciplined.* This is a tall order to fill. The teacher will have to step in from time to time.
   D. *Students are respectful of one another and the teacher in the ways that they exchange ideas.* The idea of a cohesive, respectful classroom is one we would all enjoy! Keep this choice.

A—Assimilate knowledge:

Community of learners and active learners are appropriate Lariat Words here. In addition, the way a class is organized affects the learning process, so the teacher must arrange the class and provide instruction that meets the needs of all students.

S—Scrutinize your decision:

Choice (A) supports the idea that in a community of learners, students feel free to express themselves and share a feeling of connectedness. Choice (B) also suggests an openness among students where the participants in discussions genuinely like each other and work together. Choice (D) provides an atmosphere of trust and being open to listening to others.

If students are working independently and using self-discipline, they are missing out on the advantages of working together. Reasoning behind the community of learners suggests that if students learn to work together as a "community of learners" in a classroom setting, they will carry this over to their adult lives. They will experience hands-on problem-solving, exploration, and risk-taking while working together.

The answer to this question is choice (C). This question addresses information from PPR Competency 004. The teacher understands learning processes and factors that impact student learning and demonstrates this knowledge by planning effective, engaging instruction and appropriate assessments.

Clustered Items

1. The eighth-grade team of teachers—language arts, social studies, science, and math—are planning together to provide students with excellent instruction and interdisciplinary teaching. They want to work very hard this year on teaching eighth graders to do research. All of the teachers recall how difficult doing a research paper was even in college and agree that research papers were assigned but that the research process was rarely taught. Before teaching the students, the team should:

   A. ask the students if they are interested in learning to write research papers.
   B. analyze the specific skills required to complete a research project and teach these specific skills to the students.
   C. create a rubric for the students to follow.
   D. determine topics that will interest the students and plan to research those topics themselves.

TExES Test-Taking Strategies

T—Take control:

Note that the eighth-grade team of teachers is planning on teaching students how to write research papers.

E—Examine the question:

The question, "Before teaching the students, the team should…" means prior to teaching the students how to write a research paper, what must the teachers do?

X—X-ray the choices:

Look at each choice before deciding on an answer and delete the choices that you know are <u>wrong</u>. The choices for this question are:

A. *Ask the students if they are interested in learning to write research papers.* It is doubtful the teacher would get a positive response.
B. *Analyze the specific skills required to complete a research project and teach these specific skills to the students.* This sounds like an excellent, direct teaching approach.
C. *Create a rubric for the students to follow.* The rubric doesn't sound like the right assessment tool for a research paper.
D. *Determine topics that will interest the students and plan to research those topics themselves.* Research is not always completed on subjects the students like.

A—Assimilate knowledge:

Teacher as facilitator and modeling are Lariat Words here. In addition, teachers are going to impart their knowledge on how to write research papers. They will need to agree on format, approach, acceptable materials, word processing, and final product.

S—Scrutinize your decision:

Choice (A) leaves the decision making with the students and we know the teachers are meeting prior to working with the students and modeling expectations. Choice (C) suggests using a rubric. Rubrics are evaluative tools with benchmarks. In this case the teachers are not setting performance levels for the research paper, but formulating specific skills that all students must meet. Choice (D) recommends teachers complete the research for the students.

The team wants to plan effective, engaging lessons in which the teacher not only lectures but also facilitates the learning process and in which students become active participants in this process. The teacher will need to teach students the steps in research, model good note taking skills, and establish checkpoints throughout the writing of the paper.

The answer to this question is choice (B). This question addresses information from PPR Competency 004. The teacher understands learning processes and factors that impact student learning and demonstrates this knowledge by planning effective, engaging instruction and appropriate assessments.

2. To assist the students in learning time-management skills and facilitate the projects being completed by the due date, the team decides to:
   A. post the grading scale and the number of points to be deducted for each day the project is late.
   B. have students work on the project for the entire semester so that the slowest learners will not be rushed.
   C. post signs outside each classroom door reminding the students that the research projects are due on a certain date.
   D. create a research project calendar showing what day the project begins and specific dates for sections of the project to be completed.

T—Take control:

Picture what is happening: The eighth-grade team of teachers is facilitating how to write research papers and teaching time-management skills.

E—Examine the question:

The question, "To assist the students in learning time-management skills and facilitate the projects being completed by the due date, the team decides to…" means the team must teach time-management skills so students learn to work within a deadline.

X—X-ray the choices:

Look at each choice before deciding on an answer and delete the choices that you know are wrong. The choices for this question are:

A. *Post the grading scale and the number of points to be deducted for each day the project is late.* This is a negative approach to learning.
B. *Have students work on the project for the entire semester so that the slowest learners will not be rushed.* This wouldn't be fair to the students who pace themselves and have already established good study habits.
C. *Post signs outside each classroom door reminding the students that the research projects are due on a certain date.* This choice may not be enough, as students don't always pay attention to notices.
D. *Create a research project calendar showing what day the project begins and specific dates for sections of the project to be completed.* This choice teaches students how to manage their time.

A—Assimilate knowledge:

Modeling and facilitating are Lariat Words in this scenario. In addition, teachers are going to teach students time-management skills. They will need to provide a product and model what is expected.

S—Scrutinize your decision:

Choice (A) suggests points taken off. Students will need to have some idea of what happens if their papers are submitted after the deadline, but this is a negative approach and doesn't teach time-management skills. Choice (B) suggests using the entire semester to enable students who do not work at a faster pace. This is an excellent reason to teach time-management skills. Choice (C) only gives students deadline dates and doesn't provide students with a model for time-management skills or organizational knowledge.

The team wants to prepare the students to pace themselves on a class project. The students will be unfamiliar with the requirements, so the teachers will need to model and monitor age-appropriate skills such as keeping the papers together, taking notes, and organizing the information collected for the paper. They will also need to instruct students on how to write an acceptable research paper and make the students' learning meaningful.

The answer to this question is choice (D). This question addresses information from PPR Competency 004. The teacher understands learning processes and factors that impact student learning and demonstrates this knowledge by planning effective, engaging instruction and appropriate assessments.

TExES

Decision Set

The sixth-grade teacher, Ms. Campos, is looking forward to beginning her first year of teaching. She is fluent in both English and Spanish. Each year the principal at the school notifies teachers of the students in each class who are receiving assistance through special education or bilingual education prior to the beginning of the school year so that teachers can begin planning. The principal has sent Ms. Campos the following note:

> Ms. Campos,
>
> The following students will be in your class this year and are also receiving the following special services:
>
> Tammy Cab   Special Education
>
> Ricardo Aviles   Special Education
>
> Ho Phan   English Language Learner (ELL)/first language is Vietnamese

1. Ms. Campos plans to become certified as a bilingual or ESL teacher but is not sure what she must do to get certified. For this year she wants to get assistance in ways that she can *best* meet the needs of an ELL student who speaks a language that she does not speak. How might she *best* get information about working with Ho Phan?

    A. Contact the university and see if a conversational Vietnamese class is offered.
    B. Contact the district's bilingual coordinator and ask for assistance.
    C. Contact the fifth-grade teacher and discuss the student's needs.
    D. Call the family and arrange for a home visit to meet the child and the family.

T—Take control:

Note that Ms. Campos plans to become certified as a bilingual or ESL teacher and she wants to get assistance so she can meet the needs of an ELL student who speaks a language that she does not speak.

E—Examine the question:

The question, "How might she best get information about working with Ho Phan?" means, what is the best way to find out how to assist the new student?

X—X-ray the choices:

Look at each choice before deciding on an answer and delete the choices that you know are wrong. The choices for this question are:

A. *Contact the university and see if a conversational Vietnamese class is offered.* This choice is probably not the quickest method of adapting to the needs of the student.
B. *Contact the district's bilingual coordinator and ask for assistance.* A good option, but there's a change no one there will speak Vietnamese.
C. *Contact the fifth-grade teacher and discuss the student's needs.* This sounds like an informative, productive option.
D. *Call the family and arrange for a home visit to meet the child and the family.* This would be counterproductive, because if Ms. Campos can't speak English, the student will be left to translate.

A—Assimilate knowledge:

Professional relationships are Lariat Words in this situation. In addition, the teacher is working with a student from a diverse culture and needs help in meeting the student's needs. The teacher wants to make the experience in her room meaningful and provide as much support as possible.

S—Scrutinize your decision:

Choice (A) suggests that the teacher should learn conversational Vietnamese but the student in her class will need more immediate assistance. Choice (B) suggests going to the district bilingual coordinator for assistance and this is a valid choice, but not if there isn't anyone who speaks the language. Choice (D) will not provide the teacher with language-appropriate materials and ideas.

In contacting the fifth-grade teacher and discussing strengths and weaknesses, Ms. Campos will discover the type of student Ho Phan was in her class the year before, the extent to which she required help, and the best way to make learning effective and meaningful.

The answer to this question is (C). This question addresses information from PPR Competency 012. The teacher enhances professional knowledge and skills by effectively interacting with other members of the educational community and participating in various types of professional activities.

2. Ms. Campos has worked with Spanish-speaking ELL students during student teaching. She was able to communicate with the families and wants to do all that is possible to communicate effectively with Ho Phan's family. She knows that there are other Vietnamese families in the school and thinks that a good way to involve all families is to plan an all-school event. As part of a sixth-grade interdisciplinary unit on "Borders," Ms. Campos suggests to her principal an all-school event in which each class chooses a different culture to study. For a culminating activity, there will be cultural food fair that parents, students, and teachers prepare. Ms. Campos does NOT expect this event to:

   A. involve families in meaningful school activities.
   B. allow families, students, and teachers to learn about other cultures.
   C. use diversity in the classroom as a way to enrich all students' learning experiences.
   D. improve relationships among campus, state, and local educational components.

T—Take control:

Picture what is happening: Ms. Campos wants to do all that is possible to communicate effectively with Ho Phan's family. Plans are developed for an all-school event and for a culminating activity. There will be a cultural food fair that parents, students, and teachers prepare.

E—Examine the question:

The question, "Ms. Campos does NOT expect this event to..." means, what is the one thing that Ms. Campos does not think will happen as a result of having the culminating activity?

X—X-ray the choices:

Look at each choice before deciding on an answer and delete the choices that you know are wrong. The choices for this question are:

   A. *Involve families in meaningful school activities.* This will most likely occur.
   B. *Allow families, students, and teachers to learn about other cultures.* This is also most likely to occur.
   C. *Use diversity in the classroom as a way to enrich all students' learning experiences.* This would be a very positive outcome.
   D. *Improve relationships among campus, state, and local educational components.* Since state and local components weren't mentioned, this is the one thing that probably will not occur.

A—Assimilate knowledge:

The Lariat Words here are involvement with families, diversity, and enhance one's own diversity knowledge. In addition, when planning an all-school event, the positive factors include everyone working together. This sounds like a beneficial experience because students from different cultures will have an opportunity to express themselves in a variety of ways.

S—Scrutinize your decision:

Choice (A) is excellent because one of the goals is to engage families in the various aspects of the educational program. Choice (B) shows that Ms. Campos understands the importance of learning about others' diverse backgrounds and needs. Choice (C) provides an opportunity for everyone to grow from the experience.

The all-school activity would allow students, teachers, and parents an opportunity to share in an experience that ultimately will promote better relationships and contribute to students' learning. Choice (D), which mentions improving relationships among campus, state, and local educational components, would not be a factor.

The answer to this question is choice (D). This question addresses information from PPR Competency 011. The teacher understands the importance of family involvement in children's education and knows how to interact and communicate effectively with families.

3. Ms. Campos meets all of her students and begins the school year successfully. Tammy Cab is a student with attention deficit disorder with hyperactivity (ADHD). Ms. Campos reads Tammy's Individual Education Plan (IEP) and notes that the IEP requires that Tammy be permitted to move about the classroom to do her work. She may work at her desk, standing at a table, or other places in the classroom as long as she does not disturb others. Ms. Campos knows that all sixth graders are at a developmental stage of rapid growth and physical change and all like to move about. She knows that effective instructional planning must include:

   A. strict behavior management plans to prevent the students from becoming too active in the classroom.
   B. lessons that include opportunities for students to move about the classroom for activities such as role-playing and simulations.
   C. lessons that are not focusing on higher-order thinking because at this active stage of development, students do not need to function at that level.
   D. lessons that ask students to think abstractly and to do tasks requiring the stage of thinking Piaget termed "formal operational."

T—Take control:

Note that Ms. Campos has a student with attention deficit disorder with hyperactivity (ADHD) and the IEP requires that Tammy be able to move about.

E—Examine the question:

The question, "She knows that effective instructional planning must include..." means, what is the best way to work with the student using what she knows about ADHD and the developmental characteristics of a child of this age?

X—X-ray the choices:

Look at each choice before deciding on an answer and delete the choices that you know are wrong. The choices for this question are:

A. *Strict behavior management plans to prevent the students from becoming too active in the classroom.* "Strict" management would go against what Ms. Campos knows about the students.

B. *Lessons that include opportunities for students to move about the classroom for activities such as role-playing and simulations.* This choice would allow for fun, educational opportunities that take into account all students.

C. *Lessons that are not focusing on higher-order thinking because at this active stage of development, students do not need to function at that level.* This statement is untrue.

D. *Lessons that ask students to think abstractly and to do tasks requiring the stage of thinking Piaget termed "formal operational."* This concept might be beyond this age group.

A—Assimilate knowledge:

The relevant Lariat Words here are developmentally appropriate and positive environment. In addition, the teacher is going to be working with an ADHD student and the IEP suggests moving around so long as the student doesn't bother others. The teacher is aware of the age group and must plan accordingly.

S—Scrutinize your decision:

Choice (A) suggests a strict behavior management plan and this is not what the student will require to function in the classroom. Choice (C) suggests working at a lower level of achievement, and just because the student is ADHD does not mean the student shouldn't be challenged with inquiry learning and effective learning experiences. Choice (D) is not totally out of the question, but instructional plans need to take into consideration activities in which the student can freely move around.

The student needs an instructional plan that allows learning to take place and choice (B) demonstrates that the teacher has the knowledge to set goals for the student and prepare effective lessons.

The answer to this question is (B). This question addresses information from PPR Competency 001. The teacher understands human development processes and applies this knowledge to plan instruction and ongoing assessment that motivate students and are responsive to their developmental characteristics and needs.

8–12 QUESTIONS

Single Item

1. After looking over your students' work on a recent test in government, you realize that they have many misconceptions about the way the judicial system works. You previously covered the information by having them work in cooperative groups and jigsaw the different court systems in the state. As time is limited and you want to present specific information about the court systems, the *best* approach would be to:

    A. plan a direct instruction lesson for the individuals who did not score well on the test.
    B. have the students return to their textbooks and reread the chapter about the judicial system.
    C. have the students work in pairs to find the information online.
    D. repeat the jigsaw activity with only the students who did poorly on the exam.

T—Take control:

Note that the teacher has previously used cooperative learning as a means of engaging students. However, after surveying the results of a test, the teacher realizes some students did not grasp the concepts and the teacher's time is limited.

E—Examine the question:

The question, "As time is limited and you want to present specific information about the court systems, the *best* approach would be…" is asking you what is the best approach in disseminating information to students when there is a limited amount of time.

X—X-ray the choices:

Look at each choice before deciding on an answer and delete the choices that you know are wrong. The choices for this question are:

A. *Plan a direct instruction lesson for the individuals who did not score well on the test.* This seems like a specific way to address the issue.
B. *Have the students return to their textbooks and reread the chapter about the judicial system.* The students might not be able to process the information on their own.
C. *Have the students work in pairs to find the information online.* This is not a very direct method of accomplishing the teacher's objectives.
D. *Repeat the jigsaw activity with only the students who did poorly on the exam.* If time were not a factor, then the activity would actively engage the students, but because the teacher's goal is to impact learning, this just seems repetitive.

A—Assimilate knowledge:

The relevant Lariat Words here are teacher–student interactions, instructional planning, and teacher as facilitator. In addition, the teacher has analyzed the situation and realizes that time is a factor. Previously used cooperative groups were successful, but in this situation, not for all students. The teacher understands that expectations, choice, and type of instructional strategies affect learning.

S—Scrutinize your decision:

Choice (B) suggests that the students should reread the information from the textbook. There are several things to look at. To begin with, the students might not have read the assignment in the first place; second, the students who were not as successful on the test might have a processing problem when it comes to reading. Choice (C) recommends the students work in pairs and online. This activity assumes the students will find the appropriate websites and that the information will address the areas of concern. Choice (D) has several problems. The students didn't comprehend the material in the first place using the jigsaw approach, and the jigsaw method of cooperative learning requires careful consideration when organizing the members of each group. In this case there might not be enough time, and time is a factor. Choice (A) mentions a direct teaching approach. The teacher can address the students' needs in a small-group situation and focus on specific areas of concern.

The answer to this question is choice (A). This question addresses information from PPR Competency 004. The teacher understands learning processes and factors that impact student learning and demonstrates this knowledge by planning effective, engaging instruction and appropriate assessments.

Clustered Items

During the faculty workshop prior to the start of the school year, the faculty at University High School discusses school-wide goals for the year. One of the goals selected is to maximize the instructional time available and minimize the time spent on administrative tasks. The teachers examine how a day is structured and see that one hour a day is spent during passing periods. Another large amount of time is spent with administrative tasks such as returning papers, writing notes to parents, going over tests, and taking roll.

1. Which of the following is the *best* way for teachers to maximize instructional time and minimize administrative tasks?

    A. Use prewritten notes to send home to parents where the appropriate concern is checked rather than taking the time to write notes about behavior or grades.
    B. Set up each class on the computer so that attendance and other tasks can be done quickly.
    C. Use assigned seating to be able to check for absences quickly.
    D. Have students grade a peer's paper to save the teacher time for instruction.

T—Take control:

Note that at a school-wide workshop, the faculty discusses goals and realizes administrative tasks take up a lot of a teacher's time. They want to maximize time.

E—Examine the question:

The question, "Which of the following is the best way for teachers to maximize instructional time and minimize administrative tasks?" is asking you what the best approach is to maximizing the time set aside for teaching and reducing the amount of time spent on administrative tasks.

X—X-ray the choices:

Look at each choice before deciding on an answer and delete the choices that you know are wrong. The choices for this question are:

A. *Use prewritten notes to send home to parents where the appropriate concern is checked rather than taking the time to write notes about behavior or grades.* This would certainly save time, but a personal note would be more productive.
B. *Set up each class on the computer so that attendance and other tasks can be done quickly.* This seems like an efficient way to use technology to accomplish the teacher's goal.
C. *Use assigned seating to be able to check for absences quickly.* This choice won't help teachers tackle administrative tasks besides taking attendance.
D. *Have students grade a peer's paper to save the teacher time for instruction.* The goal is not to use the students to save the teacher's time.

A—Assimilate knowledge:

The relevant Lariat Words here are technological tools for administrative tasks. In addition, teachers are to look at the way they structure their day and try to make adjustments. They are also encouraged to use technological tools to perform administrative tasks.

S—Scrutinize your decision:

Choice (A) mentions the use of a checklist and prewritten notes. This practice would be extremely impersonal. Even though it would save time, it would not provide appropriate feedback for the parents. Choice (C) suggests assigned seating, but doesn't take into account the individual differences in teaching style and student requirements. Choice (D) suggests having students grade each other's papers. In some situations students can learn by engaging in this practice, but the goal should be to involve the student in the process, not to save the teacher time. Choice (B) suggests using technology for administrative purposes which would address faculty goals.

The answer to this question is choice (B). This question addresses information from PPR Competency 006. The teacher understands strategies for creating an organized and productive learning environment and for managing student behavior.

2. A second goal selected is to improve teaching skills. The teachers discuss various ways to do this and decide that the *best* way for teachers to improve teaching skills quickly is to:

   A. attend the annual Texas State Reading Conference in order for all teachers to assist students who have reading problems.
   B. subscribe to magazines such as *The Instructor* and read about other teachers and schools.
   C. use appraisal results to set personal goals for improvement and work with a mentor.
   D. use online resources to read about recent research in teaching and try new strategies.

T—Take control:

Picture what is happening: At a school-wide workshop, the faculty discusses how to improve teaching skills.

E—Examine the question:

The question, "The teachers discuss various ways to do this and decide that the best way for teachers to quickly improve teaching skills is…" is asking you what teachers can do to improve teaching skills quickly.

X—X-ray the choices:

Look at each choice before deciding on an answer and delete the choices that you know are wrong. The choices for this question are:

   A. *Attend the annual Texas State Reading Conference in order for all teachers to assist students who have reading problems.* This choice doesn't seem to have much to do with improving teaching skills.
   B. *Subscribe to magazines such as The Instructor and read about other teachers and schools.* This could be a place for teachers to gain insight.
   C. *Use appraisal results to set personal goals for improvement and work with a mentor.* This would provide teachers with an immediate plan.
   D. *Use online resources to read about recent research in teaching and try new strategies.* This could also be a place for teachers to gain insight.

A—Assimilate knowledge:

The relevant Lariat Words here are teacher reflection, self-assessment, and professional development. In addition, teachers are always looking to improve, and in this case the faculty has gathered to discuss how it can quickly improve its teaching strategies.

S—Scrutinize your decision:

Choice (A) would give a teacher ideas, but it would be neither the quickest nor the best way to do this. Choice (B) suggests using a professional magazine such as *The Instructor*, but I think this would give ideas for teaching and not necessarily strategies for improvement. Choice (D) suggests online resources, which don't allow for a personal approach. However, looking at appraisal results as choice (C) suggests would provide teachers with immediate ideas, focusing on areas of concern with someone who can support objectives and help set personal goals.

The answer to this question is choice (C). This question addresses information from PPR Competency 012. The teacher enhances professional knowledge and skills by effectively interacting with other members of the educational community and participating in various types of professional activities.

Decision Set

The biology teacher is planning a unit on wildflowers for the spring. The teacher wants students to visit the Wildflower Center in Austin to view actual wildflowers and to study the ecological systems in place, such as the rainwater collection system. She has several sections of biology and wants to take all of the students to the Wildflower Center for a field trip.

1. District policies require teachers wanting to take field trips to complete a form requesting a field trip and necessary transportation. Because this teacher is new and has never taken a field trip, she is not aware of the district policies on field trips. She should:

    A. ask a parent volunteer to find out the procedure and file the necessary paperwork.
    B. decide that students can go in their own cars and not worry about getting buses.
    C. call the transportation director and arrange for two buses on the designated date.
    D. go to her immediate supervisor for information and assistance.

T—Take control:

Picture what is happening: A teacher wants to take her classes on a field trip but is unaware of district policies.

E—Examine the question:

The question, "Because this teacher is new and has never taken a field trip, she is not aware of the district policies on field trips. She should…" is asking you what this teacher should do to follow school district policies for field trips.

X—X-ray the choices:

Look at each choice before deciding on an answer and delete the choices that you know are wrong. The choices for this question are:

A. *Ask a parent volunteer to find out the procedure and file the necessary paperwork.* The parent would follow up on the teacher's request, but this seems to be the responsibility of the teacher.
B. *Decide that students can go in their own cars and not worry about getting buses.* This is not for the teacher to decide.
C. *Call the transportation director and arrange for two buses on the designated date.* A teacher would never be able to do this without the principal's permission.
D. *Go to her immediate supervisor for information and assistance.* This choice could provide the teacher with valuable information.

A—Assimilate knowledge:

The revelant Lariat Words here are knowledge of state educational system. In addition, when teachers are responsible for students on a field trip, they need to follow school district policy.

S—Scrutinize your decision:

Choice (A) would put the responsibility on the parent volunteer and the teacher is the one assuming the responsibility. In this case, the teacher needs to obtain appropriate paperwork, read it carefully, and sign it. Choice (B) is an inappropriate answer because of the teacher's and school's liability. Choice (C) would certainly get the teacher into trouble for not following protocol. The teacher needs to ask for help from the principal and then find out other policies on parental approval, students' absences from other classes, cell phone policies, funds required, routes to take, and late arrivals.

The answer to this question is choice (D). This question addresses information from PPR Competency 013. The teacher understands and adheres to legal and ethical requirements for educators and is knowledgeable of the structure of education in Texas.

2. Austin is too far from the school and the costs for this trip are excessive. The request for the trip is denied. The biology teacher is disappointed and frustrated. The teacher decides to discuss this again with the principal. What is the best procedure for her to schedule this meeting?

   A. After considering all of the options, she sends an e-mail to the principal requesting the meeting and listing the curricular areas that she believes will be addressed on this trip and why it is beneficial to students.
   B. Frustrated, she decides to call the curriculum director and explain to her the value of the trip and asks the curriculum director to call the principal and request a meeting with the three of them.
   C. She goes to all of the faculty members along her hallway and asks about field trips they have taken. She then writes a letter to the principal explaining that other teachers have taken trips similar to this one and requests a meeting.
   D. She examines the costs and prepares a proposal for the principal that lists the objectives, rationale, and requirements of the trip. She then proposes ways that the students might raise the money to supplement the cost of the trip and requests a meeting with the principal.

T—Take control:

Note that a teacher wants to take her classes on a field trip but the request has been denied because of the expense involved.

E—Examine the question:

The question, "What is the best procedure for her to schedule this meeting?" is asking how the teacher goes about scheduling a meeting.

X—X-ray the choices:

Look at each choice before deciding on an answer and delete the choices that you know are wrong. The choices for this question are:

   A. *After considering all of the options, she sends an e-mail to the principal requesting the meeting and listing the curricular areas that she believes will be addressed on this trip and why it is beneficial to students.* A face-to-face meeting seems like to good way to reverse a decision.
   B. *Frustrated, she decides to call the curriculum director and explain to her the value of the trip and asks the curriculum director to call the principal and request a meeting with the three of them.* This choice has some merit, and maybe the teacher is thinking the more professionals asking for the request, the better chance they have of getting the request approved.
   C. *She goes to all of the faculty members along her hallway and asks about field trips they have taken. She then writes a letter to the principal explaining that other teachers have taken trips similar to this one and requests a meeting.* This field trip is independent of what other teachers did in the past.
   D. *She examines the costs and prepares a proposal for the principal that lists the objectives, rationale, and requirements of the trip. She then proposes ways that the students might raise the money to supplement the cost of the trip and requests a meeting with the principal.* This seems like a systematic, feasible option.

A—Assimilate knowledge:

The revelant Lariat Words here are ethical requirements and knowledge of state educational systems. In addition, the teacher has been turned down and is now trying to persuade the principal. Possibly if the teacher had applied these procedures prior to the first request, the field trip would not have been denied.

S—Scrutinize your decision:

Choice (A) suggests an e-mail, but the teacher really needs to make an appointment and present a case so the field trip will still have a chance. Choice (B) suggests bringing in another person. It would certainly be appropriate for the teacher to discuss the field trip with the curriculum director, particularly because the teacher is new, and see if there are suggestions. Choice (C) would not be a suggested procedure as the rest of the faculty would certainly disapprove, plus the field trip this teacher wants to take has nothing to do with the field trips taken by other classes. The teacher needs to know how to work with supervisors and address issues. By preparing a proposal that lists the objectives, rationale, and requirements of the trip and then proposing ways that the students might raise the money to supplement the costs, the teacher understands appropriate protocol.

The answer to this question is choice (D). This question addresses information from PPR Competency 013. The teacher understands and adheres to legal and ethical requirements for educators and is knowledgeable of the structure of education in Texas.

3. Unfortunately, the teacher is not able to take her classes on the trip. She has planned the unit around the trip and now must make other plans. What is the *best* way for the teacher to use productivity tools to communicate information about the Wildflower Center for her unit?

   A. Have the students go online and look at the Wildflower Center website.
   B. Visit the Wildflower Center herself and make a video of the tour she takes.
   C. Have students create computer presentations using photographs they take of local wildflowers.
   D. Provide students with brochures from the Wildflower Center.

T—Take control:

Picture what is happening: A teacher wants to take her classes on a field trip but the request has been denied and now she must find other ways to communicate information concerning the Wildflower Center.

E—Examine the question:

The question, "What is the best way for the teacher to use productivity tools to communicate information about the Wildflower Center for her unit?" is asking how the teacher can give the students information about the Wildflower Center using resource tools.

X—X-ray the choices:

Look at each choice before deciding on an answer and delete the choices that you know are <u>wrong</u>. The choices for this question are:

A. *Have the students go online and look at the Wildflower Center website.* If the website has a vitual tour, this could be a viable option.
B. *Visit the Wildflower Center herself and make a video of the tour she takes.* Sounds good if this is allowed.
C. *Have students create computer presentations using photographs they take of local wildflowers.* Sounds fun, but it wouldn't take the place of the tour.
D. *Provide students with brochures from the Wildflower Center.* This is a good suggestion, but not as interactive as a tour.

A—Assimilate knowledge:

The relevant Lariat Words here are appropriate use of technology. In addition, the teacher has been turned down and now is trying to provide and replicate the information that would have been gained by visiting the center. I do remember reading something about productivity tools and communicating information by using a variety of resources.

S—Scrutinize your decision:

Choice (A) suggests a virtual tour and if there were no other choices available, this could work. Choice (C) recommends using the computer and producing photographs of local wildflowers. This method won't necessarily educate the students as to what the flowers *are*. Choice (D) suggests a brochure. Students would benefit by looking at the brochure, but it in no way replaces an actual trip or video presentation. If the teacher visits the Wildflower Center herself and making a video of the tour she takes, students will have an opportunity to experience the trip through the eyes of their teacher.

The answer to this question is Choice (B). This question addresses information from PPR Competency 007. The teacher understands and applies principles and strategies for communicating effectively in varied teaching and learning contexts.

4. In an effort to have students apply their knowledge beyond the school setting, become reflective thinkers, apply abstract reasoning, and become self-directed learners, the teacher will use which of the following activities as a culminating event?

   A. Select a community project to complete, such as delivering wildflowers bouquets to local nursing homes.
   B. Plant Texas bluebonnets and Indian paintbrush along the curbs of the main street that runs through the town following the directions from the National Wildflower Center.
   C. In small groups, plan and present a Texas wildflower garden for local businesses incorporating perennial wildflowers and evergreen shrubs included on the National Wildflower Center database.
   D. Complete a wildflower notebook that includes pressed species and digital images from the National Wildflower Center image file.

T—Take control:

Picture what is happening: A teacher wants her students to become reflective thinkers and use this knowledge outside the school setting.

E—Examine the question:

The question, "In an effort to have students apply their knowledge beyond the school setting, become reflective thinkers, apply abstract reasoning, and become self-directed learners, the teacher will use which of the following activities as a culminating event?" is asking what event will provide students opportunities to apply abstract reasoning and become self-directed learners.

X—X-ray the choices:

Look at each choice before deciding on an answer and delete the choices that you know are <u>wrong</u>. The choices for this question are:

   A. *Select a community project to complete such as delivering wildflowers bouquets to local nursing homes.* How would students apply abstract thinking here?
   B. *Plant Texas bluebonnets and Indian paintbrush along the curbs of the main street that runs through the town following the directions from the National Wildflower Center.* This might be difficult to execute.
   C. *In small groups, plan and present a Texas wildflower garden for local businesses incorporating perennial wildflowers and evergreen shrubs included on the National Wildflower Center database.* Students would need to utilize several skills in order to carry this out.
   D. *Complete a wildflower notebook that includes pressed species and digital images from the National Wildflower Center image file.* Good idea, but not for reflective thinking.

A—Assimilate knowledge:

The relevant Lariat Words here are developmentally appropriate, lifelong learning, and reflective thinkers. In addition, the teacher wants students to use abstract thinking, which means the activity needs to focus on higher-order thinking and opportunities to seek information and justify responses.

S—Scrutinize your decision:

Choice (A) is a wonderful suggestion and students would benefit from the philanthropic activity, but the activity would not extend nor support the teachers goals and objectives. Choice (B) suggests supporting the beautification program already established in Texas, but again, the strategy would not focus on the development of the learner. Choice (D) would provide experience working with the computer and certainly make the students more knowledgeable about technology issues, but it too lacks the reference to reflective thinking. In using small groups, planning and presenting a Texas wildflower garden for local businesses provides the students with opportunities to apply knowledge outside the school setting and use abstract thinking and reasoning.

The answer to this question is choice (C). This question addresses information from PPR Competency 001. The teacher understands human development processes and applies this knowledge to plan instruction and ongoing assessment that motivate students and are responsive to their developmental characteristics and needs.

The preceding section has attempted to provide you with a specific strategy to apply as you take the TExES certification exam. The following section is intended to provide you some "Pistol-Packing Tips" for hitting the TExES bullseye!

Pistol-Packing Tips

The following tips will offer you some practical suggestions for preparing yourself to be a successful test taker.

- **Review.** Spend time learning the important concepts from each competency.
- **Practice.** You have several practice tests available in this study guide, as well as those provided at the NES website (www.texes.nesinc.com). Spend time practicing with these materials and attempting to understand why each answer is what it is. Team up with fellow students and form study groups. After each session, treat yourself to an enjoyable activity. Take advantage of review sessions provided by your university or a nearby Educational Service Center.
- **Prepare yourself.** In addition to practicing for the test, there are several things to remember as you get ready for the important test date.
    - Take several well-sharpened No. 2 lead pencils and an eraser that does not smudge.
    - Take a photo ID to show at the door of the testing center.
    - Take your admission ticket for the test.
    - You may want to take mints, hard candy, or gum for a quick energy boost.
    - You may want to take earplugs if you are easily distracted by ambient sounds.
    - Take a watch and monitor your time. Divide your time into segments with a goal of completing a reasonable number of test items in small time blocks.
    - Plan your week preceding the test so that you will be rested and in top mental and physical condition on the day of the test. Get a good night's sleep the night before the test, have something to eat before you leave for the test site, and dress in layers to allow you to stay comfortable, no matter what the temperature in the testing center.
- **Pace yourself by marking the half-way point of your test before you begin.** When you reach that point, if you have less than half your allotted time remaining, you will need to work through the remaining items at a faster pace.
- **Analyze each question.** Temporarily skip any item that seems difficult and time consuming. Mark on your scantron or in your test booklet the items to which you should return, then move on. Don't stress yourself unnecessarily by spending too much time on one question when you can move forward with items you DO know. Remember, there is no penalty for guessing, so use your strategies and make an informed "guess."
- **Think before responding.** Earlier in this chapter, an extensive explanation was provided for utilizing the TEXAS procedure. Use this strategy as you think through each question.

- **Answer every question.** If you find you are running behind near the end of the time limit, quickly mark each remaining item with a response of your choice. There is no penalty for incorrect answers, so leave no answer blank. However, sequentially marking several items without considering the appropriate answer could result in low domain scores, since items could be clustered in some areas. In addition, some questions are weighted more heavily than others for a given domain area, so answering every question ensures a better chance of a better score in each domain.
- **Stick with your answer.** Unless you are absolutely sure you made the wrong choice initially, do NOT change an answer. Overanalyzing often causes you to choose the second best answer.
- **Watch your "bubbles."** As you record your answers on your scantron form, periodically check to make sure you are bubbling on the corresponding item number as the one you are looking at in the test booklet. As you answer your questions, mark them in the booklet as well as on the scantron. If you do find that you have mismarked your sheet, this will assist you in quickly correcting the error.

With plenty of preparation, you are now ready to be a successful test taker. Go into the test with confidence. Good luck as you move through the process of becoming a certified teacher in Texas and as you begin this new and exciting career.

CHAPTER THREE

How to Use the Tests in This Book

This book has five practice tests. The purpose of this chapter is to suggest ways for you to use each of the tests as you begin to prepare for your specific TExES PPR exam. Our recommendation is that if you score 80% or better on each test you will be well prepared to pass the actual test. The actual test has a scaled score with some questions scaled as harder than others and 10 questions that are not graded as they are being field-tested.

When taking any test in the book keep in mind that the actual TExES exam is assuming the "ideal world." Don't read your own biases into the test. Answer each question as if it were set in an ideal world. In an ideal world, all parents cooperate with the school and with the teachers. All school districts have enough money. All students want to learn. All teachers have mentors. You must leave your mental backpack at the door. This means, don't answer the questions based on what you know about schools from observing in a classroom or from your field experience (what you carry around in your brain like a backpack). The state of Texas wants to know, if the world were an ideal place, do you know what best practice is? Don't think of reasons why something won't work; instead say, "In an ideal world, what is best practice?"

The first test in the book is the Diagnostic EC–4 Pedagogy and Professional Responsibilities Test. This test has 40 questions (one half the number of questions that are graded on the real TExES PPR). The questions on this test include early childhood through fourth grade, fourth grade through eighth grade, and eighth grade through twelfth grade. Even if you are getting certified in only one of those areas, all of the tests cover the same 13 competencies. By taking the diagnostic test you can ascertain in a short amount of time which competencies are your strengths and which competencies you need to review further.

After you have taken the diagnostic test, read all of the detailed answers in order to understand why specific answers were wrong. A score of 32 out of 40 would be 80% correct.

Next, go to the diagnostic answer sheet sorted by competency found after the answer explanations for each test. This last sheet will have the answers grouped by domain and competency. By analyzing your results, the diagnostic test shows which domains and competencies you need to review or relearn before taking any other tests. Chapters 4–7 cover each of the domains and competencies and will provide you with a complete review. These chapters also suggest additional websites and resources if you require more detailed studying.

The second test you should take is the test for your specific certification area. If you are getting certified EC–4, take one of the two EC–4 practice tests. After scoring the test, read the detailed answer section. Then, analyze the domains and competencies that need additional work by recording your errors on the EC–4 answer sheets sorted by competency. If you are getting certified 4–8 do the same with the 4–8 test and if you are getting certified 8–12 do the same with the 8–12 test.

If you are getting certified at all levels, the five tests will provide you with practice at all of the levels. If you are getting certified EC–4 or 8–12, there may not be a question about the Texas Professional Development and Appraisal System (PDAS) on the EC–4 or 8–12 practice tests. By taking the 4–8 practice test, you will have a question about the PDAS. The EC–4 tests will cover indicators that are not covered on the 8–12 test. Likewise the 8–12 and 4–8 tests will cover indicators not covered on other tests. Taking all of the tests will provide you with additional knowledge about specific indicators that may be tested on the actual TExES exam. The content is different for each level but the pedagogy, which is what this test assesses, is the same for all certification levels.

The purpose of these practice tests is really threefold. First, the diagnostic test is a self-assessment instrument. It will show you which domains and competencies are strengths and which are weak areas. You can study your weak areas in Chapters 4–7. Second, you can test yourself on the specific test for your certification level to determine strengths and needs. Finally, you will continue to learn about competencies and indicators that you may not know about by taking the remaining tests and reading the detailed answer sheets.

Kaplan Tip: Take all of the tests. Read all of the detailed answer explanations. Analyze your strengths and needs on the answer sheets that are sorted by item number and sorted by competency. Study those domains and competencies that are your weak areas.

Section Two

TExES DOMAINS

CHAPTER FOUR

Domain I: Designing Instruction and Assessment to Promote Student Learning
(Includes Competencies 001–004)

The content in Domain I represents 31% of the questions on any of the Pedagogy and Professional Responsibility (PPR) exams. The focus of this domain is the teacher's ability to create appropriate instructional methods as well as the ability to implement effective assessment procedures in order to impact students' learning.

The information represented in these questions is intended to capture the teacher's knowledge regarding the following concepts:

Competency 001—The teacher understands human developmental processes and applies this knowledge to plan instruction and ongoing assessment that motivate students and are responsive to their developmental characteristics and needs.

> **In Other Words:**
>
> This competency focuses on the teacher's understanding and application of milestones in a student's growth and development as important features in planning effective instruction and the assessment of the instruction.

Teachers understand the intellectual, social, physical, and emotional developmental characteristics of students in different age groups. They must also apply their understanding of these varying characteristics by implementing appropriate instructional and assessment procedures to ensure student learning.

> Specific emphasis for grade **EC–4** teachers may include the teacher's understanding of:
> - the role that each of the following have on the child's development and learning
>   - nutrition
>   - sleep
>   - prenatal conditions
>   - family conditions
>   - emotional and physical contact with caregivers
>   - play and its role in normal development
>   - developmental stages of cognitive growth
>
> Specific emphasis for grade **4–8** teachers may include the teacher's understanding of:
> - the physical changes associated with later childhood and early adolescence and how these impact other domains
> - how development in one domain impacts other domains
>
> Specific emphasis for grade **8–12** teachers may include the teacher's understanding of:
> - physical changes associated with adolescence and how these impact other domains
> - how development in one domain impacts other domains

The teacher plans lessons that reflect an understanding of students' developmental characteristics and needs.

The teacher adapts lessons to address students' varied backgrounds skills, interests, and learning needs, including the needs of English Language Learners (ELLs).

The teacher uses effective approaches to address varied student learning needs and preferences.

> Specific emphasis for grade **EC–4** teachers may include the teacher's understanding of:
> - spontaneous activities or observations to promote learning
>
> Specific emphasis for grade **4–8** teachers may include the teacher's understanding of:
> - students' interest in peers
> - the importance of not singling out students

Domain I: Designing Instruction and Assessment to Promote Student Learning

Specific emphasis for grade **8–12** teachers may include the teachers' understanding of:
- making use of students' focus on peer relationships
- students' growing awareness of and engagement with the world beyond school

The teacher plans instruction that motivates students to want to learn and achieve.

The teacher understands the implications of students' developmental characteristics for planning appropriate instruction.

Specific emphasis for grade **EC–4** teachers may include the teacher's understanding of:
- the lifelong impact of experiences provided in early childhood through fourth grade on individual development and on society
- the wide range of developmental differences (resulting from different rates of development in different domains) and the implications for instructional planning
- how developmental characteristics of EC–4 children (attention span, need for physical activity, and movement) impact learning and performance
- the importance of helping EC–4 children apply decision making, organization, and goal-setting skills (selecting learning centers, putting materials away, completing a self-initiated project)
- young children's reliance on concrete thinking, motor and sensory input, and direct experiences for development of skills and knowledge and the implications for instructional planning and assessment
- how to use developmental characteristics and needs of EC–4 children to plan meaningful integrated and active learning and play experiences that promote the development of the whole child

Specific emphasis for grade **4–8** teachers may include the teacher's understanding of the:
- rationale for and structure of middle-level education
- middle years as transitional years when students may exhibit characteristics of younger or older children
- importance of developing crucial attitudes such as working and getting along with others, respecting diversity, making a commitment to continued schooling
- range of individual development and the implications of this for instructional planning
- challenges for students in the middle years (self-image, physical appearance, eating disorders, feelings of rebelliousness, and ways to address these challenges)
- ways involvement in risky behaviors (gangs, drugs, and alcohol) impacts development and learning
- effects of social and emotional factors (peer interactions, search for identity, questioning of principles and expectations, parental divorce, homelessness) on student development and on teaching and learning

- developmental characteristics of middle level students and how the impact of these characteristics affect learning and performance and how to use this knowledge to plan effective learning experiences and assessments
- importance of helping middle-level students apply decision-making, organizational, and goal-setting skills

Specific emphasis for grade **8–12** teachers may include the teacher's understanding of the:

- importance for students to learn and apply life skills (self-direction, decision-making, goal setting, workplace skills) to promote lifelong learning and participation in society
- wide range of individual development, the differences at this age, and the implications for instructional planning
- typical challenges of adolescence and young adulthood (self-esteem, physical appearance, eating disorders, identity formation, educational and career decisions) and effective ways to address these challenges
- ways involvement in risky behavior (gang involvement, drug and alcohol use) impacts learning and development
- importance of peers, peer acceptance and conformity to peer group norms and expectations for adolescents and the significance of peer related issues for teaching and learning
- effects of social and emotional factors (interacting with the larger community, building relationships, questioning values, exploring long-term career and life goals, parental divorce, homelessness) on student development, teaching, and learning
- ability to use knowledge of cognitive changes in 8–12 students (refinement of abstract thinking and reasoning, reflective thinking, focus on the world beyond the school setting) to plan instruction that promotes learning and development
- impact of developmental characteristics of students in grades 8–12 on learning and performance and how to use this knowledge to plan effective learning experiences and assessments

Where to find other study resources for information regarding theories of human growth and development, developmental stages, and how these apply to teaching:

http://www.theshop.net/aboatman/edtheory.htm

This site provides a nice overview of theories of learning, theorists, and resources for each of the major theorists and their theories.

http://chiron.valdosta.edu/whuitt/col/cogsys/piaget.html

This site provides a thorough overview of the theory, processes, and stages of cognitive development.

Domain I: Designing Instruction and Assessment to Promote Student Learning

www.ncac-hsv.org/stages.html

This site provides a comprehensive list of developmental characteristics and stages of children, age birth through 18.

http://tip.psychology.org/

This site is intended to make learning and instructional theory more accessible to educators. The database contains brief summaries of 50 major theories of learning and instruction.

http://childdevelopmentinfo.com/development/

This site provides information on how to help children and adolescents reach their full potential as they grow and develop.

Competency 002—The teacher understands student diversity and knows how to plan learning experiences and design assessments that are responsive to differences among students and that promote all students' learning.

> **In Other Words:**
>
> This competency focuses on the teacher's understanding of how to design appropriate lessons and assessments for the many different students being taught. Teachers must understand the differences in children's background, ethnicity, learning styles, and motivations in order to provide effective instruction.

The teacher understands the characteristics and instructional needs of students with varied backgrounds, skills, interests, and learning needs.

The teacher understands the different approaches to learning that students may exhibit and what motivates students to become active, engaged learners.

The teacher understands the cultural and socioeconomic differences and the significance of these differences for instructional planning.

The teacher understands appropriate strategies for instructing English Language Learners (ELLs).

The teacher acknowledges and respects cultural and socioeconomic differences among students when planning instruction.

Where to find other study resources for information about diversity and how to design appropriate instruction for students presenting differences in background, ethnicity, learning styles, and motivations:

http://teacher.scholastic.com/professional/teachdive/manylanguages.htm
This site provides advice about working with all children and families, fostering bilingualism, and encouraging tolerance and self-esteem.

http://oncampus.richmond.edu/academics/as/education/projects/webunits/diversity/diversity.html
This website provides information about pieces of literature that can be used within the classroom to help children learn more about diversity. Its goal is to increase awareness and help children become more open-minded to differences with special emphasis on children with special needs and children from multicultural backgrounds.

www.ri.net/gifted_talented/character.html
This site provides characteristics and behaviors of gifted children.

http://everythingesl.net
This site provides resources, teaching tips, and lesson plans for teachers of ESL students.

www.ced.appstate.edu/projects/partnership/student/diversity98/diversity.htm
This site is designed to help teachers become more aware of diversity and have a better understanding of what it is and how to deal with it in the classroom. It provides information and activities for incorporating diversity into the classroom.

www.nichcy.org
This site provides extensive information on disabilities in children.

www.kidsource.com/NICHCY/learning_disabilities.html
This site provides information about learning disabilities including the definition, incidence, characteristics, educational implications, and additional resources.

http://ericec.org/faqs.html
This site provides a significant collection of ERIC sites regarding disabilities and gifted education.

Domain I: Designing Instruction and Assessment to Promote Student Learning

Competency 003—The teacher understands procedures for designing effective and coherent instruction and assessment based on appropriate learning goals and objectives.

> **In Other Words:**
>
> This competency focuses on the teacher's understanding of the state curriculum of Texas (Texas Essential Knowledge and Skills–TEKS), how to use the curriculum to plan instruction, and the importance of selecting appropriate instructional goals and objectives.

Content and Pedagogy

The teacher understands the importance of the state content and performance standards as outlined in the Texas Essential Knowledge and Skills (TEKS).

The teacher understands relevant content of the discipline being taught, including concepts, principles, relationships, methods of inquiry, and key issues.

The teacher understands the significance of the vertical alignment of content, including prerequisite knowledge and skills.

The teacher understands how lesson content and skills connect with other disciplines and within the discipline.

The teacher understands current research on best pedagogical practices.

The teacher uses the TEKS to plan instruction.

The teacher exhibits appropriate knowledge of a subject to promote student learning.

The teacher demonstrates awareness of common student misconceptions or likely sources of student error in relation to particular content.

The teacher plans instruction that reflects an understanding of important prerequisite relationships.

The teacher plans instruction that makes connections within the discipline and across disciplines.

The teacher uses a variety of pedagogical techniques to convey information and teach skills.

  Specific emphasis for **EC–4** teachers may include:
  - hands-on exploration and guided discussions

  Specific emphasis for **4–8** teachers may include:
  - cooperative learning groups and whole class discussions

  Specific emphasis for **8–12** teachers may include:
  - self-directed inquiry

Selection of Instructional Goals and Objectives

The teacher understands the importance of developing instructional goals and objectives that are clear, relevant, meaningful, and age-appropriate.

The teacher understands the importance of developing instructional goals and objectives that can be assessed.

The teacher understands the importance of developing instructional goals and objectives that are suitable for students with varied learning needs.

  Special emphasis for **4–8** teachers may include:
  - students who think concretely in some contexts but can reason abstractly in others
  - students with varying academic backgrounds

  Special emphasis for **8–12** teachers may include:
  - students with different levels of skills in abstract thinking and reasoning

The teacher understands the importance of aligning instructional goals with campus and district goals.

The teacher develops instructional goals and objectives that are clear, relevant, meaningful, and age-appropriate.

The teacher develops instructional goals and objectives that are able to be assessed.

The teacher develops instructional goals and objectives that reflect students' age, developmental level, prior skills and knowledge, background, and interests.

The teacher develops instructional goals and objectives that reflect different types of student learning and skills.

Special emphasis for the **EC–4** teacher may include:
- learning to cooperate with others
- understanding cause-and-effect relationships

Special emphasis for the **4–8** teacher may include:
- collaborating with peers
- developing logical arguments

Special emphasis for the **8–12** teacher may include:
- workplace skills
- self-direction

Where to find other study resources for information about designing effective instruction using appropriate instructional goals and objectives:

www.tea.state.tx.us/teks
This site provides the Texas Essential Knowledge and Skills, the curriculum required for children in Texas public schools.

www.tea.state.tx.us/curriculum/ced.html
This site provides links to various areas of curriculum for students in Texas.

www.adprima.com./lesson.htm
This site provides excellent resources for designing appropriate and effective instruction.

http://my.execpc.com/~dboals/k-12.html
This site provides ideas for planning effective instruction for students grade K-12.

Competency 004—The teacher understands learning processes and factors that impact student learning and demonstrates this knowledge by planning effective, engaging instruction and appropriate assessments.

> **In Other Words:**
> This competency focuses on the teacher's understanding and use of appropriate resources to engage students in effective learning as well as the teacher's ability to understand and apply effective assessment models in order to guide instructional planning.

Resources

The teacher understands the use of appropriate materials and resources for preparing instruction, presenting lessons, and assessing learning.

The teacher understands the importance of knowing when to integrate technology into instruction and assessment.

The teacher understands the use of resources beyond the campus to help students meet academic and nonacademic needs.

The teacher uses various types of materials and other resources to aid in preparing and implementing instruction.

The teacher uses technological tools to promote learning and expand instructional options.

The teacher uses resources available outside the school (e.g., museums, businesses, community members) to enhance students' learning opportunities.

Designing Coherent Instruction

The teacher understands the importance of designing instruction that reflects the TEKS.

The teacher understands features of instruction that maximize students' thinking skills.

   Special emphasis for the **8–12** teacher may include:
   - posing problems that develop students' higher-order and abstract thinking

The teacher understands the importance of planning lessons and structuring units so that activities progress in a logical sequence.

The teacher understands how materials, technology, and other resources may be used to support instructional goals and objectives and engage students in meaningful learning.

The teacher understands the benefits of designing instruction that integrates content across disciplines.

The teacher understands the importance of engaging in continuous monitoring and self-assessment of instructional effectiveness.

The teacher plans instructional activities that progress sequentially and support stated instructional goals based on the TEKS.

The teacher selects instructional resources that support instructional goals, enhance student achievement, and engage students in learning.

Domain I: Designing Instruction and Assessment to Promote Student Learning

The teacher uses varied activities and instructional groupings to engage students in instructional content and meet instructional goals and objectives.

The teacher allocates time appropriately within lessons and units, including providing adequate opportunities for students to engage in reflection and closure.

   Special emphasis for the **EC–4** teacher may include:
- awareness of attention spans of students in grades EC–4

   Special emphasis for the **4–8** teacher may include:
- exploring content by presenting thematic units that incorporate different disciplines, grouping students in study teams, providing multicultural learning experiences, and prompting students to consider ideas from multiple viewpoints

The teacher provides students with opportunities to explore content from many perspectives.

   Special emphasis for the **EC–4** teacher may include:
- exploring content by providing an integrated curriculum, employing plan as one learning mode, permitting student choice of activities when appropriate, involving students in working on projects, designing instruction that supports students' growing ability to work cooperatively and to reflect upon other points of view

   Special emphasis for the **8–12** teacher may include:
- exploring content by providing intradisciplinary and interdisciplinary instruction encouraging students' application of knowledge and skills to the world beyond the school, designing instruction that reflects students' increasing ability to examine complex issues and ideas

Assessment of Student Learning

The teacher understands the role of assessment in guiding instructional planning.

The teacher understands the importance of creating assessments that are congruent with instructional goals and objectives.

The teacher understands the characteristics, uses, advantages, and limitations of various assessment methods and strategies.

The teacher understands the role of technology in assessing student learning.

The teacher understands the benefits of and strategies for promoting student self-assessment.

   Special emphasis for the **8–12** teacher may include:
- the importance of using ongoing self-assessment in young adulthood

The teacher understands the connection between the Texas statewide assessment program, the TEKS, needs, and instruction.

The teacher understands how to analyze data from local, state, and other assessments using common, statistical measures.

The teacher uses a variety of assessment methods, including technology, that are appropriate for evaluating student achievement of instructional goals and objectives.

The teacher communicates assessment criteria and standards to students.

The teacher designs assessments, where appropriate, that reflect real-world applications of knowledge and understanding.

The teacher promotes students' use of self-monitoring and self-assessment.

The teacher analyzes assessment results to aid in determining students' strengths.

The teacher uses assessment results to help plan instruction for groups of students or individuals.

Although the TExES exam will not ask questions specifically about developmental theorists, the teacher is expected to know these theories and how they apply to teaching. As a review, these websites are listed as references at the end of the book.

Where to find other study resources for information about engaging and motivating students in effective learning and about utilizing appropriate assessment measures:

http://lucas.tea.state.tx.us/PAI/TTB/1,3498,20,00.html
This site allows users to browse lists of lesson plans and resources which have been chosen to enrich and support teaching and learning in the classroom.

www.ed.gov/databases/ERIC_Digests/ed351150.html
This site provides teachers with information regarding portfolios and their use with young children.

www.eric.ed.gov/archives/pba.html
This site provides a copy of the brochure "What Should Parents Know about Performance Assessment."

http://teacher.scholastic.com/professional/assessment/studentprogress.htm#standardized
This site provides information about measuring student progress.

CHAPTER FIVE

Domain II: Creating a Positive Productive Classroom Environment
(Includes Competencies 005 and 006)

The content in Domain II represents 15% of the questions on any of the Pedagogy and Professional Responsibility (PPR) exams. The focus of this domain is the teacher's ability to create a classroom environment of respect and rapport that fosters a positive climate for learning, equity, and excellence.

The information represented in these questions is intended to capture the teacher's knowledge regarding the following concepts:

Competency 005–The teacher knows how to establish a classroom climate that fosters learning, equity, and excellence and uses this knowledge to create a physical and emotional environment that is safe and productive.

> **In Other Words:**
>
> This competency focuses on the teacher's understanding and application of the need for children to be taught appropriate material using age-appropriate strategies and to be actively engaged in learning. It also points out the need for the teacher to understand the importance of establishing a safe, supportive, and collaborative environment for children of all backgrounds and diversities. It addresses the need for the teacher to communicate an enthusiasm for learning.

Creating an Environment of Respect and Rapport

The teacher understands the importance of creating a learning environment in which diversity and individual differences are respected.

The teacher understands the impact of teacher-student interactions and interactions among students on classroom climate and student learning and development.

The teacher understands ways to establish a positive classroom climate that fosters active engagement in learning among students.

The teacher interacts with students in ways that reflect support and shows respect for all students.

The teacher uses strategies to ensure that interactions among students are polite, respectful, and cooperative.

Special emphasis for the **EC–4** teacher may include:
- encouraging cooperation and sharing
- teaching children to use language appropriately to express their feelings

Special emphasis for the **4–8** teacher may include:
- using knowledge of the unique characteristics and needs of 4-8 students to establish a positive, productive classroom environment (collaboration with peers, how actions and attitudes affect others)

Special emphasis for the **8–12** teacher may include:
- using knowledge of the unique characteristics and needs of 8-12 students to establish a positive, productive classroom environment (encourage respect for the community and the people in it, promote the use of appropriate language and behavior in daily interactions)

The teacher uses strategies to ensure that the classroom environment and interactions among individuals and groups within the classroom promote active engagement in learning.

Domain II: Creating a Positive Productive Classroom Environment

Establishing an Environment for Learning and Excellence

The teacher understands the importance of communicating enthusiasm for learning.

The teacher understands the necessity of communicating teacher expectations for student learning.

The teacher communicates to all students the importance of instructional content and the expectation of high-quality work.

The teacher ensures that instructional goals and objectives, activities, classroom interactions, assessments, and other elements of the classroom environment convey high expectations for student achievement.

Maintaining a Physical and Emotional Environment That Is Safe and Productive

The teacher understands features and characteristics of physical spaces that are safe and productive for learning.

The teacher understands the benefits and limitations of various arrangements of furniture in the classroom.

The teacher understands the procedures for ensuring safety in the classroom.

The teacher understands physical accessibility as a potential issue in student learning.

The teacher understands students' emotional needs and ways to address those needs.

The teacher organizes the physical environment in a way that facilitates learning.

The teacher creates a safe and inclusive classroom environment.

The teacher uses effective strategies for creating and maintaining a positive classroom environment.

The teacher respects students' rights and dignity.

Where to find other study resources for information about establishing an appropriate classroom climate that is safe and productive:

http://www.udel.edu/cte/TAbook/climate.html
This site provides information about strategies teachers can use to create an environment in which students are willing to be active participants.

http://www.ncrel.org/sdrs/areas/issues/students/earlycld/ea4lk24.htm
This site provides guidelines for maintaining an effective classroom environment.

http://das.kucrl.org/iam/assessclass.html
This site provides a checklist for assessing the classroom environment.

Competency 006–The teacher understands strategies for creating an organized and productive learning environment and for managing student behavior.

> **In Other Words:**
>
> This competency focuses on the teacher's understanding and application of procedures and routines that promote organization and productive learning. It emphasizes the teacher's understanding of the importance of collaboration, active learning, time management, and organization for learners of all ages. Further, it emphasizes the teacher's ability to use technology to assist with administative tasks and the ability to work with volunteers and paraprofessionals to enrich learning while implementing effective strategies for monitoring their performance. It focuses on the teacher's ability to apply appropriate behavior management strategies to reinforce appropriate behavior for each developmental level. It further emphasizes the teacher's ability to promote appropriate and ethical work habits in the classroom and beyond. Teachers are expected to convey high and realistic behavior expections, allowing the students to be involved in developing rules and procedures. They are able to establish clear consequences for inappropriate behavior and enforce these standards consistently.

Managing Classroom Procedures

The teacher understands how classroom routines and procedures affect student learning and achievement.

The teacher understands how to organize student groups to facilitate cooperation and productivity.

Domain II: Creating a Positive Productive Classroom Environment

The teacher understands the importance of time management for effective classroom functioning.

Special emphasis for the **EC–4** teacher may include:
- importance of creating a schedule that balances restful activities and active movement activities and that provides large blocks of time for play, projects, and learning centers
- importance of creating a schedule that considers the attention span characteristic of EC-4 children

Special emphasis for the **4–8** teacher may include:
- the importance to young adolescents of incorporating time for physical movement throughout the day

Special emphasis for the **8–12** teacher may include:
- the importance of establishing the expectation that students will arrive in class ready to begin working

The teacher understands procedures for making transitions.

The teacher understands and implements routines and procedures for managing and using materials, supplies, and technology.

Special emphasis for the **EC–4** teacher may include:
- teaching children where things belong
- teaching children how and when to share
- teaching children how to use and take care of materials, supplies, and technology

Special emphasis for the **4–8** teacher may include:
- teaching students responsibility for taking care of materials and equipment in the classroom

The teacher understands noninstructional duties (e.g., taking attendance) and procedures for performing these duties effectively.

The teacher establishes classroom rules and procedures to promote an organized and productive learning environment.

Special emphasis for the **EC–4** teacher may include:
- teaching, modeling, and monitoring students' organizational skills at an age-appropriate level (establishing regular places for classroom toys and materials, sorting blocks by shape and size during clean-up)

Special emphasis for the **4–8** teacher may include:
- teaching, modeling, and monitoring students' organizational and time management skills at an age-appropriate level (keeping related materials together, using organizational tools)

Special emphasis for the **8–12** teacher may include:
- teaching, modeling, and monitoring students' organizational and time management skills at an age-appropriate level (using effective strategies for locating information, organizing information systematically)

The teacher organizes and manages groups to ensure that students work together cooperatively and productively.

The teacher schedules activities and manages class time in ways that maximize student learning.

The teacher manages transitions to maximize instructional time.

The teacher monitors the performance of volunteers and paraprofessionals in the classroom in accordance with district policies and procedures.

The teacher uses volunteers and paraprofessionals to enhance and enrich instruction, and evaluates their effectiveness.

Managing Student Behavior

The teacher understands theories and techniques relating to managing and monitoring student behavior.

The teacher understands appropriate behavior standards and expectations for students at various developmental levels.

Domain II: Creating a Positive Productive Classroom Environment

Special emphasis for the **EC–4** teacher may include:
- teaching children to wait their turn, to cooperate with others, to use words appropriately, and to express disagreement

Special emphasis for the **4–8** teacher may include:
- demonstrating and requiring respectful treatment of others

Special emphasis for the **8–12** teacher may include:
- expecting all students to conform and contribute to an atmosphere of civility

The teacher understands the significance of district policies and procedures for managing student behavior and ensuring ethical behavior in the classroom.

The teacher understands the importance of establishing and enforcing classroom standards of student conduct and clear consequences for inappropriate behavior.

The teacher understands the value of encouraging students to work in an ethical manner and monitor their own behavior.

The teacher uses effective methods and procedures for monitoring and responding to positive and negative student behaviors.

Where to find other study resources for information about creating an organized and productive learning environment and for managing student behavior:

http://www.honorlevel.com/techniques.xml
This site provides 11 techniques for use in the classroom that will help in achieving effective group management and control.

http://osi.fsu.edu/waveseries/htmlversions/wave3.htm
This site offers suggestions for effective classroom management with a focus on organization, communication, monitoring, and instructional delivery.

http://www.theteachersguide.com/ClassManagement.htm
This site provides an extensive listing of classroom management resources.

http://www.behavioradvisor.com
This site offers thousands of tips on managing student behavior and provides step-by-step directions for implementing a great number of standard interventions.

CHAPTER SIX

Domain III: Implementing Effective, Responsive Instruction and Assessment
(Includes Competencies 007–010)

The content in Domain III represents 31% of the questions on any of the Pedagogy and Professional Responsibility (PPR) exams. The focus of this domain is the teacher's ability to effectively communicate with students in order to actively engage students in learning, to utilize technology to enhance learning, and to provide timely and meaningful feedback.

The information represented in these questions is intended to capture the teacher's knowledge regarding the following concepts:

Competency 007—The teacher understands and applies principles and strategies for communicating effectively in varied teaching and learning contexts.

> **In Other Words:**
>
> This competency focuses on the teacher's understanding and application of the importance of clear, accurate communcation for effective teaching and learning. It emphasizes the importance of using effective principles and strategies for communicating as well as using spoken and written language that is appropriate for a student's age, interest, and background. It stresses the importance of utilizing skills and strategies for engaging in appropriate questioning that leads to effective student discussions.

Communication

The teacher understands the importance of clear, accurate communication in the teaching and learning process. The teacher communicates directions, explanations, and procedures clearly, accurately, and with an appropriate level of detail, both orally and in writing.
The teacher understands principles and strategies for communicating effectively in varied teaching and learning contexts. The teacher uses effective, appropriate verbal and nonverbal interpersonal skills to reach students and communicate commitment to students.

The teacher understands and uses spoken and written language that is appropriate to students' ages, interests, and backgrounds.

The teacher understands skills and strategies for engaging in skilled questioning and leading effective student discussions.

The teacher uses effective communication techniques, including questioning and discussion techniques, to foster active student inquiry, higher-order thinking, problem solving, and productive, supportive interactions.

The teacher uses carefully framed questions to enable students to reflect on their understanding of content and to consider new possibilities.

The teacher applies skills for leading discussions that engage all students in exploring important questions and that extend students' knowledge.

Where to find other study resources for information regarding effective communication in varied teaching and learning contexts:

http://ourspecialkids.org/tgi-commstrategies.html
This site provides a concise list of strategies to use for effective communication with parents.

http://ourspecialkids.org/tgi-negotiating.html
This site provides and excellent list of strategies to assist parents in negotiating with school personnel.

http://ourspecialkids.org/tgi-commschool.html
This site provides a concise list of strategies for helping parents communicate with school personnel.

http://www.stc-india.org/articles/articles/strategies.htm
A practical guide for learning to communicate well with professionals, supervisors, and parents.

Domain III: Implementing Effective, Responsive Instruction and Assessment

Sparks-Langer, G.M., Starko, A.J., Pasch, M., Burke, W., Moody, C.D., & Gardner, T.G. (2004). Teaching As Decision Making. 2nd ed. New Jersey: Pearson/Merrill Prentice Hall. pp. 18–19; 315; 338–341.

Textbook that provides excellent strategies for communication.

Competency 008—The teacher provides appropriate instruction that actively engages students in the learning process.

> **In Other Words:**
>
> This competency focuses on the teacher's understanding and application of the importance of selecting appropriate instructional activities and assignments for all students. It emphasizes the importance of presenting content to students in relevant and meaningful ways as well as promoting students, intellectual involvement through appropriate instructional groupings, effective motivational strategies, and effective structuring and pacing of lessons in order to promote student engagement and learning.

Engaging Students in Learning

The teacher understands the criteria for selecting appropriate instructional activities and assignments for students with varied characteristics and needs and is able to create lessons with a clearly defined structure around which activities are organized.

Specific emphasis for grade **EC–4** teachers may include the teacher's ability to:
- relate content to students' play activities or background experiences

The teacher understands the importance of promoting students' intellectual involvement with content and their active development of understanding. The teacher creates activities and assignments that are appropriate for students and that actively engage them in the learning process.

Specific emphasis for grade **4–8** teachers may include the teacher's ability to:
- teach, model, and monitor age-appropriate study skills (using graphic organizers, outlining, note-taking, summarizing, test taking) and structuring research projects appropriately (teach students the steps in research, establish checkpoints during research projects, help students use time-management tools)

The teacher understands strategies and techniques for using instructional groupings to promote student learning.

The teacher understands different types of motivation, factors affecting student motivation, and effective motivational strategies in varied learning contexts.

The teacher understands techniques for structuring and pacing lessons in ways that promote student engagement and learning.

The teacher understands the need to encourage students' self-motivation and active engagement in learning.

The teacher selects and uses instructional materials, resources, and technologies that are suitable for instructional goals and that engage students cognitively.

The teacher represents content effectively and in ways that link with students' prior knowledge and experience.

The teacher uses flexible grouping to promote productive student interactions and enhance learning.

The teacher paces lessons appropriately and flexibly in response to student needs.

The teacher engages students intellectually by teaching meaningful content in ways that promote all students' active and invested participation in the learning process.

Specific emphasis for grade **EC–4** teachers may include the teacher's ability to:
- stimulate reflection, critical thinking, and inquiry among students (provide opportunities to manipulate materials and to test ideas and hypotheses, provide repetition for increased conceptual understanding, support the concept of play as a valid vehicle for learning)

Specific emphasis for grade **4–8** teachers may include the teacher's ability to:
- stimulate reflection, critical thinking, and inquiry among grade 4–8 students (engage students in structured hands-on problem-solving activities that are challenging; encourage exploration and risk-taking; create a learning community that promotes positive contributions, effective communication and the respectful exchange of ideas)
- enhance learning for students by providing instruction that encourages the use and refinement of higher-order thinking skills (prompting students to explore ideas from diverse perspectives, structuring active learning experiences involving cooperative learning problem solving, open-ended questioning, and inquiry; building students' capacity to learn through in-depth study and research)

Specific emphasis for grade **8–12** teachers may include the teacher's ability to:
- enhance learning for students by providing instruction that encourages the use and refinement of higher-order thinking skills (prompting students to explore ideas from diverse perspectives, structuring active learning experiences involving cooperative learning problem solving, open-ended questioning, and inquiry; building students' capacity to learn through in-depth study and research)

Domain III: Implementing Effective, Responsive Instruction and Assessment

Where to find other study resources for information about regarding active student engagement and motivation in the learning process:

www.kidsource.com/kidsource/content2/Student_Motivation.html
This website examines motivation as an important ingredient in student learning.

http://www.nwrel.org/request/oct00/textonly.html
This website provides extensive information on the role of student engagement and motivation in the learning process.

http://www.mccallie.org/student_engagement.htm
This website provides a list of the characteristics of student engagement and how teachers can foster this in students.

http://www.gse.uci.edu/renewal/Challenge/engage.html
This website provides an article discussing the challenges of student engagement.

Competency 009—The teacher incorporates the effective use of technology to plan, organize, deliver, and evaluate instruction for all students.

> **In Other Words:**
>
> This competency focuses on the teacher's ability to incorporate effective materials, resources, and technologies that are appropriate and engaging for students in varied learning situations.

The teacher understands the use of instructional materials, resources, and technologies that are appropriate and engaging for students in varied learning situations and utilizes them appropriately throughout learning experiences.

Where to find other study resources for information about the use of technology for effective planning, organization, delivery, and evaluation of instruction for all students:

http://www.iste.org/resources
This website, sponsored by the International Society for Technology Education, provides listings of current web sites, books, and periodicals that relate to educational technology. You may choose an online resource topic and discover a vast array of information from lesson plans to job postings.

http://nces.ed.gov/pubsearch/pubsinfo.asp?pubid=2004014

This website provides a report examining the use of computers and the internet by American children and adolescents between the ages of 5 and 17. The report examines the overall rate of use, the ways in which children and teens use the technologies, where the use occurs (home, school, and other locations), and the relationships of these aspects of computer and internet use to demographic and socioeconomic characteristics such as children's age and race/ethnicity and their parents' education and family income.

http://www.mff.org/edtech

This website offers a series of articles related to the use of educational technology in k–12 education.

http://learnweb.harvard.edu/ent/home

This website is designed to help educators develop, enact, and assess effective ways of using new technologies.

Competency 010—The teacher monitors student performance and achievement; provides students with timely, high-quality feedback; and responds flexibly to promote learning for all students.

> **In Other Words:**
> This competency focuses on the teacher's understanding and ability to provide effective feedback in a timely aand constructive manner in order to guide each student's learning. It emphasizes the teacher's flexibility and responsiveness in the teaching/learning process in order to enhance student learning.

Providing Feedback to Students

The teacher understands characteristics of effective and timely feedback for students and uses appropriate language and formats to provide each student with feedback that is accurate, constructive, substantive, and specific.

The teacher understands how to use constructive feedback to guide each student's learning and is able to promote students' ability to use feedback to guide and enhance their learning.

The teacher bases feedback on high expectations for student learning.

Domain III: Implementing Effective, Responsive Instruction and Assessment

Demonstrating Flexibility and Responsiveness

The teacher understands the significance of teacher flexibility and responsiveness in the teaching/learning process and responds flexibly to various situations, such as lack of student engagement in a learning activity or the occurrence of an unanticipated learning opportunity.

The teacher understands situations in which teacher flexibility can enhance student learning and adjusts instruction based on ongoing assessment of student understanding.

Specific emphasis for grade **4–8** teachers may include the teacher's understanding of:
- the importance of using different illustrations and/or language to re-explain something students have not understood

The teacher uses alternative instructional approaches to ensure that all students learn and succeed.

Where to find other study resources for information about providing timely and high-quality feedback to students:

http://www.ih.k12.oh.us/

This website provides information from the Ohio teacher certification standards regarding providing effective feedback to students.

http://www.rdg.ac.uk/Handbooks/Teaching_and_Learning/Useful_distinctions.html

This website provides examples of how to provide effective feedback to students.

CHAPTER SEVEN

Domain IV: Fulfilling Professional Roles and Responsibilities
(Includes Competencies 011–013)

The content in Domain III represents 23% of the questions on any of the Pedagogy and Professional Responsibility (PPR) exams. The focus of this domain is the teacher's understanding of the importance of family involvement in students' education. In addition, teachers understand the importance of ongoing professional development and knowledge of and adherence to legal and ethical requirements in Texas.

The information represented in these questions is intended to capture the teacher's knowledge regarding the following concepts:

Competency 011—The teacher understands the importance of family involvement in children's education and knows how to interact and communicate effectively with families.

> **In Other Words:**
>
> This competency focuses on the teacher's understanding and ability to involve the families of students in an appropriate manner by demonstrating sensitivity to diverse characteristics, backgrounds, and needs. It emphasizes working and communicating with families on a regular basis through effective parent-teacher conferences, sharing information regarding student progress, responding to family concerns, and engaging families in various aspects of the instructional program.

The teacher understands the importance of families' involvement in their children's education.

The teacher understands effective methods for working and communicating with families in varied contexts and is able to interact appropriately with families that have diverse characteristics, backgrounds, and needs.

The teacher applies procedures for conducting effective parent–teacher conferences.

The teacher communicates with families on a regular basis to share information about students' progress and responds appropriately to families' concerns.

The teacher engages families in their children's education and in various aspects of the instructional program.

Where to find other study resources for information about interacting and communicating effectively with families:

www.nea.org/neatoday/9709/chat.html

This website provides a transcript of a conversation between the founder/president of Home and School Institute (HIS) and the NEA editor regarding the importance of communicating with families.

www.nwrel.org/scpd/sirs/3/cu6.html

This website provides a review of the literature about parent involvement and examines the role of parental involvement on student achievement, student attitude and behavior, and sense of community.

http://www.pta.org/parentinvolvement/index.asp

This website provides information regarding parent involvement from the perspective of the National Parent–Teacher Association (PTA).

Competency 012—The teacher enhances professional knowledge and skills by effectively interacting with other members of the educational community and participating in various types of professional activities.

> **In Other Words:**
>
> This competency focuses on the teacher's understanding and ability to interact with other educators and contribute to the school and district. It emphasizes the importance of ongoing professional development in order to enhance content knowledge and pedagogical skills.

Domain IV: Fulfilling Professional Roles and Responsibilities

Interacting with Other Educators and Contributing to the School and District

The teacher understands types of interactions among professionals in a school (e.g., vertical teaming, horizontal teaming, team teaching, mentoring) and the significance of these interactions in order to maintain supportive and cooperative relationships with colleagues.

The teacher understands appropriate ways for working and communicating effectively with other professionals in varied educational contexts and engages in collaborative decision making and problem solving with other educators to support students' learning and well-being.

The teacher understands the roles and responsibilities of specialists and other professionals at the building and district levels (e.g., department chairperson, principal, board of trustees, curriculum coordinator, special education professional) and communicates effectively and appropriately with other educators in varied contexts.

The teacher understands the available educator support systems (e.g., mentors, service centers, state initiatives, universities).

The teacher understands the various ways in which teachers may contribute to their school and district and assumes professional responsibilities and duties outside the classroom as appropriate (e.g., serve on committees, volunteer to participate in events and projects).

The teacher understands the value of participating in school activities.

The teacher collaborates professionally with other members of the school community to achieve school and district educational goals.

The teacher participates in decision making, problem solving, and sharing ideas and expertise.

Continuing Professional Development

The teacher understands the importance of participating in professional development activities to enhance content knowledge and pedagogical skill and participates in various types of professional development opportunities (e.g., conferences, workshops, working with mentors, and other support systems).

The teacher understands the importance of documenting self-assessments and uses evidence of self-assessment (e.g., portfolio) to identify strengths, challenges, and potential problems; improve teaching performance; and achieve instructional goals.

The teacher understands characteristics, goals, and procedures associated with teacher appraisal.

The teacher understands the importance of using reflection and ongoing self-assessmemt to enhance teaching effectiveness.

The teacher enhances content and pedagogical knowledge through a variety of activities (e.g., reading journals, joining professional associations, attending conferences, engaging in coursework).

The teacher uses appropriate resources and support systems inside and outside the school to address professional development needs.

Where to find other study resources for information about interacting with educators and contributing to the school and district:

www.ncrel.org/sdrs/areas/issues/envrnmnt/go/94-4over.htm

This website explores changes in our assumptions about effective professional development, new visions of teaching and learning, and the implications of these new approaches for schools. It describes alternative strategies for effectively finding and using time to support professional development needs and discusses the accompanying policy implications.

http://www.eduscapes.com/tap/

This website provides a variety of information to assist teachers with professional development in a wide variety of areas.

www.sedl.org/pitl/pic/reflection.html

This website provides strategies for guiding teachers' efforts to improve student learning through reflection of their own teaching practices.

http://knowledgeloom.org

This website provides a venue for teachers to review current research, view stories about real teachers, schools, and districts as well as providing the opportunity for participation in online events and discussions.

Competency 013—The teacher adheres to legal and ethical requirements for educators and is knowledgeable of the structure of education in Texas.

> **In Other Words:**
>
> This competency focuses on the teacher's understanding of the legal and ethical requirements of Texas education as well as how to use to this knowledge to guide behavior in education-related situations. It emphasizes the importance of adhering to ethical guidelines in relation to confidentiality, maintaining accurate records, advocating for students and the profession, and adhering to required procedures for administering state and district mandated assessments.

Domain IV: Fulfilling Professional Roles and Responsibilities

The teacher understands legal requirements for educators (e.g., those related to special education, students' and families' rights, student discipline, equity, and child abuse).

The teacher understands ethical guidelines for educators in Texas (e.g., in relation to confidentiality, interactions with students and others in the school community).

The teacher uses knowledge of legal and ethical guidelines to guide behavior in education-related situations.

The teacher understands policies and procedures in compliance with the Code of Ethics and Standard Practices for Texas as adopted by the State Board for Educator Certification.

The teacher understands procedures and requirements for maintaining accurate student records and is able to maintain these records.

The teacher understands the importance of adhering to required procedures for administering state and district-mandated assessments.

The teacher understands the structure of the education system in Texas, including relationships between campus, local, and state components and uses the knowledge of this structure to seek information and assistance in addressing issues.

The teacher serves as an advocate for students and the profession.

Where to find other study resources for information about the legal and ethical requirements and the structure of education in Texas:

http://www.tea.state.tx.us
This Texas Education Agency site provides extensive information regarding all aspects of teaching in Texas.

http://www.sbec.state.tx.us
This State Board for Educator Certification site provides extensive information for all teachers in Texas.

http://www.aft.org/lessons/resources.html
This site lists resources relevant to the provision of quality public education.

http://www.aft.org/edissues/Idea.htm
This site offers excellent information regarding laws governing students with disabilities' rights, featuring many positive changes.

http://www.ed.gov/pubs/OR/ResearchRpts/whos.html

This site discusses teachers' views on control over school policy and classroom practices.

http://www.aft.org/parentpage

This site provides extensive information on academic standards, communication with school staff, class size, school discipline, and discipline.

Section Three

DIAGNOSTIC AND PRACTICE TESTS AND ANSWERS

Diagnostic All-level Pedagogy and Professional Responsibilities Test Answer Sheet

Remove (or photocopy) this answer sheet and use it to complete the practice test.
(See answer key following the test when finished.)

1. Ⓐ Ⓑ Ⓒ Ⓓ
2. Ⓐ Ⓑ Ⓒ Ⓓ
3. Ⓐ Ⓑ Ⓒ Ⓓ
4. Ⓐ Ⓑ Ⓒ Ⓓ
5. Ⓐ Ⓑ Ⓒ Ⓓ
6. Ⓐ Ⓑ Ⓒ Ⓓ
7. Ⓐ Ⓑ Ⓒ Ⓓ
8. Ⓐ Ⓑ Ⓒ Ⓓ
9. Ⓐ Ⓑ Ⓒ Ⓓ
10. Ⓐ Ⓑ Ⓒ Ⓓ

11. Ⓐ Ⓑ Ⓒ Ⓓ
12. Ⓐ Ⓑ Ⓒ Ⓓ
13. Ⓐ Ⓑ Ⓒ Ⓓ
14. Ⓐ Ⓑ Ⓒ Ⓓ
15. Ⓐ Ⓑ Ⓒ Ⓓ
16. Ⓐ Ⓑ Ⓒ Ⓓ
17. Ⓐ Ⓑ Ⓒ Ⓓ
18. Ⓐ Ⓑ Ⓒ Ⓓ
19. Ⓐ Ⓑ Ⓒ Ⓓ
20. Ⓐ Ⓑ Ⓒ Ⓓ

21. Ⓐ Ⓑ Ⓒ Ⓓ
22. Ⓐ Ⓑ Ⓒ Ⓓ
23. Ⓐ Ⓑ Ⓒ Ⓓ
24. Ⓐ Ⓑ Ⓒ Ⓓ
25. Ⓐ Ⓑ Ⓒ Ⓓ
26. Ⓐ Ⓑ Ⓒ Ⓓ
27. Ⓐ Ⓑ Ⓒ Ⓓ
28. Ⓐ Ⓑ Ⓒ Ⓓ
29. Ⓐ Ⓑ Ⓒ Ⓓ
30. Ⓐ Ⓑ Ⓒ Ⓓ

31. Ⓐ Ⓑ Ⓒ Ⓓ
32. Ⓐ Ⓑ Ⓒ Ⓓ
33. Ⓐ Ⓑ Ⓒ Ⓓ
34. Ⓐ Ⓑ Ⓒ Ⓓ
35. Ⓐ Ⓑ Ⓒ Ⓓ
36. Ⓐ Ⓑ Ⓒ Ⓓ
37. Ⓐ Ⓑ Ⓒ Ⓓ
38. Ⓐ Ⓑ Ⓒ Ⓓ
39. Ⓐ Ⓑ Ⓒ Ⓓ
40. Ⓐ Ⓑ Ⓒ Ⓓ

CHAPTER EIGHT

Diagnostic All–level Pedagogy and Professional Responsibilities Test

1. Pedro is a fifth-grade student who appears tired and restless. His teacher, Mr. Burnside, observes that Pedro falls asleep at his desk and his homework assignments are usually late or incomplete. Mr. Burnside arranges a meeting with Pedro's mother and during the conference she confides that she is temporarily parenting on her own. Because she works a late shift at a local store, it is often late when she picks Pedro up from the babysitter's. What suggestion should Mr. Burnside make when discussing the situation with Pedro's mother?

    A. Reinforce how factors affecting the physical growth and health of a child have an impact on a student's cognitive development.
    B. Suggest that Pedro's mother limit her hours at work or find another means of employment.
    C. Suggest he will simplify Pedro's homework until his mother is no longer working nights.
    D. Suggest a highly recommended day care center in the community for Pedro's mother to consider.

2. Jenny, a slim, self-motivated 12-year-old, is actively involved in school as well as outside activities. Jenny tells her best friend that she dislikes her body and thinks she needs to go on a fasting diet. Her teacher overhears the conversation. What should be the teacher's *first* step?

   A. Disregard the conversation, knowing that Jenny is just looking for attention and is probably not really serious about going on a diet.
   B. Immediately contact Jenny's parents and share with them the conversation.
   C. Speak with Jenny in a private conference, sharing with her the information she overheard, and offer to be a sounding board.
   D. Talk to Jenny's friend about the conversation and tell her about several excellent websites Jenny might use.

3. Mr. Hutchinson, a fourth-grade teacher, is planning a social studies unit on the annexation of Texas to the United States. Mr. Hutchinson explains unit expectations and shares with the students that they will be working on projects in cooperative learning groups as well as on individual activities. At the completion of the unit, Mr. Hutchinson uses rubrics to assess the students. He has several students who work quite diligently on the group projects, but when it comes to individual projects, they do not respond as well. Mr. Hutchinson arranges individual conferences. When discussing the problem with the students during individual conferences, Mr. Hutchinson should:

   A. compare the students' individual work to that of the other students in the class.
   B. lower his expectations for these students so they can complete projects on time.
   C. emphasize the importance of goal-setting and completing assignments.
   D. have the students team up with other students who have a good record of completing assignments.

4. Students in a seventh-grade history class have been discussing Stephen F. Austin's contributions to the state of Texas. Mr. Radcliffe has several English Language Learner (ELL) students in his class. Which of the following shows that Mr. Radcliffe understands student diversity issues?

   A. Having the ELL students work with English-proficient partners to create dialogue or scenes about Stephen F. Austin and then dramatize the events.
   B. Having the ELL students complete a timeline of Austin's contributions to the state of Texas.
   C. Having the ELL students meet together and conduct research to learn more about Stephen F. Austin and then give a report.
   D. Having the ELL students create a map about the settling of Texas and the contributions made by Stephen F. Austin.

GO ON TO THE NEXT PAGE

5. Casey, a fourth grade student, was experiencing difficulty with word recognition skills and was not performing at the expected grade level. After the administration of a series of tests, it was determined that Casey has mild mental retardation. His teacher can *best* address his problem by:

   A. adjusting the program to meet Casey's needs and appropriate instructional objectives.
   B. providing more challenging activities so Casey will improve on his word recognition skills.
   C. keeping a list of the words that Casey knows and drill him on them daily.
   D. focusing mainly on limiting the amount of classroom work Casey is given so he has more time to work on vocabulary definitions.

6. Ms. Justin asks her students to word process their papers. However, several students in the class have physical disabilities. Each student who has been diagnosed has an Individualized Education Program (IEP). Ms. Justin's *primary* responsibility would be:

   A. to limit the amount of time the students sit at the computer.
   B. to meet objectives as outlined on the student's IEP.
   C. to require the student to complete only half of the assignment.
   D. to provide a buddy system for the students who need help and let that student do all of the word processing.

7. Ms. Patton plans a fifth-grade language arts poetry unit. She presents specific poems that she wants the children to read. She has several gifted and talented students in the class. Which of the following would be the *most* likely choice of activities for the bright students?

   A. Read the poem aloud using gestures to convey meaning and encourage the students to copy the actions.
   B. Ask students to self-select and dramatize a poem.
   C. Ask the students to copy the poem so they can enter it in their portfolios.
   D. Give a poem to a student and have him or her read it in class.

8. Dialogue journals have become a regular part of Mr. Wheeler's seventh-grade math class. Mr. Wheeler uses the journals to talk to his students through writing. He encourages his students to write informally about their math assignments. He suggests they ask questions, write about what they understand, or write about what they do not understand. What *primary* benefit are the journals to the students?

   A. They are a way to reduce the number of teacher-made tests.
   B. They are a means to compare what they are learning to what others in the class are learning.
   C. They are a way to use material at a conference and gain the feeling of collaboration.
   D. They are a means of self-evaluation to determine what they learned and where they still need the most help.

9. Ms. Fidler teaches seventh grade in a low socioeconomic community. Several students are slow to respond to questions and can't keep track of the assignments. Ms. Filder perceives the students to be less capable because of their low socioeconomic status. What should Ms. Fidler do to change her perception?

   A. Engage in self-reflection and realize that her own behaviors may be the cause of the students' slow achievement.
   B. Have all the students tested to determine if they have a learning disability.
   C. Demand less work from the students so they can excel on the work they submit.
   D. Let the high achievers in the class model how to respond to questions.

10. Students in Ms. Gonzalez's sixth-grade English class are asked to read and actively engage in discussion after the completion of a story or book. Ms. Gonzalez regularly asks questions such as, "Justify your reasons for making the previous statement," "Critique the following conversation that took place between the main characters in the book," "Establish the way you think the author should have ended the book," or "Predict what you think will happen in the next chapter." In asking these questions of her students, Ms. Gonzalez's focus should be on:

    A. checking to make sure the students read the assigned material.
    B. encouraging the use of higher-order thinking skills.
    C. gathering information and discovering students' knowledge, interests, and experiences.
    D. receiving literal interpretations of the material students are to be reading.

GO ON TO THE NEXT PAGE

11. Kwame, an eighth-grade student who has difficulty using his arms and his legs, is confined to a wheelchair. Kwame's disability prompted his teacher, Ms. Goodwin, to approach the principal about providing a computer device for Kwame. Ms. Goodwin's actions demonstrate that:

    A. she was frustrated with Kwame's lack of skill and wished Kwame could keep up with the rest of the class.
    B. she knows how to work with school administration to foster an effective, purposeful classroom climate.
    C. she understands the importance of creating a classroom climate that addresses Kwame's emotional needs and respects his rights.
    D. she shows how knowledgeable she is when it comes to technology.

12. In addition to supporting Kwame by providing a computer device, Ms. Goodwin addresses his wheelchair needs. In making accommodations for his wheelchair, what would be the *most* important thing Ms. Goodwin could do in the classroom?

    A. Have Kwame select where he wishes to sit in the classroom.
    B. Position Kwame next to Ms. Goodwin's desk so his wheelchair doesn't interfere with the rest of the class.
    C. Make sure the classroom is free of obstructive articles so Kwame can move around where he needs to be.
    D. Have a special desk made for Kwame so he feels less intrusive.

13. When students in Mr. Smith's eighth-grade science class get ready for laboratory assignments, Mr. Smith begins by connecting the present lesson to prior learning and explaining lesson objectives. By organizing the class in this manner, Mr. Smith knows:

    A. the rationale for appropriate middle-level education and understands how to address the characteristics and needs of young adolescents.
    B. students learn best in an atmosphere in which routines are present and procedures are well established.
    C. how to use diversity in the classroom to enrich all students' learning experiences.
    D. how to take advantage of all of the science equipment that is provided by the school district.

14. Mr. Mendon uses the jigsaw format for cooperative learning groups, but one of the students in his class, Carl, has poor study skills and struggles with difficulty in reading. What procedures should Mr. Mendon follow to ensure that Carl is a contributing member of the group?

    A. Because this technique relies on "expert" groups, make sure that Carl is paired with a capable peer when the group meets so he is productive in his endeavors.
    B. Take Carl aside and explain that his reading skills are not on grade level so he may wish to sit in on the group but work on an outside assignment.
    C. Offer to tutor Carl while the group meets so his reading skills improve.
    D. Provide an opportunity for Carl to demonstrate his skill in mathematics so the class can see that he is capable.

15. Ms. Nicholson carefully plans her history lectures well in advance of her classes, and while teaching covers all the important points. She spends in excess of 30 minutes many days lecturing to the students. She has noticed that the students seem bored and listless and are unsuccessful on history tests. After an observation from her principal, which of the following suggestions might the principal offer?

    A. Allow the students to alternate presenting information in the class so they will be ensured of understanding the textbook information.
    B. Reduce teacher-centered and direct instruction time to allow for group work and individual activities.
    C. Focus more on a question-and-answer routine so Ms. Nicholson can assess which students read the assignment and which ones did not.
    D. Increase the amount of lecture time, as students are obviously not listening to the information that is being delivered.

16. When teachers organize students into cooperative groups, all of the following except which should be decided and discussed before group work begins?

    A. Ways students work together to develop the feeling of a cohesive group.
    B. If a conflict among students should arise, ways the students might solve the problem.
    C. Using good listening and questioning skills.
    D. All the possibilities for cooperative learning and the advantages and disadvantages of cooperative learning.

17. While reading a story, students in Ms. Barrientos's fifth-grade class have been working on the strategy of predicting and making judgments. Several students are not happy with the decisions they have made. Ms. Barrientos suggests that the students should base their decisions on logic, and then support those decisions with story details and/or personal experience. The *best* way for Ms. Barrientos to clearly communicate this strategy would be to:

    A. tell students to reread the story so they have a better understanding before they make further predictions.
    B. have Ms. Barrientos read a part of the story with the class and model how to make appropriate predictions.
    C. group students according to those who make accurate decisions with those who have difficulty, and then have the group share their answers.
    D. suggest easier books for students to read so they can be successful.

18. Students in Ms. Rios's fourth-grade social studies class were given a reading assignment on the colonies in the Western Hemisphere. As a follow-up assignment, which of the following would *best* demonstrate that Ms. Rios understands the need for higher-order thinking skills and inquiry learning?

    A. List hardships faced by immigrants in the Western Hemisphere.
    B. Review specific reasons why Europeans migrated and be ready to share these findings with the class the next day.
    C. Compare and contrast the reasons people immigrated.
    D. Create a timeline showing the span of time it took for the migration.

19. To become a successful teacher, Ms. Huling realizes she has to assess classroom goals and management skills such as deciding the right amount of time for instruction, group work, individualizing, and planning. Which of the following would NOT show that Ms. Huling monitors her instructional effectiveness?

    A. She omits those activities that have little to offer.
    B. She examines her instructional goals and objectives and adjusts lessons accordingly.
    C. She assesses students' knowledge so she isn't spending time on concepts they have already learned.
    D. She reduces the amount of wait time after asking a question so the lessons can stay right on target.

20. Juan entered Mr. Gonzales's room early one morning and slipped into his seat very quietly. When Mr. Gonzales asked Juan if there were anything wrong, Juan tried to explain that although he understood spoken English, he was having a difficult time reading the assigned material. Which of the following practices would help Juan the *most*?

    A. Have the students read silently; then discuss the assignment.
    B. Have Mr. Gonzales give a lecture on the assignment and then tell students to read as much as they can at home.
    C. Have Juan move his desk to the front of the room.
    D. Pair Juan with a classmate when reading and have them alternate reading to each other.

21. Mr. Hardy's fifth-grade science class has been discussing the solar system. As an extension activity, Mr. Hardy has his students use the computer. He recommends a website that correlates with the current state-adopted textbook. What is the *major* benefit to the students in using the computer?

    A. Problems on the computer are sometimes open-ended and students can engage in inquiry learning.
    B. The program enhances and supports Mr. Hardy's instructional strategies.
    C. By using the program, the time given to science can be extended.
    D. It can provide a substitute for one of Mr. Hardy's lectures.

22. Ms. Langston is a new English teacher at Dobie Middle School. One of the first activities she plans is a survey that will assess the students' knowledge of English skills. She identifies the specific skill and then asks if the students have little knowledge, some knowledge, or mastery of the skill. By using this survey, Ms. Langston demonstrates she understands:

    A. the importance of understanding diversity in the classroom.
    B. the need for students to take an active role in their own learning environment.
    C. the importance of being able to use a checklist.
    D. the importance of students answering higher-order thinking questions.

23. Mr. Hart is preparing a test for his eighth grade science class. He plans on including matching questions, multiple-choice items, and short explanation items. Which of the following is NOT an advantage of this type of testing?

   A. Students are tested over a lot of content.
   B. Teachers can easily score or grade the tests.
   C. Students can be tested over material in a shorter amount of time than essay tests.
   D. Teachers tend to write questions at the knowledge base of cognitive thinking.

24. Ms. Chen uses performance-based assessment to help assess her seventh-grade English class. Several parents have expressed concerns and are unsure of this form of evaluation. To alleviate these concerns, Ms. Chen should:

   A. invite the parents to a meeting and explain the advantages of performance-based assessment.
   B. prepare a letter describing authentic assessment and send it home with the students.
   C. publicize on the school website that a member of the school board will be available to address questions or concerns.
   D. explain to the parents that the teacher is a recent graduate from a nearby university and is aware of the current methods of assessment.

25. Parents of a student in Ms. Scott's class have requested a conference. They have noticed their child's grades are not what they had been earlier in the semester and discipline problems are surfacing more often. Which of the following is NOT an action Ms. Scott should take during the conference?

   A. Respect what the parents have to say about the student and be prepared to listen.
   B. Show documentation of grades, detention slips, or referral notices.
   C. Prepare to have the counselor or vice principal available if necessary.
   D. Confront the parent with behavior problems that have been occurring in class.

26. A sixth-grade student has been getting very angry and yelling at his friends. It takes just the slightest provocation to get him irritated. Several of the other students express concern and tell the teacher that they are afraid of him. What is the *first* step the teacher should take?

   A. Recommend that the student immediately visit the school counselor.
   B. Talk to the student and see if the teacher can determine why the student is getting so upset.
   C. Call the parents and ask them to see if they can figure out what is wrong with their child.
   D. Suggest the student talk to one of the student's best friends because peers are so important at this age.

27. Mr. Collins enjoys his weekends because it gives him time to read articles in professional journals to which he subscribes. The *primary* value of subscribing to the journals would be:

   A. to enhance his own knowledge of what is happening in the field of teaching.
   B. to get new ideas for articles for submission, thus improving his resume.
   C. to copy ideas so he doesn't have to plan so many lessons.
   D. to enhance his status at the school by promoting the value of educational commitment.

28. Ms. Allen has been teaching Special Education for many years. She and Ms. Denton, another Special Education teacher, have always worked together and complement each other's teaching styles. However, Ms. Denton is being transferred to another school, and Mr. Forester has been assigned to Ms. Allen's room. During a lunch break, Mr. Forester told Ms. Allen that he really isn't looking forward to his new assignment. What course of action should Ms. Allen take?

   A. Ms. Allen should wait and see what happens when Mr. Forester arrives in her room.
   B. Ms. Allen should immediately confront Mr. Forester and tell him she really doesn't want him in the room either.
   C. Ms. Allen should go to the curriculum supervisor and explain what Mr. Forester said.
   D. Ms. Allen should ask her principal if Ms. Denton can stay with her and if Mr. Forester can be the one transferred.

29. It would be very unusual if one did not see Mr. Gratz, an eighth-grade mathematics teacher, at a sporting event. He seemingly never misses an opportunity to either take tickets or hand out programs. Mr. Gratz's presence indicates that he:

   A. enjoys being seen at school functions and hopes to be hired as a coach.
   B. realizes the value of participating in school activities.
   C. understands the need for students in middle school to interact with their peers.
   D. is trying to get on the good side of the students so they will like him as a teacher.

30. Adam is a new student at Craddick Middle School who has just recently been confined to a wheelchair. His parents are unsure of regulations and requirements for their son. Ms. Reese explains that under the Individuals with Disabilities Education Act (IDEA) the *primary* action the school must take is to:

   A. maintain a folder with information on a student's disability.
   B. guarantee all children with disabilities access to a free and appropriate public education.
   C. provide wheelchairs for disabled parents who attend school events.
   D. encourage all students to be actively involved at all times and guarantee an interdisciplinary education.

31. Leticia's parents asked if they could inspect and review their child's education records that were maintained by the school. They were getting ready to move and knew that Leticia's records would follow her to the new school. Which of the following indicates the school followed appropriate procedures?

   A. The parents were allowed to look at the student's education records because Leticia was transferring to a new school.
   B. The parents were told they could not view the student's records because the information is kept very confidential.
   C. The parents were told they could not view the records, but Leticia would be allowed to see them once she reached the age of 18.
   D. The parents were told they would need a court order before viewing the records, and once it was received they would be welcome to look at them.

GO ON TO THE NEXT PAGE

Clustered Items Begin Here

32. Ms. Murray, a seventh-grade history teacher, was developing a unit on the Holocaust. She researched information on the Internet and found a website that was specifically designed for teachers who were interested in this period of history. Ms. Murray consulted the Texas Essential Knowledge and Skills (TEKS) to make sure the information correlated with state requirements. What was the significance of Ms. Murray using the TEKS?

    A. She wanted to demonstrate she could write detailed lesson plans while using the TEKS.
    B. She wanted to see if there were lesson plans on the Internet that were based on the TEKS, and if not she would submit ones that she wrote.
    C. She wanted to make contact with the provider of the website to see if the lessons could be adapted for the TEKS.
    D. She understood the importance of using the TEKS to guide instructional goals and objectives.

33. Ms. Murray wants her students to understand how the political, economic, and social impact of World War II affected individuals, families, and communities. Ms. Murray uses the jigsaw method of cooperative learning to explore information about the Holocaust. She divides the class into groups of five students. Each student researches an assigned topic, meets with students in the other groups who have the same assignment, and then comes back to his or her jigsaw group and presents a report. Which one of the following is NOT a benefit of this method of teaching?

    A. Each student's part is essential for the final product to be a success.
    B. The organization of the group discourages dominance of a particular student.
    C. The jigsaw method encourages listening, active learning, and group participation.
    D. The jigsaw method allows for a relaxation in grades as all students receive an overall assessment of their work.

GO ON TO THE NEXT PAGE

34. Ms. Murray's final project on the Holocaust was a rather somber one, yet left the children with a very pointed message about that time in world history. One of the concentration camps held mostly children. However, with the help of several courageous adults, the children found a way to write prose and poetry that was later published in a book. Ms. Murray assigned each student in the room a piece of work completed by one of the children in the concentration camp. Ms. Murray had each student design a butterfly that was made specifically for the child whose work he or she were reading and attach the butterfly to the ceiling. As the project came to an end, Ms. Murray read off the names of the children who lived and who died. Ms. Murray had the students discuss their reaction to the treatment the children received. By allowing her students to become emotionally involved with a child of the Holocaust, Ms. Murray understands:

A. that life has many challenges that will need to be met.
B. that children in Texas need to be compared to children who were involved in the Holocaust.
C. that learning takes place through intellectual involvement and active engagement in the learning process.
D. that all children should develop an interest in history.

End Clustered Items Here

Decision Set Begins Here

35. As part of an integrated unit, Ms. Garcia's fourth-grade students will take a field trip and participate in the Texas Beach Clean-up. Ms. Garcia has personally been involved with the clean-up for several years. She would like her class to share in the commitment and enthusiasm of keeping the earth clean, and at the same time feel the sense of accomplishment that comes after being involved in a valuable experience. Which of the following would be the *best* approach for Ms. Garcia to take?

    A. Honor the students' requests to bring a friend from another class, and tell the student's teacher that it is for a very worthy cause.
    B. Tell the students how good they are going to feel after they have been involved in the beach clean-up.
    C. Respect students' requests to be teamed with the person of choice.
    D. Model enthusiasm and express excitement about the project and the active role students can take in their own community and state.

36. Before going to the beach, Ms. Garcia divides the class into groups of four. In each group, one student will hold the large trash bags, two students will pick up trash, and one student will record items that are collected. Prior to starting the beach project, the students are given directions as to the length of time each group will have, how they will rotate, and specific duties each student will incur. However, one of the students in the class has limited visibility, yet Ms. Garcia wants to make sure the student has an opportunity to participate in the beach clean-up. She discusses the situation with a visual impairment specialist to determine if there is something specific she needs to know and how the needs of the child can be met during the trip. In talking to the specialist, Ms. Garcia demonstrates which of the following?

    A. She knows she must include the student on the trip, but doesn't want it to be a bother and disturb the fun for the rest of the students.
    B. She knows legal requirements for educators and adheres to guidelines in education-related situations.
    C. She realizes the importance of skilled questioning for students with learning disabilities.
    D. She demonstrates an awareness of appropriate classroom management and behavior standards.

GO ON TO THE NEXT PAGE

37. At the beginning of each school year, Ms. Garcia presents management techniques to the class. One of the rules she uses is just a single-word format. For instance, when a visitor walks into the room, all she does is say the word "visitor" and because Ms. Garcia has previously presented her expectations concerning someone visiting the class, the students know how they are to conduct themselves. As the students are making plans for the field trip, Ms. Garcia guides a discussion on establishing rules for conduct while the class is at the beach. She expects the students to meet her expectations when she uses the word "beach." In establishing rules prior to taking the trip, Ms. Garcia shows she practices:

   A. effective communication skills and techniques which are paramount in keeping a group of students functioning.
   B. classroom management where the students are the ones who make the policies.
   C. communicating with as few words as possible.
   D. grouping according to the students' behavior patterns.

38. Ms. Garcia plans on using the school's digital cameras while on the field trip. She will post the pictures she takes on the school website and send several pictures to the community newspaper. Before she completes this project, Ms. Garcia needs to check with the local school district policies to ensure compliance with copyrighted material. By doing this Ms. Garcia shows she understands the importance of:

   A. involving school personnel in making important decisions.
   B. following appropriate guidelines for using technology.
   C. checking the laws and guidelines that are relevant to her professional development.
   D. maintaining a structured, well-managed learning environment for all students.

39. After the field trip, Ms. Garcia facilitates the creation of a slide show using the pictures taken at the beach. The students are excited about the final product and invite the parents to a "show." Creating the slide show will benefit the students by:

   A. substituting the slide show for a live performance in front of the class for the parents.
   B. allowing the students an opportunity to communicate their beach trip experience in a varied format.
   C. allowing the students to interact more closely with their teacher.
   D. providing an opportunity to see if film making and editing is a possible career choice.

40. Several parents who attended the Parent Night belong to a local service organization. One of the parents contacted Ms. Garcia and asked if she would come to their next meeting to present the slide show and talk about the students' involvement in the beach clean-up. By accepting the invitation to speak at a local service function, Ms. Garcia showed:

   A. she felt comfortable assuming a public speaking role.
   B. she knew this would enable her students to engage in future beach clean-ups.
   C. she knew how to assert her authority as a teacher.
   D. she knew how to interact and communicate effectively with family members as well as community resources.

Decision Set Ends Here

CHAPTER NINE

Diagnostic Test Answers and Explanations

1. A

This question addresses information from PPR Competency* 001.

The teacher understands human developmental processes and applies this knowledge to plan instruction and ongoing assessment that motivate students and are responsive to their developmental characteristics and needs.

Eliminate (B) because it is not Mr. Burnside's responsibility to solve the problem for Pedro's mother. Eliminate (C) as this is not best practice and would unfairly show favoritism to Pedro. Eliminate choice (D) because, again, it is giving advice. Mr. Burnside needs to discuss during the conference with Pedro's mother that children at this stage of development are approaching adolescence and physical changes are taking place. He should reinforce that most children at this age require more sleep, not less, and that Pedro's behavior of falling asleep is affecting his ability to function in the classroom. Mr. Burnside may need to suggest resources that Pedro's mother can use during her husband's absence. Mr. Burnside should suggest that he and Pedro's mother keep in close connect to stay on top of the situation. Choice (A) is the correct response.

*Competency statements copyright © 2003 by the Texas State Board for Educator Certification and National Evaluation Systems, Inc. (NES ®). Reprinted by permission.

2. C

This question addresses information from PPR Competency 001.

The teacher understands human developmental processes and applies this knowledge to plan instruction and ongoing assessment that motivate students and are responsive to their developmental characteristics and needs.

This is a priority-setting question as you are to determine the *first* thing Jenny's teacher needs to do. Eliminate (A) because students at this age are concerned with their physical appearance and can cause harm to themselves. Eliminate (B) as it would be best to find out if Jenny is really serious, and it would alarm her parents if she were just trying to impress her friend. Choice (D) suggests the problem exists and it is Jenny's problem and not the friend's. Students at this stage of development are showing signs of puberty and physical changes are taking place. Her teacher should set aside a time to talk to Jenny and explain that no one has a perfect shape and that she should try to like her body as it is because it is a part of who she is. She might suggest talking to the counselor or letting her know that she is available if Jenny would like to talk to her again. Choice (C) is the correct response.

3. C

This question addresses information from PPR Competency 001.

The teacher understands human developmental processes and applies this knowledge to plan instruction and ongoing assessment that motivate students and are responsive to their developmental characteristics and needs.

Eliminate (A) because it would be unprofessional to compare one student's achievement with another. Eliminate (B) because lowering expectations would not be best practice and it would show preference. Choice (D) suggests teaming. Although pairing students is usually a good instructional strategy it would not be advisable in this situation. Children at this stage of development usually perform quite well in group situations, and they like the interaction with each other. Therefore, it is not surprising that Mr. Hutchinson's students do well with the group activities. However, it will be helpful for him when conferencing with the recalcitrant students to first review the learning objectives for the specific assignments. He can then guide the students in completing the activities in small segments using goal-setting skills and rubrics and also use frequent positive reinforcement for the completed tasks. Choice (C) is the correct response.

Diagnostic EC–4 Pedagogy and Professional Responsibilities Test Answers and Explanations

4. A

This question addresses information from PPR Competency 002.

The teacher understands student diversity and knows how to plan learning experiences and design assessments that are responsive to differences among students and that promote all students' learning.

Eliminate (B) because a timeline is the lowest level of cognitive development and does not address the student's needs. Eliminate (C) because, although the students might enjoy working in a group, unless there is someone who is able to speak English, the action on the part of the teacher suggests Mr. Radcliffe is not aware of the needs of ELL students. Choice (D) will not further the development of English and the activity becomes a form of busy work. First of all, Mr. Radcliffe must realize the importance of becoming acquainted with each student's culture and then building on that culture. Because most English Language Learner (ELL) students require more time for learning activities than other students, Mr. Radcliffe has arranged activities for his ELL students to create dialogue and then dramatize their work. In doing so, the students and their English-proficient partner will have time to discuss unfamiliar material and work on translating or clarifying meaning. Choice (A) is the correct response.

5. A

This question addresses information from PPR Competency 002.

The teacher understands student diversity and knows how to plan learning experiences and design assessments that are responsive to differences among students and that promote all students' learning.

This is a priority-setting question, as you are to determine how the teacher can *best* address Casey's problem. Eliminate (B) because challenging Casey so he will improve will only cause him to be more frustrated. Eliminate (C) because rote-learning will probably not help Casey. Choice (D) is not appropriate in Casey's situation because the teacher wants to develop Casey's understanding of material read and not just ask him to memorize definitions. Casey has mild retardation, which means he is just slower to learn. Casey's teacher can specifically help him improve his reading skills by concentrating on pronunciation and word meanings. In addition, his teacher will need to discover things he does well and build on those interests and skills. The teacher can help Casey by presenting the information he must learn in small segments, by varying instructional strategies, making use of in-class time rather than assigning out-of-class work, and being less concerned with how much content is covered and more concerned with what he is learning. Choice (A) is the correct response.

6. B

This question addresses information from PPR Competency 002.

The teacher understands student diversity and knows how to plan learning experiences and design assessments that are responsive to differences among students and that promote all students' learning.

This is a priority-setting question. You are to determine Ms. Justin's *primary* responsibility. Eliminate (A) because the student may not be required to work at the computer and Ms. Justin will need to follow Individual Education Plan (IEP) requirements. Eliminate (C) because Ms. Justin is making the student work at the computer without consulting the IEP. Choice (D) suggests a buddy; however, if the student is able to work at the computer, a paraprofessional would be assisting in most cases. Choice (B) is the correct response.

7. B

This question addresses information from PPR Competency 002.

The teacher understands student diversity and knows how to plan learning experiences and design assessments that are responsive to differences among students and that promote all students' learning.

This is a priority-setting question. You are asked to decide the *most* likely activities for the bright students. Eliminate (A) because the activity is at the lower level of cognitive development and the gifted student should be performing at a higher level. Eliminate (C) because this activity does not challenge the gifted student. Eliminate (D) because just reading a poem would, again, have the Gifted and Talented (GT) student performing at a lower level of cognitive development. However, the emphasis when teaching and working with Gifted and Talented students should be on inquiry learning and problem solving. It is helpful if the students are included in the planning of their objectives. The students need to be challenged and encouraged to develop their own skills. Ms. Patton demonstrates her knowledge of students who are Gifted and Talented and plans accordingly. Choice (B) is the correct response.

Diagnostic EC–4 Pedagogy and Professional Responsibilities Test Answers and Explanations

8. D

This question addresses information from PPR Competency 003.

The teacher understands procedures for designing effective and coherent instruction and assessment based on appropriate learning goals and objectives.

This is a priority-setting question as you are asked to determine the *primary* benefit of using journals. Eliminate (A) as the journals do not take the place of teacher-made tests. Eliminate (B) because teachers are not supposed to compare students' work. Choice (C) suggests using the journals as a source for teacher–student conferences. There is a possibility the teacher would make a reference to the journal during a conference, but not for the purpose of collaboration. Dialogue journals are an effective means of assessment as they provide an understanding of each student's growth. Because a dialogue journal is a written record of a student's reaction and observation, Mr. Wheeler uses the journals as a way of connecting with the student's thoughts, feelings, and progress. The students are able to reflect on their own progress and converse about their strengths and weakness. Choice (D) is the correct response.

9. A

This question addresses information from PPR Competency 004.

The teacher understands learning processes and factors that impact student learning and demonstrates this knowledge by planning effective, engaging instruction and appropriate assessments.

Eliminate (B) because it would not be sound educational practice to request having all students tested for learning disabilities. Eliminate (C) as Ms. Fidler would not be able to evaluate the students for individual growth and needs. Eliminate (D) because this has nothing to do with Ms. Fidler changing her perception. Ms. Fidler will need to reflect on her own bias and examine how her perceptions are affecting the students. She may want to examine the climate of the classroom and make sure the atmosphere is one of encouragement and productivity. Choice (A) is the correct response.

10. B

This question addresses information from PPR Competency 004.

The teacher understands learning processes and factors that impact student learning and demonstrates this knowledge by planning effective, engaging instruction and appropriate assessments.

Eliminate (A) as the questions Ms. Gonzalez asked do not correspond to the interpretation of factual information. Eliminate (C) because Ms. Gonzalez is not asking about students' interests and experiences. Choice (D) should be eliminated because Ms. Gonzalez is not asking students to summarize material read. Ms. Gonzalez is encouraging her students to think at the highest level of questioning and to stimulate their intellectual development. By asking these questions, she wants students to respond with their own opinions and make value judgments. Choice (B) is the correct response.

11. C

This question addresses information from PPR Competency 005.

The teacher knows how to establish a classroom climate that fosters learning, equity, and excellence and uses this knowledge to create a physical and emotional environment that is safe and productive.

Eliminate (A) because the teachers' action do not indicate a frustration level had been reached. Eliminate (B) because, although she was able to work with the principal, her actions do not demonstrate this choice. This question is about accommodations and not about the climate of the classroom. Choice (D) should be eliminated because other than the computer devise, you do not know Ms. Goodwin's expertise about computers. There are numerous physical and health conditions that limit students from being able to participate in a classroom without some type of assistance. The Individuals with Disabilities Education Act (IDEA) emphasizes normalizing the environment for students with disabilities and providing for the least restrictive environment for these students. By introducing the computer device to Kwame, Ms. Goodwin shows she has familiarized herself with Kwame's impairment and made adjustments in the classroom. She realized the importance of providing a safe nurturing environment that addressed Kwame's emotional needs and respected his rights and dignity. Choice (C) is the correct response.

Diagnostic EC–4 Pedagogy and Professional Responsibilities Test Answers and Explanations

12. C

This question addresses information from PPR Competency 005.

The teacher knows how to establish a classroom climate that fosters learning, equity, and excellence and uses this knowledge to create a physical and emotional environment that is safe and productive.

This is a priority-setting question. You are asked what would be the *most* important thing Ms. Goodwin could do to address Kwame's wheelchair needs. Eliminate (A) because allowing Kwame to select where he wishes to sit may not be the most appropriate accommodation. Eliminate (B) since Ms. Goodwin's desk may be at a complete disadvantage for Kwame. Choice (D) would have to be included on Kwame's Individual Education Plan (IEP) if special furniture were to be made. Ms. Goodwin will need to examine the physical layout of her classroom and make sure that it is free of articles of obstruction so Kwame is able to freely move around. By doing so she will be in compliance with The Individuals with Disabilities Education Act (IDEA) that emphasizes normalizing the environment for students with disabilities and providing for the least restrictive environment for these students. Choice (C) is the correct response.

13. B

This question addresses information from PPR Competency 006.

The teacher understands strategies for creating an organized and productive learning environment and for managing student behavior.

Eliminate (A) because Mr. Smith is not addressing characteristics of eighth-grade students. Eliminate (C) because diversity was not mentioned. Choice (D) suggests equipment usage, and although the laboratory is mentioned, it wouldn't have anything to do with the organization of the class. Depending on the content being taught, routines are comfortable for the teacher and the students because the students know what to expect. Students will take a more active role in their own learning because they realize what is going on in the classroom. Choice (B) is the correct response.

14. A

This question addresses information from PPR Competency 006.

The teacher understands strategies for creating an organized and productive learning environment and for managing student behavior.

Eliminate (B) because, although Carl has difficulty reading, he can still be a contributing member of the group. Eliminate (C) because Carl should be working with the group in whatever capacity he can and the tutoring for reading will need to be scheduled at a different time. Eliminate choice (D) because demonstrating success in another subject will not meet the objective of being a contributing member of a group. Mr. Mendon will need to pair Carl with a capable peer and then closely monitor the work Carl is submitting. Choice (A) is the correct response.

15. B

This question addresses information from PPR Competency 006.

The teacher understands strategies for creating an organized and productive learning environment and for managing student behavior.

Eliminate (A) because you don't know how Ms. Nicholson is conducting the discussion interactions in the class. Eliminate (C) because the focus on question-and-answer strategies is not designed to ferret out those who read the assignment and those who did not. Choice (D) suggests increasing lecture time, but students are already failing to respond to the amount of time Ms. Nicholson spends in a direct-teaching mode. Ms. Nicholson's use of lectures can be useful; however, she is devoting too much time without varying strategies and providing for student-centered activities. Instead of the heavy concentration on teacher-centered instruction, she can arrange for activities for individuals and small groups in which students have time for inquiry learning and interactive instruction. Choice (B) is the correct response.

16. D

This question addresses information from PPR Competency 006.

The teacher understands strategies for creating an organized and productive learning environment and for managing student behavior.

This is a priority-setting question asking you to select a choice that would be *incorrect*. Therefore, in this question we already know that three out of the four choices are correct. Keep (A) because teachers do need to discuss working together prior to the groups convening. Keep (B) because it is helpful to discuss how to handle conflict before problems occur. Keep (C) because all students need to know about good listening and questioning skills. When the process is well planned and organized, the outcome for cooperative learning is a positive experience. Students do need to discuss prior to working in a group ways the group can be cohesive, how they might resolve conflicts, and good listening and questioning skills. The teacher needs to decide ahead of time if the grouping will be heterogeneous ability, homogeneous ability, learning styles or personality traits, random or student generated. There would be very little advantage for the student to use class time discussing the different types of groups. Choice (D) is the correct response.

Diagnostic EC–4 Pedagogy and Professional Responsibilities Test Answers and Explanations

17. B

This question addresses information from PPR Competency 007.

The teacher understands and applies principles and strategies for communicating effectively in varied teaching and learning contexts.

Eliminate (A) because reading the story again will not guarantee that the students will have a better understanding. Eliminate (C) because this practice tends to reinforce the negative. Choice (D) is not appropriate for this activity. By first reading the story with the students and then modeling how to make appropriate predictions, Ms. Barrientos can demonstrate the anticipated outcome for the students. She is showing through her actions what is expected from the students. Choice (B) is the correct response.

18. C

This question addresses information from PPR Competency 007.

The teacher understands and applies principles and strategies for communicating effectively in varied teaching and learning contexts.

This is a priority-setting question. You are to determine which assignment would *best* demonstrate higher-order thinking. Eliminate (A) because making lists is a lower-level form of cognitive development. Eliminate (B) because students are looking for factual information. Eliminate choice (D) because the students are performing a lower-level form of cognitive development. Ms. Rios understands that using questions at the highest level of thinking stimulates learning and facilitates intellectual development. Choice (C) is the correct response.

19. D

This question addresses information from PPR Competency 008.

The teacher provides appropriate instruction that actively engages students in the learning process.

This is a priority-setting question asking you to select a choice that would be *incorrect*. Therefore, in this question we already know that three out of the four choices are correct. Keep (A) because activities with limited value have no place in the curriculum. Keep (B) since Ms. Huling is monitoring her teaching. Keep (C) because there is no need to teach students what they already know. One way to make better use of time is to eliminate activities that are of little value and are just time consuming. Activities need to be carefully planned so time is not lost owing to lack of organization or poor transitions. Students, however, require time to think about a question that has just been asked so reducing wait time would not be a good instructional practice, and would indicate Ms. Huling monitors the effectiveness of her instruction. Choice (D) is the correct response.

20. D

This question addresses information from PPR Competency 008.

The teacher provides appropriate instruction that actively engages students in the learning process.

This is a priority-setting question as you are to determine which practice would be *most* beneficial to Juan. Eliminate (A) because Juan probably needs to engage in reading aloud or lip movement so he can "hear" what he is reading. Eliminate (B) because it places reading time in an out-of-school setting. Eliminate (C) because moving his desk to the front of the room will not assist Juan in learning to read. If Juan is having difficulty, the teacher can assign a classmate to help him whereby they can alternate reading to each other. Choice (D) is the correct response.

21. B

This question addresses information from PPR Competency 009.

The teacher incorporates the effective use of technology to plan, organize, deliver, and evaluate instruction for all students.

This is a priority-setting question. You are to determine the *major* benefit for the students in using the computer. Eliminate (A) because, although higher-order thinking and inquiry learning may take place when working on the computer, there is no guarantee it will occur. Eliminate (C) because this would not be Mr. Hardy's goal. Eliminate (D) because Mr. Hardy is not looking for a substitute for a lecture. Because Mr. Hardy is using a website that correlates with the current state-adopted textbooks, he realizes the program will support the instructional strategies and activities he is presently using. Choice (B) is the correct response.

22. B

This question addresses information from PPR Competency 010.

The teacher monitors student performance and achievement; provides students with timely, high-quality feedback; and responds flexibly to promote learning for all students.

Eliminate (A) because if you selected this choice as your answer, you are reading into this question because diversity is not an issue that is addressed. Eliminate (C) because the process of using a checklist would not be as important as the information Ms. Langston receives. Choice (D) should be eliminated because the questions are benchmarks, and are not asking for problem-solving answers. By having the students use a checklist to determine knowledge of English, Ms. Langston provides an opportunity for the students to take an active role in their own learning. The students can identify areas of need and set goals for future performance. Ms. Langston can use the students' assessment for improvement in her own instruction. Choice (B) is the correct response.

23. D

This question addresses information from PPR Competency 010.

The teacher monitors student performance and achievement; provides students with timely, high-quality feedback; and responds flexibly to promote learning for all students.

This is a priority-setting question asking you to select a choice that would be *incorrect*. Therefore, in this question we already know that three out of the four choices are correct. Keep (A) because a wide range of content is usually assessed. Keep (B) as the items are easily scored. Keep (C) because the items are usually answered quickly. Mr. Hart understands he is primarily using this type of testing to evaluate students' knowledge of facts and definitions. If he wishes to test for higher-order thinking and problem solving, he will use other forms of assessment. Choice (D) is the correct response.

24. A

This question addresses information from PPR Competency 010.

The teacher monitors student performance and achievement; provides students with timely, high-quality feedback; and responds flexibly to promote learning for all students.

Eliminate (B) because the parents may never see the letter. Eliminate (C) because this would usually not be a school board issue. Choice (D) will probably not impress the parents and is not appropriate. Activities such as plays, skits, dramatizations, newspaper articles, and book reviews are all examples of activities that are assessed on performance. Activities such as these are not easily assessed by traditional methods of testing. When Ms. Chen meets with the parents, she should be prepared to explain the advantages of performance-based assessment. Choice (A) is the correct response.

25. D

This question addresses information from PPR Competency 011.

The teacher understands the importance of family involvement in children's education and knows how to interact and communicate effectively with families.

This is a priority-setting question asking you to select a choice that would be *incorrect*. Therefore, in this question we already know that three out of the four choices are correct. Keep (A) because Ms. Scott should listen to what the parents have to say. Keep (B) because a teacher needs to be prepared with student's records. Keep (C) because assistance may be required if a difficult situation should arise. Any time a parent requests a meeting, the teacher needs to prepare copies of grade sheets and documentation of all kinds. In addition, the teacher needs to inform the vice principal or counselor prior to the meeting in case support is necessary. The goal for the meeting will be to find a solution to the student's problem by working with the parents in an amicable way rather than in a confrontational manner. Choice (D) is the correct response.

26. B

This question addresses information from PPR Competency 011.

The teacher understands the importance of family involvement in children's education and knows how to interact and communicate effectively with families.

This is a priority-setting question. You are asked to determine the *first* step a teacher should take. Eliminate (A) because the teacher may be able to take care of the problem. Eliminate (C) because the problem may exist only in a particular situation and the teacher needs to determine, if possible, the reason for the provocation before getting the parents involved. Choice (D) is not the first step and would not be a recommendation a teacher would make. In this case, the teacher should first discuss the situation with the student to determine if there is something specific that is bothering the student. If the problem concerns behavior that is not handled by this conference, then a meeting with the counselor and parents would be in order. Choice (B) is the correct response.

27. A

This question addresses information from PPR Competency 012.

The teacher enhances professional knowledge and skills by effectively interacting with other members of the educational community and participating in various types of professional activities.

This is a priority-setting question. You are asked to determine the *primary* value of subscribing to journals. Eliminate (B) because, although it may be an end result, it would not be professional or the primary reason. Eliminate (C) because, although he is reading the journals and gaining ideas, he wouldn't want to copy just so he doesn't have to plan his lessons. Choice (D) does not show professionalism and therefore should not be a concern. Professional journals contain educational issues and provide new ideas in the field of education. Mr. Collins's main reason for subscribing to professional journals is to enhance his knowledge of current happenings. Choice (A) is the correct response.

28. A

This question addresses information from PPR Competency 012.

The teacher enhances professional knowledge and skills by effectively interacting with other members of the educational community and participating in various types of professional activities.

Eliminate (B) because she would not be demonstrating professionalism. Eliminate (C) since it would not be a situation for the curriculum supervisor to handle. Choice (D) would be an inappropriate request. Rather than be offended by Mr. Forrester's remark, Ms. Allen should wait until they have had an opportunity as a team to plan, share ideas, and deliver current instruction. If a problem still exists, then further action might be warranted. Choice (A) is the correct response.

Diagnostic EC–4 Pedagogy and Professional Responsibilities Test Answers and Explanations

29. B

This question addresses information from PPR Competency 012.

The teacher enhances professional knowledge and skills by effectively interacting with other members of the educational community and participating in various types of professional activities.

Eliminate (A) because there is not enough information on which to base this decision. Eliminate (C) because, although this is an important point, it has nothing to do with Mr. Gratz's reason for attending the school events. Choice (D) is an inappropriate action. Mr. Gratz understands the value of interacting with students and parents in situations other than the classroom. It gives him an opportunity to become acquainted on a more personal basis. Choice (B) is the correct response.

30. B

This question addresses information from PPR Competency 013.

The teacher understands and adheres to legal and ethical requirements for educators and is knowledgeable of the structure of education in Texas.

This is a priority-setting question. You are to determine the *primary* action the school should take under IDEA act. Eliminate (A) as this would not be the primary action under IDEA requirements. Eliminate (C) because the act covers students, not parents. Eliminate (D) because, while students should be actively involved, the act does not pertain to these matters. According to the Individuals with Disabilities Education Act (IDEA), the state must develop and implement policies that ensure a free appropriate public education (FAPE) to all children with disabilities. The school district must be consistent with the state and federal statues and provide for wheelchair accessibility. Choice (B) is the correct response.

31. A

This question addresses information from PPR Competency 013.

The teacher understands and adheres to legal and ethical requirements for educators and is knowledgeable of the structure of education in Texas.

Eliminate (B) because the parents are allowed to view the records if they have given written permission. Eliminate (C) because with written permission the parents can view the records, and Leticia has the same privilege once she reaches the age of 18. Eliminate (D) because a court order is necessary only if the records need to be viewed without consent. The Family Educational Rights and Privacy Act (FERPA) is a federal law that protects the privacy of student education records; however, FERPA gives parents certain rights with respect to their children's education records and allows parents to inspect them and view the records kept by the school. The school would allow the parents to look at the student's education records under the law. Choice (A) is the correct response.

32. D

This question addresses information from PPR Competency 003.

The teacher understands procedures for designing effective and coherent instruction and assessment based on appropriate learning goals and objectives.

Eliminate (A) because the significance would be if she uses the TEKS to guide her lesson plans and not that she could write detailed plans while using the TEKS. Eliminate (B) because this question is not about submitting plans if internet lessons aren't correlated. Eliminate (C) because it would not be the publisher's responsibility to adapt information to the TEKS. Ms. Murray understands the curriculum she uses is based on the Texas Essential Knowledge and Skills (TEKS). All instruction, activities, and assignments must correlate with the state requirements. Before adapting the information she discovered on the internet, she wanted to make sure it correlated with state requirements. Choice (D) is the correct response.

33. D

This question addresses information from PPR Competency 004.

The teacher understands learning processes and factors that impact student learning and demonstrates this knowledge by planning effective, engaging instruction and appropriate assessments.

This is a priority-setting question asking you to select a choice that would be *incorrect*. Therefore, in this question we already know that three out of the four choices are correct. Keep (A) because each student is essential for the final product to be a success. Keep (B) because the way the jigsaw method is organized, it is difficult for one student to dominate. Keep (C) because the jigsaw method involves students in all aspects of learning. Cooperative learning provides a way for students to work together. Teachers base students' grades on how committed the students are when working on a project, the involvement of each student, and the quality of work that is submitted. Assessment is determined for the individual as well as a group. It is not a time for teachers to relax grading standards. Choice (D) is the correct response.

34. C

This question addresses information from PPR Competency 008.

The teacher provides appropriate instruction that actively engages students in the learning process.

Eliminate (A) because Ms. Murray is not teaching about life's challenges. Eliminate (B) since she is not teaching comparison. Eliminate (D) because not all children will develop the same interest in history and historical events. Ms. Murray planned activities that would involve the students intellectually and emotionally in the learning process and kept students actively engaged. Choice (C) is the correct response.

Diagnostic EC–4 Pedagogy and Professional Responsibilities Test Answers and Explanations

35. D

This question addresses information from PPR Competency 008.

The teacher provides appropriate instruction that actively engages students in the learning process.

This is a priority-setting question as you are to determine which approach would be *best* so students will become motivated and feel a sense of accomplishment. Eliminate (A) because, while the students might have more fun bringing a friend from another class, this field trip to the beach is not a social gathering. Ms. Garcia wants the students to discover something about themselves and not just the fun of a field trip with a friend. Eliminate (B) because the idea of the trip is for the students to become motivated and feel a sense of pride. Eliminate (C) because the person of choice may not be the best selection for teaming on the trip and also defeat the purpose as in the first choice. Ms. Garcia's excitement for the beach clean-up provides a role model for the students and shows enthusiasm toward community involvement and the valuable experience that can result. Choice (D) is the correct response.

36. B

This question addresses information from PPR Competency 013.

The teacher understands and adheres to legal and ethical requirements for educators and is knowledgeable of the structure of education in Texas.

Eliminate (A) because the teacher should be concerned about the student with limited visibility and not with how much fun the other students are having. Eliminate (C) because there is no reference to asking skilled questions. Eliminate (D) because, although she is using good management skills in arranging the groups, there is not a connection between the needs of the student with limited visibility and the choice. Ms. Garcia is, however, demonstrating that she knows legal requirements for educators and adheres to guidelines in education-related situations by contacting the specialist. Choice (B) is the correct response.

37. A

This question addresses information from PPR Competency 007.

The teacher understands and applies principles and strategies for communicating effectively in varied teaching and learning contexts.

Eliminate (B) because Ms. Garcia established her own classroom management. Eliminate (C) because using a lesser amount of words to communicate doesn't answer the question about prior expectations. Eliminate (D) because ability grouping is not an issue with this question. Ms. Garcia understands the importance of using effective strategies for communicating. By modeling effective behavior and using language and techniques that are age appropriate, there will be less disruption of activities during the beach clean-up. Choice (A) is the correct response.

38. B

This question addresses information from PPR Competency 009.

The teacher incorporates the effective use of technology to plan, organize, deliver, and evaluate instruction for all students.

Eliminate (A) because other school personnel were not mentioned. Eliminate (C) because the school privacy laws have nothing to do with her professional development. Eliminate (D) because she is interested in privacy laws and the structured learning environment is not addressed. Prior to using technology, the teacher must be aware of the laws of computer software material. By contacting the local school district, Ms. Garcia shows she is following the appropriate guidelines. Choice (B) is the correct response.

39. B

This question addresses information from PPR Competency 009.

The teacher incorporates the effective use of technology to plan, organize, deliver, and evaluate instruction for all students.

Eliminate (A) because the teacher's goal is not to avoid having the students perform in front of the class. Eliminate (C) because, although the students will be working closely with the teacher, this would not be the major benefit. Eliminate (D) because providing an opportunity for career selection could result from this experience, it certainly would not be the reason for creating a slide show presentation. However, allowing the students an opportunity to communicate their beach trip experience in a varied format is an effective use of technology and use of productivity tools. Choice (B) is the correct response.

40. D

This question addresses information from PPR Competency 011.

The teacher understands the importance of family involvement in children's education and knows how to interact and communicate effectively with families.

Eliminate (A) because we don't have enough information. Eliminate (B) because speaking at a community function will not ensure Ms. Garcia of anything that concerns the beach clean-up. Eliminate (C) because asserting herself as a teacher is not her objective. Ms. Garcia is interacting with the community in a professional manner. She demonstrated the importance of working with families and getting everyone involved. Choice (D) is the correct response.

Diagnostic EC–4 Pedagogy and Professional Responsibilities Test Answers and Explanations

Diagnostic Test Answers Sorted by Competency

Question	Domain	Competency	Answer	Did You Answer Correctly?
1	1	1	A	
2	1	1	C	
3	1	1	C	
4	1	2	A	
5	1	2	A	
6	1	2	B	
7	1	2	B	
8	1	3	D	
32	1	3	D	
9	1	4	A	
10	1	4	B	
33	1	4	D	
11	2	5	C	
12	2	5	C	
13	2	6	B	
14	2	6	A	
15	2	6	B	
16	2	6	D	
17	3	7	B	
18	3	7	C	
37	3	7	A	
19	3	8	D	
20	3	8	D	
34	3	8	C	
35	3	8	D	
21	3	9	B	
38	3	9	B	
39	3	9	B	
22	3	10	B	
23	3	10	D	
24	3	10	A	
25	4	11	D	
26	4	11	B	
40	4	11	D	
27	4	12	A	
28	4	12	A	
29	4	12	B	
30	4	13	B	
31	4	13	A	
36	4	13	B	

What competencies did you do well in?
What competencies do you need to work on?

Practice Test One Answer Sheet

Remove (or photocopy) this answer sheet and use it to complete the practice test.
(See answer key following the test when finished.)

1. Ⓐ Ⓑ Ⓒ Ⓓ
2. Ⓐ Ⓑ Ⓒ Ⓓ
3. Ⓐ Ⓑ Ⓒ Ⓓ
4. Ⓐ Ⓑ Ⓒ Ⓓ
5. Ⓐ Ⓑ Ⓒ Ⓓ
6. Ⓐ Ⓑ Ⓒ Ⓓ
7. Ⓐ Ⓑ Ⓒ Ⓓ
8. Ⓐ Ⓑ Ⓒ Ⓓ
9. Ⓐ Ⓑ Ⓒ Ⓓ
10. Ⓐ Ⓑ Ⓒ Ⓓ
11. Ⓐ Ⓑ Ⓒ Ⓓ
12. Ⓐ Ⓑ Ⓒ Ⓓ
13. Ⓐ Ⓑ Ⓒ Ⓓ
14. Ⓐ Ⓑ Ⓒ Ⓓ
15. Ⓐ Ⓑ Ⓒ Ⓓ
16. Ⓐ Ⓑ Ⓒ Ⓓ
17. Ⓐ Ⓑ Ⓒ Ⓓ
18. Ⓐ Ⓑ Ⓒ Ⓓ
19. Ⓐ Ⓑ Ⓒ Ⓓ
20. Ⓐ Ⓑ Ⓒ Ⓓ

21. Ⓐ Ⓑ Ⓒ Ⓓ
22. Ⓐ Ⓑ Ⓒ Ⓓ
23. Ⓐ Ⓑ Ⓒ Ⓓ
24. Ⓐ Ⓑ Ⓒ Ⓓ
25. Ⓐ Ⓑ Ⓒ Ⓓ
26. Ⓐ Ⓑ Ⓒ Ⓓ
27. Ⓐ Ⓑ Ⓒ Ⓓ
28. Ⓐ Ⓑ Ⓒ Ⓓ
29. Ⓐ Ⓑ Ⓒ Ⓓ
30. Ⓐ Ⓑ Ⓒ Ⓓ
31. Ⓐ Ⓑ Ⓒ Ⓓ
32. Ⓐ Ⓑ Ⓒ Ⓓ
33. Ⓐ Ⓑ Ⓒ Ⓓ
34. Ⓐ Ⓑ Ⓒ Ⓓ
35. Ⓐ Ⓑ Ⓒ Ⓓ
36. Ⓐ Ⓑ Ⓒ Ⓓ
37. Ⓐ Ⓑ Ⓒ Ⓓ
38. Ⓐ Ⓑ Ⓒ Ⓓ
39. Ⓐ Ⓑ Ⓒ Ⓓ
40. Ⓐ Ⓑ Ⓒ Ⓓ

41. Ⓐ Ⓑ Ⓒ Ⓓ
42. Ⓐ Ⓑ Ⓒ Ⓓ
43. Ⓐ Ⓑ Ⓒ Ⓓ
44. Ⓐ Ⓑ Ⓒ Ⓓ
45. Ⓐ Ⓑ Ⓒ Ⓓ
46. Ⓐ Ⓑ Ⓒ Ⓓ
47. Ⓐ Ⓑ Ⓒ Ⓓ
48. Ⓐ Ⓑ Ⓒ Ⓓ
49. Ⓐ Ⓑ Ⓒ Ⓓ
50. Ⓐ Ⓑ Ⓒ Ⓓ
51. Ⓐ Ⓑ Ⓒ Ⓓ
52. Ⓐ Ⓑ Ⓒ Ⓓ
53. Ⓐ Ⓑ Ⓒ Ⓓ
54. Ⓐ Ⓑ Ⓒ Ⓓ
55. Ⓐ Ⓑ Ⓒ Ⓓ
56. Ⓐ Ⓑ Ⓒ Ⓓ
57. Ⓐ Ⓑ Ⓒ Ⓓ
58. Ⓐ Ⓑ Ⓒ Ⓓ
59. Ⓐ Ⓑ Ⓒ Ⓓ
60. Ⓐ Ⓑ Ⓒ Ⓓ

61. Ⓐ Ⓑ Ⓒ Ⓓ
62. Ⓐ Ⓑ Ⓒ Ⓓ
63. Ⓐ Ⓑ Ⓒ Ⓓ
64. Ⓐ Ⓑ Ⓒ Ⓓ
65. Ⓐ Ⓑ Ⓒ Ⓓ
66. Ⓐ Ⓑ Ⓒ Ⓓ
67. Ⓐ Ⓑ Ⓒ Ⓓ
68. Ⓐ Ⓑ Ⓒ Ⓓ
69. Ⓐ Ⓑ Ⓒ Ⓓ
70. Ⓐ Ⓑ Ⓒ Ⓓ
71. Ⓐ Ⓑ Ⓒ Ⓓ
72. Ⓐ Ⓑ Ⓒ Ⓓ
73. Ⓐ Ⓑ Ⓒ Ⓓ
74. Ⓐ Ⓑ Ⓒ Ⓓ
75. Ⓐ Ⓑ Ⓒ Ⓓ
76. Ⓐ Ⓑ Ⓒ Ⓓ
77. Ⓐ Ⓑ Ⓒ Ⓓ
78. Ⓐ Ⓑ Ⓒ Ⓓ
79. Ⓐ Ⓑ Ⓒ Ⓓ
80. Ⓐ Ⓑ Ⓒ Ⓓ

CHAPTER TEN

Practice EC–4 Pedagogy and Professional Responsibilities Test I

1. In Ms. Tyler's kindergarten class, the children were pouring liquid from a short, wide container into a tall, thin container. Max, a student in the class, insisted that the tall container held more liquid. Using what she knows and understands about the human developmental process, Ms. Tyler's *best* assessment of this class activity would be that:

   A. most children at this stage of cognitive development are unable to conserve quantities.
   B. Max probably has a form of delayed development and it may take several years to reach the same development as his peers.
   C. not all children are at the same stage of development at the same time and Max may need some tutoring to help him develop appropriately.
   D. children at this stage of development are egocentric, so Ms. Tyler needs to make adjustments in the activity.

2. Each day during the language arts period of her kindergarten class, Ms. Hageman reads a story to her students and then asks the students to retell, act out, or dictate their favorite part of the story. Based on what Ms. Hageman knows about students at this stage of their development, her *primary* goal for this activity should be to:

   A. ensure adequate material is included in the students' folders.
   B. provide for the wide range of individual developmental differences and the results of developmental planning.
   C. provide alternate activities that can be divided between Ms. Hageman and her aide.
   D. create a wide range of individual activities so that all children are well occupied.

3. During the block set aside for science in her kindergarten class, Ms. Anderson involves the students in many activities. She plans these activities based on the children's development. Which of the following instructional strategies would *best* meet the needs of students in her kindergarten science class?

   A. Let children study the history of science and the contributions that scientists make.
   B. Let children create lists of trees found on the school ground.
   C. Let children construct tables and charts about the monthly weather changes.
   D. Let children explore their shadows on a sunny day and then draw around the shadows.

4. Jose is an active four-and-a half-year-old. He has just entered a preschool setting for the first time. Ms. Nohl observes that he shies away from the other children. In addition, she notes he has no interest in developing a leadership role or in joining the others while they are playing at the centers. Ms. Nohl's *best* assessment of Jose's actions as he plays with other students would be:

   A. Jose is severely mentally retarded.
   B. Jose is not developmentally ready for cooperative play and a sense of belonging with the other children.
   C. Jose's home environment is rich with educational materials that stimulate him and he is just bored.
   D. Jose is too advanced in his play and probably should be promoted to first grade.

GO ON TO THE NEXT PAGE

5. Ms. Werner is a first-year teacher who has recently graduated from a nearby university. In her professional development classes she studied the role of cognitive development. She learned that children pass through hierarchical stages. The children she will be teaching fall into the concrete operational stage of development. Using this knowledge, how can she *best* approach instructional planning?

   A. Wait for children to reach a more cognitively advanced level before introducing certain concepts.
   B. Carefully observe the children's activities and materials and plan appropriate instruction to meet the required goals.
   C. Request testing of the students to determine if they meet the criteria for the concrete operational stage of development.
   D. Plan different strategies and see which ones the children like best.

6. Maureen, a first grader, has been diagnosed with a developmental expressive language disorder and is considered to have a developmental delay. Test results indicate her speech lags approximately two years behind that of her peers. Her parents have no trouble understanding her, but her teacher, Ms. Trundle, is having a difficult time communicating with her. Ms. Trundle will receive the *most* beneficial assistance from which of the following?

   A. Discussing with the first grade level team her frustration and lack of knowledge in dealing with Maureen's disorder.
   B. Checking out books on speech and language disorders and reading up on the educational implications.
   C. Inviting the special education teacher to come to her class and asking her to design an Individualized Educational Program (IEP).
   D. Collaborating with the district's speech and language therapist to help develop goals and techniques for effective therapy at school as well as at home.

7. Ms. Lee, a first-year teacher, is formulating a unit on Native Americans. As she plans her instructional strategies, she hopes to have the children who come from different cultural and ethnic groups understand the culture of the Native Americans. Ms. Lee decides to discuss the situation with her mentor, and asks for advice in meeting the needs of all of the students. Which of the following would NOT be a recommendation by the mentor?

   A. Try varied approaches to teaching and organizing classes and see if one works better than another.
   B. Try to include a variety of activities so children are given a choice or a preference.
   C. Encourage the students to participate in discussions and then correct them when appropriate English is not used.
   D. Be an informed teacher and build as much as possible on every student's culture.

8. At the beginning of each year, Ms. Patterson uses "Me Containers" as an introductory activity. She especially likes this activity because each year her class is made up of a diverse population. Each student in the class is directed to bring a small box or bag containing articles that explains something about him or her. For instance, they should include something that explains a hobby, a special trip, or a special person. She advises the students to limit what they bring to five or fewer items. She encourages the children in the class to ask each other questions about their special items. She spreads the activity over several days and begins the activity by bringing her own "Me Container." The *primary* advantage of this activity would be:

   A. to develop a sense of community by providing insight into each individual in the class.
   B. to allow students an opportunity to see what other students bring to class for "show and tell."
   C. to provide a learning experience where students, particularly those who have difficulty speaking English, can practice their oral language skills.
   D. to provide an opportunity for students to ask each other questions, thus developing good questioning techniques.

9. As Jennifer was learning to talk, her parents realized she was developing a speech problem. Although it was not severe, Jennifer would say "wabbit" for rabbit, and "wunning" for running. Now that she is in school, her speech problem does not affect her reading, but Jennifer is beginning to withdraw from oral activities and the students in the class make fun of her. Jennifer's teacher can *best* help her by:

   A. suggesting that Jennifer not use the words with which she is having difficulty.
   B. discussing Jennifer's difficulty with the class when Jennifer is out of the room, and asking them not to mention it to her.
   C. being sensitive to Jennifer's speech problem and applying skills that Jennifer has acquired while going to speech therapy.
   D. insist that Jennifer interact with the other children so she can build confidence.

GO ON TO THE NEXT PAGE

Practice EC-4 Pedagogy and Professional Responsibilities Test I

Clustered Items Begin Here

10. During a rock unit, Ms. Jackson has students in her first-grade class study the concept that some rocks are harder than others depending on the kind of mineral from which they are made. Several students in the class are English Language Learners (ELLs). She can *best* meet the needs of these students by:

    A. arranging for children to drop rocks into a pail of water and see which ones float.
    B. having children look in magazines to find people using rocks and then discuss orally what the people are doing with the rocks.
    C. demonstrating hardness and softness of rocks by showing how hard rocks can scratch or make a mark on softer rocks.
    D. asking the students to make a list of hard rocks and soft rocks.

11. Ms. Jackson extends the rock unit and incorporates music into her program. Children place small rocks in plastic or cardboard containers and shake them. They hit rocks together and use sticks to tap rocks. Favorite songs are sung while children play their instruments. However, Ms. Jackson realizes from past experience that some children may become overly excited, with the instruments disturbing other classes. In establishing the classroom climate and managing student behavior, Ms. Jackson needs to remember that:

    A. children at this age level need to be interested in music.
    B. children need to be involved in cooperative learning.
    C. children are too young to incorporate musical technology.
    D. children need to be taught procedures and routines.

12. Ms. Jackson has her first-grade class use centers while she is involved in teaching the guided reading program. The technology center is set up as an extension of her rock unit. The textbook publishing company has a website that is directly related to the teaching of rocks. Children have choices of finding out how to safely gather rocks, putting a rock puzzle together, or learning new vocabulary associated with rocks. Which of the following is a *primary* reason Ms. Jackson has the students use a computer rather than just looking at books on rocks?

    A. It satisfies the technology component of the Texas Essential Knowledge and Skills (TEKS).
    B. It provides for a variety of resources when studying the concept of rocks.
    C. It keeps the children well occupied while Ms. Jackson is working with guided reading.
    D. It ensures that the students will develop a more active role in science.

Clustered Items End Here

GO ON TO THE NEXT PAGE

13. Ken, a fourth-grade student, asks to leave the class each day around the time the teacher will be having a discussion about the silent reading assignment. His teacher realizes an avoidance pattern is developing and makes it a point to conference with the student. Ken confides in his teacher and tells her he doesn't like reading. His teacher conducts an Informal Reading Inventory, and after analyzing the results, discovers that Ken has no problem with word recognition skills and very few comprehension problems during oral reading, but after reading a passage silently, Ken is unable to answer questions or tell the teacher what he has been reading. What should the *next* approach be in helping Ken?

    A. Provide Ken with instructional strategies so he is able to take an active part in the reading process.
    B. Ask Ken if he is paying attention while he reads silently.
    C. Ask another student in the class to read to Ken so he will learn how reading is supposed to sound.
    D. Discuss Ken's problem with his parents and ask them to read with him at home.

14. Following the guidelines outlined by the Texas Essential Knowledge and Skills (TEKS) for science and social studies, Ms. Allen's first-grade class is studying the movement of water and the process of accumulation as it flows into the lakes. Because there is a lake in close proximity to the school, several of the children ask if they can visit the lake as a class. After discussing the request with the principal, Ms. Allen proceeds with making plans. Prior to the field trip, Ms. Allen brainstorms about other lakes the children have visited. They talk about how big the lakes are and the source of the water. They discuss ways water from rivers and lakes is used. Ms. Allen creates a word web on the board with the words children used to describe lakes. They look at a map of Texas that includes rivers, lakes, and the Gulf of Mexico and trace the paths of the river with their fingers. They talk about melting snow, rain, and creeks. After the field trip and in small groups, they make a clay model of a lake and simulate the process of accumulation and evaporation. Which instructional goals and objectives would *best* be supported by the inclusion of such a variety of activities?

    A. Exploring content from integrated and varied sources, thus meeting individual needs and enhancing learning.
    B. Providing students with an opportunity to improve oral and written communication skills.
    C. Providing students with an opportunity to connect with the teacher on an informal basis.
    D. Facilitating the students' abilities to recall pertinent information.

15. The *most* important reason for Ms. Allen to consult the Texas Essential Knowledge and Skills (TEKS) would be to:

   A. address the children's need for outdoor activity.
   B. address the students' need for self-reflection.
   C. address the students' need for interacting with other students.
   D. address expectations for students as described by the state of Texas.

16. At the beginning of the school year, Ms. Lovell, a second-grade teacher, sets up independent centers. She also conducts her reading using guided reading. While meeting with each group, the rest of the class works in centers. For the centers to remain effective, Ms. Lovell must evaluate the appropriateness of the materials in the center and make sure they are meeting the varied students' needs. How should she approach this task?

   A. Assign a student who regularly finishes the work at the center to help the other students with their work.
   B. Verify that each center has materials that encourage children to explore, to meet the students' needs, and to promote independence.
   C. Have ample worksheets available so the center will not run out of material.
   D. Have each student assess his or her own work and then share with Ms. Lovell the results.

17. Teachers spend a great deal of time planning for the school day and preparing stimulating lessons. When implementing daily lesson plans, it is important for the teachers to:

   A. make sure everything that is planned is completed so there is no holdover for the next day.
   B. make sure that the lessons are easy enough so the students don't have a lot of questions.
   C. make sure that at the end of a lesson, the teachers allow for students' self-reflection and bring closure.
   D. make sure the teachers tell the students exactly what they learned during the lesson so they can share the information with their parents.

18. Ms. Boone, a third-grade teacher, was planning a lesson in which the students use concrete square unit models to find the area of a shape. She purchased dry beans and one-inch grid paper and made tiles out of construction paper to use in conjunction with the lesson. To begin the strategy, she directed the children to cover a portion of the grid paper with beans and discover the number of pieces used. Next, she directed them to use the tiles and repeat the process. She then explained that the number of square units needed to cover a figure was called the area. She went on to teach perimeter using the same procedure. For a reinforcement activity, Ms. Boone divided the class into groups of two and directed the partners to take turns choosing flat objects they found throughout the classroom. They were first to estimate and then to establish the number of tiles it would take to cover the object completely. She inquired as to whether they thought the area and perimeter could ever be the same. Ms. Boone's *primary* goal for this lesson was:

   A. to plan a lesson whereby Ms. Boone was able to cover all of the material she had hoped to cover and in the allotted amount of time.
   B. to stimulate the children's reflection and promote critical thinking and inquiry.
   C. to ensure that the students were aware of mathematical terms such as area and perimeter.
   D. to teach the students to recognize the pattern of symmetry when they see it.

19. Ms. Boone realizes that learning varies from student to student. By using manipulatives, she will focus *primarily* on which style of learning?

   A. Auditory
   B. Individual
   C. Kinesthetic
   D. Linguistic

20. A student in Ms. Barber's class loves to read. However, when it comes to reading orally, the student frequently mispronounces words and stumbles over fairly easy material. The other students get impatient and several laugh when errors are made. During a parent–teacher conference, the student's parents are made aware of the problem and ask if they can be of any help. Which of the following would be the *best* advice Ms. Barber can give the parents?

   A. Suggest the parents read with the student and keep track of mistakes that the child makes.
   B. Suggest to the parents that while the child is reading, they should stop when an error is made and correct the mistake at that time.
   C. Suggest that the parents and child read together, but make the situation as natural and stress free as possible.
   D. Suggest to the parents that they check books out of the library they think their child will enjoy.

GO ON TO THE NEXT PAGE

21. Ms. Hart, a first-year teacher, has a habit of orally outlining the day's events and activities at the beginning of each class day. After the first three weeks she realizes that several students are experiencing difficulty in remembering the assignments. Her mentor suggests that children need a variety of formats in which to learn and some children are probably visual learners. Which of the following would NOT be of benefit to visual learners?

   A. Using graphic organizers
   B. Writing the assignment on the board
   C. Providing a variety of visuals in the classroom
   D. Taping lessons so the children can listen to their assignments

22. Ms. Kumar enjoys teaching mathematics to her first-grade students. For the children to become actively involved in the learning process, she uses concrete objects such as blocks to create sets of tens and ones when teaching the concept of place value. The children, however, are easily distracted and tend to make configurations other than what Ms. Kumar expects. Ms. Kumar can *best* alleviate this problem in future lessons by:

   A. allowing only those students who used the blocks appropriately to have use of them during the following lesson.
   B. modeling for the students the appropriate procedures and specifying expectations.
   C. motivating the children to do their best with the blocks so they can have more play time.
   D. alternating different ways for the children to learn the place value concept.

23. Ms. Gallager, a third-grade teacher, wishes to reinforce the idea of community by using a hands-on activity. She divides the class into groups of four and distributes popsicle sticks and masking tape. She directs the students to make a structure using the materials provided. The group must work in complete silence. Afterwards, the entire class discusses how they communicated without talking and came up with the following ideas:

- Respect everyone in the group.
- Try out new ideas.
- Take responsibility for your own actions.

Having students work in a group and then discuss their reaction to the group work is *most* likely to help them:

A. understand that life has many challenges that will need to be met.
B. use self-reflection to develop a sense of involvement and responsibility.
C. compare and contrast those students who readily work well in a group to those that don't offer as much support.
D. develop a form of management for the class that ultimately will result in the selection of leaders.

24. Mr. Craddick is a highly successful fourth-grade teacher who rarely experiences behavior problems. When discussing his reasons for success with the members of the fourth-grade planning team, he suggests that his room arrangement is largely responsible. He explains that he moves desks around depending on the activity. He rarely has the desks in rows because he feels as though it limits student participation. During whole-group discussion he arranges the seats in a U-shape format so students are able to see each other and when working in groups, students' desks are clustered. Depending on the activity and the arrangement required, the *most* important thing to remember is to:

A. maintain an arrangement whereby the children are pleased so discipline problems are reduced.
B. maintain an arrangement that allows for easy access to the students and one in which the teacher can monitor the students on a continuous basis.
C. arrange the room so a neat, orderly environment can be maintained.
D. arrange the room so the students who create the most problems are all seated at the front where the teacher has direct eye contact.

25. Flora is a gifted and talented student in a fourth-grade science class. Flora's teacher uses cooperative groups and wonders if this method of instruction is beneficial for bright students. The *primary* consideration Flora's teacher needs to realize is that:

   A. Flora can benefit from group work, but the group will need to be monitored for productiveness and fairness.
   B. Flora cannot meet her potential by being placed in cooperative groups.
   C. Flora is just being polite and is probably complaining to her parents and friends.
   D. Flora should be allowed to always take a lead role in the cooperative groups and in this way she will feel less frustrated.

26. Kelly attends an early childhood center in her neighborhood. Kelly has been taught to share her toys with others and in most cases behaves very well. However, when it comes time for centers in school, Kelly runs to the beanbag chair, which is located in the reading center and claims it is hers. Her teacher can change this behavior by:

   A. telling Kelly she may not use the center until she changes her behavior.
   B. holding a discussion with the class and explaining the rules of the reading area and particularly the beanbag chair.
   C. modeling turn-taking and then monitoring Kelly closely.
   D. allowing the children to determine how they will resolve the problem of the beanbag chair.

27. Ms. Webb, along with other kindergarten teachers at Crockton Elementary, plans the day with large blocks of time, and establishes a routine when the students first begin school. She knows students need structure so she organizes tasks such as watering the plants, feeding the ferret, putting away equipment, and cleaning up after painting. Ms. Webb can *most* effectively have students follow a routine by:

   A. adding new tasks on a daily basis so more children have a task of their own to complete.
   B. empowering a student who has shown leadership to direct the clean-up.
   C. making adjustments for the youngest students in the class and excusing them from participating.
   D. developing a sense of responsibility among the class so they take pride in being a member of group.

28. Ms. McIntyre enjoys using trade books as well as the state-approved basal for her reading instruction. However, she thinks the students are not as engaged in the reading process as she wants them to be. During the weekly planning session, another teacher suggests that she might try using Literature Circles. She divides the class into small groups who then meet to discuss some literature they have all read. They ask each other thought-provoking questions, discuss their favorite parts, or talk about how the book relates to their lives. Ms. McIntyre uses this approach because:

   A. group members assume responsibility for their own learning and the learning of others.
   B. some of the students have not read the book and it will help those individuals process the material if they are discussing it in a group situation.
   C. by having the students work in groups, it allows her to have more time for planning and organizing her lessons.
   D. she will be allowing students the practice of using their social skills in a group situation.

29. Which of the following factors has been shown to be *most* important in developing a well-organized functioning kindergarten classroom?

   A. Receiving administrative support on setting up a schedule.
   B. Planning large blocks of time that allow for task completion and that reflect interests and abilities of the students.
   C. Showing a willingness to work closely with other kindergarten teachers in the building.
   D. Limiting the amount of time students are engaged in free play.

30. Mr. Santini intends to record grades electronically using a computer program provided by the school district. What is the *primary* benefit of using the software?

   A. This will ensure that Mr. Santini will be able to spend more time with his students.
   B. It will motivate students to turn their work in on time.
   C. By modeling the use of the computer, Mr. Santini provides a role model.
   D. The computer program provides grades to be kept in an efficient and organized manner.

31. The *primary* consideration when placing a paraprofessional in the classroom is:

   A. the development of a close personal relationship with parents.
   B. the clarification of the role and responsibility the paraprofessional will have in the classroom.
   C. the development of a separate curriculum when the paraprofessional is working with the class.
   D. the benefits the community will receive by having paraprofessionals in a school setting.

32. Mario is a student in Mr. Larson's science class. Mario makes comments or asks questions that disrupt class discussion. In addition, he mumbles while others are talking, makes crude remarks, and laughs at inappropriate times. It appears Mario is seeking attention from his peers, and he sees interrupting as a way of gaining peer status. Which of the following is likely to be the *most* effective and direct way of dealing with Mario?

   A. Reduce Mario's ability to make contact with his peers by placing him at the back of the classroom.
   B. Send Mario out of the room so the interruptions will stop.
   C. Occasionally give Mario the attention he desires.
   D. Continue teaching, ignoring the behavior if possible, and then have a private conference with Mario at the first opportunity.

33. Ms. Cory has a difficult time keeping her third-grade class quiet. She has tried various approaches and decides to ask her mentor to observe her class in hopes of discovering a solution. After the observation, her mentor discusses the following observations:

   - Children are out of their seats sharpening pencils, passing notes, and randomly going to centers.
   - Classroom rules are not visible.
   - Ms. Cory yells above the children to get their attention.

What would be the most important *first* step Ms. Cory should take?

   A. Post a list of classroom rules and ask the students to read them.
   B. Clearly define and model expectations for behavior that include a well-established routine.
   C. Tell the students what they have been doing wrong and then suggest ways they can alter their behavior.
   D. Invite the principal to her class while she talks about discipline.

34. Mr. Scott, a fourth-grade teacher, plans a lesson in which he provides an opportunity for students to read with dramatic intonation. He can *best* do this by:

   A. choosing a student with excellent intonation to read to the class.
   B. slowing down and speeding up several times during a paragraph.
   C. infusing his voice with excitement when he comes to exclamation marks and modeling how reading should sound.
   D. putting on a recording of the story and have the students read along.

35. Mr. Peterson's fourth-grade social studies class was discussing the population expansion that has occurred in Texas. They talked about how new businesses are springing up in every town and city, but along with that growth there are always problems. Mr. Peterson asks the class to predict how they think Texas will meet the challenges brought on by the growth of the state. In responding to the previous question, Mr. Peterson is hoping for what kind of response?

   A. He wants the students to answer the question with specific details using the social studies book as a reference.
   B. He wants the students to ask him what he thinks so he can make the lesson more interesting.
   C. He wants to know the students' backgrounds on the topic of economic growth.
   D. He wants the students to engage in active, inquiry learning and higher-order thinking.

36. Mr. Peterson continues with his questioning on the population expansion in Texas. According to Bloom's Taxonomy, the highest-order question Mr. Peterson asks is:

   A. What city in the state of Texas has the most pollution?
   B. Which of the following cities has the highest population?
   C. Is pollution in Austin higher during the summer or winter months?
   D. What effect will the population expansion in Texas have on your lives 15 years from now?

37. Ms. Prentice, a third-grade language arts teacher, wants to encourage her students to write Haiku poetry. She demonstrates several poems, showing examples on the overhead projector. The class as a whole writes several poems under the guidance of Ms. Prentice. She next explains how the students will compose their own haikus. Ms. Prentice's *likely* purpose for using the overhead and demonstrating the strategy of poetry writing is to:

   A. integrate technology into the lesson.
   B. model and communicate expectations.
   C. encourage students to become poets.
   D. provide samples of students' work for the class poetry book.

38. If a teacher has developed skilled questioning techniques, the teacher should:

    A. concentrate on the quantity rather than the quality of questions.
    B. ask questions that help children see relationships among ideas.
    C. always ask each child the same number of questions.
    D. promote a healthy environment in the classroom by asking just the children who raise their hands to answer a question.

39. Mr. Patel notices that Chris is having a particularly bad day. He is late for school, he forgets his homework, and he gets into an argument on the playground. During math, Chris appears frustrated with the assignment. Mr. Patel quietly goes over to Chris and places a hand on his shoulder. In performing this gesture Mr. Patel's *most* likely reason is that he is:

    A. irritating Chris even further.
    B. illustrating the concept of overlapping.
    C. monitoring closely Chris's seatwork assignment.
    D. communicating that he understands by using nonverbal skills.

40. Ms. Dresden explains to the students that they will be using a new group discussion method called Reciprocal Teaching where she will first model reading and understanding, and then each student will have an opportunity to lead the discussion of a selection the class has read. The teacher's *primary* objective for using this method is to:

    A. promote intellectual involvement and stimulate active student engagement and learning.
    B. provide an alternative to the usual pattern of reading.
    C. demonstrate good oral reading practices.
    D. prepare the students in the use of a new method for an up-coming teacher evaluation.

41. Ms. Farr, a second-grade social studies teacher, plans on using a direct mode of teaching when she introduces the concepts of major land forms and bodies of water. Which one of the following is NOT an advantage of this method of teaching?

    A. The teacher is able to cover content in a shorter amount of time.
    B. The teacher controls what is to be taught.
    C. The information presented is clear and to the point.
    D. Students make most of the decisions about what they want to learn.

42. As Mr. Olsen's class discusses the Western Hemisphere, he wants to make sure he is promoting student engagement in the classroom. Which of the following would *best* demonstrate this?

   A. Mr. Olsen asks students to work in groups and to write a script in which a present-day newscaster interviews a French fur trapper.
   B. Mr. Olsen contacts a professor at the local university and invites the professor to lecture to the class on his trips to the Western Hemisphere.
   C. Mr. Olsen asks students to make a list of questions they would ask Christopher Columbus.
   D. Mr. Olsen's students read an assignment in the textbook and report to the class.

43. As a first-grade teacher, Ms. Franks realizes the importance of keeping good records. She is particularly dedicated to observing student endeavors during reading. She uses anecdotal records to keep track of strategies, miscues, interests, and work habits. She records what the child says or does. In using anecdotal records, Ms. Franks should ask herself which of the following questions?

   A. Did I record enough conversation today?
   B. How can I utilize the information I have observed to determine students' grades?
   C. What does this information reveal and how can I use it to plan for my students' instructional program?
   D. Did I observe everything on my checklist today?

Clustered Items Begin Here

44. In Ms. Routman's fourth-grade class, all of the students participate in an Author Study. She selects paperback books that are on the students' interest and ability levels as well as on CD-ROM. Then, letting children select a book, she divides the students into pairs according to their selections. Each student is responsible for reading a book of choice. The team may approach the Author Study in various ways. Some of the activities Ms. Routman suggests are:

   - read other books by the author.
   - write a letter to a living author.
   - simulate a letter and response from a deceased author.
   - write a dialogue journal between yourself and a character in the book.

GO ON TO THE NEXT PAGE

What should Ms. Routman's *primary* role be while the children are working in small groups?

A. Consult with each set of partners and offer to help them with their project.
B. Walk around the room and monitor the students to see if they are actively engaged and on task.
C. At the student's request, use the computer to find pertinent information.
D. Summarize material for students who are having difficulty reading the assigned material.

45. Another part of the Author Study assignment is to e-mail a partner and discuss his or her likes and dislikes about the book. At the completion of the project, the team will present their Author Study by way of a dramatization, a poster board, or talk show format. Ms. Routman asks the students to self-assess their work by completing a rubric. They are asked:

- Is your presentation neat?
- Is your presentation easy to understand?
- Did the presentation meet the goals and objectives?
- Did I participate equally with my partner?

Ms. Routman understands the Author Study project will require work and cooperation between team members. The majority of the students want to do well for the sake of learning, but several students are not as enthusiastic as she would like. To keep the students motivated and involved in their own learning process, Ms. Routman should:

A. assure everyone ahead of time that they will all get As for the Author Study project.
B. encourage the students to do their best work and offer praise.
C. invite parents to a special showing and select the best Author Studies.
D. make sure there is a student who is motivated internally and one who is motivated externally when pairing the groups.

46. The Author Study teaching strategy that Ms. Routman has chosen to use will *most likely*:

A. promote school and parent relationships.
B. teach students how to use the computer more effectively.
C. encourage students' self-motivation and foster independent learning.
D. discourage students from wanting to work on their own.

Clustered Items End Here

47. Because technology is assuming an ever-increasing role in our lives, teachers must continue to explore and evaluate new equipment and the effectiveness of it in the classrooms. In one of Mr. Smith's professional journals, mention was made of the Educational Technologies Providing Increased Learning Opportunities for Texas Students (Ed Tech PILOTS). He became quite interested as this program examines applications of technology in K–12 schools. It also examines the effectiveness in meeting educational goals and objectives in the areas of teaching and learning as well as other areas of concern for educators and then provides the Texas Education Agency (TEA) with their results. What would Mr. Smith's *first* step be if he were interested in finding out more about Ed Tech PILOTS?

   A. Set up a meeting with the principal of his school.
   B. Call Ed Tech PILOTS and arrange a meeting for his school.
   C. Purchase a piece of equipment that has been recommended to TEA and explore its feasibility in his own classroom.
   D. Write a letter to the parents to see if they can help fund the purchase of some technology in the classroom.

48. When instructing students on the use of word-processing programs, which of the following is NOT a *primary* element to be considered?

   A. Saving one's work on a disk.
   B. Listing advantages of word processing.
   C. Rearranging paragraphs and sentences.
   D. Learning the keyboard.

49. When Ms. Sidle, the school librarian, was ordering new materials for the library, she wanted to make sure she appropriated the right amount of funds for current technology. The *primary* goal in selecting the right software and programs for the school would be to:

   A. select material that would meet campus and students' needs.
   B. select material that would be useful, attractive, and fun to use.
   C. select a program that incorporates all of the objectives and includes reproducible worksheets.
   D. select material that parents would enjoy.

50. Ms. Beyers had a favorite assignment she used at the beginning of each year. She instructed the students, while they were supervised, to explore the Internet and look for information about the world's happenings on the day they were born. They were to record their findings and report the results to the class. If they had difficulty locating information, Ms. Beyers and her aide would be of assistance. Which of the following is a major benefit of this type of activity?

   A. It will provide for excellent reading material for the entire class.
   B. It provides the teacher with information on the students' capabilities of using the computer.
   C. It provides the teacher with historical data that she can use during the year.
   D. It promotes students' understanding of the Internet and links to other information.

51. Ms. Boone regularly uses rubrics as a means of assessing her students. The *primary* purpose of using a rubric is that it:

   A. eliminates the need for letter grades.
   B. provides criteria for task assessment.
   C. provides results on multiple-choice and true-false tests.
   D. makes allowances for students who are quite creative.

52. The *main* advantage of using a norm-referenced or standardized test is that:

   A. parents can be well informed of a student's mastery of specific skills.
   B. teachers can use the information provided from the products created to assess their students.
   C. students are compared with a representative sample of other students who are at the same age or grade level.
   D. students' performances on the questions will indicate if objectives have been met.

53. Ms. Mills, a second grade teacher, uses portfolios as an alternative approach to traditional testing and grading systems. Ms. Mills initiates the portfolio at the beginning of each school year. In convincing her grade team to use portfolios as well, which of the following is the *biggest* advantage for using portfolios?

   A. Portfolios show continuous growth over time and provide students with a means of self-assessment.
   B. Portfolios contain examples of a student's best work.
   C. Portfolios can be shown to other students so they can decide what to keep and what to discard.
   D. Portfolios help teachers spot problem areas with their own instruction.

54. Ms. Morris, a third-grade teacher, is completing a chapter on fractions. She uses the state-adopted books for mathematics. She guides students through the assigned textbook pages and practice exercises and then assesses what they have learned. Which of the following activities would *best* assess the assignment?

   A. A standardized test
   B. A chapter test
   C. An interview between the teacher and student
   D. A dramatization

55. Ms. Alvarez incorporates authentic assessment in her classroom. She frequently requires students to apply what they know to class assignments rather than just recall information. In addition, she asks students to demonstrate their knowledge of a task instead of taking a multiple-choice test. The *primary* reason for using authentic assessment is that:

   A. she wants to assess the students' performance and achievement in as natural a setting as possible and in situations that reflect the real world.
   B. she doesn't feel qualified to prepare traditional tests.
   C. students complain about having to study for multiple choice and matching tests.
   D. she likes to observe her students perform and she doesn't feel responsible then for having to teach to a specific test.

56. Ms. Alvarez also believes in self-evaluation for her students and often asks them to complete statements during the day as to what they learned, what they discovered, or what they were excited about. What *major* benefit of this type of procedure should the students hope to see?

   A. Students reflect on their own learning and assume responsibility for assessing their own work.
   B. It provides time with the teacher on a one-to-one basis in a teacher–student conference.
   C. It gives students an opportunity to compare their work with that of the rest of the class.
   D. Students can say what they think they want the teacher to hear.

GO ON TO THE NEXT PAGE

57. Ms. Donnely realizes the value of effective communication between teachers and parents or guardians. She sends home notes, holds conferences, and posts weekly assignments and upcoming events on the school website. Her *primary* goal should be to:

   A. find a means of communication that is easier than a face-to-face conference.
   B. enhance her professional image.
   C. share her teaching ideas with her colleagues.
   D. provide a means of effective communication that keeps parents abreast of goals and objectives.

58. Ms. Stanfield's student teacher, Ms. Gaines, has been with her class since the beginning of the semester and is just about to complete her student teaching requirements. During the semester Ms. Gaines has taken an active role in working with the students, and with Sarah in particular. Because she has become so involved, she asks Ms. Stanfield if she can attend Sarah's parent–teacher conference. Ms. Stanfield's response should be to:

   A. explain to the parents ahead of time the active role Ms. Gaines has had and ask if they would approve of her sitting in during the conference.
   B. tell Ms. Gaines to plan on sitting in at the conference because the parents will undoubtedly approve of her being there.
   C. tell her that she'll need to wait until she gets her own class.
   D. suggest Ms. Gaines ask the principal for permission.

59. Mr. Gonzales has just had a new Asian student enter his third-grade class. The student speaks English with proficiency, but indicates to his teacher that his parents still speak their native language and do not understand English. It is time for parent–teacher conferences and Mr. Gonzales wishes to meet with the parents. What is the *most* appropriate action for Mr. Gonzales to take?

   A. Ask the parents to attend the conference with someone other than their own child who speaks their native language as well as English.
   B. Request an interpreter who is provided by the school district to attend the parent–teacher conference.
   C. In the parent's native language, provide a written report.
   D. Disregard the conference because the student is doing very well.

GO ON TO THE NEXT PAGE

60. Ms. Bondalino learns in a parent–teacher conference that a parent who has three small children to support has just been laid off. Ms. Bondalino suggests that a local family service agency might be able to help and arranges a meeting with the counselor, parent, and member of the agency. What should be the *primary* goal of this meeting?

   A. Discuss the advantages of working with the agency and share success stories.
   B. Address long-term goals for the family.
   C. Provide a list of services the agency can provide.
   D. Evaluate the most immediate needs of the family and express interest in helping.

61. One elementary school in a suburban setting became concerned about the increases in the number of discipline problems they were having. Children were developing a less caring attitude, students were in more fights, attendance was down, and teachers as well as parents were puzzled as to what to do. The principal asked Mr. Hanson if he would chair a committee to come up with solutions. Mr. Hanson's *primary* goal for the first meeting should be:

   A. to foster a clear exchange of ideas from all concerned.
   B. to allow all partners to present their side of the issue on why there were problems.
   C. to enforce a stricter code of discipline for the students.
   D. to list the infractions that have taken place and determine appropriate action.

62. Ms. Ruda has been the third-grade team leader for the last four years. She is ready for a change and would like one of the other teachers to assume the responsibility. What should Ms. Ruda's *first* approach be?

   A. Go to the principal and discuss the possible change.
   B. Discuss her proposal with the rest of the teachers and tell them she is overworked.
   C. Continue the leadership for another year as none of the teachers is interested in assuming the role.
   D. Talk to other grade-level team leaders in the school about her situation.

63. Ms. Anthony routinely assesses her teaching style, instructional strategies, and strengths and weakness. Which one of the following questions would NOT support the idea of self-assessment and reflective teaching?

   A. What materials and resources would be most appropriate for this lesson?
   B. What is the best teaching strategy for this lesson?
   C. How long will this lesson take?
   D. How can I meet all of the children's needs?

Practice EC-4 Pedagogy and Professional Responsibilities Test I

64. Ms. Joseson is a new teacher at her school who has just moved from another state. During a team meeting at which Ms. Joseson is present, several teachers express a concern that the strategies and ideas she is implementing do not reflect the Texas Essential Knowledge and Skills (TEKS). How can they *best* assist Ms. Joseson?

    A. Meet regularly with the grade-level team and together set goals, determine objectives, and engage in an exchange of ideas.
    B. Provide the teacher with a copy of the TEKS and suggest she use them.
    C. Refer her to a website that has excellent lesson plans.
    D. Share lesson plans and offer to observe.

65. Ms. Selensky is preparing for an observation from her principal. She is a very conscientious teacher and wants to make sure the lesson goes well. She has a concern, however, about a particular part of the lesson cycle. What approach should she take?

    A. Prior to the observation, provide a list of all her problems outlining all the areas of concern.
    B. Prior to the observation, discuss with the students the goals and objectives of the lesson and ask them to be on their best behavior.
    C. Prior to the observation, provide the principal with unit plans.
    D. Discuss the problem area ahead of time with the principal, and ask the principal to help evaluate the difficulty she is experiencing.

66. Each year, Mr. Dolezal attends the Texas State Teachers Association (TSTA) annual conference. A new teacher has arrived at his school and he shares with him why he attends the conference. What is Mr. Dolezal's *primary* reason for attending the meetings?

    A. It gives him an opportunity to present the latest ideas on teaching.
    B. He understands the value of attending meetings as a means to grow professionally and exchange ideas with others in the profession.
    C. It provides an opportunity to see former colleagues.
    D. It provides an opportunity to get off campus for several days and to come back refreshed.

GO ON TO THE NEXT PAGE

67. Mr. Gunderson started his teaching career much later than most of his colleagues. He enjoys teaching but feels inadequate when it comes to incorporating technology in his classes. He wants his students to be exposed to the many uses that the field of technology offers in order to enhance productivity in class. Which of the following would be the *most* important step he could take?

   A. Explore online the many facets of technology.
   B. Subscribe to an educational journal that focuses mainly on technology.
   C. Consult the technology coordinator in his district and ask for suggestions.
   D. Participate in lively discussions with his friends as to their choices of technology.

68. Latoya had never missed a day of school. For this reason, her parents were very surprised when her report card came home showing she had been absent. Concerned, her parents went to the school, but after discussing the situation with appropriate school personnel, the absence was verified. After looking at the date in doubt, they realized it was the day her grandmother came to visit and Latoya asked to be taken to school an hour late, but still in time to not be counted absent. The school would not back down from their decision. What would be the *next* step for the parent?

   A. Demand that the school retract the absence or they will take Latoya out of school.
   B. Request a formal hearing based on parental rights, and if the school still won't make adjustments, place a statement with the record stating the parents' view.
   C. Request a meeting with the superintendent and complain about the treatment.
   D. Disregard the error and explain to Latoya that errors do happen.

69. Ms. Tapely accepted a position in a small rural community and was preparing for parent–teacher conferences for the first time. She was really looking forward to the exchange that would take place. Many of the children's best friends were related so they came together for the conference. Two mothers arrived outside Ms. Tapely's door, and she motioned them to come in. She proceeded to hold the conference with both mothers present. In revealing confidential information concerning the students with both mothers in the room, Ms. Tapely demonstrated that she:

   A. was not well versed in rural customs and the interrelationship among families.
   B. was a very poor teacher and should be reprimanded.
   C. was not following the Code of Ethics and Standard Practices for Texas Educators.
   D. was an enthusiastic teacher and the parents probably were going to talk about the grades anyway.

GO ON TO THE NEXT PAGE

70. Every year Markam Elementary School publishes a directory listing the students' names, addresses, and telephone numbers. The directory is completed after the start of school and then sent home with the students. The students find the directory very helpful when they need to contact another student concerning a class project or homework assignment. However, inadvertently, parents were not notified of the directory. The *major* error made was that:

   A. students thought additional information should have been included such as honors and awards they received so they asked for a reprinting.
   B. under the Family Educational Rights and Privacy Act (FERPA), schools must notify parents that the directory will be sent out and then give parents time to request nondisclosure of information.
   C. names of students were left out and students became very upset because they were not included in the directory.
   D. parents were upset because they had given permission the year before and thought that covered all the elementary school years.

Decision Set Begins Here

Ms. Barrett is a first-year teacher in a fourth-grade class. The class makeup is 56% girls and 44% boys and it is composed of African-American, Hispanic-American, Indian-American, and Anglo-American students. The class is heterogeneously grouped according to academic ability.

Ms. Barrett's class is studying about the cultural differences in Texas. Part of this unit of study will focus on celebrations and ethnic traditions that have become an important element in the state of Texas. Several celebrations the students will study will be Juneteenth, Cinco de Mayo, Charo Days, Oktoberfest, Diez y Seis de Septiembre, and Thung Trung Thu. To begin the unit, Ms. Barrett connects prior learning by reminding the students that earlier in the year they had been studying about the Tigua Indians and their ancient heritage. Ms. Barrett is excited about the project because it promotes a feeling of ownership and belonging in the community.

71. Which of the following assignments would *best* enhance students' learning and help with an awareness of social and cultural factors?

   A. Write a letter to a prominent person in the community and request information on festivals.
   B. Look up local civic groups that are listed in the phonebook.
   C. As a class project, plan a mini-festival that centers on the diverse cultural heritage in Texas and invite leaders of the community to come and help celebrate.
   D. Complete worksheets in which students match the name of the celebration to a description.

72. Which of the following activities would demonstrate that Ms. Barrett understands the needs of an English Language Learner (ELL) in the classroom?

    A. Asking the student to write a paper on the geographic differences of each ethnic group.
    B. Asking the student to identify characteristics of leaders from several ethnic and cultural groups.
    C. Asking the student to describe how the migration of his or her culture is different from the migration of other cultures.
    D. Asking an English-speaking student to pair with the ELL student while working on the unit.

73. Ms. Barrett plans on having the students research information on cultural differences in their own communities, and then do a follow-up report outside of school. She realizes that in doing so students may need to use the telephone, public library, or Internet. How should Ms. Barrett approach the fact that some of the families may not have access to these facilities?

    A. Allow students to select their best method so they won't feel obligated to use just one means of research.
    B. Suggest the student pair up with another student and use his or her phone or home computer.
    C. Discuss with parents at the first parent meeting the requirements for the year and the many occasions on which students will need to use a computer at home.
    D. Explain to students that the technology requirement is a small portion of their grade, and if they do well on the rest of the class during the six weeks they will not need to worry about their grades.

74. Ms. Barrett has a student in her class who has been diagnosed with attention deficit/hyperactivity disorder (ADHA). Instead of sitting quietly in his seat working on materials for the unit, Todd is running around. Which of the following suggestions is the *least* effective in dealing with the student's disability?

    A. Provide for periods of mobility in the room such as stretch breaks.
    B. Try to change the child's habits of constant mobility by suggesting he sit still for longer periods of time.
    C. Role-play how to carry out the rules of the room and model appropriate behavior.
    D. Focus on a positive environment and review the student's behavior management plan.

GO ON TO THE NEXT PAGE

75. When discussing the different cultures, Ms. Barrett divides the class into small groups. Each group will be assigned a specific culture and will be required to do research and then report on the specifics of each culture. Conducting the class in this manner supports the instructional practice that teachers, in using cooperative learning, would *most* likely:

   A. assume a facilitating role.
   B. guide activities with lectures.
   C. provide the students with a checklist of duties prior to group activity.
   D. determine group members based on grades.

Decision Set Ends Here

Decision Set Begins Here

Ms. Ling, a third-grade teacher, is preparing a unit for her social studies class on communities. Students will work together in groups to discuss the components that are needed to make a community. With the individual portion of the unit, Ms. Ling will require students to demonstrate their understanding of communities by planning a community of their own. She designs a packet that outlines requirements for the assignment and includes Internet resources where students can turn to for assistance. She sends the packet home with the students and posts the information on the school's website.

76. Before posting the information on the website, Ms. Ling must adhere to which of the following guidelines?

   A. The legal and ethical requirements regarding copyright, privacy, and acceptable use policies.
   B. The TEKS goals and objectives and state clearly which objectives she will cover so students will do well on the TAKS test.
   C. Her own background and prior teaching experience so parents will understand why she is asking the students to plan their own community.
   D. A logical sequential unit so parents will have a greater understanding of students' requirements.

77. Ms. Ling firmly believes in equity for all students and particularly appreciates the gender differences in her class. Because of this, the *most* important thing Ms. Ling should remember is:

   A. when it comes time for the parents to help, make sure there are the same number of male and female adults helping with the project.
   B. to point out that most government employees are male, but in some communities women are also hired.
   C. to expect all students, regardless of their gender, to meet the same expectations.
   D. to design the cooperative groups so there are always exactly the same number of boys as there are girls.

78. In addition to attention to gender, Ms. Ling wants to make provisions for Marvin, a new student, who is confined to a wheelchair. She reviews The Individuals with Disabilities Education Act (IDEA) and realizes that she must:

   A. always pair Marvin with an understanding classmate who will help him maneuver his wheelchair.
   B. contact the other parents in the class and inform them of her plans for Marvin.
   C. communicate clear expectations so Marvin will not think he is receiving special treatment.
   D. ensure a free, appropriate education for all children with disabilities.

79. About a week before configuring the cooperative groups, the principal informs Ms. Ling that she will have a new student from Mexico. After visiting with the curriculum supervisor and the technology coordinator, Ms. Ling discovers that computerized language translators are available that translate assignments students wrote in their native language into English. She plans to use the language translator and several websites as well to enhance instruction for the new student. Ms. Ling has demonstrated that *primarily* she knows how to:

   A. develop a close personal relationship with the school personnel.
   B. incorporate effective use of technology to help students meet instructional goals.
   C. meet the challenges that come her way.
   D. be a well-rounded teacher with many capabilities and avenues for resources.

80. For the culminating event, Ms. Ling invites the parents to a "Community Show" so they are able to share in the excitement of seeing the completion of students' projects and accomplishments. She includes the parents in the culminating event because:

A. she wants feedback on her instruction.
B. she wants to engage families and parents in the educational program.
C. she will get ideas for any necessary changes or adaptations in next year's community project.
D. she knows students will more readily accept preparing a short presentation if their parents are attending.

Decision Set Ends Here

CHAPTER ELEVEN

Practice EC–4 Pedagogy and Professional Responsibilities Test I Answers and Explanations

1. A

This question addresses information from PPR Competency* 001:

The teacher understands human developmental processes and applies this knowledge to plan instruction and ongoing assessment that motivate students and are responsive to their developmental characteristics and needs.

This is a priority-setting question. You are to determine the *best* assessment for a class activity based on developmental stages and the role of cognitive development. Eliminate (B) because the teacher would be jumping to conclusions based on an activity involving different containers. Eliminate (C) because even though not all children are at the same stage of development at the same time, tutoring at this age would not provide the results for which Ms. Tyler is looking. The cognitive thinking in choice (D) is too advanced. Children at this age are in the preoperational stage and most are unable to conserve or to think what something was like before it occurred. Choice (A) is the correct response.

---

*Competency statements copyright © 2003 by the Texas State Board for Educator Certification and National Evaluation Systems, Inc. (NES ®). Reprinted by permission.

2. B

This question addresses information from PPR Competency 001:

The teacher understands human developmental processes and applies this knowledge to plan instruction and ongoing assessment that motivate students and are responsive to their developmental characteristics and needs.

This is a priority-setting question. You must determine Ms. Hageman's *primary* goal for requiring the students to perform one of the activities. Eliminate (A) because, although Ms. Hageman certainly would desire adequate material in the students' folders, the answer has no connection to the goal and the activity. Eliminate (C) because the teacher and the aide might be sharing the responsibility during language arts, but this would not be the primary goal. Choice (D) mentions a wide range of activities but does not meet educational goals and expectations as teachers do not plan instructional strategies just so their students are occupied. Because children at this age possess a wide range of individual differences, the kindergarten program should expose students to a broad range of activities. Children need experiences through which they can explore their own potential and that encourage self-expression. Choice (B) is the correct response.

3. D

This question addresses information from PPR Competency 001:

The teacher understands human developmental processes and applies this knowledge to plan instruction and ongoing assessment that motivate students and are responsive to their developmental characteristics and needs.

This is a priority-setting question. You've been asked to determine which would *best* meet the needs of the kindergarten students. Eliminate (A) because children at this age are not developmentally ready to study the history of science. Ms. Anderson, however, could talk about scientists and mention important discoveries. Eliminate (B) because making lists is a form of low-level learning. The teacher wants the students engaged, and children at this age would have a difficult time creating lists on their own. Eliminate choice (C) because, although children at this age do discuss charts and graphs, most could not create them. In this situation, Ms. Anderson has effectively analyzed how the developmental characteristics of students in kindergarten affect or impact students' learning. She selected an activity that would meet these developmental needs in which children would enjoy physical activity and learn best through play, exploration, and discovery. Choice (D) is the correct response.

Practice EC–4 Pedagogy and Professional Responsibilities Test I Answers and Explanations

4. B

This question addresses information from PPR Competency 001:

The teacher understands human developmental processes and applies this knowledge to plan instruction and ongoing assessment that motivate students and are responsive to their developmental characteristics and needs.

This is a priority-setting question. You are asked to look carefully at how Ms. Nohl *best* assesses Jose's actions while children are at play. Eliminate (A) as there is no basis for Ms. Nohl to make this judgment. Eliminate (C) because Ms. Nohl does not have enough information to make this observation and the question does not have anything to do with the home environment. In choice (D), if Jose were that advanced in his play, he would undoubtedly be leading the other students during play centers rather than showing reticent behavior. Children at this age pass through stages at a different rate of development. At this particular time, Jose is probably not ready to interact socially with the other students, and Ms. Nohl will continue to observe him. Choice (B) is the correct response.

5. B

This question addresses information from PPR Competency 001:

The teacher understands human developmental processes and applies this knowledge to plan instruction and ongoing assessment that motivate students and are responsive to their developmental characteristics and needs.

This is a priority-setting question. You are to determine how the teacher can *best* approach instructional planning. This question requires you to know something about the concrete operational stage of development. Children at this stage range in age from 7 to 11 and are beginning to think more logically. Eliminate choice (A) because even though all children are individuals by nature, Ms. Werner realizes that she must plan for the whole child and the whole class. She knows from her Professional Development classes that she shouldn't wait for a child to advance to a higher cognitive level. Eliminate (C) because Ms. Werner will rely on her knowledge of human growth and development to guide her planning and use testing procedures to show academic growth. Eliminate choice (D) because Ms. Werner will need to plan activities based on children's developmental needs and not on activities the children like. Ms. Werner should carefully observe her students and make sure the requirements she makes are reasonable for the age level. She can keep anecdotal records on the students and create a routine for observing. Choice (B) is the correct response.

6. D

This question addresses information from PPR Competency 001:

The teacher understands human developmental processes and applies this knowledge to plan instruction and ongoing assessment that motivate students and are responsive to their developmental characteristics and needs.

Eliminate (A) because this is a question about developmental delays, and choosing to express frustration with the grade level team will not assist Maureen and her language disorder. Eliminate (B) as the most beneficial help even though it would be an admirable action for Ms. Trundle to take. Choice (C), inviting the Special Education teacher to come to her class and asking her to design an IEP, indicates Ms. Trundle realizes the need for help from the school's specialist, but that it would not be proper professional judgment. Because Maureen has already been diagnosed with a developmental expressive language disorder, Ms. Trundle's main response will be to collaborate with the district to find ways to make the learning environment one where Maureen will experience success. Choice (D) is the correct response.

7. C

This question addresses information from PPR Competency 002:

The teacher understands student diversity and knows how to plan learning experiences and design assessments that are responsive to differences among students and that promote all students' learning.

This is a priority-setting question asking you to select a choice that would be *incorrect*. Therefore, in this question we already know that three out of the four choices are correct. Keep choice (A) because the teacher is trying different approaches and there will not be just one best approach when planning instructional strategies for a diverse classroom. Keep choice (B) as giving students a choice is a recommended procedure in given situations. Choice (D) is also an excellent strategy when working with children from different cultures, for Ms. Lee will better understand the students in her class. Choice (C) is something the mentor would NOT recommend. Ms. Lee will want to encourage the students to participate in discussions, but she should not try to correct the children during the discussion. Choice (C) is the correct response.

Practice EC–4 Pedagogy and Professional Responsibilities Test I Answers and Explanations

8. A

This question addresses information from PPR Competency 002:

The teacher understands student diversity and knows how to plan learning experiences and design assessments that are responsive to differences among students and that promote all students' learning.

This is a priority-setting question, which means you have to select which is the *primary* advantage of using "Me Containers" as an activity. Eliminate (B), for this activity is not the time for show and tell or to bring favorite toys from home. Eliminate (C) as a primary reason even though the experience would be beneficial for non English-speaking students. Choice (D) mentions asking each other questions and Ms. Patterson will certainly be encouraging students to inquire about the other students' selections and choices, but not for the benefit of developing good questioning techniques. Ms. Patterson has selected an activity that will allow community building in the classroom. She provides an opportunity for children to share something about themselves and their family. Choice (A) is the correct response.

9. C

This question addresses information from PPR Competency 002:

The teacher understands student diversity and knows how to plan learning experiences and design assessments that are responsive to differences among students and that promote all students' learning.

This is a priority-setting question in which you must decide how Jennifer's teacher can *best* assist with her speech problem. Eliminate (A) because asking Jennifer to use the words she struggles with will only increase her anxiety and withdrawal from activities. Eliminate (B) even though Jennifer's teacher may talk to the class about Jennifer's problem, there are better ways to assist Jennifer. Choice (D) is similar to the first choice in that the teacher is forcing an issue rather than trying to find a way to assist. Jennifer's teacher will need to work collaboratively with the speech and language pathologist. The teacher's goal will be to transfer skills learned during therapy to the classroom and work with Jennifer within the context of the school curriculum. Choice (C) is the correct response.

10. C

This question addresses information from PPR Competency 002:

The teacher understands student diversity and knows how to plan learning experiences and design assessments that are responsive to differences among students and that promote all students' learning.

This is a priority-setting question as you must decide how to *best* meet the needs of the English Language Learners (ELLs). Eliminate (A) because it is only asking students to carry out an activity and will not address hardness. Eliminate (B) because it also is not a good choice if the teacher is trying to find an activity for ELL students because this activity requires word-recognition and verbalizing results. Choice (D) is a low-level cognitive activity and again requires oral discussion. Ms. Jackson wants the ELL students to grasp the concept of hardness. She can best do this by demonstrating or modeling the concept rather than using printed material the students are unable to read. Choice (C) is the correct response.

11. D

This question addresses information from PPR Competency 006:

The teacher understands strategies for creating an organized and productive learning environment and for managing student behavior.

Eliminate choice (A) because this choice has little to do with classroom management and the level of activity. Eliminate (B) because the question has nothing to do with cooperative learning activities. Choice (C) assumes that these children are not able to incorporate musical technology and the question is asking about classroom climate. Ms. Jackson realizes that children need many approaches to learning so she has provided for a fun activity while teaching the rock unit. However, the students will need to be taught how they are supposed to conduct themselves when making music with the rocks and sticks. Ms. Jackson will need to establish procedures and routines prior to starting the activity. Choice (D) is the correct response.

Practice EC–4 Pedagogy and Professional Responsibilities Test I Answers and Explanations

12. B

This question addresses information from PPR Competency 009:

The teacher incorporates the effective use of technology to plan, organize, deliver, and evaluate instruction for all students.

This is a priority-setting question asking you to determine the teacher's *primary* reason for having the students use the computer. Eliminate (A) because although it does satisfy the TEKS, it wouldn't be the primary reason for having students use technology. Eliminate (C) because, even though having students work on the computer keeps them occupied while Ms. Jackson is teaching other students during guided reading, it would not be a primary reason. Choice (D) should be eliminated because the word "ensure" sets the tone that to incorporate technology, students will be more active in science and no teacher can predict those results. Ms. Jackson is providing for a variety of resources during the rock unit. By extending the program with the use of the computer, Ms. Jackson is allowing students to interact with technology. She has shown she understands how to acquire and evaluate electronic information. Choice (B) is the correct response.

13. A

This question addresses information from PPR Competency 003:

The teacher understands procedures for designing effective and coherent instruction and assessment based on appropriate learning goals and objectives.

Eliminate (B) as this question indicates the teacher is quite insensitive to Ken's problem and would embarrass him in front of the class. Eliminate (C) as an approach to helping Ken. Teachers do request students to read aloud in class, but not as a remedial approach. Eliminate choice (D), as it suggests that Ken's parents should handle the problem. The results of the Informal Reading Inventory indicate that Ken has a problem with silent reading. Ken's teacher should provide teaching strategies such as a Think-a-Loud, Imagery, or the SQ3R Method so Ken will be able to participate more actively in the reading process. Choice (A) is the correct response.

14. A

This question addresses information from PPR Competency 003:

The teacher understands procedures for designing effective and coherent instruction and assessment based on appropriate learning goals and objectives.

This is a priority-setting question. You are asked to determine what goals and objectives would *best* be supported by Ms. Allen's choice of activities. Eliminate (B) as an answer to this question because even though students are discussing, they are not addressing written communication. Eliminate (C), as Ms. Allen would not select this type of activity to get to know her students better. Choice (D) is asking about lower-level skills and Ms. Allen would not ask students to recall specifics about the trip even though she will question them about their experiences. Ms. Allen is using an integrated curriculum approach in which achievement of a wide range of objectives is delivered through a variety of modes. Students have the opportunity to explore, inquire, and problem solve. Choice (A) is the correct response.

15. D

This question addresses information from PPR Competency 003:

The teacher understands procedures for designing effective and coherent instruction and assessment based on appropriate learning goals and objectives.

Eliminate (A) because, even though the students were involved in outdoor activities, Ms. Allen would not consult the TEKS for this purpose. Eliminate (B) as an answer to this question even though self-reflection is desirable when meeting individual needs. Choice (C) is not a reason to consult the TEKS. When developing her lesson plans, Ms. Allen wants to make sure that her goals and objectives correlate with the state-adopted requirements, the TEKS. By referring to these standards, Ms. Allen has an awareness of what students should know and be able to master. Choice (D) is the correct response.

16. B

This question addresses information from PPR Competency 003:

The teacher understands procedures for designing effective and coherent instruction and assessment based on appropriate learning goals and objectives.

Eliminate (A) because Ms. Lovell is trying to evaluate the appropriateness of the centers. Eliminate (C) as worksheets are not considered a recommended activity. Choice (D) suggests the students self-assess and in some cases she will want students to reflect on what they are learning, but she will not use this method to determine if the materials she places in the centers are appropriate. She must, however, make sure the activities are organized, meaningful, and related to instructional objectives. In addition, she must make sure that the directions she places at the centers are available so students are able to work independently and that the arrangement of the center will accommodate several students at one time. Choice (B) is the correct response.

Practice EC–4 Pedagogy and Professional Responsibilities Test I Answers and Explanations

17. C

This question addresses information from PPR Competency 003:

The teacher understands procedures for designing effective and coherent instruction and assessment based on appropriate learning goals and objectives.

Eliminate (A) because effective teachers over-plan to make sure they have addressed their goals and objectives and realize that not all activities must be completed on a specific time and a specific day. Eliminate (B) as this is a negative response and assumes teachers are not concerned about higher-order thinking and discovery learning. Choice (D) has the teacher telling the students what they learned, rather than asking students to restate or self-reflect during the closure of a lesson. The teachers can question students as to what they learned or what they discovered about the lesson. In bringing closure to a lesson, the teachers as well as the students can restate the main points and concepts, thus prompting self-learning and reflection. Choice (C) is the correct response.

18. B

This question addresses information from PPR Competency 004:

The teacher understands learning processes and factors that impact student learning and demonstrates this knowledge by planning effective, engaging instruction and appropriate assessments.

This is a priority-setting question. You are to determine the *primary* goal for a lesson. Eliminate (A) as Ms. Boone is really stimulating critical thinking and wasn't trying to fit a lesson into an allotted amount of time. Eliminate (C) because even though Ms. Boone's goal is for students to understand area and perimeter, she is hoping to engage the students in learning and not just provide an awareness. Choice (D) has nothing to do with symmetry. Ms. Boone could have used a direct teaching approach to instruct the students about area and perimeter. Instead, she introduced the lesson by incorporating manipulatives and further extended the lesson through inquiry and discovery learning. Choice (B) is the correct response.

TExES

19. C

This question addresses information from PPR Competency 004:

The teacher understands learning processes and factors that impact student learning and demonstrates this knowledge by planning effective, engaging instruction and appropriate assessments.

This is a priority-setting question. You are to determine the *primary* focus of a learning style. Eliminate (A) because the auditory learner will be listening for correct instructions and procedures. Eliminate (B) as this is not a learning style. Choice (D) is talking about language, and, again, is not a learning style. Ms. Boone realizes the importance of addressing learning styles in the classroom. She understands that some children learn best by doing and being physically involved, which addresses the kinesthetic learner. Choice (C) is the correct response.

20. C

This question addresses information from PPR Competency 004:

The teacher understands learning processes and factors that impact student learning and demonstrates this knowledge by planning effective, engaging instruction and appropriate assessments.

This is a priority-setting question asking, What is the *best* advice a teacher would give parents in helping their child learn to read? Eliminate (A) because Ms. Barber would recommend parents read with their children; however, she would not recommend keeping track of mistakes the child makes during this time together. Eliminate (B) as stopping to correct a child during reading is not considered best practice. Eliminate choice (D) as it suggests the parents are going to make choices for their child. Ms. Barber can recommend getting a library card for their child and then, together, selecting books that are at the child's interest and reading level. Ms. Barber should keep the parents well informed of the student's progress and suggest that when they work with the student they provide a supportive and stress-free climate. It is important for the parents to make this experience as enjoyable as possible so the student will have a positive experience. Choice (C) is the correct response.

Practice EC–4 Pedagogy and Professional Responsibilities Test I Answers and Explanations

21. D

This question addresses information from PPR Competency 004:

The teacher understands learning processes and factors that impact student learning and demonstrates this knowledge by planning effective, engaging instruction and appropriate assessments.

This is a priority-setting question asking you to select a choice that would be *incorrect*. Therefore, for this question we already know that three out of the four choices are correct. Keep choice (A) because the instructional strategy of providing graphic organizers is an excellent choice and benefits a visual learner. Keep choice (B) because students who learn visually need to be able to receive directions in as many ways as possible. Keep choice (C) because it addresses best practice for helping a visual learner. Because Ms. Hart has been delivering instruction orally prior to talking to the mentor, she should not try taping lessons. The children who are having difficulty do not learn best by auditory means. Instead, Ms. Hart should try using visual techniques to inform students of the routine and procedures. Choice (D) is the correct response.

22. B

This question addresses information from PPR Competency 004:

The teacher understands learning processes and factors that impact student learning and demonstrates this knowledge by planning effective, engaging instruction and appropriate assessments.

This is a priority-setting question. You are asked to make a decision on how Ms. Kumar can *best* alleviate the problem of students becoming distracted during the use of manipulatives. Eliminate (A) because it tends to focus on the negative and reinforces misbehavior for those children who didn't use the blocks appropriately. Eliminate (C) because it is a form of bribery and it doesn't deal with the issue at hand. The students are to meet Ms. Kumar's expectations when working with the blocks. Choice (D) suggests that Ms. Kumar find other ways, in addition to working with blocks, to teach the concept of place value. It is a good suggestion but doesn't address the problem of children becoming distracted. Ms. Kumar needs to analyze the lesson and ask what she might do differently so the students will remain on-task the next time they use the concrete blocks. She must model appropriate use of the blocks and continuously reinforce desired expectations. Choice (B) is the correct response.

23. B

This question addresses information from PPR Competency 005:

The teacher knows how to establish a classroom climate that fosters learning, equity, and excellence and uses this knowledge to create a physical and emotional environment that is safe and productive.

This is a priority-setting question as you are to determine the *most* likely reason for working in a group and then discussing the reaction to group work. Eliminate choice (A) because most students at this age do not have the ability to understand life challenges that must be met. Eliminate choice (C) as this form of classroom management will cause more problems and not build the concept of community that Ms. Gallager is hoping to establish. Choice (D) recommends selecting class leaders and developing classroom management. During the course of the year, Ms. Gallager will have students involved in many activities that require leadership, but the choice doesn't address the question. In reinforcing the idea of community, Ms. Gallager has the students use discovery and self-reflection. The students were able to determine the skills required to function as part of a group. Choice (B) is the correct response.

24. B

This question addresses information from PPR Competency 005:

The teacher knows how to establish a classroom climate that fosters learning, equity, and excellence and uses this knowledge to create a physical and emotional environment that is safe and productive.

This is a priority-setting question. You are asked to determine the *most* important point when arranging a room. Eliminate (A) as Mr. Craddick's goal is to teach students; therefore, pleasing students is not his highest priority. Eliminate (C) because learning can take place in an atmosphere other than one that is neat and orderly. Choice (D) suggests all students sit near the front, and much of the time, Mr. Craddick may be walking around the room and conducting lessons from different areas in the room. Mr. Craddick realizes that the success he has as a teacher has come from careful planning and good room arrangement. He arranges the desks in the room so as to permit orderly movement that is consistent with the instruction and activities. Choice (B) is the correct response.

Practice EC–4 Pedagogy and Professional Responsibilities Test I Answers and Explanations

25. A

This question addresses information from PPR Competency 005:

The teacher knows how to establish a classroom climate that fosters learning, equity, and excellence and uses this knowledge to create a physical and emotional environment that is safe and productive.

This is a priority-setting question. You are to establish the *primary* consideration for gifted and talented students during cooperative groups. Eliminate (B) because Flora should be challenged to perform at her potential and she can do this in groups as well as on individual assignments. Eliminate (C) because there is nothing to indicate Flora is unhappy about working in cooperative groups with the rest of the class. Choice (D) suggests that Flora should *always* have the lead role. The word always should be a clue that this choice may not be the best answer. Research on gifted and talented students suggests that cooperative groups can be effective if the teacher monitors closely to ensure that a productive climate exists and GT students are working according to their level of ability. The teacher also needs to make sure that the brighter students do not end up doing all of the work. Choice (A) is the correct response.

26. C

This question addresses information from PPR Competency 005:

The teacher knows how to establish a classroom climate that fosters learning, equity, and excellence and uses this knowledge to create a physical and emotional environment that is safe and productive.

Eliminate (A) because Kelly is in an early childhood center and is in the process of learning appropriate behavior. This answer focuses on the negative and that will not help Kelly overcome her behavior. Eliminate (B) because children at this age need to be shown how to share rather than just have a discussion and an explanation of rules. Eliminate choice (D) as most children at this age are not equipped with problem-solving skills. Centers provide an opportunity for children to be active, self-selecting, and problem solvers. Kelly's teacher will need to model appropriate behavior, establish procedures and routines, and then find a way to monitor Kelly at the centers. Kelly can be shown how to share and can be taught to express how she feels about the centers and the beanbag chair. Choice (C) is the correct response.

27. D

This question addresses information from PPR Competency 006:

The teacher understands strategies for creating an organized and productive learning environment and for managing student behavior.

This is a priority-setting question. You are asked to determine how the teacher can *most* effectively have the students follow a routine. Eliminate (A) because students need consistency and if new tasks are added on a daily basis they may not have enough time to become established in a routine. Eliminate (B) because it is not the teacher's objective to empower any student, particularly at the kindergarten level. Choice (C) makes allowances for children who are younger than the rest of the class and this practice will not teach students to share in responsibilities. Routines and procedures guide the climate and behavior of a classroom. If routines are established at the beginning of the year, they save time and provide a comfort level for children. Students like to know what they are to do and when they are to do it. Choice (D) is the correct response.

28. A

This question addresses information from PPR Competency 006:

The teacher understands strategies for creating an organized and productive learning environment and for managing student behavior.

Eliminate (B) because the purpose of grouping students in the Literature Circles is to share ideas and have the students assume responsibility for what they have read. The procedure would not be effective if some students had not read the books. Eliminate (C) because Ms. McIntyre should be going from one Literature Circle to another while the students are meeting and should not be planning future lessons at this time. Choice (D) suggests that the Literature Circles are a time for social engagements and students are to be engaged in an exchange of ideas. Ms. McIntyre uses the Literature Circles as a means for students to share material they have all read. She realizes the effectiveness group work can have and monitors a discussion format in which students might ask each other questions, talk about other books, discuss the author, and find out likes and dislikes. Choice (A) is the correct response.

Practice EC–4 Pedagogy and Professional Responsibilities Test I Answers and Explanations

29. B

This question addresses information from PPR Competency 006:

The teacher understands strategies for creating an organized and productive learning environment and for managing student behavior.

This is a priority-setting question because you are to determine what contributes the *most* to a well-functioning kindergarten classroom. Eliminate choice (A) because the teacher will want to be in charge of his or her own classroom and schedule activities according to what the other kindergarten classrooms are doing. Eliminate (C) because even though the ability to work closely with school personnel is a very important quality for teachers to possess, it doesn't necessarily affect the well-organized classroom. Eliminate choice (D) because it is more concerned with management than with organizational skills. Kindergarten children function well when they have sufficient time to complete activities. They need large blocks of time that are balanced with teacher-directed activities and a quiet time routine. Choice (B) is the correct response.

30. D

This question addresses information from PPR Competency 006:

The teacher understands strategies for creating an organized and productive learning environment and for managing student behavior.

This is a priority-setting question. You are asked to determine the *primary* benefit of using software to record grades electronically. Eliminate (A) because a computer program will not ensure Mr. Santini will have more time for students. Eliminate (B) because it suggests that students will turn grades in on time and the question has nothing to do with the students. Choice (C) has Mr. Santini setting an example, and although this is admirable, it would not be the primary benefit. Utilizing an efficient software program can help the teachers with organizational skills and increase the level of professionalism. Choice (D) is the correct response.

31. B

This question addresses information from PPR Competency 006:

The teacher understands strategies for creating an organized and productive learning environment and for managing student behavior.

This is a priority-setting question as you are to determine the *primary* consideration for placing a paraprofessional in the classroom. Eliminate (A) because, although the schools are encouraged to develop working relationships with the family, this would not be a responsibility of a paraprofessional. Eliminate (C) because the paraprofessional is supposed to be working with the teacher and not on a separate program. Choice (D) suggests the community will benefit and it really is the students who benefit by having an additional person in the classroom to support the learning environment. Paraprofessionals assume a variety of roles depending on the school district. One important consideration when placing a paraprofessional is to clarify the roles and the responsibilities of the person to be placed, and then provide an ongoing evaluation and supervision for support. Choice (B) is the correct response.

32. D

This question addresses information from PPR Competency 006:

The teacher understands strategies for creating an organized and productive learning environment and for managing student behavior.

This is a priority-setting question as you are to determine the *most* effective and direct way of dealing with Mario. Eliminate (A) because just placing Mario in the back of the room does not address his problem of disrupting the class. Eliminate (B) because it is only a temporary solution and does not keep Mario engaged in learning. Choice (C) only adds to the problem that exists. Mr. Larson needs to guard against overreacting. He should try to ignore Mario and go on with his teaching. If the behavior continues, he should try to find a time as soon as possible to talk to Mario and find out why he is behaving in such a manner. Choice (D) is the correct response.

Practice EC–4 Pedagogy and Professional Responsibilities Test I Answers and Explanations

33. B

This question addresses information from PPR Competency 006:

The teacher understands strategies for creating an organized and productive learning environment and for managing student behavior.

This is a priority-setting question for you are asked to determine the *first* step Ms. Cory should take to address the classroom management problems. Eliminate (A) because just posting a set of rules for third-grade students does not mean they will read them. Eliminate (C) because telling third-grade students what they have been doing wrong is not creating a positive environment. Eliminate choice (D) because it shifts the responsibility of discipline to the principal. Ms. Cory will find her management problems reduced if she clarifies expectations. She needs to establish well-defined classroom rules that include following directions. Choice (B) is the correct response.

34. C

This question addresses information from PPR Competency 007:

The teacher understands and applies principles and strategies for communicating effectively in varied teaching and learning contexts.

This is a priority-setting question. You are to determine the *best* way to show dramatic intonation. Eliminate (A) because unless that student really understands intonation, the students will not hear the tones Mr. Scott is hoping to provide. Eliminate choice (B) because slowing down and speeding up is not going to be effective. Choice (D) could be an acceptable answer, but choice (C) is better because modeling first hand and in person how he wants the students to sound is better than using a tape recording. By infusing his voice with excitement and meaning, Mr. Scott is demonstrating clear, accurate communication and modeling how he wants his students to read. Choice (C) is the correct response.

35. D

This question addresses information from PPR Competency 007:

The teacher understands and applies principles and strategies for communicating effectively in varied teaching and learning contexts.

Eliminate (A) because Mr. Peterson wants to engage the students in skilled questioning and using the social studies book to find the answers to specific details does not reflect higher-order thinking. Eliminate (B) because Mr. Peterson is not concerned with what he thinks; he wants students to explore and extend their knowledge. Choice (C) refers to what the students know and not what they predict. Mr. Peterson is asking students to use higher-order thinking skills to problem solve and engage in inquiry learning. Choice (D) is the correct response.

36. D

This question addresses information from PPR Competency 007:

The teacher understands and applies principles and strategies for communicating effectively in varied teaching and learning contexts.

Eliminate (A) because according to Bloom's Taxonomy, the question asked would be knowledge based. Eliminate (B) because it asks students to rank cities and not engage in any type of inquiry, which again is knowledge based. Choice (C) asks students to compare and contrast, which does ask students to explore content. However, it comes under the category of analysis in Bloom's Taxonomy so it is not the highest ordered question. Consistent with Bloom's Taxonomy, Mr. Peterson wants his students to use previously learned criteria and make a judgment or support a decision. It falls in the category of evaluation and is the highest level in Bloom's Taxonomy. Choice (D) is the correct response.

37. B

This question addresses information from PPR Competency 007:

The teacher understands and applies principles and strategies for communicating effectively in varied teaching and learning contexts.

Eliminate (A) because Ms. Prentice is just using an overhead projector, so even though this is a low-level form of technology, it would not address the most likely strategy for communicating information. Eliminate (C) because, although Ms. Prentice would like to have students become writers, this would not be the reason for using the overhead projector. Eliminate choice (D) because although providing samples for the class poetry book may be an end result, it would not be the reason for using the overhead. Ms. Prentice shows she understands the importance of good communication skills and the effectiveness of providing examples during instruction. Choice (B) is the correct response.

38. B

This question addresses information from PPR Competency 007:

The teacher understands and applies principles and strategies for communicating effectively in varied teaching and learning contexts.

Eliminate (A) because a good teacher is concerned not with the quantity but with the quality of questions. Eliminate (C) because teachers understand all students need to be involved in the learning process and the activity will dictate the types of questions. It would be difficult for a teacher to keep track of the number of questions asked of each child. Choice (D) would have just the opposite effect of promoting a healthy environment, because teachers realize all students need to be engaged and not just the ones who raise their hands. A good teacher makes sure that the questions asked are grade and content appropriate. In addition, the question must have a direct relationship with the subject matter that is being presented. Choice (B) is the correct response.

Practice EC–4 Pedagogy and Professional Responsibilities Test I Answers and Explanations

39. D

This question addresses information from PPR Competency 007:

The teacher understands and applies principles and strategies for communicating effectively in varied teaching and learning contexts.

This is a priority-setting question because you are to assume the *most* likely reason that Mr. Patel quietly places his hand on Chris's shoulder. Eliminate (A) because we don't know if it is irritating Chris. Eliminate (B) because it has nothing to do with the process of overlapping. Choice (C) could be observed without placing a hand on Chris' shoulder. Mr. Patel realizes Chris is experiencing a bad day and communicates his understanding by using a quiet, nonverbal manner. Choice (D) is the correct response.

40. A

This question addresses information from PPR Competency 008:

The teacher provides appropriate instruction that actively engages students in the learning process.

This is a priority-setting question. You are asked to determine Ms. Dresden's *primary* reason for using reciprocal teaching. Eliminate (B) because, although the teaching strategy does represent a diversion from the normal routine, that would not be the primary reason for using the activity. Eliminate (C) because there are other activities that would measure oral reading practices. Ms. Dresden could select choice (D), preparing the students in the use of a new method for a teacher evaluation, but it would not be the primary objective. Ms. Dresden is incorporating a technique whereby she and the students vary the roles in the instructional process. She is hoping to stimulate intellectual development and active student engagement. She also hopes to address the development of appropriate thought processes while reading and with good questioning techniques. Choice (A) is the correct response.

41. D

This question addresses information from PPR Competency 008:

The teacher provides appropriate instruction that actively engages students in the learning process.

This is a priority-setting question asking you to select a choice that would be *incorrect*. Therefore, in this question we already know that three out of the four choices are correct. Keep choice (A) because this is an advantage of using the direct method of teaching. It is considered a "stand and deliver" form of teaching whereby the teacher knows the material, imparts it directly to the students, models what he or she is teaching, and then asks students to restate what has been learned. Keep choice (B) because the teacher has command of what is being taught and can regulate or modify according to student or teacher needs. Choice (C) also is an advantage of the direct method of teaching. The direct-teaching approach is designed for the teacher to present information the students need in a direct manner. In choice (D) students do not interact as much and do not make the decision about what they want to learn. Choice (D) is the correct response.

42. A

This question addresses information from PPR Competency 008:

The teacher provides appropriate instruction that actively engages students in the learning process.

This is a priority-setting question as you are asked how *best* to demonstrate promoting student engagement in the classroom. Eliminate (B) because, although the students would profit from hearing about the professor's experiences, the students would be listening rather than actively involved. Eliminate (C) because making a list is at the lowest level of cognitive development and the assignment is rather limiting. Eliminate choice (D) because it suggests the students are busy reading the assignment, but it doesn't tell us what type of report is to be presented. Mr. Olsen cannot be sure that all students will read the assignment even if it is required. By arranging his students in instructional groups, Mr. Olsen is providing a means for students to take control of their own learning. Mr. Olsen is keeping the students engaged in the learning process. Choice (A) is the correct response.

43. C

This question addresses information from PPR Competency 008:

The teacher provides appropriate instruction that actively engages students in the learning process.

Eliminate (A) because the purpose of evaluating students is not to see how much they talk during a given class day. Eliminate (B) because, although the first part of the question would be beneficial for the teacher, he or she is not so much interested in grades as to how the student is performing. With choice (D), you get the idea that everything on the checklist must be seen during that specific day. Ms. Franks plans on using the recorded information in the anecdotal records to monitor students' progress and pinpoint problem areas. If the records are used over time, they will give her an overall picture of how the students are doing. Choice (C) is the correct response

Practice EC–4 Pedagogy and Professional Responsibilities Test I Answers and Explanations

44. B

This question addresses information from PPR Competency 008:

The teacher provides appropriate instruction that actively engages students in the learning process.

This is a priority-setting question. You are to determine Ms. Routman's *primary* role during the group effort. Eliminate (A) because Ms. Routman is supposed to be monitoring and evaluating the students and not offering to do their work, as this choice suggests. Eliminate (C) as the Author Study is a group effort and each member of the team should assume responsibility. In this case, with supervision, one or both members could research the Internet for information on their selected author. Choice (D) again places the teacher in the middle of the project. Although students will be engaged in their own learning processes, Ms. Routman still needs to monitor the students' learning and make sure they are on target with intended goals and objectives. Choice (B) is the correct response.

45. B

This question addresses information from PPR Competency 008:

The teacher provides appropriate instruction that actively engages students in the learning process.

This is a question about motivation. Eliminate (A) as Ms. Routman would undoubtedly fail to see students working to their potential if they knew prior to completing a project that the grade they would receive would be an A. Eliminate (C) as a reason to keep all students motivated. As a culminating activity, Ms. Routman could sponsor a Parent Night during which all students would have an opportunity to explain the purpose of the assignment and showcase their work. Choice (D) suggests the students are equally divided between those who are internally and externally motivated. As a teacher, Ms. Routman's realizes that not all students are motivated by the same factors. Her goal would be to have the students seek a depth of knowledge and understanding of an author and the works created by the artist because they wish to learn more about literature and not to receive some extrinsic reward. Ms. Routman has given the students a challenging task. She hopes to create a positive climate of learning to support their hard endeavors. She frequently walks around the room and offers praise and encouragement. Choice (B) is the correct response.

46. C

This question addresses information from PPR Competency 008:

The teacher provides appropriate instruction that actively engages students in the learning process.

This is a priority-setting question as you are to determine the *most* likely result of using the Author Study strategy. Eliminate (A) as no mention was made of involving the parents. If, as in the previous question, Ms. Routman had hosted a Parent Night, then she would have been promoting family relationships. Eliminate (B) for, even though the students may learn more about the computer during their research efforts, this would not be Ms. Routman's ultimate goal. Choice (D) suggests a positive experience working in groups. However, if the groups have been monitored closely and evaluation is ongoing, students will have divided their efforts with both individual and group work. Ms. Routman hopes that by letting the students take ownership of their projects the experience will foster independent learning and self-motivation. Choice (C) is the correct response.

47. A

This question addresses information from PPR Competency 009:

The teacher incorporates the effective use of technology to plan, organize, deliver, and evaluate instruction for all students.

This is a priority-setting question. You are to determine Mr. Smith's *first* step in finding out more about the computer program. Eliminate (B) as Mr. Smith has made an assumption that the school board is interested in the Ed Tech PIOTS program prior to making contact with appropriate personnel. Eliminate (C) because, although it would demonstrate Mr. Smith's knowledge of computers, it would tend to focus more on his lack of knowledge in acquiring school equipment and the inappropriateness of the decision. Choice (D) also suggests an inappropriate move on the part of Mr. Smith. Even though Mr. Smith has discovered information in an area in which he is interested, he needs to go through the proper channels. In this case, he needs to contact the principal of the school about the feasibility of using this educational tool. Choice (A) is the correct response.

Practice EC–4 Pedagogy and Professional Responsibilities Test I Answers and Explanations

48. B

This question addresses information from PPR Competency 009:

The teacher incorporates the effective use of technology to plan, organize, deliver, and evaluate instruction for all students.

This is a priority-setting question. Three out of the four choices include information students need to know when they are word-processing which means you are looking for a negative response. Keep choice (A) because saving work to a disk is one of the first things students need to be taught when using the computer and word processing papers or other work. Keep choice (C) because students will find out how easy it is to create something on the computer and then rearrange it if needed. Choice (D) is a must when using the computer. Students will need to have instruction on the use of the computer when they are getting ready to word process their written work. However, having a list of advantages would not be considered a key element. Choice (B) is the correct response.

49. A

This question addresses information from PPR Competency 009:

The teacher incorporates the effective use of technology to plan, organize, deliver, and evaluate instruction for all students.

This is a priority-setting question. You will need to determine the *primary* goal in selecting the right software programs for a school. Eliminate (B) because although students may be more readily attracted to software that is fun as well as useful, Ms. Sidle will need to keep in mind the appropriate objectives. Eliminate (C) because it incorporates appropriate objectives, but does not include developmentally appropriate practices. When choosing software for the school library, Ms. Sidle will have to make decisions based not on whether the programs look good or are fun to use, but rather what is right for the students and will meet their needs. Choice (A) is the correct response.

50. D

This question addresses information from PPR Competency 009:

The teacher incorporates the effective use of technology to plan, organize, deliver, and evaluate instruction for all students.

Eliminate (A) because the instructional strategy was not designed for informal reading for the entire class. Eliminate (B) because Ms. Beyers will assess the students' knowledge using a more direct evaluative approach. Choice (C) tends to deviate from the goals of the assignment. In using the computer as a research tool, it provides a different avenue of learning and contributes and extends the students' knowledge base. Choice (D) is the correct response.

51. B

This question addresses information from PPR Competency 010:

The teacher monitors student performance and achievement; provides students with timely, high-quality feedback; and responds flexibly to promote learning for all students.

This is a priority-setting question. You are to determine the *primary* reason Ms. Boone would choose to use rubrics. Eliminate (A) because rubrics do not replace other forms of assessment. They are written descriptions of a standard or a measure to be met. Eliminate (C) because rubrics do not assess multiple-choice or true–false tests. Eliminate choice (D) because, although rubrics are designed to assess a process or a product and a student who is creative may seem to have an advantage, rubrics if used in the appropriate manner, assess certain criteria and not creativity. Ms. Boone chooses to incorporate rubrics as a form of assessment and will make sure they are congruent with instructional goals. Rubrics lend themselves to task assessment and in some situations it is quite helpful if the students are participants in deciding the quality of the task. Choice (B) is the correct response.

52. C

This question addresses information from PPR Competency 010:

The teacher monitors student performance and achievement; provides students with timely, high-quality feedback; and responds flexibly to promote learning for all students.

Eliminate (A) as standardized tests are not used to measure mastery of specific skills as in criterion-referenced tests such as an Informal Reading Inventory. Eliminate (B) because there are no products produced with a standardized test. Choice (D) suggests essay questions and standardized tests are usually multiple-choice type. The main advantage of using norm-referenced tests is that the results are used to make comparisons. The scores indicate how well a student performs in comparison to other students of the same age. This information guides local and state curriculum and school programs. Choice (C) is the correct response.

Practice EC–4 Pedagogy and Professional Responsibilities Test I Answers and Explanations

53. A

This question addresses information from PPR Competency 010:

The teacher monitors student performance and achievement; provides students with timely, high-quality feedback; and responds flexibly to promote learning for all students.

This is a priority-setting question. You are asked to determine what is the *biggest* advantage for using portfolios. Eliminate (B) because portfolios do not always contain a student's best work. Many times students are encouraged to include in the portfolio examples of all of their work so a pattern of growth will be indicated. Eliminate (C) because portfolios would not be shown to other students so they could decide what to keep and what to discard. Choice (D) suggests that teachers spot problem areas in their own teaching. Teachers inadvertently may discover problem areas in their instruction, but most of the time teachers will use another means of assessing their own strengths and weaknesses. There are many types of portfolios, but the way Ms. Mills utilizes them is to indicate students' growth. By starting at the first of the year to gather samples, she will have a record of the students' accomplishments and development. Choice (A) is the correct response.

54. B

This question addresses information from PPR Competency 010:

The teacher monitors student performance and achievement; provides students with timely, high-quality feedback; and responds flexibly to promote learning for all students.

This is a priority-setting question, for you are asked to determine which activity would *best* assess the assignment. Eliminate (A) because standardized tests are used for some sort of comparison and in this situation, Ms. Morris's objective is to discover if she were successful in teaching her objectives. Eliminate (C) because Ms. Morris utilized the state-adopted book for mathematics and expects feedback on the basis of what she has been teaching. Eliminate (D) because Ms. Morris would find dramatization difficult to use with math assessment. Because Ms. Morris uses the state-adopted math book, she wishes to determine the students' knowledge and see if what they have learned is congruent with instructional goals and objectives. Choice (B) is the correct response.

55. A

This question addresses information from PPR Competency 010:

The teacher monitors student performance and achievement; provides students with timely, high-qualify feedback; and responds flexibly to promote learning for all students.

Eliminate (B) because even though the teacher doesn't feel qualified to use traditional methods of testing there needs to be a balance of different types of assessment methods in the classroom. Eliminate (C) because, the teacher would not allow the students to determine the type of assessment she will use in the classroom. (Eliminate (D) because she should not be teaching to a specific test in the first place, even though she might enjoy watching the students perform. The teacher is carefully monitoring student performance and achievement. In using authentic assessment, students are often required to engage in higher-order thinking and incorporate many skills. The teacher uses this type of assessment in contexts that closely resemble real world situations. Choice (A) is the correct response.

56. A

This question addresses information from PPR Competency 010:

The teacher monitors student performance and achievement; provides students with timely, high-quality feedback; and responds flexibly to promote learning for all students.

This is a priority-setting question for you are asked to determine the *major* benefit of having students reflect and restate what they learned during the day. Eliminate (B) because, although it does provide time with the teacher on an individual basis, it would not be the major reason. Eliminate (C) because this would not be best practice. Eliminate choice (D) because it suggests the teacher might not be attuned to what the students would be doing. Ms. Alvarez asks the student to self-assess because it will help the student discover what they know and ultimately enhance their own learning. Choice (A) is the correct response.

57. D

This question addresses information from PPR Competency 011:

The teacher understands the importance of family involvement in children's education and knows how to interact and communicate effectively with families.

This is a priority-setting question. You are asked to determine the teacher's *primary* goal in communicating with parents. Eliminate (A) because a face-to-face meeting is usually a desired objective but not always possible. Eliminate (B) because Ms. Donnely should not be thinking about her professional image in relationship to communicating with parents. In choice (C), Ms. Donnely might share ideas, but it wouldn't be the primary goal. Ms. Donnely has discovered how beneficial the school website can be not only for herself, but also for the students and parents. The website is an effective means of communication. She must also realize that not all families have access to computers at home, so she will need to provide alternate means of informing parents. Choice (D) is the correct response

Practice EC–4 Pedagogy and Professional Responsibilities Test I Answers and Explanations

58. A

This question addresses information from PPR Competency 011:

The teacher understands the importance of family involvement in children's education and knows how to interact and communicate effectively with families.

Eliminate (B) because Ms. Stanfield has made an irresponsible decision, as she would need the parent's approval. Eliminate (C) because Ms. Gaines may have important information she can share with the parents and needs to be given the opportunity. Choice (D) gets the principal involved and this is a decision to be made by the parents. Parent–teacher conferences are a time to inform parents of their student's progress and to exchange ideas. Ms. Stanfield takes appropriate steps in asking for approval prior to the conference to see if the parents have any objection to her student teacher participating in the conference. She doesn't want any surprises for the parents and wants the parents to feel comfortable discussing their child's situation with someone with whom they are not familiar. Choice (A) is the correct response.

59. B

This question addresses information from PPR Competency 011:

The teacher understands the importance of family involvement in children's education and knows how to interact and communicate effectively with families.

This is a priority-setting question for you are to decide the *most* appropriate action for Mr. Gonzales to take about meeting with the new student's parents. Eliminate (A) because there may not be anyone else on whom the student's parents can rely. Eliminate (C) because the parents are probably not able to read English. Choice (D) is not best practice or a professional decision. Mr. Gonzales realizes he will need to seek help in conveying information to the student's parents so he follows appropriate procedures and requests an interpreter. Choice (B) is the correct response.

60. D

This question addresses information from PPR Competency 011:

The teacher understands the importance of family involvement in children's education and knows how to interact and communicate effectively with families.

This is a priority-setting question. You are asked the *primary* goal of the meeting. Eliminate (A) because the success a family service agency has had with other families has no connection with this parent. Eliminate (B) because right now the family is probably dealing with a day-to-day crisis. Choice (C) would be helpful but the family needs more immediate assistance. When intervention is required, school personnel can assist in helping the family, but any intervention should emphasize the needs of the entire family. The most important point is to communicate effectively with the family and address their concerns. Choice (D) is the correct response.

61. A

This question addresses information from PPR Competency 011:

The teacher understands the importance of family involvement in children's education and knows how to interact and communicate effectively with families.

This is a priority-setting question. You are asked Mr. Hanson's *primary* goal for the first meeting. Eliminate (B) as allowing everyone to discuss the reasoning behind the problems will only cause more disturbances and is a negative response. Eliminate (C) because having a stricter code of discipline may not alleviate the problem. Choice (D) focuses only on the negative and not the positive. Mr. Hanson's primary goal will be to get the committee involved in decision-making. He will want to discuss improving the climate of the school and talk about changes that need to be addressed. Choice (A) is the correct response.

62. A

This question addresses information from PPR Competency 012:

The teacher enhances professional knowledge and skills by effectively interacting with other members of the educational community and participating in various types of professional activities.

This is a priority-setting question. You are to determine Ms. Ruda's *first* approach in finding a replacement as grade-level team leader. Eliminate (B) because, although Ms. Ruda no longer wants to assume the leadership role, the principal or other administrative leaders may wish to have her continue. Eliminate (C) as it doesn't really solve Ms. Ruda's dilemma. Choice (D) suggests talking to other grade-level team leaders, but what they do and what is correct for her may be very different. Ms. Ruda has assumed a large responsibility by being team leader for so many years. Rather than discuss the possible change she desires with other team members or teachers in the school, she would most likely benefit by discussing her proposal first with the principal, particularly if she had been appointed to the position. Choice (A) is the correct response.

Practice EC–4 Pedagogy and Professional Responsibilities Test I Answers and Explanations

63. C

This question addresses information from PPR Competency 012:

The teacher enhances professional knowledge and skills by effectively interacting with other members of the educational community and participating in various types of professional activities.

This is a priority-setting question asking you to select a choice that would be *incorrect*. Therefore, in this question we already know that three out of the four choices are correct. Keep (A) as Ms. Anthony will address the question of appropriate materials and resources every day. Keep (B) because Ms. Anthony will determine goals and objectives and then determine the instructional strategy that will best meet those goals. Keep choice (D) because the primary goal will be to meet the needs of all of the students. Ms. Anthony needs to be concerned with the appropriate needs, strategies, goals, and resources when self-assessing. Only after she has made these decisions should she determine approximate length of time for the activities. Choice (C) is the correct response.

64. A

This question addresses information from PPR Competency 012:

The teacher enhances professional knowledge and skills by effectively interacting with other members of the educational community and participating in various types of professional activities.

This is a priority-setting question. You are to determine how the rest of the teachers can *best* assist Ms. Joseson, the new teacher. Eliminate (B) because just handing Ms. Joseson a list will not provide the support she needs. Eliminate (C) as a best choice. However, if there are websites that Ms. Joseson can use to help her plan instructional strategies and meet the TEKS objectives, the teachers should inform her. Choice (D) would only tend to make her more aware of her negligence and cause friction among the teachers. The teachers will have an opportunity during the weekly grade-level meeting to explain to Ms. Joseson the importance of the Texas Essential Knowledge and Skills (TEKS), and how, by incorporating them into the lessons, they help students meet state expectations. Choice (A) is the correct response.

65. D

This question addresses information from PPR Competency 012:

The teacher enhances professional knowledge and skills by effectively interacting with other members of the educational community and participating in various types of professional activities.

Eliminate (A) because, although writing down the problem may help Ms. Selensky, the principal might not observe the specific areas of concern she has outlined. Eliminate (B) because, although Ms. Selensky has a concern, telling the students to be on their best behavior will not provide a realistic class setting. Choice (C) suggests providing unit plans, but the principal will be interested in what is happening on a daily basis. Ms. Selensky indicates she is proactive and assumes responsibility for her own growth and development. In discussing ahead of time her area of concern, the principal will know to carefully observe this part of the lesson. The principal can then offer constructive criticism and provide suggestions for improvement. Choice (D) is the correct response.

66. B

This question addresses information from PPR Competency 012:

The teacher enhances professional knowledge and skills by effectively interacting with other members of the educational community and participating in various types of professional activities.

This is a priority-setting question. You are to determine the *primary* reason Mr. Dolezal will be attending the meetings. Eliminate (A) because he will probably be seeking other colleagues' latest teaching strategies and ideas. Eliminate (C) because, although this will occur, it should not be the primary reason for attending. Choice (D) does not address professional development needs. State and national associations represent teachers' interests, so by attending the conference, Mr. Dolezal knows this will give him an opportunity for contact with other teachers and help him grow professionally. Choice (B) is the correct response.

Practice EC–4 Pedagogy and Professional Responsibilities Test I Answers and Explanations

67. C

This question addresses information from PPR Competency 012:

The teacher enhances professional knowledge and skills by effectively interacting with other members of the educational community and participating in various types of professional activities.

Eliminate (A) because technology is the area with which he feels the most unfamiliar. Eliminate (B) because even though it is a good suggestion, it probably will not address Mr. Gunderson's most immediate needs. Choice (D) will provide Mr. Gunderson with a lot of useful information, but it may be difficult for him to sort out what he needs and what will be best for his class objectives. Mr. Gunderson's desire to provide up-to-date technology can be satisfied by contacting the technology coordinator for support on how to integrate technology into the curriculum. Choice (C) is the correct response.

68. B

This question addresses information from PPR Competency 013:

The teacher understands and adheres to legal and ethical requirements for educators and is knowledgeable of the structure of education in Texas.

This is a priority-setting question as you are to determine the *next* step for the parents. Eliminate (A) because the parents will probably not get anywhere by demanding something be done. Eliminate (C) because the superintendent would not be the first line of administration the parents should consult. Choice (D) would prepare Latoya for disappointment, but the parents have legal rights. Under the Family Educational Rights and Privacy Act (FERPA), parents or eligible students have the right to request that a school corrects records that they believe to be inaccurate or misleading. If the school decides not to amend the record, the parent or eligible student then has the right to a formal hearing. After the hearing, if the school still decides not to amend the record, the parent or eligible student has the right to place a statement with the record setting forth his or her view about the contested information. Choice (B) is the correct response.

69. C

This question addresses information from PPR Competency 013:

The teacher understands and adheres to legal and ethical requirements for educators and is knowledgeable of the structure of education in Texas.

Eliminate (A) because a rural setting should not have affected the decision made by Ms. Tapely. Eliminate (B) because Ms. Tapely made a poor choice, but it doesn't mean she is a poor teacher. Choice (D) assumes Ms. Tapely was not in violation. Under the Code of Ethics and Standard Practices for Texas Educators, it states that the educator shall not reveal confidential information concerning students unless disclosure serves lawful professional purposes or is required by law. In this case, Ms. Tapely was in error because she continued with the conference with both mothers present. Choice (C) is the correct response.

70. B

This question addresses information from PPR Competency 013:

The teacher understands and adheres to legal and ethical requirements for educators and is knowledgeable of the structure of education in Texas.

This is a priority-setting question. You have been asked to determine the *major* error that has occurred. Eliminate (A) because the omitted information was not pertinent. Eliminate (C) because omitted names could be sent home as a separate list and would not constitute a major problem. Eliminate choice (D) because it can be addressed at a parent night and a letter to the parents. It would be a concern to the students and parents, but not the major problem. Under the Family Educational Rights and Privacy Act, schools may disclose, without consent, directory information such as a student's name, address, telephone number, date and place of birth, honors and awards, and dates of attendance. However, schools must tell parents and eligible students about directory information and allow parents and eligible students a reasonable amount of time to request that the school not disclose directory information about them. Schools must notify parents and eligible students annually of their rights under FERPA. Choice (B) is the correct response.

71. C

This question addresses information from PPR Competency 002:

The teacher understands student diversity and knows how to plan learning experiences and design assessments that are responsive to differences among students and that promote all students' learning.

This is a priority-setting question as you are to determine which assignment would *best* enhance students' learning. Eliminate (A) because, although community involvement is important, writing a letter is not the best activity that would enhance students' learning. Eliminate (B) because this activity is a very low-level form of cognitive development as well. Eliminate choice (D) because worksheets are at the lowest level of cognitive development. In planning a mini-festival, the teacher shows how to use diversity in the classroom. In addition, students will have an opportunity to research specific cultures and develop an awareness of the many interesting factors in each cultural. Choice (C) is the correct response.

Practice EC–4 Pedagogy and Professional Responsibilities Test I Answers and Explanations

72. D

This question addresses information from PPR Competency 002:

The teacher understands student diversity and knows how to plan learning experiences and design assessments that are responsive to differences among students and that promote all students' learning.

Eliminate (A) because the student is already having difficulty with the English language and would experience further difficulty if trying to write a paper. Eliminate (B) because most ELL students would not have the background for completing the assignment. Choice (C) shows a lack of understanding on Ms. Barrett's part as most ELL students would find it difficult to compare cultures. However, by asking the English-speaking student to work with the ELL student during the unit, Ms. Barrett shows she is responsive to cultural differences among students. Choice (D) is the correct response.

73. A

This question addresses information from PPR Competency 002:

The teacher understands student diversity and knows how to plan learning experiences and design assessments that are responsive to differences among students and that promote all students' learning.

Eliminate (B) because the teacher is asking students to complete work in an off-campus situation. The assumption is also being made that the students get along and that the parents would approve. Eliminate (C) because suggesting assignments will require the use of a computer and put pressure on parents who may not be able to meet those needs. Choice (D) is not using good judgment or practice. Not all families have access to the telephone, library, or Internet, so several choices need to be allowed to provide for these differences. Choice (A) is the correct response.

74. B

This question addresses information from PPR Competency 013:

The teacher understands and adheres to legal and ethical requirements for educators and is knowledgeable of the structure of education in Texas.

This is a priority-setting question asking you to select a choice that would be *incorrect*. Therefore, in this question we already know that three out of the four choices are correct. Keep (A) as motion and moving are advocated for a student with ADHA. Keep (C) because, by modeling appropriate behavior the student will know what is expected. Keep (D) because providing a positive attitude and reviewing the student's behavior management plan will reinforce appropriate goals and objectives. Ms. Barrett may need reinforcement or support to help her function with Todd, but forcing him to try to sit for longer periods of time would be in violation of his plan and be discriminatory toward the student. Choice (B) is the correct response.

75. A

This question addresses information from PPR Competency 004:

The teacher understands learning processes and factors that impact student learning and demonstrates this knowledge by planning effective, engaging instruction and appropriate assessments.

This is a priority-setting question as you are to determine the *most* likely activity for cooperative learning. Eliminate (B) as lectures are a stand-and-deliver form of teaching and the students are to be working in groups. Eliminate (C) because Ms. Barrett should have spent time developing a rubric and going over the responsibilities of each group member, rather than just presenting a checklist. Choice (D) would be an inappropriate action if taken by Ms. Barrett. When working with cooperative learning, the teacher's role becomes one of facilitating and supervising the work being done in groups. Choice (A) is the correct response.

76. A

This question addresses information from PPR Competency 013:

The teacher understands and adheres to legal and ethical requirements for educators and is knowledgeable of the structure of education in Texas.

Eliminate (B) because, while Ms. Ling will keep as her goal the students' performance on the TAKS test, it would not be the reason for adhering to guidelines or posting website information. Choice (C) suggests Ms. Ling should include her own background knowledge while presenting the unit, but again, it would not be the main reason for posting information on the website. Eliminate choice (D) because most parents will not be concerned about a unit's logical sequence. However, Ms. Ling should know and adhere to legal requirements concerning the posting of information on a website. Choice (A) is the correct response.

77. C

This question addresses information from PPR Competency 002:

The teacher understands student diversity and knows how to plan learning experiences and design assessments that are responsive to differences among students and that promote all students' learning.

This is a priority-setting question as you are to determine the *most* important thing for Ms. Ling to remember about gender differences. Eliminate (A) because the equity situation refers to a school setting and not to parents. Eliminate (B) because the statement is biased. Choice (D) may not always be possible, but she should never show bias when planning cooperative groups. Ms. Ling demonstrates knowledge of students and shows she understands the importance of organizing her class so that all students are able to meet class expectations regardless of gender differences. Choice (C) is the correct response.

Practice EC–4 Pedagogy and Professional Responsibilities Test I Answers and Explanations

78. D

This question addresses information from PPR Competency 013:

The teacher understands and adheres to legal and ethical requirements for educators and is knowledgeable of the structure of education in Texas.

Eliminate (A) because, although this would be helpful, another student should not always have the responsibility of assisting Marvin. Eliminate (B) because Marvin's presence in the classroom has no bearing on other students' parents. Choice (C) should be eliminated because special treatment is not a part of IDEA. According to the Individuals with Disabilities Education Act (IDEA) all children must be assured of a free appropriate education for all children with disabilities. Choice (D) is the correct response.

79. B

This question addresses information from PPR Competency 009:

The teacher incorporates the effective use of technology to plan, organize, deliver, and evaluate instruction for all students.

This is a priority-setting question as you must determine what Ms. Ling has *primarily* demonstrated. Eliminate (A) because, although she is working closely with the curriculum supervisor and technology coordinator, developing a close relationship is not a priority. Eliminate (C) because meeting challenges is a personal matter and should not be an issue in her role as a teacher. Eliminate (D) because she is just meeting expectations. Ms. Ling demonstrated that she incorporated technology and provided instruction for the new student. She realized she needed to build on the student's culture because many students from a different background don't see a connection between the new culture and the one from which they just moved. Choice (B) is the correct response.

80. B

This question addresses information from PPR Competency 011:

The teacher understands the importance of family involvement in children's education and knows how to interact and communicate effectively with families.

Eliminate (A) because inviting parents to a program is not the time to solicit feedback on instruction. Eliminate (C) as she needs to self-assess when all activities have been completed and not during a parental visit. Eliminate choice (D) because the students should be motivated to do their work even if their parents would not be attending the special event. Choice (B) is the correct response.

Practice Test 1 Answers, EC-4 PPR Sorted by Competency

Question	Domain	Competency	Answer	Did You Answer Correctly?	Question	Domain	Competency	Answer	Did You Answer Correctly?
1	1	1	A		37	3	7	B	
2	1	1	B		38	3	7	B	
3	1	1	D		39	3	7	D	
4	1	1	B		40	3	8	A	
5	1	1	B		41	3	8	D	
6	1	1	D		42	3	8	A	
7	1	2	C		43	3	8	C	
8	1	2	A		44	3	8	B	
9	1	2	C		45	3	8	B	
10	1	2	C		46	3	8	C	
71	1	2	C		12	3	9	B	
72	1	2	D		47	3	9	A	
73	1	2	A		48	3	9	B	
77	1	2	C		49	3	9	A	
13	1	3	A		50	3	9	D	
14	1	3	A		79	3	9	B	
15	1	3	D		51	3	10	B	
16	1	3	B		52	3	10	C	
17	1	3	C		53	3	10	A	
18	1	4	B		54	3	10	B	
19	1	4	C		55	3	10	A	
20	1	4	C		56	3	10	A	
21	1	4	D		57	4	11	D	
22	1	4	B		58	4	11	A	
75	1	4	A		59	4	11	B	
23	2	5	B		60	4	11	D	
24	2	5	B		61	4	11	A	
25	2	5	A		80	4	11	B	
26	2	5	C		62	4	12	A	
11	2	6	D		63	4	12	C	
27	2	6	D		64	4	12	A	
28	2	6	A		65	4	12	D	
29	2	6	B		66	4	12	B	
30	2	6	D		67	4	12	C	
31	2	6	B		76	4	13	A	
32	2	6	D		68	4	13	B	
33	2	6	B		69	4	13	C	
34	3	7	C		70	4	13	B	
35	3	7	D		74	4	13	B	
36	3	7	D		78	4	13	D	

What competencies did you do well in?
What competencies do you need to work on?

Practice Test Two Answer Sheet

Remove (or photocopy) this answer sheet and use it to complete the practice test.
(See answer key following the test when finished.)

1 Ⓐ Ⓑ Ⓒ Ⓓ	21 Ⓐ Ⓑ Ⓒ Ⓓ	41 Ⓐ Ⓑ Ⓒ Ⓓ	61 Ⓐ Ⓑ Ⓒ Ⓓ
2 Ⓐ Ⓑ Ⓒ Ⓓ	22 Ⓐ Ⓑ Ⓒ Ⓓ	42 Ⓐ Ⓑ Ⓒ Ⓓ	62 Ⓐ Ⓑ Ⓒ Ⓓ
3 Ⓐ Ⓑ Ⓒ Ⓓ	23 Ⓐ Ⓑ Ⓒ Ⓓ	43 Ⓐ Ⓑ Ⓒ Ⓓ	63 Ⓐ Ⓑ Ⓒ Ⓓ
4 Ⓐ Ⓑ Ⓒ Ⓓ	24 Ⓐ Ⓑ Ⓒ Ⓓ	44 Ⓐ Ⓑ Ⓒ Ⓓ	64 Ⓐ Ⓑ Ⓒ Ⓓ
5 Ⓐ Ⓑ Ⓒ Ⓓ	25 Ⓐ Ⓑ Ⓒ Ⓓ	45 Ⓐ Ⓑ Ⓒ Ⓓ	65 Ⓐ Ⓑ Ⓒ Ⓓ
6 Ⓐ Ⓑ Ⓒ Ⓓ	26 Ⓐ Ⓑ Ⓒ Ⓓ	46 Ⓐ Ⓑ Ⓒ Ⓓ	66 Ⓐ Ⓑ Ⓒ Ⓓ
7 Ⓐ Ⓑ Ⓒ Ⓓ	27 Ⓐ Ⓑ Ⓒ Ⓓ	47 Ⓐ Ⓑ Ⓒ Ⓓ	67 Ⓐ Ⓑ Ⓒ Ⓓ
8 Ⓐ Ⓑ Ⓒ Ⓓ	28 Ⓐ Ⓑ Ⓒ Ⓓ	48 Ⓐ Ⓑ Ⓒ Ⓓ	68 Ⓐ Ⓑ Ⓒ Ⓓ
9 Ⓐ Ⓑ Ⓒ Ⓓ	29 Ⓐ Ⓑ Ⓒ Ⓓ	49 Ⓐ Ⓑ Ⓒ Ⓓ	69 Ⓐ Ⓑ Ⓒ Ⓓ
10 Ⓐ Ⓑ Ⓒ Ⓓ	30 Ⓐ Ⓑ Ⓒ Ⓓ	50 Ⓐ Ⓑ Ⓒ Ⓓ	70 Ⓐ Ⓑ Ⓒ Ⓓ
11 Ⓐ Ⓑ Ⓒ Ⓓ	31 Ⓐ Ⓑ Ⓒ Ⓓ	51 Ⓐ Ⓑ Ⓒ Ⓓ	71 Ⓐ Ⓑ Ⓒ Ⓓ
12 Ⓐ Ⓑ Ⓒ Ⓓ	32 Ⓐ Ⓑ Ⓒ Ⓓ	52 Ⓐ Ⓑ Ⓒ Ⓓ	72 Ⓐ Ⓑ Ⓒ Ⓓ
13 Ⓐ Ⓑ Ⓒ Ⓓ	33 Ⓐ Ⓑ Ⓒ Ⓓ	53 Ⓐ Ⓑ Ⓒ Ⓓ	73 Ⓐ Ⓑ Ⓒ Ⓓ
14 Ⓐ Ⓑ Ⓒ Ⓓ	34 Ⓐ Ⓑ Ⓒ Ⓓ	54 Ⓐ Ⓑ Ⓒ Ⓓ	74 Ⓐ Ⓑ Ⓒ Ⓓ
15 Ⓐ Ⓑ Ⓒ Ⓓ	35 Ⓐ Ⓑ Ⓒ Ⓓ	55 Ⓐ Ⓑ Ⓒ Ⓓ	75 Ⓐ Ⓑ Ⓒ Ⓓ
16 Ⓐ Ⓑ Ⓒ Ⓓ	36 Ⓐ Ⓑ Ⓒ Ⓓ	56 Ⓐ Ⓑ Ⓒ Ⓓ	76 Ⓐ Ⓑ Ⓒ Ⓓ
17 Ⓐ Ⓑ Ⓒ Ⓓ	37 Ⓐ Ⓑ Ⓒ Ⓓ	57 Ⓐ Ⓑ Ⓒ Ⓓ	77 Ⓐ Ⓑ Ⓒ Ⓓ
18 Ⓐ Ⓑ Ⓒ Ⓓ	38 Ⓐ Ⓑ Ⓒ Ⓓ	58 Ⓐ Ⓑ Ⓒ Ⓓ	78 Ⓐ Ⓑ Ⓒ Ⓓ
19 Ⓐ Ⓑ Ⓒ Ⓓ	39 Ⓐ Ⓑ Ⓒ Ⓓ	59 Ⓐ Ⓑ Ⓒ Ⓓ	79 Ⓐ Ⓑ Ⓒ Ⓓ
20 Ⓐ Ⓑ Ⓒ Ⓓ	40 Ⓐ Ⓑ Ⓒ Ⓓ	60 Ⓐ Ⓑ Ⓒ Ⓓ	80 Ⓐ Ⓑ Ⓒ Ⓓ

CHAPTER TWELVE

Practice EC–4 Pedagogy and Professional Responsibilities Test II

1. Seven-year-old Heather is involved in a game on the playground when one of the other children doesn't follow the rules of the game. Heather immediately runs to the teacher and "tattles" on the student. Heather's teacher needs to understand that some children at this stage of development:

    A. like to get their peers into a lot of trouble by telling things about their friends.
    B. are developing a sense of conscience and feel the need to play by the rules.
    C. value sports a great deal so are concerned with how the peer group views the situation rather than with the actual rules of the game.
    D. are in a more highly advanced stage of discipline and want the teacher to clearly see both sides of the game.

2. According to Piaget, children pass through a series of hierarchical stages in which they exhibit similar characteristics. Children between the ages of two and seven are in which stage of development?

    A. Sensorimotor
    B. Preoperational
    C. Concrete operations
    D. Formal operations

3. Ms. Gillis's third-grade students have become quite argumentative over who was going to put things away at the end of an activity. At the suggestion of a colleague, Ms. Gillis decides to hold a class discussion and ask the students how they think the class should handle this problem. Ms. Gillis guides the creation of a chart that focuses on specific goal-setting responsibilities. Throughout the following week, Ms. Gillis sees a dramatic change for the better. Based on the interactions of the teacher and students, Ms. Gillis indicates she understands:

   A. the importance of having students take care of discipline problems.
   B. the importance of taking advice from a colleague.
   C. the importance of making charts and following through with the contents of the chart.
   D. the importance of helping children apply decision-making skills.

4. Ms. Pape's kindergarten class takes a field trip to the zoo. During the trip Ms. Pape has an opportunity to ask students questions focusing on different animals they have seen. While promoting spontaneous learning, Ms. Pape shows she uses knowledge of developmental characteristics and needs of the students to:

   A. let children decide what they want to do while they are on a field trip.
   B. promote the development of the child and extend thinking and knowledge.
   C. observe what students really know about zoo animals.
   D. use this time to evaluate students in the large-group activity and how they interact with each other.

5. Sandra is a student in Ms. Fite's early childhood class. When asked to perform an activity, she often tells Ms. Fite that she can't do something or that the activity is too hard. Ms. Fite encourages Sandra and provides a nurturing environment so Sandra will develop a more positive self-image. Ms. Fite realizes that Sandra's negative attitude and emotional development greatly affect:

   A. the privileges Sandra will receive, as they are based on a good attitude.
   B. after-school activities.
   C. development in other areas.
   D. her attitude at home with siblings.

GO ON TO THE NEXT PAGE

Practice EC-4 Pedagogy and Professional Responsibilities Test II

6. During the first week of school Ms. Fletcher observes that Anita, a very young second-grade student, is having a difficult time following directions and completing assignments. After several "forgetful" incidents at school, Ms. Fletcher, along with Anita's parents and the principal, make the decision to return Anita to the first-grade classroom. Those involved in making the decision recognized that:

   A. Anita needed more time to develop her short-term memory.
   B. Anita was not developmentally ready for the challenges of second grade.
   C. Anita would continue to create problems in the class unless she was with students her own age or younger.
   D. Anita was a rather lazy child and needed an extra year to become motivated.

7. Ms. Hoke uses a lesson format in which students change the endings of stories by composing new endings. Ms. Hoke models how the students should respond. Several students have been diagnosed as English Language Learners (ELLs), so meeting the needs of these students is important. Which of the following would NOT be an appropriate strategy to use for ELL students?

   A. While presenting instructions, pause and ask questions to make sure everyone understands the assignment.
   B. Provide some "hints" on ideas students might use.
   C. Suggest students work on their own, and after they complete the assignment check their work to see if they understood the assignment.
   D. Arrange for special needs students to work with a competent peer.

8. When students were going to centers in the kindergarten class, one of the teachers told Kolby to build a tower instead of always playing in the kitchen center. The teacher's remark indicates that:

   A. the teacher liked how Kolby utilizes the blocks and the kitchen area was undoubtedly occupied.
   B. the teacher was showing favoritism.
   C. the teacher was hoping Kolby would take a leadership role in the class.
   D. the teacher was stereotyping on the basis of gender.

GO ON TO THE NEXT PAGE

9. In Ms. Lovell's kindergarten class, students were sitting on the floor in a large circle. Bryan was overheard saying to Robert, the new Chinese student, that he talked funny. To teach students to respect each other's diversity, Ms. Lovell should respond by saying:

   A. "Bryan, that is very rude. Would you please apologize to Robert and then go sit someplace else until you can talk nicely?"
   B. "Children, did you just hear Bryan? Let's not make remarks like that anymore."
   C. "Robert is learning to speak English. Maybe we'd all like to learn several Chinese words."
   D. "Bryan, do you know any other language besides English? If so, why don't you share with us some of those words."

10. Several children in Ms. Earl's class have food allergies. During health class, the students discussed their specific allergies and talked about the similarities and differences in their experiences with these allergies. She then compared the allergies to similarities and differences in culture. In building on these differences, Ms. Earl shows she knows how to:

    A. enrich students' learning experience by accepting differences.
    B. encourage cooperation among all of the students.
    C. teach nutrition and appropriate diets for children.
    D. teach students about all of the food allergies people may incur.

11. Ms. Marion teaches in an inner-city school. Her prior teaching experience was in an affluent suburban setting where diversity was not much of an issue. Because of her former teaching experience and lack of exposure to diversity, plus reading research articles indicating that children from low-socioeconomic conditions may suffer from poor self-esteem and substandard reading skills, Ms. Marion assumed the articles' conclusions applied to the students in this school. However, after working with the students and meeting the parents, just the opposite was occurring in this school district. Ms. Marion's reaction indicates a greater need for teachers to:

    A. do more research on inner-city schools using websites.
    B. alternate teaching in schools classified as lower socioeconomic and higher socioeconomic to get a better idea of diversity.
    C. write papers on inner-city schools and submit them to the latest education journals.
    D. broaden their own understanding and appreciation of diversity.

GO ON TO THE NEXT PAGE

12. Mr. Bond correlates the instructional strategies with the Texas Essential Knowledge and Skills (TEKS) as he prepares lessons for the third-grade class. During a direct-teaching approach, he uses instructional objectives and prior knowledge to initiate a lesson. He continues by presenting skills and modeling lesson requirements. After closing the lesson, Mr. Bond asks the students to explain how they could relate the lesson to their own lives. In asking this, it shows Mr. Bond understands the importance of:

    A. utilizing this period of time to reiterate TEKS standards so students will understand the importance of the lesson.
    B. engaging in the process of reflection.
    C. fostering a sense of social interaction among the class.
    D. motivating students who did not understand the lesson to want to learn more.

13. Ms. Woods, a second-grade teacher, taught a science lesson on observing light. Children became familiar with words such as transparent, translucent, and opaque. While conducting experiments, students were using materials such as plastic wrap, flashlights, books, paper, and water. The lesson specified that after the experiments were completed the students should determine which objects let light through and which didn't. The last question in the lesson asked students to formulate a hypothesis about the experiments and justify their answers. Ms. Woods chose not to ask the last question because for most students:

    A. the question was not age appropriate.
    B. the question contained vocabulary words the students had not used before.
    C. the lesson did not hold their interest and their attention was elsewhere.
    D. the answer was unclear because the objectives of the lesson were not covered appropriately.

14. The Texas Essential Knowledge and Skills (TEKS) are used when Ms. Delgado prepares her health lessons. The *primary* significance of Ms. Delgado correlating her lesson to the state requirements is that:

    A. the principal will be observing and evaluating the lesson plans; therefore each lesson must correlate with the TEKS.
    B. the grade-level team shares lesson plans and ideas.
    C. the appropriate goals and objectives are used as a basis for instructional planning.
    D. the lessons support campus and district goals.

15. Mr. Perry's objective for the geography assignment is to study geographic features of Texas. Mr. Perry makes sure the lesson is relevant and meaningful to the students. Which of the following activities would *best* address Mr. Perry's objective?

   A. Plan a stimulating lecture on the four major regions of Texas.
   B. Give a test covering the four major regions and let students draw the landforms and bodies of water on the test.
   C. Provide a variety of books and magazines from the school library. Then require students to present a report on one of the regions.
   D. Have students create a brochure about the geographic areas using Internet links specifically designed for this purpose.

16. As a requirement of the Texas Essential Knowledge and Skills (TEKS) for a fourth-grade social studies class, students will be asked to apply critical thinking skills and use problem-solving and decision-making processes. How might the teacher *best* accomplish this goal?

   A. Require the students to answer factual questions about one of the celebrations that occurs in Texas.
   B. Encourage students to illustrate pictures of their favorite celebration.
   C. Request students to compare and contrast how the celebrations in their town are alike and how they are different.
   D. Use a variety of resources including the Internet and prepare a timeline on the inception of the celebrations and traditions in their area.

17. Ms. Griffen, a fourth-grade teacher, has a banner in the front of her room that says, A QUESTION IS AN INVITATION TO SPEAK. Ms. Griffen follows up on the banner message by using an activity in which no one may make a statement. When a question is asked, it must be answered by another question. Ms. Griffen's goal in using this form of discussion exercise is to:

   A. promote inquiry through conceptual understanding.
   B. formulate questions to be used on the students' next test.
   C. assess what the students know and don't know.
   D. activate prior knowledge of important details.

18. When visitors walk into Mr. Hanson's kindergarten room, what is one *primary* activity that should NOT be observed?

   A. Interactions between large and small groups as well as students working individually.
   B. Students' artwork decorating the walls and displayed for all to see.
   C. A supportive environment where students are actively engaged in learning.
   D. A climate of competition between the students.

19. Each morning Ms. Morrison's first-grade class begins with the daily goals. In a discussion format, children discover new vocabulary words, predict weather, and learn about exciting events. What is the *greatest* advantage of Ms. Morrison following a routine?

   A. It creates a way for teachers to assess students' skills in a large-group setting.
   B. It encourages students to take turns, share new ideas, and cooperate with each other.
   C. It ensures that all students will have an opportunity to talk that day.
   D. It provides an opportunity for students to respond to factual questions.

20. Mr. Ganther, a new fourth-grade teacher, is eagerly awaiting the first day of school. Before classes begin, however, room arrangement decisions will need to be made. In deciding on where the desks should go, it is important for Mr. Ganther to remember that:

   A. the room should be arranged in the "best" way.
   B. the arrangement should be flexible and meet the needs of the students.
   C. the arrangement should leave little room for social interaction to take place.
   D. the teacher's desk should always be placed in the front of the room so careful monitoring can take place.

21. As children work at their seats, Ms. Corning walks around the room straightening papers, books, and utensils on the children's desks and requires their feet to be flat on the floor. The environment in the classroom *primarily* shows a lack of understanding that children need:

   A. a classroom that addresses their emotional and social well-being.
   B. a neat and orderly atmosphere in which to learn.
   C. a classroom that incorporates diversity.
   D. a classroom that demonstrates effective use of administrative tasks.

22. Mr. Sanchez teaches in a self-contained classroom in which history immediately follows the language arts block. Several students continue working on their writing assignment after the history lesson has started. Which of the following would *best* help Mr. Sanchez achieve a smooth transition between subject areas?

   A. Informing students of all assignments at the beginning of the day.
   B. Maximizing the amount of time between subjects so everyone will have time to finish what he or she is doing.
   C. Making sure he has everyone's attention before he begins the next subject area.
   D. Letting the students continue writing while he is teaching history so they can complete their assignments.

23. Mr. Robbins uses the computer to keep track of expenditures that he accumulates over the year. He also uses a program that creates seating charts and makes certificates. The *most* likely benefit of the computer programs Mr. Robbins uses is to provide:

   A. a way for Mr. Robbins to receive in-service hours for the amount of time he spends using computer programs for in-school business.
   B. a means of communication with the teachers around the state.
   C. a means for managing the administrative workload that is required of teachers.
   D. a means of assessing a program for inclusion in the school district.

24. Mr. Mason realizes the health unit that was planned is rather all-inclusive and is looking forward to having Ms. Sappington, a paraprofessional, assist in the classroom. The paraprofessional will be able to help with everything *except*:

   A. providing assistance for personal care and other physical needs of the students.
   B. creating new, alternative instruction without any direction from the teacher or certified personnel.
   C. facilitating interactions between students.
   D. adapting lessons under Mr. Mason's guidance.

25. During center time in Ms. Mehan's kindergarten class, the students rotate to activities that have been introduced during shared reading time. Several children at a time are at each center and are working on beginning sounds with magnetic letters, retelling a story with a flannel board, drawing pictures based on an incident from the story just read, or dictating what the picture is showing. During the time students are at centers, Ms. Mehan's *most* important role is to:

   A. make sure students are on task by asking specific questions about the story that was read during the shared reading experience.
   B. make sure students are communicating with each other and building friendships.
   C. rotate to each center, observe students' behavior, and make sure students are on task and productive.
   D. encourage children to talk about what they like best at school and who their best friend might be.

GO ON TO THE NEXT PAGE

26. Mr. Matthew's third-grade class operated in a rather unorganized manner. Mr. Matthews didn't believe in strict rules and routines, but rather in letting students form their own idea of a functioning "community." As a result, disorder persisted throughout the day, and the principal spent more time than was desired trying to settle disputes. Mr. Mathew's *primary* problem was caused by:

   A. his not selecting appropriate class leaders who would help the "community" establish guidelines.
   B. a lack of appropriate parental authority and control, which carries over to the school environment.
   C. a lack of a supportive administration who would try to work with Mr. Matthew's philosophy of teaching.
   D. a lack of effective, consistent rules and routines that need to be implemented at the beginning of the year.

27. During the weekly spelling test, Roger asks Mr. Mitchell if he can get another pencil. While he is looking in his locker he sneaks a peek at the list of spelling words he has tucked under a book. Mr. Mitchell is aware of what he is doing. What is the *best* strategy for Mr. Mitchell to take?

   A. Value the results of the spelling test as a major grade and tell Roger he will need to study harder next time.
   B. Ask Roger to leave the door of his locker open during the next spelling test so the temptation is minimized.
   C. Provide a competitive environment so Roger will realize he needs to study harder instead of cheat.
   D. Discuss the cheating incident with Roger and find effective means to help him study for the next spelling test.

28. Anand was repeatedly disrupting Ms. Carter's fourth-grade class. After receiving many warnings, Anand, his desk, and his belongings were relocated to an area outside the principal's office. Anand was told he would need to apologize to the class for his behavior and ask permission to return to the class. After several weeks of forced withdrawal, Anand requested he be allowed back in the classroom. In addition to the above modification, which of the following is the *best* strategy for Ms. Carter to use?

   A. Create a positive environment for Anand and provide him with coping strategies that can be used when he begins to get off track with his behavior.
   B. Ignore Anand's behavior because the disruption is taking time away from the rest of the students' instructional period.
   C. Make an issue in front of the class so Anand will be embarrassed enough to modify his own behavior and want to start learning.
   D. Keep track of the time Anand is wasting in having to be disciplined and, with parental approval, make Anand stay after school and make up the time.

29. Ms. Roland frequently has to remind her kindergarten students of the classroom rules and procedures. When Billy turns all of the chairs over she says, "Please put the chairs back in the upright position. Chairs are for sitting on." This action is *most* likely based on which of the following?

   A. Children should have the opportunity to arrange furniture in the room.
   B. Children should be given manageable tasks to complete and a certain amount of time in which to complete the task.
   C. Children need a physical environment that is flexible and one that will meet their developmental needs.
   D. Teachers need to discipline and interact with students by using appropriate language and communication skills.

30. Teachers must engage students in tasks that will require them to apply the higher-order thinking skills they have learned. Higher-order thinking is NOT requiring the student to:

   A. think critically and consider alternatives.
   B. relate information the students already know and apply it to real-world situations.
   C. think intuitively and use their imagination or make a judgment.
   D. understand and remember factual information.

31. During closure of a lesson on multiplication, Ms. Lam wants students to reflect on what they learned. She asks them the meaning of regrouping and then proceeds to ask if they can find a new way to regroup the apples with which they have been working. Another teacher presenting the same lesson asks his students to define multiplication during closure. In comparing the two teaching styles, Ms. Lam is *mainly* demonstrating the importance of:

   A. creating a positive classroom environment in which all students are able to learn.
   B. using everyday objects to enhance students' learning.
   C. extending students' knowledge through exploring content.
   D. seeing which students are ready for a pop-quiz the next day.

32. Several students in a fourth-grade class have learning disabilities. Which of the following would NOT be an acceptable practice when communicating expectations?

   A. Proceed from a simple to a more complex concept when explaining new material.
   B. Tell the students to remain seated until the entire assignment is completed.
   C. Give clear, easy-to-follow directions, breaking the assignment into small but doable steps.
   D. Get the students' attention before presenting information.

33. Ms. Davis has an English Language Learner in the class. Rita is working hard at learning English, but Ms. Davis spends a great deal of time using gestures, eye contact, and other forms of nonverbal contact in communicating with Rita. What action should Ms. Davis take to facilitate Rita's learning the English language?

   A. Ms. Davis should tell Rita she will need to stop using nonverbal means of communicating and try hard to start using English.
   B. Ms. Davis should ask Rita's parents to make an appointment with a speech-language pathologist to see if they can get Rita on a fast track of learning.
   C. Ms. Davis should encourage Rita to try to use English to communicate by placing Rita in pairs or a small group of peers.
   D. Ms. Davis should leave Rita alone and realize that when she is ready she will start speaking English.

Clustered Items Begin Here

34. Mr. Ardito, a third-grade teacher, uses a discussion format while teaching about the solar system. During the discussion he asks opened-ended questions to stimulate and encourage student participation. After the discussion, Mr. Ardito explains that the students will be working in cooperative learning groups and then carefully outlines the group goals. Mr. Ardito is an effective teacher, but research shows that the one *primary* problem teachers have when asking questions is:

   A. calling on only those students who have their hands raised to answer the question.
   B. having a specific goal and objective for each question that is asked.
   C. establishing rules and procedures prior to class discussion so students know how they are to respond.
   D. asking students to respond too quickly to questions by not allowing enough wait time for students to think about their answers.

35. When making decisions on group assignments, Mr. Ardito should place students according to the following with the *exception* of:

   A. placing students according to their achievement levels.
   B. placing students according to interests.
   C. placing students in groups who are culturally diverse.
   D. placing students with their best friends.

GO ON TO THE NEXT PAGE

36. During cooperative learning groups, Mr. Ardito became so involved in facilitating one group that another group completed the assignment and students were exhibiting off-task behavior. Mr. Ardito's *biggest* mistake was that he:

　A. had not given students enough work to do so consequently they were off-task.
　B. had not monitored carefully enough the pacing of the group assignment.
　C. tried using a cooperative learning activity and this method of grouping is often not effective.
　D. had not tried the appropriate form of cooperative learning because if he had, students would not have been off-task.

Clustered Items End Here

37. Ms. Harlan's second-grade science class is learning about force. The students have been directed to use the marbles to see if they can move a marble with another marble, and then blow on the marble to see if they are able to affect how fast or how slowly the marble rolls. By asking these questions, Ms. Harlan is:

　A. promoting student engagement through creative discussion and student involvement.
　B. trying to see how much students know about marbles and their physical properties.
　C. creating a fun activity so students will enjoy science and look forward to each lesson.
　D. focusing attention on students' ability to blow marbles.

38. Mr. Bates hopes to intrinsically motivate the students during the course of the year. Which of the following would be *most* appropriate?

　A. Have parents reward the students when their work is complete.
　B. Have students set goals and keep track of the progress they are making.
　C. Promise students a popcorn party if everyone does really well on the next spelling test.
　D. Pair students together such that the ones who complete their work on time are matched with those who have trouble turning in their assignments at the appropriate time.

GO ON TO THE NEXT PAGE

39. Ms. Garcia regularly uses computer jargon such as input device, online, network, password, modem, and disk drive with the students. In doing so, Ms. Garcia's *primary* purpose is to:

   A. show the students how much knowledge she has gained from taking the latest technology class offered through the in-service program.
   B. practice using computer jargon so she stays current on the latest technological advances.
   C. demonstrate knowledge of current technology and effectively incorporate it in the classroom.
   D. add to the word-wall in the room computer words the students have recently heard, seen on the computer, or used themselves.

40. Mr. Castillo, a language arts teacher, uses a website that correlates with one of the state-adopted language arts series. The *main* reason for using this website is that it:

   A. provides lesson plans that take the place of the weekly plans required by the school's principal.
   B. satisfies the school's technology requirement because instead of going to in-service meetings, teachers can provide proof they use technology when turning in lesson plans.
   C. provides a source of technology for the students so they stay on top of current trends.
   D. provides resources and ideas that extend the current reading program the school district has selected.

41. Ms. Mackie's kindergarten class has a computer in the room and students are free to use it independently during center time. Which of the following would be the *most* appropriate activity for children at this age level?

   A. The students will read a story and then answer questions asked by the paraprofessional.
   B. The students will name the parts of the computer.
   C. The students will match shapes by color and size.
   D. The students will dictate a story to an aide and the aide will word process the information into the computer.

Clustered Items Begin Here

42. Mr. Garlington's fourth-grade social studies class was preparing to study the Alamo. Which of the following activities would be the *most* appropriate in integrating technology and using it in problem-solving situations that emphasize collaboration?

    A. Using school resources such as the library, videos, and CDs to prepare a timeline of the events leading up to and including the battle at the Alamo.

    B. Selecting an online article about a main character who fought at the Alamo and write a report on the hardships they incurred.

    C. Presenting artwork that students have created along with a one-page word-processed report.

    D. Using an approved website to take a computerized virtual museum field trip to the Alamo and then as a group project create a brochure recruiting men to fight for the Texas Revolution.

43. Under supervised instruction, Mr. Garlington directs the students to research the Internet for information about the Alamo and events surrounding the famous site. Students are to choose a person who was at the Alamo during the time of the siege, and while working in pairs, write a letter home to that individual's relatives describing the Alamo experience. Mr. Garlington's *main* emphasis on this assignment is for the student to:

    A. develop good keyboarding skills so in the future assignments can be word processed more rapidly.

    B. develop collaboration and teamwork using technology applications.

    C. use the computer to improve higher-order thinking skills.

    D. experience another form of technology in addition to calculators, videos, and CD-ROM.

44. After teaching a lesson, Mr. Garlington evaluates the effectiveness of the instruction to see if adjustments are needed in his overall goals and objectives. Which of the following questions is *least* important?

    A. Did I cover the appropriate material in the right amount of time so I can stay on target with the unit?

    B. Were the objectives appropriate to the students' abilities?

    C. Did I factor in the appropriate amount of "wait time" after asking questions?

    D. Was the way I delivered the lessons appropriate for the activities required?

45. When Mr. Garlington assesses the students' final products, he uses authentic assessment rather than traditional testing methods. Which of the following is NOT an advantage of authentic assessment?

   A. It is a measure of students' progress as it relates to curricular objectives and occurs in natural settings under natural situations.
   B. It is a replacement for other forms of assessment.
   C. It is used to assess instructional activities and encourage higher-order thinking.
   D. It is used as a tool for students to engage in self-reflection and reveals students' strengths and weakness.

Clustered Items End Here

46. The teacher has been observing four-year-old Manny during clean-up. Manny has been losing control of his emotions when asked to put things away or when changing from one activity to another. The teacher has come to the conclusion that once Manny has settled into a routine, he doesn't like to make changes. Which of the following would indicate that his teacher understands his needs?

   A. Give Manny a few more minutes to go from one activity to another.
   B. Point out another student to Manny in hopes that he will model that student's behavior.
   C. Put Manny in time-out and tell him he needs to start behaving himself.
   D. Refer Manny to the school counselor to determine if he is developing a behavioral problem.

47. Ms. Peterson, a fourth-grade language arts teacher, utilizes many forms of assessment. Checklists are used to record information and questionnaires are applied when students are interviewed about books they've read. Other forms of authentic assessment as well as norm-referenced tests and criterion-referenced tests are also implemented throughout the year. Which of the following should Ms. Peterson use as the *ultimate* goal when selecting the appropriate assessment tool?

   A. Measuring the students' performance against goals and objectives.
   B. Helping students advance to the next grade.
   C. Making sure that the students are achieving similar grades on the tests, so Ms. Peterson can make adjustments in her approaches.
   D. Satisfying local and state requirements which are based on standards.

48. At the beginning of each school year, Ms. Soto invites parents to come to the school for Parent Night. What is the *most* important message to communicate?

   A. Ms. Soto should tell the parents about the family reach programs that are available in the community.
   B. Ms. Soto should describe activities during which parents will be needed and provide a schedule where they can sign up.
   C. Ms. Soto should promote the value of working together and building a relationship between school and home.
   D. Ms. Soto should discuss the goals and objectives she'll be going over during parent–teacher conferences.

49. Several parents whose children were experiencing difficulty with reading requested a meeting with the school principal. Their main purpose was not to admonish the school for lack of teaching, but to gain insight into ways they could help their own children. They particularly wanted addresses for Internet sites they could depend on for sound educational advice. The principal understood their concern and set up a meeting with the district's technology coordinator, who recommended several excellent websites. What is the *greatest* advantage of Internet information for parents?

   A. The sites will help the parents diagnose their child's reading problem.
   B. The sites will supply parents with appropriate terminology so they can be more informed during parent–teacher conferences.
   C. The sites offer parents instantaneous access to related topics and provide support for parents.
   D. The sites provide links to other schools so parents can compare their school with other schools.

50. Each year Mr. Cantu's principal asks him if a student teacher can be placed under his supervision and each year he agrees. The *primary* advantage of having a student teacher is:

   A. to provide an extra set of hands to help with the daily activities.
   B. to interact in a professional manner and share the commitment of the teaching profession.
   B. to give the teacher time to work on obtaining additional certification.
   D. to capitalize on the pre-service teacher's presence at the school in case a substitute teacher is needed.

GO ON TO THE NEXT PAGE

51. The *primary* objective for professional collaboration during an Individualized Education Program (IEP) meeting is:

   A. to share information about a student and develop goals that will be beneficial for the student.
   B. to select a leader for the IEP group in order for meetings to function in a smooth, professional manner.
   C. to make sure the parent is satisfied with the outcome of the meeting.
   D. to be able to provide a sounding board for all teachers involved so they can inform each other about their problems.

52. Nadia, a young girl in Ms. Kincaid's third-grade class, has a noticeable nasal quality to her speech. From the beginning of the school year, Ms. Kincaid found it extremely irritating whenever Nadia would speak. Ms. Kincaid went to a colleague to share her feelings and ask for advice on how to deal with her feelings toward Nadia. In confiding with someone, Ms. Kincaid showed she:

   A. revealed personal, secure information about one of the students, thus violating the Code of Ethics.
   B. created a problem if the colleague reveals Ms. Kincaid's concern to the rest of the teachers because they may view Nadia differently from now on.
   C. is very insensitive to Nadia' problem and should have talked to Nadia to see if she would try to speak without a nasal quality.
   D. examined her true feelings about her bias and should use this reflection to improve her professional attitude.

53. Mr. Caldwell received a notice about a conference in Houston. He knows he should attend, but doesn't like leaving his students with a substitute. He brings his dilemma to the principal before he makes a decision. What advice should the principal give to Mr. Caldwell?

   A. He should recommend that Mr. Caldwell research and see if important speakers will be attending the conference.
   B. He should tell Mr. Caldwell to prepare for a substitute because he hasn't missed any days so far this year and the time away from school will be restful.
   C. He should stress the importance of attending professional meetings because of the valuable information he can acquire and the interaction that occurs between colleagues.
   D. He should tell Mr. Caldwell to stay with his class and get the information from one of the other colleagues who will attend the conference.

54. Ms. Jennings received her appraisal results from the last observation and was very disappointed with the outcome. What would be the *first* step Ms. Jennings should take to rectify her poor results?

   A. Make an appointment with the person who made the observation and together go over the evaluation, asking for constructive feedback.
   B. Talk to other colleagues and see what their appraisal results were like.
   C. Go over the appraisal results very carefully to see if she can determine exactly what she did that was inappropriate.
   D. Go to the superintendent and express her dissatisfaction with the person who did the appraisal, telling the superintendent that this is the second year in a row that she has had poor results and she wants something done about it.

55. Before students at Dobie Elementary School are allowed to use the Internet, students and parents are asked to sign an Acceptable Use Policy. In doing so the school is:

   A. meddling in the students' and parents' personal lives.
   B. encouraging students to find inappropriate websites.
   C. protecting the students and avoiding unwelcome use of inappropriate websites.
   D. providing a topic for discussion during the next Parent Night.

56. The Individuals with Disabilities Education Act (IDEA) gives parents and students rights. Which of the following would be in violation of that act?

   A. Inform parents of the IEP meeting and facilitate a phone call or conference call.
   B. Conduct an evaluation on the student because of the severity of the problem, and then obtain permission from the parents to proceed with the interventions.
   C. Inform parents that other persons with special knowledge of their child may accompany them to an IEP meeting.
   D. Inform parents that if they wish to have an independent evaluator assess their child they may do so at no cost to them.

57. Mr. Romero is making arrangements for Kurt, a visually impaired student, who will be joining his classroom. Which of the following would NOT appropriately meet Kurt's needs?

   A. The room should be free of mobiles, decorations, and hanging plants that can impair the vision of the student.
   B. The teacher should make provisions to have books with large print as well as tapes available for the student.
   C. The teacher should monitor students who need magnifying glasses or other equipment to make sure they are able to utilize as much of the materials in the room as possible.
   D. The teacher should make every effort to supplement oral presentations with visual presentations.

58. Ms. Curtin has taught first grade for 10 years and has a real interest in becoming a counselor. What would be the *most* appropriate course of action for Ms. Curtin to take?

   A. Arrange a meeting with the principal and ask for advice on whether or not she should continue to teach or become a counselor.
   B. Visit with the school's counselor and ask about the job and what specific courses she should take.
   C. Enroll in courses at the local university and see if the material is satisfying.
   D. Contact the State Board for Educator Certification (SBEC) for requirements.

59. Larry's parents had always considered him to be a very talented child. They even spoke with his second-grade teacher and requested testing for the Gifted and Talented program. The results indicated, however, that Larry had not met all of the criteria. His teacher was surprised and commented to the parents that it was probably the fault of the GT teacher because she was in a bad mood on the day the testing was done. In making that remark, the teacher was not:

   A. using the steps specified for teachers when working with GT students.
   B. following ethical guidelines according to the Code of Ethics.
   C. in compliance with the No Child Left Behind Act.
   D. in compliance with FERPA.

Decision Set Begins Here

Ms. Brown's second-grade class is beginning an integrated unit that will focus on important information about the state of Texas, particularly on its historical figures. Ms. Brown introduces information about heroes, biographers, songs, and legends that she finds available from a variety of sources. During the language arts period, Ms. Brown reads poetry and stories that relate to famous Texans. During geography, they look at maps of Texas and discover famous trails, and during math they compare such data as the number of Mexican soldiers and Texas soldiers who fought at the Alamo.

60. As the class continues to study about Texas and famous Texans, Ms. Brown asks students if they can identify various community or state landmarks. The students are quick to point out that there are several schools as well as streets named after significant individuals. Ms. Brown's *main* purpose in using familiarity of landmarks is to:

   A. integrate historical facts so children will do well on the TAKS.
   B. impact students' learning by planning activities that include the community and the student.
   C. increase time spent on history because it is Ms. Brown's favorite subject, and she wants to help students develop this desire for the past.
   D. provide a means whereby students will experience success using higher-order thinking skills.

61. Ms. Brown wants to extend the unit on famous Texans by integrating a writing component. Using prior knowledge of biographies, Ms. Brown plans on teaching the concept of autobiography. She models a short history on her life and provides instruction on how to begin writing about oneself. By building on the known, such as biographies, and asking students to formulate the idea of writing about oneself, Ms. Brown expects the instructional strategy will:

   A. help students learn something about themselves they had forgotten.
   B. ensure a smooth functioning day because students like to talk about themselves and writing will be even more fun.
   C. help students remember to look for additional historical landmarks in the local community.
   D. make the lesson more meaningful and relevant because it will link to students' experiences.

62. Ms. Brown's use of large-class discussion for both the historical landmarks and the autobiography shows she understands the importance of:

   A. learning how much students know about the local community and state and local landmarks.
   B. fostering a feeling of competitiveness so more students will become engaged in the discussion.
   C. varying the roles of both teacher and student while promoting intellectual involvement.
   D having discussions with students on an informal basis.

Ms. Brown next encourages students to do their best by sharing with the students a new bulletin board called "The Wall of Fame." She begins by putting pictures of famous people on the wall, and informs the students that once their autobiographies are complete they too will join the "Wall of Fame." Students must first write their stories during computer time, and then, using the school's digital camera, have their pictures input into the computer.

63. Before the students can begin on their autobiographies, they must first conduct an interview with their parents or guardians, asking such questions as "How did I get my name?" or "Where was I born?" Ms. Brown's *primary* objective for this exercise would be to:

   A. encourage students to learn to speak to adults.
   B. provide a history for the students so they will have a record of pertinent information.
   C. develop friendships among the class based on similarities.
   D. engage the parents in various aspects of the educational experience.

64. Ms. Brown provides explicit instruction on how the students are to work at the computer while word processing their papers. The final product will have their story and their picture along side it. Ms. Brown effectively uses this strategy to:

   A. create an interest in the use of technology.
   B. produce a professional document that will enhance the room's appearance.
   C. give students additional practice in keyboarding and word processing.
   D. provide a motivational activity that will create a sense of pride and ownership.

65. For students to submit quality work using the computer it is important for Ms. Brown to:

   A. outline her behavioral objectives before the students use the computer.
   B. tell the students to take their autobiographies home to their parents for proofreading help.
   C. suggest they pair with a friend to make sure they are on target for the assignment.
   D. help students write their story if they are having trouble thinking of things to say.

66. Ms. Brown has several students in her class who are identified as Gifted and Talented. During the "Wall of Fame" project, which of the following approaches would *best* meet the needs of the Gifted and Talented students in the classroom?

   A. Ask the GT students to help other students if they complete their assignments before the rest of the class.
   B. Assign the GT partners to interview each other for additional information and tape record the question-and-answer format.
   C. Suggest that the GT students bring along a book from home they would like to read.
   D. Create a matching worksheet covering famous Texans who wrote biographies.

67. Ms. Brown also has several English Language Learner (ELL) students. Which of the following would be the *best* approach in adapting the program for ELL students while working on the "Wall of Fame" assignment?

   A. Disregard the assignment because it is too difficult for an ELL student.
   B. Ask the ELL student's parents to come to class and answer questions about the student.
   C. Dictate their story line by line and ask for help from the classroom aide or Ms. Brown.
   D. Pair the ELL student with another student in the class who has a similar background and use some of that student's information.

68. Before the project is complete, Ms. Brown wants to communicate effectively with parents and share information on each student's progress. What form of communication would be the *most* effective?

   A. Send home a written report on the work the students have done so far and ask the students to return it the next day along with a parent's signature.
   B. Arrange a meeting with each of the parents and go over what the students have done and what they have left to do.
   C. Tell the students to report the progress they have made to their parents and have them specifically explain the remaining tasks.
   D. Place a phone call to each of the parents, ask if they have questions, and leave a message on the answering machine if they are not available to talk to in person.

GO ON TO THE NEXT PAGE

Practice EC-4 Pedagogy and Professional Responsibilities Test II

69. What would be the *most* appropriate assessment technique when evaluating the autobiography product?

   A. Ms. Brown should create a checklist to make sure all questions are answered and all tasks are complete.
   B. Ms. Brown should develop a rubric prior to the start of the unit on famous Texans so students will know the requirements.
   C. Ms. Brown should write a paragraph evaluating the autobiography product and send it home with the students.
   D. Ms. Brown should create a test that encompasses questions about famous people as well as items that should be included in an autobiography.

Decision Set Ends Here

Decision Set Begins Here

Mr. Cummings, a second-grade teacher, designs a unit on multicultural literature to foster an appreciation of other people's cultures and diverse backgrounds. To begin with, Mr. Cummings selects literature that accurately reflects a group's culture and values. He then collects an array of material that provides information on the many facets of different cultures. In addition, he visits several websites to look for lesson plans and ideas for the unit.

70. Mr. Cummings engages students in a discussion over previously read stories with multicultural themes and the current material they are reading for the unit. Mr. Cumming's *main* reason for including this instructional strategy is that it:

   A. enables students to convey to the teacher what they were doing prior to the lesson.
   B. connects prior learning and increases understanding of content.
   C. enhances a student's ability to memorize facts and use the facts at a later date to answer pertinent questions.
   D. allows students to take risks when answering questions and increases their self-esteem.

71. Mr. Cummings organized the unit so it will relate to other subjects. Mr. Cummings spends time researching instructional strategies to make sure the activities meet the objectives. Mr. Cumming's *primary* purpose in formulating a structured unit is:

   A. to have students learn about a lot of curriculum at one time.
   B. to provide a means for students to experience other opinions and biases so they can formulate their own thoughts.
   C. to organize everything for a 4- to 6-week unit and not have to plan again for awhile.
   D. to relate the various components of the required curriculum in a structured sequence.

GO ON TO THE NEXT PAGE

72. In searching for ideas for art, Mr. Cummings finds lesson plans on several websites that are easily adaptable for his unit. By acquiring information on the internet, Mr. Cummings shows he understands the importance of:

   A. using those lesson plans so he doesn't have to write as many.
   B. incorporating technology to plan and organize lessons.
   C. finding information on the Internet so the job of teaching art is simplified.
   D. placing his own art lessons on the Internet.

73. Mr. Cumming's *main* purpose in incorporating a variety of materials and resources into the unit is that it:

   A. creates a large block of time so students will remain occupied.
   B. provides opportunities for students to explore content from many perspectives and to value other viewpoints.
   C. provides students a situation to use the school's library.
   D. provides a means for students to become experts on the art, music, and language of a culture other than their own.

74. Which of the following is NOT a recommended adaptation or modification for an ELL student during the multicultural unit?

   A. Increase the amount of oral discussion on the books the class is reading and provide explanations for new vocabulary words.
   B. Require the student to write down all new vocabulary words and try to memorize them.
   C. Use illustrations to help clarify the meanings of the words and begin with something the students have previously heard or read.
   D. Use role-playing or small-group work if the books lend themselves to this type of activity.

75. After reading folktales, traditional stories, biographies, poetry, and other pieces of multicultural literature, Mr. Cummings and another second-grade teacher establish a plan whereby their own students will write personal stories using the computer, and, when complete, e-mail them to their "story buddy." Mr. Cumming's *primary* reason for having students develop personal narratives and share them is to:

   A. make learning meaningful and relevant for the students.
   B. have another teacher share in the responsibility of the unit.
   C. encourage students to recall facts by extending the unit.
   D. stimulate students to be good storytellers.

GO ON TO THE NEXT PAGE

76. Mr. Cummings prepares a letter to send home to the parents containing unit information and the technology requirement. In the letter he explains how the computer will be used for part of the unit objectives, but there are alternative means of research if a computer is not available. By sending a letter to the parents about the upcoming unit expectations, it shows that Mr. Cummings knows to:

  A. limit parental involvement because the work the students submit may not be their own.
  B. plan instruction based on cultural and socioeconomic differences.
  C. discourage complaining that the children never have enough homework.
  D. communicate with parents about using modern technology and set a role model for the parents to follow.

77. When Mr. Cummings contacted the other grade-level teacher and asked about sharing the storytelling activity, Mr. Art said he would if Brent, an ADHD student in Mr. Cummings class, was not paired with anyone in his class. Mr. Cummings can *most* appropriately handle the situation by:

  A. agreeing with Mr. Art and tell him there will be an alternative place for Brent to go.
  B. explaining how a management system now in place has had a positive effect on Brent's behavior.
  C. suggest that Mr. Art come to the class to observe Brent to see if he can come up with new suggestions.
  D. ask the special education teacher to come to class that day and monitor Brent.

78. Jose was reading to his grandmother when she realized the story's setting was the same village where she was reared. Jose wants her to come to class and share her own story and bring her famous guacamole recipe. By allowing Jose's grandmother to visit the class, Mr. Cumming's *primary* consideration is:

  A. to obtain a copy of the famous guacamole recipe.
  B. to make Jose feel a part of the inner circle in the class and be more readily accepted.
  C. to let the parents and grandparents share in the teaching responsibilities, thus forming a community of educators.
  D. to build a relationship that establishes a connection between teachers and caregivers.

79. When Jose's grandmother arrives at school with the guacamole, Mr. Cummings overhears various slang remarks from one of the other teachers about how the grandmother is dressed. Discouraged by the racial bias and damaging implications, Mr. Cummings requests a meeting with the principal and school board. By addressing the issue of diversity with the school administration, Mr. Cummings:

   A. caused more problems by bringing the issue of racial bias to the forefront.
   B. plans to monitor more closely the attitudes and intent of his colleagues.
   C. used good judgment in seeking assistance rather than trying to confront the issue on his own.
   D. clearly defines what multicultural education requires.

80. At the completion of the project, Mr. Cummings instructs the students to reflect on their roles and participation in the project. This is done by conducting individual interviews. The *main* reason for using this type of assessment is that it will:

   A. provide feedback on Mr. Cummings's instructional strategies.
   B. promote self-assessment and help the students enhance their own learning as they reflect on what they learned.
   C. help Mr. Cummings make changes and adaptations for the next unit he is about to teach.
   D. provide Mr. Cummings with a means with which to evaluate mastery of the TEKS.

Decision Set Ends Here

CHAPTER THIRTEEN

Practice EC–4 Pedagogy and Professional Responsibilities Test II Answers and Explanations

1. B

This question addresses information from PPR Competency* 001:

The teacher understands human developmental processes and applies this knowledge to plan instruction and ongoing assessment that motivate students and are responsive to their developmental characteristics and needs.

Eliminate (A) because children at this age are sensitive to the feelings of others, so Heather probably was not trying to get anyone in trouble. Eliminate (C) because we don't know what kind of game the students are playing. Choice (D) suggests some abstract thinking but many children at this stage are not ready for this cognitive development. Children at this stage of development are prone to tattling on each other. Researchers say that it isn't so much out of concern for the rules of the game, but that students are developing a conscience and are following through with their beliefs. Choice (B) is the correct response.

---

*Competency statements copyright © 2003 by the Texas State Board for Educator Certification and National Evaluation Systems, Inc. (NES ®). Reprinted by permission.

2. B

This question addresses information from PPR Competency 001:

The teacher understands human developmental processes and applies this knowledge to plan instruction and ongoing assessment that motivate students and are responsive to their developmental characteristics and needs.

Eliminate (A) as the Sensorimotor stage lasts for approximately 2 years. Eliminate (C) because the child is between 7 and 11 years of age. In choice (D), the child is between 11 and 15 years of age, and in the Preoperational stage the child is between 2 and 7 years of age. Children at this age are in the Preoperational stage of development. Choice (B) is the correct response.

3. D

This question addresses information from PPR Competency 001:

The teacher understands human developmental processes and applies this knowledge to plan instruction and ongoing assessment that motivate students and are responsive to their developmental characteristics and needs.

Eliminate (A) because, although teachers do want students to get along, they do not expect students to handle all of the discipline problems. Eliminate (B) because even though teachers realize the importance of working with colleagues, that is not the focus in this situation. Choice (C) suggests that chart making is the answer. Even though charts may help keep the class organized, we don't see a reference to interactions between the teacher and students as the question asks. At this age, children need help in applying decision-making skills. Students need to set goals, be shown how to meet those goals, and follow through with their responsibilities. Choice (D) is the correct response.

4. B

This question addresses information from PPR Competency 001:

The teacher understands human developmental processes and applies this knowledge to plan instruction and ongoing assessment that motivate students and are responsive to their developmental characteristics and needs.

Eliminate (A) because many children at this stage of development would not be able to make logical decisions or reach a consensus on what they want to see. Eliminate (D) because, although this may occur this is not the main objective of the field trip. Choice (C) suggests Ms. Pape wants to question the students on factual information. Ms. Pape uses the field trip to integrate meaningful experiences and involve the students in active learning. She could have asked the students the same questions in a classroom setting; however, by giving the students the opportunity to actually see the animals and capitalizing on the natural environment, Ms. Pape shows she understands the needs of her students. Choice (B) is the correct response.

5. C

This question addresses information from PPR Competency 001:

The teacher understands human developmental processes and applies this knowledge to plan instruction and ongoing assessment that motivate students and are responsive to their developmental characteristics and needs.

Eliminate (A) because privileges should not be connected to behavior. Eliminate (B) because after-school activities usually do not have a connection to what is occurring during the school setting. Choice (D) occurs in the home setting so should not be tied to what is happening in school. Sandra is experiencing a negative self-image and this will affect her emotional and social development. The best thing that Ms. Fite can do is provide a nurturing environment in which Sandra feels she can take risks. Choice (C) is the correct response.

6. B

This question addresses information from PPR Competency 001:

The teacher understands human developmental processes and applies this knowledge to plan instruction and ongoing assessment that motivate students and are responsive to their developmental characteristics and needs.

Eliminate (A) because Anita undoubtedly was involved in play when she forgot to do several tasks. Eliminate (C) as there is no indication that Anita was causing problems with her classmates. Choice (D) suggests Anita was lazy, but the work may have been too difficult or she was not able to process the information. Because Anita was a very young second-grade student, she probably entered school too early and wasn't developmentally ready for it. By returning to first grade, she will have the opportunity to develop and perform at the level of students closer to her own age. Choice (B) is the correct response.

7. C

This question addresses information from PPR Competency 002:

The teacher understands student diversity and knows how to plan learning experiences and design assessments that are responsive to differences among students and that promote all students' learning.

This is a priority-setting question asking you to select a choice that would be *incorrect*. Therefore, in this question we already know that three out of the four choices are correct. Keep choice (A) because presenting instructions, pausing, and making sure everyone is on-task is an excellent instructional strategy. Keep (B) because additional help might provide the support the ELL student needs. Choice (D) is a highly recommended strategy for supporting the diverse learner. English Language Learner students need direction, so suggesting that a student work on his own and then checking to see what he might have accomplished would not be an effective strategy. Choice (C) is the correct response.

8. D

This question addresses information from PPR Competency 002:

The teacher understands student diversity and knows how to plan learning experiences and design assessments that are responsive to differences among students and that promote all students' learning.

Eliminate (A) and (B) because you do not have enough information for this choice. Choice (C) would have to mention something about asking Kolby to take the lead for you to make this choice. The teacher may have had a good reason for Kolby playing with the blocks, but the remark came across as stereotyping. Kolby might possibly really like to play in the kitchen center and could be dominating the area, but his teacher should have maneuvered him to another play area without the biased remark. Choice (D) is the correct response.

9. C

This question addresses information from PPR Competency 002:

The teacher understands student diversity and knows how to plan learning experiences and design assessments that are responsive to differences among students and that promote all students' learning.

Eliminate (A) because the teacher is supposed to be teaching and modeling acceptance. Eliminate (B) because it is a negative response. Choice (D) puts Bryan on the spot and it appears the teacher is trying to embarrass him. The teacher can take this opportunity to teach a lesson in diversity by asking Robert to share something of his culture and let the children enjoy each other's differences. In doing so, children will look at Robert as being able to do something special rather than different. She is modeling acceptance and respect for someone else's background and needs. Choice (C) is the correct response.

10. A

This question addresses information from PPR Competency 002:

The teacher understands student diversity and knows how to plan learning experiences and design assessments that are responsive to differences among students and that promote all students' learning.

Eliminate (B) because we don't see any mention of Ms. Earl trying to get the students to work together even though it is a desired quality. Eliminate (C) because, even though Ms. Earl is instructing the class on nutrition, it isn't the reason for comparison of allergies and culture. Eliminate (D) because it isn't Ms. Earl's responsibility to inform her students of all of the allergies that people may incur. She has designed lessons based on learning experiences and differences. Ms. Earl realized that children are accepting of each other when they understand the problem. She capitalized on the fact that there were already differences in the class with regard to food allergies and could then transition into the differences in diversity. In doing so she was using the experience to enrich students' learning about each other's differences and culture. Choice (A) is the correct response.

Practice EC–4 Pedagogy and Professional Responsibilities Test II Answers and Explanations

11. D

This question addresses information from PPR Competency 002:

The teacher understands student diversity and knows how to plan learning experiences and design assessments that are responsive to differences among students and that promote all students' learning.

Eliminate (A) because not all websites would address the socioeconomic situation in which Ms. Marion found herself. Eliminate (B) because, although the choice suggests alternating between various schools to gain a better idea of diversity, each school would be different and the diversity problems and behaviors would be unique to that school. Choice (C) would provide interesting statistics on inner-school schools, but it doesn't answer Ms. Marion's greatest need. Many low-socioeconomic schools do have a problem with low reading scores and parental involvement, but is not to say that all schools report low performance. Ms. Marion needed to examine her own understanding and appreciation of diversity and should have researched information concerning the school district prior to starting her new position. If she had done so she would have realized the school had an effective program in place. Choice (D) is the correct response.

12. B

This question addresses information from PPR Competency 003:

The teacher understands procedures for designing effective and coherent instruction and assessment based on appropriate learning goals and objectives.

Eliminate (A) because most third-grade students do not have a perception of TEKS and standards. Eliminate (C) because closure is not the time for social interaction. Choice (D) is inappropriate as Mr. Bond will probably need to reteach part of the lesson if students are unsure of what they learned. Mr. Bond realizes that to complete the lesson cycle he not only needs to introduce the lesson by stating objectives and connecting prior learning, but if he wants students to see the connection of the lesson to their own lives, he also needs to have students reflect on what they learned, thus restating the objectives. Choice (B) is the correct response.

13. A

This question addresses information from PPR Competency 003:

The teacher understands procedures for designing effective and coherent instruction and assessment based on appropriate learning goals and objectives.

Eliminate (B) because Ms. Woods could have introduced the students to the new vocabulary during the lesson and then involved them in looking up the meaning. Eliminate (C) because if the question is important enough to ask, Ms. Woods would have stopped the lesson until she had the attention of all students. Choice (D) suggests objectives were not covered, and Ms. Woods would have checked for understanding during closure. If this were the case, she would have gone into more detail or would have retaught the lesson. Ms. Woods used an already prepared lesson when teaching about light. Children interacted during the lesson as they conducted the experiments, but she realized the last question was probably not appropriate for this age group so she chose not to use it. Choice (A) is the correct response.

14. C

This question addresses information from PPR Competency 003:

The teacher understands procedures for designing effective and coherent instruction and assessment based on appropriate learning goals and objectives.

This is a priority-setting question. You are to determine the *primary* reason for correlating the TEKS to the lesson. Eliminate (A) as a primary reason even though the lesson for an evaluation should be based on TEKS objectives. Eliminate (B) because, while the grade-level team would require the shared lessons to be based on TEKS objectives, Ms. Delgado would not use that as a primary reason. Choice (D) suggests local and campus goals and the TEKS are state requirements. Ms. Delgado understands the significance of the TEKS and of prerequisite knowledge and skills in determining instructional goals and objectives. Choice (C) is the correct response.

15. D

This question addresses information from PPR Competency 004:

The teacher understands learning processes and factors that impact student learning and demonstrates this knowledge by planning effective, engaging instruction and appropriate assessments.

This is a priority-setting question. You are to determine which activity would *best* address Mr. Perry's objective. Eliminate (A) because lecturing to students about maps would not be as engaging as other instructional strategies. Eliminate (B) because testing, although important, would not answer the question of making the lesson relevant and meaningful. Choice (C) might be included in part of the study on maps, but it is still not as engaging. However, creating a brochure using the Internet site would be far more meaningful and relevant than taking a test or giving a report. Choice (D) is the correct response.

Practice EC–4 Pedagogy and Professional Responsibilities Test II Answers and Explanations

16. C

This question addresses information from PPR Competency 004:

The teacher understands learning processes and factors that impact student learning and demonstrates this knowledge by planning effective, engaging instruction and appropriate assessments.

This is a priority-setting question. You are to determine how the teacher will *best* accomplish the goal of applying critical thinking skills. Eliminate (A) because answering factual questions is at the lowest level of Bloom's Taxonomy, and is thus not considered problem solving. Eliminate (B) because illustrating pictures of their favorite celebration is also considered at the lowest level of cognitive development. Choice (D) suggests using the Internet and then preparing a timeline. Preparing a timeline, answering questions, or illustrating pictures are all activities requiring students to function at a low cognitive level. However, comparing and contrasting how celebrations are alike is an activity fourth-grade students could be required to do and they would be using problem-solving and decision-making skills. Choice (C) is the correct response.

17. A

This question addresses information from PPR Competency 004:

The teacher understands learning processes and factors that impact student learning and demonstrates this knowledge by planning effective, engaging instruction and appropriate assessments.

Eliminate (B) as a possible answer because Ms. Griffen would present an instructional strategy if she wanted students to formulate questions, thus discovering more about their own knowledge of content. Eliminate (C) because, as a result of the exercise, Ms. Griffen would tend to learn something about the students' knowledge. Eliminate choice (D) because Ms. Griffen is not searching for factual information. Ms. Griffen wants students to use critical thinking and inquiry as a means of learning. By asking students to ask questions only, students will not only need to understand a concept but to apply knowledge as well. Choice (A) is the correct response.

18. D

This question addresses information from PPR Competency 005:

The teacher knows how to establish a classroom climate that fosters learning, equity, and excellence and uses this knowledge to create a physical and emotional environment that is safe and productive.

This is priority-setting question asking you to select a choice that would be *incorrect*. Therefore, in this question we already know that three out of the four choices are correct. You must determine the *primary* thing you would NOT see walking into a Mr. Hanson's kindergarten class. Keep choice (A) because interaction of all kinds is a cornerstone of the kindergarten curriculum. Keep (B) because by displaying children's artwork, they take pride in their accomplishments. Choice (C) suggests a classroom in which one would see respect for individual differences and active student learning. A kindergarten classroom should be one of interaction, full of students' artwork and conducted in a supportive environment. Even though students are expected to do their best, the climate should be free of competition. Choice (D) is the correct response.

19. B

This question addresses information from PPR Competency 005:

The teacher knows how to establish a classroom climate that fosters learning, equity, and excellence and uses this knowledge to create a physical and emotional environment that is safe and productive.

This is a priority-setting question as you are determine what the *greatest* advantage would be of Ms. Morrison following a routine. Eliminate (A) because a large group setting is not the best way to assess students. Eliminate (C) because teachers usually don't have trouble getting kindergarten students to talk. Choice (D) suggests answering factual questions and the discussion format is usually meant for discovery learning. By using the same routine each day, students in Ms. Morrison class learn a pattern. The more the children participate in the daily discussion, the more comfortable they will become sharing their ideas and taking turns talking. Ms. Morrison is encouraging cooperation and encouraging students to use language to express themselves. Choice (B) is the correct response.

Practice EC–4 Pedagogy and Professional Responsibilities Test II Answers and Explanations

20. B

This question addresses information from PPR Competency 005:

The teacher knows how to establish a classroom climate that fosters learning, equity, and excellence and uses this knowledge to create a physical and emotional environment that is safe and productive.

Eliminate (A) because there is not one best way for a room to be arranged. It all depends on the activities. Eliminate (C) because, even though Mr. Ganther will not welcome distraction and uninvited talking, social interaction will occur in the classroom. Choice (D) suggests that the teacher's desk should always be placed in the front of the room, but Mr. Ganther may teach from different parts of the room depending on the instructional strategies and activities that are occurring. Mr. Ganther knows how to arrange the room for a productive learning environment and recognizes the benefits and limitations of some room arrangements. The ultimate goal is for learning to take place. Choice (B) is the correct response.

21. A

This question addresses information from PPR Competency 005:

The teacher knows how to establish a classroom climate that fosters learning, equity, and excellence and uses this knowledge to create a physical and emotional environment that is safe and productive.

Eliminate (B) because classroom organization, although desirable, is not necessarily a key factor that must be present for children to learn. Eliminate (C) because diversity is not an issue at this point. Choice (D) focuses entirely on organizational skills being the prime consideration in the classroom. It appears that Ms. Corning is more concerned about how the classroom looks and is meeting her own needs of organization rather than the emotional needs of the students. The teacher needs to create a safe, nurturing environment that addresses emotional and social needs and respects students' rights and dignity. Choice (A) is the correct response.

22. C

This question addresses information from PPR Competency 006:

The teacher understands strategies for creating an organized and productive learning environment and for managing student behavior.

Eliminate (A) because, while Mr. Sanchez probably does inform students of the activities it would be difficult for most students to remember all of the assignments if they are given at one time. In addition, it isn't addressing the transition problem. Eliminate (B) because instead of maximizing time, Mr. Sanchez should teach time management skills. Choice (D) only contributes to the problem. Mr. Sanchez should, however, get everyone's attention by having materials used for the language arts block put away before beginning the next subject. Choice (C) is the correct response.

23. C

This question addresses information from PPR Competency 006:

The teacher understands strategies for creating an organized and productive learning environment and for managing student behavior.

This is a priority-setting question. You are to determine the *most* likely benefit of the computer programs. Eliminate (A) because in-service hours are most likely not based on time spent on the computer. Eliminate (B) because, although being on a list serve or building a distribution list with other teachers is an advantage, this would not be the primary reason. Eliminate choice (D) because with Mr. Robbin's utilization of the complete program, the school district has most likely already given approval for its use. Teachers need to be aware of the timesaving programs that are available to help them with the administrative tasks such as taking attendance, grades, and communicating with parents. Choice (C) is the correct response.

24. B

This question addresses information from PPR Competency 006:

The teacher understands strategies for creating an organized and productive learning environment and for managing student behavior.

This is a priority-setting question asking you to select a choice that would be *incorrect*. Therefore, in this question we already know that three out of the four choices are correct. You are to determine the one thing a paraprofessional is not supposed to do. Keep (A) since personal care and physical needs are tasks provided if needed. Keep (C) because paraprofessionals do help with the interaction in a classroom. Choice (D) is a possibility if required. Paraprofessionals contribute a great deal to the classrooms; however, they should not create new, alternative instruction without the direction of the teacher or another certified individual. Choice (B) is the correct response.

25. C

This question addresses information from PPR Competency 006:

The teacher understands strategies for creating an organized and productive learning environment and for managing student behavior.

Eliminate (A) because asking questions concerning the story would have occurred during the shared reading time. Eliminate (B) because although Ms. Mehan is supposed to be monitoring, it wouldn't be to build friendships. Choice (D) would be inappropriate. Ms. Mehan's most important role is to monitor student behavior while the students are at the centers and provide an environment in which students are on-task and learning is occurring. Choice (C) is the correct response.

Practice EC–4 Pedagogy and Professional Responsibilities Test II Answers and Explanations

26. D

This question addresses information from PPR Competency 006:

The teacher understands strategies for creating an organized and productive learning environment and for managing student behavior.

This is a priority-setting question as you are to determine Mr. Matthew's *primary* problem of management. Eliminate (A) because it suggests that student leaders are to establish guidelines. Eliminate (B) because the parents are not responsible for the lack of order in the classroom. Eliminate choice (C) because it puts the responsibility on the administration. Mr. Matthew's form of governing might be effective if rules and procedures had been established along with his guidance. Because third-grade students study community, they need to know how groups of people work together, but Mr. Matthews initially will need to instill a sense of order. Choice (D) is the correct response.

27. D

This question addresses information from PPR Competency 006:

The teacher understands strategies for creating an organized and productive learning environment and for managing student behavior.

This is a priority-setting question as you are to determine what Mr. Mitchell is supposed to do about Roger's cheating. Eliminate (A) because studying harder may not alleviate Roger's main problem. Eliminate (B) because it reinforces the negative behavior. Choice (C) will continue to cause Roger more problems. Roger needs help, not competition. Mr. Mitchell should provide a spelling strategy that will help him with more difficult words, and pair him with a peer who can assist him. Choice (D) is the correct response.

28. A

This question addresses information from PPR Competency 006:

The teacher understands strategies for creating an organized and productive learning environment and for managing student behavior.

This is a priority-setting question. You are to determine the *best* strategy for disciplining Anand. Eliminate (B) because it suggests ignoring Anand. Undoubtedly, Ms. Carter has tried that strategy and did not have success. Eliminate (C) because embarrassing Anand in front of the class is not good educational practice. Choice (D) is an option if there were not a better choice. Having Ms. Carter keep track of the minutes wasted puts the burden on her, so providing coping strategies for Anand to use makes him the responsible person. Choice (A) is the correct response.

29. D

This question addresses information from PPR Competency 007:

The teacher understands and applies principles and strategies for communicating effectively in varied teaching and learning contexts.

This is a priority-setting question. You are to determine why Ms. Roland *most* likely exercised the management skill. Eliminate (A) because arranging the furniture is not left to the students. Eliminate (B) because the situation doesn't appear to be based on a pacing problem. Choice (C) mentions a flexible environment, but isn't dealing with the student's problem of turning over chairs. Instead of just telling Billy to put the chairs in back in the upright position, Ms. Roland tells Billy what she wants and then explains why she is asking him to carry out the task. In doing so she uses appropriate language skills. Choice (D) is the correct response.

30. D

This question addresses information from PPR Competency 007:

The teacher understands and applies principles and strategies for communicating effectively in varied teaching and learning contexts.

This is a priority-setting question as you are to decide which of the choices does not reflect higher-order thinking. When we think of higher-order thinking we think of Bloom's Taxonomy, which categorizes cognitive thinking into the following six categories: Knowledge, Comprehension, Application, Analysis, Synthesis, and Evaluation. The first three choices focus mainly on higher-order thinking skills. Choice (A) requires students to think critically, choice (B) requests students to relate what they know to other knowledge, and choice (C) asks students to think intuitively. All three ask students to inquire and make decisions, whereas choice (D) talks about factual information and requires students to remember facts. Choice (D) is the correct response.

31. C

This question addresses information from PPR Competency 007:

The teacher understands and applies principles and strategies for communicating effectively in varied teaching and learning contexts.

This is a priority-setting question. You are to determine what Ms. Lam is *mainly* demonstrating by the type of question she is asking. Eliminate (A) because, although we know that Ms. Lam wants her students to reflect, we don't have enough information to determine anything about the classroom atmosphere. Eliminate (B) because, although using apples does provide something with which students can relate, it is not of greatest importance. Choice (D) is the type of question the other teacher might ask, but it doesn't correlate with reflecting. Ms. Lam wants her students to think creatively and extend their content knowledge. She does this by asking higher-order thinking level questions. Choice (C) is the correct response.

32. B

This question addresses information from PPR Competency 007:

The teacher understands and applies principles and strategies for communicating effectively in varied teaching and learning contexts.

This is a priority-setting question asking you to select a choice that would be *incorrect*. Therefore, in this question we already know that three out of the four choices are correct. Keep choice (A) because, proceeding from a simple to a more complex concept is good teaching practice for all students. Keep (C) because most students, and particularly students with learning disabilities, would profit from this instructional practice. Keep (D), as it also is a must for all students, particularly those who may have a learning disability. However, asking students with learning disabilities to remain seated is in direct conflict with recommended procedures. Choice (B) is the correct response.

33. C

This question addresses information from PPR Competency 007:

The teacher understands and applies principles and strategies for communicating effectively in varied teaching and learning contexts.

Eliminate (A) because Rita is probably already trying hard, but just isn't confident enough to experiment with the English language in front of the whole class. Eliminate (B) because the goal is not to rush Rita, but for her to be successful. Choice (D) should be eliminated because it appears that Rita will need some assistance to encourage her to try speaking English. Leaving Rita alone, admonishing her in front of her peers, or taking her to a speech-language pathologist will not solve Rita's language problem. Ms. Davis can pair Rita with a helpful peer who can provide a comfort zone and afford her opportunities to try English. Choice (C) is the correct response.

34. D

This question addresses information from PPR Competency 007:

The teacher understands and applies principles and strategies for communicating effectively in varied teaching and learning contexts.

This is a priority-setting question as you are to decide the *primary* problem that occurs when the teacher asks questions. Eliminate (A) because, although it is not the best practice to call on just those students whose hands are raised, it is not the primary problem. Eliminate (B) because some questions can be open-ended questions that focus on problem solving. Eliminate (C) because, although it is good practice, it doesn't answer the question. However, it takes students time to digest the question that has been asked and to come up with an appropriate, plausible answer. Not all students formulate their answers or thoughts as quickly as others, which increases the need for wait time. Choice (D) is the correct response.

35. D

This question addresses information from PPR Competency 008:

The teacher provides appropriate instruction that actively engages students in the learning process

This is a priority-setting question asking you to select a choice that would be *incorrect*. Therefore, in this question we already know that three out of the four choices are correct. Keep (A) because placing students according to achievement levels is considered appropriate when putting students in cooperating learning groups. Keep (B) because it is appropriate to place students according to interests. Keep (C) because placing students who are culturally diverse will assist them as well as the other students in learning about their culture and facilitate the student's learning of the English language at a faster pace. Cooperating learning groups should be determined on the basis of the task and what will be required of the group. They can also be determined on the basis of interest and include students who are diverse. However, it is best not to determine cooperative groups on the basis of friendships. Choice (D) is the correct response.

36. B

This question addresses information from PPR Competency 008:

The teacher provides appropriate instruction that actively engages students in the learning process.

This is a priority-setting question. You are to determine what Mr. Ardito's *biggest* mistake might have been. Eliminate (A) since we do not have enough information to make this decision. Eliminate (C) because we already know that he is an effective teacher and that placing students in cooperative groups is an accepted form of working with students. Eliminate (D) because we aren't informed as to the grouping procedure that was implemented. Mr. Ardito became so involved in the one group that he completely let time get away from him. He should have monitored the pacing more closely so off-task behavior wouldn't have occurred. Choice (B) is the correct response.

37. A

This question addresses information from PPR Competency 008:

The teacher provides appropriate instruction that actively engages students in the learning process.

Eliminate (B), as a discussion is not taking place. Eliminate (C) because having fun may have been a result of the activity, but would not be the main reason for asking the questions. Eliminate (D) because Ms. Harlan is not concerned about ability when blowing marbles. Ms. Harlan's main purpose in providing this type of activity and in asking questions of students is to create a way for students to learn yet be actively involved in the process. She could have just talked about the lesson on force, but the students might not have understood it as well. By verbalizing the answers, they are involved in the lesson. Choice (A) is the correct response.

Practice EC–4 Pedagogy and Professional Responsibilities Test II Answers and Explanations

38. B

This question addresses information from PPR Competency 008:

The teacher provides appropriate instruction that actively engages students in the learning process.

This is a priority-setting question. You are to determine the *most* appropriate instructional strategy for intrinsically motivating students. Eliminate (A) because, although we want to build relationships with parents, Mr. Bates is the person who should be motivating students in the classroom. Eliminate (C) because it is a form of extrinsic motivating. Eliminate choice (D) because there is no guarantee that intrinsic motivation will occur. For students to become motivated intrinsically, the desire to learn must come from within. Instead of completing work for rewards, some students may need help in setting goals and then charting their progress. Choice (B) is the correct response.

39. C

This question addresses information from PPR Competency 009:

The teacher incorporates the effective use of technology to plan, organize, deliver, and evaluate instruction for all students.

This is a priority-setting question. You are to determine the *primary* reason Ms. Garcia uses technology jargon. Eliminate (A) because she isn't interested in impressing the students. Eliminate choice (B) because she will not stay current just by using the jargon. Choice (D) is a good practice but not the primary reason. All students are to have contact with technology, so Ms. Garcia wishes to have the students become familiar with computer terminology and does so when it is task appropriate and grade-level appropriate. She is demonstrating her basic knowledge and incorporating it in the classroom. Choice (C) is the correct response.

40. D

This question addresses information from PPR Competency 009:

The teacher incorporates the effective use of technology to plan, organize, deliver, and evaluate instruction for all students.

This is a priority-setting question. You are asked to determine the *main* reason for using a website that correlates with the state-adopted series. Eliminate (A) because the lessons suggested on the website are used only to extend previously planned instruction. Eliminate (B) because using technology in lessons does not meet the requirements for in-service meetings. Eliminate (C) because, while using technology is part of the TEKS objectives, incorporating a website will not necessarily keep students current. Teachers do benefit in using technology for some lessons and it does help them keep current, but the main reason for including technology is to extend the lessons with additional resources. In Mr. Castillo's case, the language arts program provided additional activities and students were able to benefit from these extensions. Choice (D) is the correct response.

41. C

This question addresses information from PPR Competency 009:

The teacher incorporates the effective use of technology to plan, organize, deliver, and evaluate instruction for all students.

This is a priority-setting question. You are to determine which activity would be *most* appropriate for a student in a kindergarten class. Eliminate (A) because, although some kindergarten students are able to read, many students are not ready for this skill. Eliminate (B) because if kindergarten students are to become familiar with the computer, just naming the parts of a computer would not be best practice or necessarily age appropriate. Choice (D) is a possibility but certainly not the main reason. Technology is a part of the kindergarten curriculum. Students are expected to use a variety of input devices and proper keyboarding techniques that are grade-level appropriate. Some students are capable of working on computer programs and reading, but the most appropriate activity for Ms. Mackie's kindergarten students would be to work on an activity that extends the current curriculum. Choice (C) is the correct response.

42. D

This question addresses information from PPR Competency 009:

The teacher incorporates the effective use of technology to plan, organize, deliver, and evaluate instruction for all students.

This is a priority-setting question. You are to determine the *most* appropriate activity. Eliminate (A) because the technology used corresponds to a low level of cognitive development. Eliminate (B) because students would just be finding an article and writing a report. Eliminate (C) because the students are using technology only to word process. Students would have little problem finding information on the Internet about the Alamo and creating timelines or reports, but the most interactive assignment would involve taking a virtual museum field trip and as a class collaborating on the creation of a brochure to recruit soldiers. Choice (D) is the correct response.

Practice EC–4 Pedagogy and Professional Responsibilities Test II Answers and Explanations

43. B

This question addresses information from PPR Competency 009:

The teacher incorporates the effective use of technology to plan, organize, deliver, and evaluate instruction for all students.

Eliminate (A) because developing word-processing skills would not be a major emphasis for the assignment. Eliminate (C) because another instructional strategy would be implemented to develop higher-order thinking skills. Eliminate (D) because, although Mr. Garlington does want the students interested in technology, the main emphasis is on the students. As a teacher, it is Mr. Garlington's responsibility to incorporate the effective use of current technology and implement activities that emphasize collaboration and teamwork, and at the same time integrate TEKS requirements. Mr. Garlington's meets these expectations when he makes the assignment to research the Internet and work in pairs to complete an assignment. Choice (B) is the correct response.

44. A

This question addresses information from PPR Competency 010:

The teacher monitors student performance and achievement; provides students with timely, high-quality feedback; and responds flexibly to promote learning for all students.

This is a priority-setting question asking you to select a choice that would be *least* important. Therefore, in this question we already know that three out of the four choices are correct. Keep (B) because goals and objectives should be evaluated for effectiveness. Keep (C) because providing for appropriate "wait time" is best practice. Keep (D) because a teacher may provide wonderful instruction, but the activities that follow might not be appropriate. Although it is important to stay on-target and use time efficiently, for Mr. Garlington to evaluate his lesson, he should be asking himself questions about the objectives and if they are appropriate for the students. He should make sure to factor in "wait time" so students are learning in a nurturing environment, and he needs to know if he used the right medium through which to teach the students. Choice (A) is the correct response.

45. B

This question addresses information from PPR Competency 010:

The teacher monitors student performance and achievement; provides students with timely, high-quality feedback; and responds flexibly to promote learning for all students.

This is a priority-setting question asking you to select a choice that would be *incorrect*. Therefore, in this question we already know that three out of the four choices are correct. Keep (A) because one of the major advantages of authentic assessment is the correlation to the curriculum. Keep (C) because authentic assessment is used to evaluate products and processes. Keep (D) because students can use results from the assessments to determine areas of needed growth. Teachers like to use authentic assessment because it relates to the specific curriculum they are using; however, it does not replace other forms of assessment that have definite purposes in which to measure students' abilities. Choice (B) is the correct response.

46. A

This question addresses information from PPR Competency 010:

The teacher monitors student performance and achievement; provides students with timely, high-quality feedback; and responds flexibly to promote learning for all students.

Eliminate (B) because the teacher should not be comparing Manny to another student. Eliminate (C) because time-out may be an effective means of discipline, but Manny needs to know the reason he is in time-out and then receive instructions on how he can and should make adaptations with his behavior. Eliminate (D) because Manny is an early-childhood student and is exhibiting behavioral characteristic of that age. Students at this stage of development like routines and sameness. Manny is probably not ready to change so quickly to another activity. The teacher can begin by giving him a little more time as he goes from one activity to another and hopefully he'll begin to make the transitions in the expected amount of time. Choice (A) is the correct response.

47. A

This question addresses information from PPR Competency 010:

The teacher monitors student performance and achievement; provides students with timely, high-quality feedback; and responds flexibly to promote learning for all students.

This is a priority-setting question as you are to determine the *ultimate* goal in selecting appropriate assessment tools. Eliminate (B) because, although Ms. Peterson wants all of her students to advance, the assessment tool should not be tied to that objective. Eliminate (C) because Ms. Peterson should not be comparing students' grades. Eliminate (D) because even though Ms. Peterson does have to satisfy standards developed by the district and the state, she wouldn't use that as the ultimate goal. Ms. Peterson must make sure that the assessment tools she uses measure the task the students are completing and that the tasks are congruent with the classroom goals and objectives. Choice (A) is the correct response.

Practice EC–4 Pedagogy and Professional Responsibilities Test II Answers and Explanations

48. C

This question addresses information from PPR Competency 011:

The teacher understands the importance of family involvement in children's education and knows how to interact and communicate effectively with families.

This is a priority-setting question. You are to determine the *most* important message that should be communicated to the parents. Eliminate (A) because Ms. Soto would be making the implication that the parents needed assistance from the family reach programs. Eliminate (B) because, even though Ms. Soto would like assistance, she should not be overly exuberant when recruiting help. Eliminate (D) because parent–teacher conferences are conducted on an individual basis. There are many things that Ms. Soto will want to talk about, but she needs to communicate the value of working together where everyone is involved in the students' learning. Choice (C) is the correct response.

49. C

This question addresses information from PPR Competency 011:

The teacher understands the importance of family involvement in children's education and knows how to interact and communicate effectively with families.

Eliminate (A) because the parents are not interested in assessing the students' reading skills themselves. Eliminate (B) because the terminology, even though helpful, is not their ultimate goal. Eliminate (D) because the parents aren't wishing to compare schools. If the parents are asking about websites, they already have some familiarity with the computer. They are requesting websites that will refer them to related topics and support in the area of reading. Choice (C) is the correct response.

50. B

This question addresses information from PPR Competency 012:

The teacher enhances professional knowledge and skills by effectively interacting with other members of the educational community and participating in various types of professional activities.

This is a priority-setting question as you are to determine the *primary* advantage of having a student teacher in the classroom. Eliminate (A) because, although helpful, there are greater advantages. Eliminate (C) because the time needed for additional certification should not be taken during school hours. Eliminate (D) because student teachers are not to be used as substitutes on a regular basis. There are many advantages to having a student teacher. It is true they are a second pair of hands, and in some schools they do allow the student teacher to substitute, but the primary advantage is the interaction between the student and cooperating teacher. Both have the opportunity to share the experience of teaching in a professional manner. The cooperating teacher and the student teacher share an opportunity to discuss pedagogy and instructional strategies. Choice (B) is the correct response.

51. A

This question addresses information from PPR Competency 012:

The teacher enhances professional knowledge and skills by effectively interacting with other members of the educational community and participating in various types of professional activities.

This is a priority-setting question for you are to determine the *primary* reason for the cooperation among participants involved in an IEP meeting. Eliminate (B) because leadership should already have been established. Eliminate (C) because there is no guarantee that parents will be satisfied at the end of an IEP meeting. Eliminate (D) because the IEP meeting is centered on an individual student and not teachers' problems. The primary goal of an IEP meeting is for everyone to share information concerning the student and their work toward developing goals that will help improve the performance of the student involved. Choice (A) is the correct response.

52. D

This question addresses information from PPR Competency 012:

The teacher enhances professional knowledge and skills by effectively interacting with other members of the educational community and participating in various types of professional activities.

Eliminate (A) because she didn't reveal personal information, just a personal quality. Eliminate (B) because Ms. Kincaid would probably not have selected the colleague if she thought the information shared in a private conversation would be told to others. Eliminate (C) because Nadia may not be able to change the nasal quality in her voice. Ms. Kincaid was having a difficult time working with a particular student, so she decided to seek the advice of a colleague. In doing so, she engaged in self-reflection and assessed her problems. In realizing the source of her irritability and in sharing the bias toward Nadia, she may be able to come up with solutions on how to deal with the situation. Choice (D) is the correct response.

Practice EC–4 Pedagogy and Professional Responsibilities Test II Answers and Explanations

53. C

This question addresses information from PPR Competency 012:

The teacher enhances professional knowledge and skills by effectively interacting with other members of the educational community and participating in various types of professional activities.

Eliminate (A) because there are reasons other than the presence of important speakers that merit going to the conference. Eliminate (B) because leaving the school for a needed rest is not a recommendation the principal should be offering. Eliminate (D) because the colleague may be going to different meetings than ones Mr. Caldwell would select. The principal should make sure Mr. Caldwell understands the importance of attending professional meetings to enhance his knowledge and skills, which in turn results in long-lasting benefits. Choice (C) is the correct response.

54. A

This question addresses information from PPR Competency 012:

The teacher enhances professional knowledge and skills by effectively interacting with other members of the educational community and participating in various types of professional activities.

This is a priority-setting question as you are to determine Ms. Jennings' *first* step in improving her evaluation. Eliminate (B) because it would not be professional to compare results. Eliminate (C) because, in going over the results by herself, Ms. Jennings may miss the most important areas of concern. Eliminate (D) because complaining about the results of her observation would not be professional. Ms. Jennings should make an appointment with the person who made the observation and go over the evaluation. She will receive feedback on specific areas of concern. Choice (A) is the correct response.

55. C

This question addresses information from PPR Competency 013:

The teacher understands and adheres to legal and ethical requirements for educators and is knowledgeable of the structure of education in Texas.

Eliminate (A) because the school is concerned only with the safety of the student. Eliminate (B) because the AUP policy is not providing unacceptable websites, but just a safeguard whereby the school will notify the student and parent if inappropriate behavior were to result. Eliminate (D) because there is no connection between signing the AUP and a parent–teacher night. Even though schools provide supervision, students are adept at using the Internet. In signing the Acceptable Use Policy, both students and parents are aware of the regulations when using the computer. Choice (C) is the correct response.

56. B

This question addresses information from PPR Competency 013:

The teacher understands and adheres to legal and ethical requirements for educators and is knowledgeable of the structure of education in Texas.

Eliminate (A) because parents are to be notified. Eliminate (C) because a person with special knowledge about the student may be invited to the IEP meeting. Eliminate (D) because parents may choose to have an independent evaluator assess their child and it is to be at no extra cost to the parents. Parents must give permission, however, before an evaluation is conducted so answer (C) is in violation. Choice (B) is the correct response.

57. D

This question addresses information from PPR Competency 013:

The teacher understands and adheres to legal and ethical requirements for educators and is knowledgeable of the structure of education in Texas.

This is a priority-setting question asking you to select a choice that would be *incorrect*. Therefore, in this question we already know that three out of the four choices are correct. Keep (A) because the room should be free of visuals that would interfere with Kurt's visibility. Keep (B) because the teacher should provide as much help as possible for a student who has difficulty with standard equipment. Keep (C) because the teacher may not know when Kurt will need additional assistance. Teachers who have visually impaired students in the classroom should make sure the student's visibility is not blocked and provide as many devices and aids as possible. However, they would not want to provide visual presentations in place of oral presentations because the student is visually impaired. Choice (D) is the correct response.

58. D

This question addresses information from PPR Competency 013:

The teacher understands and adheres to legal and ethical requirements for educators and is knowledgeable of the structure of education in Texas.

This is a priority-setting question. You are asked to determine the *most* appropriate course of action for Ms. Curtin. Eliminate (A) because the decision to become a counselor will be a personal choice. Eliminate (B) because the school counselor may have attended a different school and requirements change. Eliminate (C) because it could be a waste of time and money. Ms. Curtin's desire to become a counselor would require her to contact the State Board for Educator Certification (SBEC) to make sure she is aware of the exact requirements. She could then contact the university from where she will receive her certification to continue with her plans. Choice (D) is the correct response.

Practice EC–4 Pedagogy and Professional Responsibilities Test II Answers and Explanations

59. B

This question addresses information from PPR Competency 013:

The teacher understands and adheres to legal and ethical requirements for educators and is knowledgeable of the structure of education in Texas.

Eliminate (A) because the question doesn't pertain to specific steps a teacher should follow, but to confidentiality. Eliminate (C) because this has nothing to do with the No Child Left Behind Act. Eliminate (D) because FERPA involves the family but with other issues. The Code of Ethics specifically states that "the educator shall not harm others by knowingly making false statements about a colleague or the school system." In this case, Larry's teacher made a poor choice in talking about the GT teacher. Choice (B) is the correct response.

60. B

This question addresses information from PPR Competency 004:

The teacher understands learning processes and factors that impact student learning and demonstrates this knowledge by planning effective, engaging instruction and appropriate assessments.

This is a priority-setting question as you are asked to determine the *main* purpose in using familiarity of landmarks. Eliminate (A) because although these facts are important, it should not be the main reason. Eliminate (C) because, although history is Ms. Brown's favorite subject, that would not be the main purpose in discussing famous landmarks. Eliminate choice (D) because you don't have enough information on the type of questioning Ms. Brown is using. Ms. Brown wants to make sure the students have an opportunity to learn about resources in the community and how these contacts impact their learning. Choice (B) is the correct response.

61. D

This question addresses information from PPR Competency 008:

The teacher provides appropriate instruction that actively engages students in the learning process.

Eliminate (A) because the purpose of the strategy is to engage the students in learning. It is not to remember a number of personal facts. Eliminate (B) because, although Ms. Brown would like a smoothly functioning day, it wouldn't be the purpose of the exercise. Eliminate (C) because the students are writing about themselves. Ms. Brown will probably need to remind the students to look for historical landmarks at another time. Ms. Brown begins by modeling an autobiography before they begin to write their own stories. They have already been introduced to biographies so the lesson will be more relevant and meaningful. Choice (D) is the correct response.

62. C

This question addresses information from PPR Competency 008:

The teacher provides appropriate instruction that actively engages students in the learning process.

Eliminate (A) because historical information does not correlate with the importance of large-group discussion. Eliminate (B) because competition is inappropriate here. Eliminate (D) because informality is not a goal or objective for large discussions. Ms. Brown realizes the importance of varying the roles of teacher and student. She also understands that students will be more involved intellectually if they are engaged in the lessons. Choice (C) is the correct response.

63. D

This question addresses information from PPR Competency 011:

The teacher understands the importance of family involvement in children's education and knows how to interact and communicate effectively with families.

This is a priority-setting question. You are to determine the *primary* objective for the exercise. Eliminate (A) because the adults they are speaking to are their parents so risk-taking should not be a factor. Eliminate (B) because many students' parents have kept childhood records. Eliminate (C) because the teacher did not design the objectives around friendships. In requiring students to ask their parents or caregivers for information, Ms. Brown understands the importance of involving the family in the educational process. Choice (D) is the correct response.

64. D

This question addresses information from PPR Competency 004:

The teacher understands learning processes and factors that impact student learning and demonstrates this knowledge by planning effective, engaging instruction and appropriate assessments.

Eliminate (A) because, although this may turn out to be an advantage, it is not the main objective. Eliminate (B) because, although Ms. Brown is undoubtedly interested in how the room appears, she would have greater goals for the resulting product. Eliminate (C) because keyboarding practice is usually structured during computer time or at the computer lab. Ms. Brown wants this activity to be as self-directed as possible, for in doing for oneself, learning becomes more meaningful and students take a sense of ownership and pride in their accomplishment. Choice (D) is the correct response.

Practice EC–4 Pedagogy and Professional Responsibilities Test II Answers and Explanations

65. A

This question addresses information from PPR Competency 006:

The teacher understands strategies for creating an organized and productive learning environment and for managing student behavior.

Eliminate (B) as not all parents are qualified to help with proofreading skills. Eliminate (C) because the friend may not be knowledgeable about required deadlines. Eliminate (D) because, although Ms. Brown will monitor closely, she expects students to complete their own work. Ms. Brown shows she understands the need to communicate her expectations prior to the students' working on the computer to eliminate as many problems as possible. Choice (A) is the correct response.

66. B

This question addresses information from PPR Competency 002:

The teacher understands student diversity and knows how to plan learning experiences and design assessments that are responsive to differences among students and that promote all students' learning.

This is a priority-setting question. You are asked to decide which approach would *best* meet the needs of the GT students. Eliminate (A) because, although GT students are capable, they may not always want the responsibility of helping classmates. Eliminate (C) because the GT students need to have challenging assignments, and just bringing a book to read may not meet their needs. Eliminate (D) because the assignment is a lower-level form of cognitive development and not challenging for the students. Assignments for the Gifted and Talented students need to be challenging. Conducting additional interviews and then taping the assignment allows for a more meaningful activity than helping the other students, reading, or completing worksheets. Choice (B) is the correct response.

67. C

This question addresses information from PPR Competency 002:

The teacher understands student diversity and knows how to plan learning experiences and design assessments that are responsive to differences among students and that promote all students' learning.

Eliminate (A) because it would be better to adapt the assignment than to disregard it completely. Eliminate (B) because the students' parents may not be able to speak any English. Eliminate (D) because sharing background is not appropriate. By dictating their stories line by line, ELL students will have the opportunity to work at a slower pace and receive additional help as they work on their stories. Choice (C) is the correct response.

68. A

This question addresses information from PPR Competency 011:

The teacher understands the importance of family involvement in children's education and knows how to interact and communicate effectively with families.

This is a priority-setting question. You are asked to determine the *most* effective form of communication. Eliminate (B) because, although Ms. Brown would like to visit with each parent in a face-to-face conference, she would not find it to be effective use of her time. Eliminate (C) because Ms. Brown has no guarantee that the students will relay the information to their parents. Eliminate (D) because the task is not time effective. Sending progress reports home and requesting a signature is the most efficient form of communication. Choice (A) is the correct response.

69. B

This question addresses information from PPR Competency 010:

The teacher monitors student performance and achievement; provides students with timely, high-quality feedback; and responds flexibly to promote learning for all students.

This is a priority-setting question for you are to determine the *most* appropriate assessment technique. Eliminate (A) because a checklist will not be definitive and usually does not include standards of expected performance. Eliminate (C) because students do not always take home what the teacher has given to them. Eliminate (D) because Ms. Brown is not testing for factual information on each autobiography. Authentic assessment provides students with information on how they have completed the curricular portion of their studies. Rubrics are an excellent form of authentic assessment because criteria are established prior to the activity, and students know ahead of time what the requirements will be. Choice (B) is the correct response.

70. B

This question addresses information from PPR Competency 008:

The teacher provides appropriate instruction that actively engages students in the learning process.

This is a priority-setting question for you have been asked to determine the *main* reason for using previously read stories. Eliminate (A) because prior experience and prior learning are two different things. Eliminate (C) because students have not been asked to learn facts. Eliminate (D) because reading previously read stories encourages comprehension and understanding, so risk-taking should not be a factor. Students will have a greater understanding of the new multicultural literature because they have had prior exposure to stories involving different cultures when they were introduced to literature in their basals. Choice (B) is the correct response.

Practice EC–4 Pedagogy and Professional Responsibilities Test II Answers and Explanations

71. D

This question addresses information from PPR Competency 003:

The teacher understands procedures for designing effective and coherent instruction and assessment based on appropriate learning goals and objectives.

This is a priority-setting question. You have been asked to determine the *primary* purpose in formulating a structured unit. Eliminate (A) because, although students are introduced to a lot of content, it would not be the primary purpose in formulating the unit. Eliminate (B) because presenting content so students can experience bias is inappropriate. Eliminate (C) because, although the unit had been planned previously, Mr. Cummings will still need to evaluate his goals and objectives on a daily basis and readjust instructional strategies where needed. Mr. Cummings realizes the importance of planning the unit in a structured sequence so he can build on each lesson and then meet his stated goals and objectives. Choice (D) is the correct response.

72. B

This question addresses information from PPR Competency 009:

The teacher incorporates the effective use of technology to plan, organize, deliver, and evaluate instruction for all students.

Eliminate (A) because Mr. Cummings should not plan on using the lesson plans found on the Internet to substitute entirely for his own. Eliminate (C) because information on the Internet will not guarantee simplifying the teaching of art. Eliminate (D) because it suggests that Mr. Cummings is searching the Internet so he can submit his own lesson plans. While he may ultimately end up following through with this plan, it does not define the importance of acquiring information. Because technology plays such an important role in teaching, Mr. Cummings demonstrates he knows how to apply procedures for locating information on the Internet and to make sure it is accurate, appropriate, and congruent with what he plans to teach. Choice (B) is the correct response.

73. B

This question addresses information from PPR Competency 003:

The teacher understands procedures for designing effective and coherent instruction and assessment based on appropriate learning goals and objectives.

This is a priority-setting question for you are to determine Mr. Cumming's *main* purpose for incorporating a variety of material into the unit. Eliminate (A) because the teacher's goal is not to just have students occupied as they should be engaged and learning. Eliminate (C) because, although the students will get to experience more time in the library researching information, it would not be the main purpose for using a variety of materials. Eliminate (D) because students would not become experts in the short amount of time they will spend learning about a new culture. It is important during the multicultural unit for students to be given the opportunity to explore content from different perspectives. Choice (B) is the correct response.

74. B

This question addresses information from PPR Competency 002:

The teacher understands student diversity and knows how to plan learning experiences and design assessments that are responsive to differences among students and that promote all students' learning.

This is a priority-setting question asking you to select a choice that would be *incorrect*. Therefore, in this question we already know that three out of the four choices are correct. Keep (A) because the ELL student needs to hear discussion and vocabulary definitions. Keep (C) because illustrations help reinforce the content being covered. Keep (D) because role-playing is an excellent strategy for helping the ELL student. ELL students will profit from as much oral contact as possible, but writing vocabulary words and memorizing them would not actively engage them in the learning process. Choice (B) is the correct response.

Practice EC–4 Pedagogy and Professional Responsibilities Test II Answers and Explanations

75. A

This question addresses information from PPR Competency 004:

The teacher understands learning processes and factors that impact student learning and demonstrates this knowledge by planning effective, engaging instruction and appropriate assessments.

This is a priority-setting question. You are asked to determine the *primary* reason for having students develop personal narratives and then share them. Eliminate (B) because, although team-teaching has advantages, it would not be the primary reason for the activity. Eliminate (C) because recalling factual information is not an objective for the instructional strategy. Eliminate (D) because even though students may enjoy the act of storytelling, it would not be the primary reason. Teachers understand that creating stories, word processing them, and then sharing their creation with a buddy will help them connect what they are doing to something they have learned in the past, thus making their own activity more meaningful. Choice (A) is the correct response.

76. B

This question addresses information from PPR Competency 011:

The teacher understands the importance of family involvement in children's education and knows how to interact and communicate effectively with families.

Eliminate (A) because it is a negative response and the purpose of explaining unit expectations is not to limit parental involvement, but to detail expectations. Eliminate (C) because most students would not be complaining if they did not have enough homework. Eliminate choice (D) because it is not Mr. Cummings' responsibility to be a role model for the parents. Not all families have the means with which to purchase the latest technology, so Mr. Cummings shows awareness by indicating there are alternative ways to complete the assignment. Choice (B) is the correct response.

77. B

This question addresses information from PPR Competency 012:

The teacher enhances professional knowledge and skills by effectively interacting with other members of the educational community and participating in various types of professional activities.

This is a priority-setting question. You are to determine the *most* appropriate way to handle the situation of Mr. Art not wanting Brent paired with one of his students. Eliminate (A) because Brent would miss out on the instruction. Eliminate (C) because having Mr. Art come to observe Brent would not be an appropriate action. Eliminate (D) because bringing in the special education teacher would only magnify Brent's problem. Mr. Art is quite inappropriate when he asks Mr. Cummings not to pair Brent with one of his students. Mr. Cummings handles it nicely by telling him that he and Brent have developed a management system where Brent is now effectively working in the classroom, thus eliminating the need for any further action. Choice (B) is the correct response.

78. D

This question addresses information from PPR Competency 011:

The teacher understands the importance of family involvement in children's education and knows how to interact and communicate effectively with families.

This is a priority-setting question. You are to determine Mr. Cumming's *primary* consideration. Eliminate (A) because, although the recipe might be good and famous, it should not be the primary consideration. Eliminate (B) because other methods of nurturing should provide an atmosphere of acceptance for Jose. Eliminate (C) because even though the parents and grandparents may have a lot to offer and can share, it should not be the primary consideration. Mr. Cummings understands the importance of engaging the family in the educational process so he sanctions having Jose's grandmother come to the classroom. Choice (D) is the correct response.

79. C

This question addresses information from PPR Competency 013:

The teacher understands and adheres to legal and ethical requirements for educators and is knowledgeable of the structure of education in Texas.

Eliminate (A) because, although the issue of racial bias is not always an easy one to work with, Mr. Cummings felt the need to act on the situation. Eliminate (B) because it is not Mr. Cummings responsibility to monitor his colleague's attitudes on diversity. Eliminate (D) because it does not answer the question. Mr. Cummings is aware that racial bias exists, but he wishes to handle it in a professional manner and through the proper channels. Choice (C) is the correct response.

Practice EC–4 Pedagogy and Professional Responsibilities Test II Answers and Explanations

80. B

This question addresses information from PPR Competency 010:

The teacher monitors student performance and achievement; provides students with timely, high-quality feedback; and responds flexibly to promote learning for all students.

This is a priority-setting question. You are to determine the *main* reason for using interviews as a method of assessment. Eliminate (A) because although by conducting interviews Mr. Cummings will gain an understanding of how well he has presented objectives and goals, it is not the main reason. Eliminate (C) because, even though Mr. Cummings will make adjustments the next time he teaches a unit, he would not use the interviews to make those decisions. Choice (D) is an inappropriate type of assessment when evaluating the TEKS. In having students self-reflect on the assignment, they will have an opportunity to determine their own strengths and weaknesses and what they might need to focus on in the future. Choice (B) is the correct response.

Practice Test 2 Answers, EC-4 PPR Sorted by Competency

Question	Domain	Competency	Answer	Did You Answer Correctly?	Question	Domain	Competency	Answer	Did You Answer Correctly?
1	1	1	B		32	3	7	B	
2	1	1	B		33	3	7	C	
3	1	1	D		34	3	7	D	
4	1	1	B		35	3	8	D	
5	1	1	C		36	3	8	B	
6	1	1	B		37	3	8	A	
7	1	2	C		38	3	8	B	
8	1	2	D		61	3	8	D	
9	1	2	C		62	3	8	C	
10	1	2	A		70	3	8	B	
11	1	2	D		39	3	9	C	
66	1	2	B		40	3	9	D	
67	1	2	C		41	3	9	C	
74	1	2	B		42	3	9	D	
12	1	3	B		43	3	9	B	
13	1	3	A		72	3	9	B	
14	1	3	C		44	3	10	A	
71	1	3	D		45	3	10	B	
73	1	3	B		46	3	10	A	
15	1	4	D		47	3	10	A	
16	1	4	C		69	3	10	B	
17	1	4	A		80	3	10	B	
60	1	4	B		48	4	11	C	
64	1	4	D		49	4	11	C	
75	1	4	A		63	4	11	B	
18	2	5	D		68	4	11	D	
19	2	5	B		76	4	11	B	
20	2	5	B		78	4	11	D	
21	2	5	A		50	4	12	B	
22	2	6	C		51	4	12	A	
23	2	6	C		52	4	12	D	
24	2	6	B		53	4	12	C	
25	2	6	C		54	4	12	A	
26	2	6	D		77	4	12	B	
27	2	6	D		55	4	13	C	
28	2	6	A		56	4	13	B	
65	2	6	A		57	4	13	D	
29	3	7	D		58	4	13	D	
30	3	7	D		79	4	13	C	
31	3	7	C		59	4	13	B	

What competencies did you do well in?
What competencies do you need to work on?

Practice Test Three Answer Sheet

Remove (or photocopy) this answer sheet and use it to complete the practice test. (See answer key following the test when finished.)

1 Ⓐ Ⓑ Ⓒ Ⓓ	21 Ⓐ Ⓑ Ⓒ Ⓓ	41 Ⓐ Ⓑ Ⓒ Ⓓ	61 Ⓐ Ⓑ Ⓒ Ⓓ
2 Ⓐ Ⓑ Ⓒ Ⓓ	22 Ⓐ Ⓑ Ⓒ Ⓓ	42 Ⓐ Ⓑ Ⓒ Ⓓ	62 Ⓐ Ⓑ Ⓒ Ⓓ
3 Ⓐ Ⓑ Ⓒ Ⓓ	23 Ⓐ Ⓑ Ⓒ Ⓓ	43 Ⓐ Ⓑ Ⓒ Ⓓ	63 Ⓐ Ⓑ Ⓒ Ⓓ
4 Ⓐ Ⓑ Ⓒ Ⓓ	24 Ⓐ Ⓑ Ⓒ Ⓓ	44 Ⓐ Ⓑ Ⓒ Ⓓ	64 Ⓐ Ⓑ Ⓒ Ⓓ
5 Ⓐ Ⓑ Ⓒ Ⓓ	25 Ⓐ Ⓑ Ⓒ Ⓓ	45 Ⓐ Ⓑ Ⓒ Ⓓ	65 Ⓐ Ⓑ Ⓒ Ⓓ
6 Ⓐ Ⓑ Ⓒ Ⓓ	26 Ⓐ Ⓑ Ⓒ Ⓓ	46 Ⓐ Ⓑ Ⓒ Ⓓ	66 Ⓐ Ⓑ Ⓒ Ⓓ
7 Ⓐ Ⓑ Ⓒ Ⓓ	27 Ⓐ Ⓑ Ⓒ Ⓓ	47 Ⓐ Ⓑ Ⓒ Ⓓ	67 Ⓐ Ⓑ Ⓒ Ⓓ
8 Ⓐ Ⓑ Ⓒ Ⓓ	28 Ⓐ Ⓑ Ⓒ Ⓓ	48 Ⓐ Ⓑ Ⓒ Ⓓ	68 Ⓐ Ⓑ Ⓒ Ⓓ
9 Ⓐ Ⓑ Ⓒ Ⓓ	29 Ⓐ Ⓑ Ⓒ Ⓓ	49 Ⓐ Ⓑ Ⓒ Ⓓ	69 Ⓐ Ⓑ Ⓒ Ⓓ
10 Ⓐ Ⓑ Ⓒ Ⓓ	30 Ⓐ Ⓑ Ⓒ Ⓓ	50 Ⓐ Ⓑ Ⓒ Ⓓ	70 Ⓐ Ⓑ Ⓒ Ⓓ
11 Ⓐ Ⓑ Ⓒ Ⓓ	31 Ⓐ Ⓑ Ⓒ Ⓓ	51 Ⓐ Ⓑ Ⓒ Ⓓ	71 Ⓐ Ⓑ Ⓒ Ⓓ
12 Ⓐ Ⓑ Ⓒ Ⓓ	32 Ⓐ Ⓑ Ⓒ Ⓓ	52 Ⓐ Ⓑ Ⓒ Ⓓ	72 Ⓐ Ⓑ Ⓒ Ⓓ
13 Ⓐ Ⓑ Ⓒ Ⓓ	33 Ⓐ Ⓑ Ⓒ Ⓓ	53 Ⓐ Ⓑ Ⓒ Ⓓ	73 Ⓐ Ⓑ Ⓒ Ⓓ
14 Ⓐ Ⓑ Ⓒ Ⓓ	34 Ⓐ Ⓑ Ⓒ Ⓓ	54 Ⓐ Ⓑ Ⓒ Ⓓ	74 Ⓐ Ⓑ Ⓒ Ⓓ
15 Ⓐ Ⓑ Ⓒ Ⓓ	35 Ⓐ Ⓑ Ⓒ Ⓓ	55 Ⓐ Ⓑ Ⓒ Ⓓ	75 Ⓐ Ⓑ Ⓒ Ⓓ
16 Ⓐ Ⓑ Ⓒ Ⓓ	36 Ⓐ Ⓑ Ⓒ Ⓓ	56 Ⓐ Ⓑ Ⓒ Ⓓ	76 Ⓐ Ⓑ Ⓒ Ⓓ
17 Ⓐ Ⓑ Ⓒ Ⓓ	37 Ⓐ Ⓑ Ⓒ Ⓓ	57 Ⓐ Ⓑ Ⓒ Ⓓ	77 Ⓐ Ⓑ Ⓒ Ⓓ
18 Ⓐ Ⓑ Ⓒ Ⓓ	38 Ⓐ Ⓑ Ⓒ Ⓓ	58 Ⓐ Ⓑ Ⓒ Ⓓ	78 Ⓐ Ⓑ Ⓒ Ⓓ
19 Ⓐ Ⓑ Ⓒ Ⓓ	39 Ⓐ Ⓑ Ⓒ Ⓓ	59 Ⓐ Ⓑ Ⓒ Ⓓ	79 Ⓐ Ⓑ Ⓒ Ⓓ
20 Ⓐ Ⓑ Ⓒ Ⓓ	40 Ⓐ Ⓑ Ⓒ Ⓓ	60 Ⓐ Ⓑ Ⓒ Ⓓ	80 Ⓐ Ⓑ Ⓒ Ⓓ

CHAPTER FOURTEEN

Practice 4–8 Pedagogy and Professional Responsibilities Test III

Decision Set Begins Here

The following letter was sent to a fifth-grade teacher from the parents of a student:

> Dear Teacher:
>
> Our son complains about homework every night. It is a battle to get him to sit down to do the work. Once he begins, he complains that he does not understand the assignment. We want to do what is best for Jerry. Can you please give us some direction about what we should do?
>
> Sincerely,
> Mr. and Mrs. Johnson

1. What is the *best* thing for the teacher to do?

    A. Meet with the student and ask him to explain why the homework is such a problem and contact the parents to explain what the student told her in the teacher–student conference.

    B. Meet with the building principal and ask her for a suggestion on how to handle this situation with the parents.

    C. Modify the homework assignments for this student and give him work that is easier to complete so that the parents will not be faced with the nightly battle over homework.

    D. Contact the parents and set up a parent–teacher–student conference for the teacher to go over the homework policy and discuss possible solutions with the parents after hearing from the student.

2. The teacher looks at her homework assignments for that week and sees that the homework assignments in math cover adding fractions with like denominators. She has been teaching fractions in class and her objective is for students to add fractions with like denominators. She wants to make sure that:

   A. the objectives for her instruction and her homework assignments are congruent and that the students are not being expected to work problems independently at home that are too difficult.
   B. the math homework is at a level just above what the students can work in class because this will provide them with motivation.
   C. the lessons she plans for the class are challenging and require them to apply skills that have not yet been introduced in the classroom.
   D. the homework assignments and the classroom instruction are congruent and the lessons taught in the classroom introduce the concepts after students first have an opportunity to work the problems at home.

3. Later during the week a new student enters the teacher's classroom. The new student is from Vietnam and is fluent in both English and Vietnamese. The teacher is delighted to have this student in her classroom, primarily so that:

   A. she will be able to talk to his parents in parent–teacher conferences without the need for the district to hire an interpreter.
   B. she had a good friend who was killed in the Vietnam conflict and she wants to learn more about the country and the war that took a loved one.
   C. she can talk to the student about Vietnamese culture and improve her own knowledge of his culture and background.
   D. she will not have to modify her lessons to accommodate his learning because the other students in her class are all English speakers and do not require any adaptations.

4. The students in the class welcome the new student and he is quickly making new friends. This is important because the teacher knows that for middle school students:

   A. peers relationships play an important role and having good friends and peer acceptance is important for success in school.
   B. having friends means that students are less likely to be risk takers and troublemakers.
   C. peers can often help a new student follow the school rules and teach the new student the classroom rules so that behavior management is not a problem.
   D. the parents rarely know what is happening at school and having friends will provide the new student a group to depend on for assignments and information.

Decision Set Ends Here

GO ON TO THE NEXT PAGE

Decision Set Begins Here

The new social studies teacher is planning to teach a unit on Texas. He begins planning the unit by examining the TEKS and thinking about the unit's goals and objectives. He wants all of the students to enjoy the unit and learn about the state they live in. However, it is a week into the unit, and many students are struggling.

5. Which of the following is *best* for the teacher to try?

    A. Have the students outline the chapter in the book on the history of Texas so that they can show that they are reading the chapters.
    B. Assign homework for the students to read the chapter on the history of Texas and write a summary of the chapter.
    C. Have the students write an essay titled "What I know about Texas" so that the teacher can use this as a type of assessment to see what prior knowledge the students have about the state and connect new knowledge to existing knowledge.
    D. Pull the students having trouble out of the unit and let them work on another unit until they can learn to catch up with the rest of the class.

6. As the teacher plans the activities for the unit, which of the following activities would develop higher-order thinking?

    A. Watching the movie *The Alamo* and discussing it in class with a group of peers.
    B. Making a timeline of the history of the state of Texas from the beginning of Texas as a republic until it became a state.
    C. Defining the terms in the book that are in italics and putting them in your social studies dictionary.
    D. Presenting a short skit with your group depicting what problems faced the early Texans and how they coped with these problems.

Decision Set Ends Here

7. The students in the seventh grade range in height from 4 feet to 6 feet. School picture day is coming and the students are to be lined up from tallest to shortest so that the photographer can quickly take the group picture with the tallest students standing in the back. The seventh-grade teacher goes to the principal and requests that this not be done because he knows:

   A. students at this age are focused on their self-image and this procedure will do more harm than good by calling attention to those students who have had a growth spurt and those who have not.
   B. students in middle school are not babies and will be happy to line up in the appropriate place when asked to do so.
   C. asking students to line up this way is very disruptive to the classroom instruction and the teacher does not want to waste instructional time by having the students do this.
   D. because the tallest students were in the back of the picture last year, students have requested that this year the short students sit on the top step of the bleachers with the taller students kneeling in front.

8. The middle school math teacher is a first-year teacher. She is a chaperone for the fall dance in the school cafeteria. The night of the dance she notices that among almost all of the couples dancing, taller girls are dancing with shorter boys. She knows this is because:

   A. the older girls in middle school are the ones who will ask the younger boys to dance.
   B. girls at this age have a growth spurt almost two years before boys and will be taller, stronger, and more mature than the boys.
   C. girls in the eighth grade are usually more mature and taller than the boys in the sixth grade.
   D. taller boys are embarrassed by their height and do not want to go out on the dance floor and dance.

9. A parent has asked the classroom teacher how this middle school is different from the junior high school she attended as a student. She has never had a student in middle school and wonders if this is just a new name for the old junior high school. The classroom teacher does NOT list which of the following as a trait of the middle school concept?

   A. Subject centered
   B. Allows for flexible scheduling with large blocks of time
   C. Organizes teachers into interdisciplinary teams with a common planning period
   D. Emphasizes both affective and cognitive development of students

10. Because the math teacher knows that most middle-level students are at the concrete operational stage of cognitive development, she uses knowledge of this developmental characteristic to plan lessons. Which lesson is *best* for these students?

    A. Students at the concrete operational stage of cognitive development learn best when the instruction is in a lecture format.
    B. Students at the concrete operational stage of cognitive development learn best when asked to read the text and then discuss it in class.
    C. Students at this stage of cognitive development learn abstract concepts best by having the information presented to them visually by the teacher. An overhead projector works well.
    D. Students at this stage of cognitive development learn abstract concepts best through the use of hands-on learning and so manipulatives would be excellent to use in math.

11. Several students in the fourth-grade classroom come from very low socioeconomic status homes. Two are homeless and two live with relatives. None of these students have any prior experience with computers. The classroom teacher believes that all of the children should learn to use a computer and requires them to use the computer for a research project. An aide is available for part of the day and monitors the students working on three computers in the classroom. What is the *best* way for the teacher to help these students?

    A. Modify the research project for these students so that they do not have to use the computer for research but will just use the encyclopedias in the school library.
    B. Contact the parents and ask that they take the students to the public library where computers are available and learn some computer skills.
    C. Have the aide do the computer search for the students so that they do not take too much time on the computer.
    D. Plan some direct instruction lessons for these students to teach them specific computer skills that will then allow them to use the computer as a research tool.

12. The eighth-grade teacher spends the beginning of each year getting to know each student in her classroom. She observes how the students process information and then tries to plan differentiated instruction for students who need assistance with learning. Which of the following is the *best* differentiated instruction?

    A. Use whole-class instruction so that all of the students understand the concepts being taught.
    B. Modify the amount of time available for some students to complete an assignment.
    C. Realize that some students will not grow academically and having expectations about those students will only end in disappointment
    D. Have parents read over the assignments with the students at home in order to assist their learning.

13. An eighth-grade teaching team is working together planning a unit on Liberia. The students read the novel *Beyond the Mango Tree*, a book about a young girl from Boston living in Liberia with her parents. What is the *best* way for the teachers to plan to integrate social studies into the unit?

   A. List the content that each class needs to cover.
   B. Decide what students will write about for English and what facts need to be learned for social studies and combine these.
   C. Develop a list from the social studies textbook and the English textbook and plan to build a unit about these with the novel as the centerpiece.
   D. Examine themes and skills that overlap English and social studies and would be meaningful to middle school students.

14. In planning the unit the teachers want to use other resources to help the students learn about the country of Liberia. Which of the following resources would be *least* effective?

   A. A graduate student at the university who is from Liberia and who has agreed to talk to the class.
   B. The World Wide Web where students can research Liberia.
   C. Primary resources such as letters written by Liberians and newspapers from Liberia.
   D. A social studies textbook.

15. The science teacher is setting up her classroom for a simulated inquiry science lesson comparing whale blubber, feathers, and skin to determine the best insulator in cold water. Students will be placed in small cooperative learning groups. Each group will have a stop watch, plastic bags with blubber and feathers in them, and a container of ice water. What is the *least* important consideration in setting up the desks in the classroom for this lesson?

   A. Safety
   B. Accessibility
   C. Visibility
   D. Permanence

16. The emotional climate of the classroom is important for student learning. The sixth-grade teacher wants to assess the climate of the classroom. What is the *best* way to determine if the classroom climate is conducive to learning?

   A. Examine the end–of-year results on the Texas Assessment of Knowledge and Skills (TAKS) and use those statistics as feedback about the climate.
   B. Observe if the students are working on-task for a majority of the instructional time.
   C. Examine the interactions between the teacher and the students and see if there is mutual respect and a nurturing of all students.
   D. Examine the strategies that are used in the classroom.

GO ON TO THE NEXT PAGE

17. The seventh-grade English teacher wants to let his students know how much he expects of them. What is the *best* way to communicate those high expectations?

   A. "I know you will do well on this assignment because you know a lot about this topic and are interested in it. We will be covering this information through various activities that you can choose among and in ways that you will feel are important to you."
   B. "I know that you will do wonderfully on this assignment because your teacher last year told me she covered the concept very thoroughly."
   C. "I know you will do well today because your mid-term report cards will be out next week and this is the last assignment for you to do well on to bring up your grades."
   D. "I know you will do well on this assignment because I have covered it well and expect you to refer to the notes we took yesterday."

18. The fourth-grade teacher is a first-year teacher and is having difficulty with behavior management. She talks with her mentor and is given advice. Which of the following is the *least* likely to help with the problem?

   A. Have three to five rules for behavior management created by students and teacher.
   B. Wait several weeks before she begins to enforce the rules and consequences.
   C. Present and explain the rules and consequences on the first day of school.
   D. By day three, have the students practice the appropriate behavior through role playing.

19. Later that month the fourth-grade teacher wants to monitor how well her behavior plan is working. She can accomplish this *best* by:

   A. recording behaviors and responses on a behavior log spreadsheet with the students' names, date, time, and the teacher responses. Analyze the patterns and responses.
   B. seeing if the same students are always having consequences and modify the reward system for them.
   C. asking the class to respond to the question, "What do you like about our rules?"
   D. requiring the students with behavior problems to write a paper about the problem and the solution. Send these papers to the parents.

20. The science teacher has few behavior problems in the science lab. Students begin on time and finish on time. What method would help a teacher establish this time-on-task in the classroom so that time is not wasted?

   A. Post the time allowed for each project or assignment, and then at given intervals post how much time is remaining on the chalk board.
   B. Penalize students who do not finish an assignment on time by deducting points for every minute that they require to finish.
   C. Require that unfinished work be taken home and finished for homework.
   D. Reduce the time students have at computer lab for every minute that they spend in finishing assigned work.

21. A fifth-grade teacher is correcting a student who has broken a class rule by damaging school property. The student responds, "I didn't do it." The teacher saw the student scratch an initial on the desk. The teacher should say:

   A. "I know you did it. Why do you say you did not do it?"
   B. "I know you did it. I saw you do it. The consequence for this is to repair the damaged desk or pay for it. We will discuss your choice after school."
   C. "I saw you writing initials on the desk. Let's go down to the principal's office and talk about this."
   D. "I know you did it. But this time I will not penalize you because that is a banged up old desk anyway."

22. The seventh-grade math teacher is not pleased with the quality of work that some of the students are turning in for a grade. He has tried to communicate what he wants the students to know and do. Which communication would be *best*?

   A. "I want you to try and remember the following things in order to raise your grade on the next math papers." He verbally lists 8 to 12 things to remember.
   B. "Let's improve these scores. I want you to help me make a rubric to use for your math papers."
   C. "I think some of you will get a real surprise when you get back your next math grade!"
   D. "Does this look like an A paper to you? I don't think so!"

23. As part of a discussion about current affairs in Liberia, the teacher wants her students to problem-solve ways that Liberia can recover from the recent civil unrest. What is the *best* question to ask?

    A. "What ways can you think of that the government in Liberia can prevent the civil unrest? Remember that there is not one correct answer to a question like this. Let me hear your thoughts about this complex question."
    B. "I know that you all have wonderful ideas about ways to make Liberia a safe place today. Give me your best idea."
    C. "What do you think, class? I can think of at least four ways to make Liberia safer. One way rhymes with the word "goat." Tell me some ways."
    D. "I want everyone to think about this for a few minutes. No talking. Then we will write the best ideas on the board. Later, we can send these in a letter to the government."

24. After the opening activity each morning, the sixth-grade teacher has the students work on an assignment in their learning logs. Learning logs are a type of journal. Today the learning log topic is "irregular fractions." What is the *most* effective way for the teacher to communicate the assignment to the students?

    A. Write the term "irregular fractions" on the board and ask the students to write all they know about this term in their learning logs.
    B. Tell the students to go to the glossary of their math books and copy the definition of this term. Then check that definition with the class dictionaries.
    C. Write the assignment on an overhead transparency and read it to the students. Then turn off the projector while students continue to work.
    D. Write the assignment on a chart tablet and place the chart on an easel stand where everyone can see it. Read the assignment to the class and then ask for questions before work begins.

25. The seventh-grade Texas history teacher on the middle school team uses different instructional techniques throughout the year. For the next unit, she wants students to be actively engaged in learning. Which instructional technique is *most* likely to produce active, involved learning?

    A. Direct instruction
    B. Didactic instruction
    C. Inquiry instructional
    D. Traditional instruction

26. Throughout the unit, the Texas history teacher plans to team with the English language arts teacher. Students will be writing persuasive speeches for Texas heroes for English class and will be researching Texas missions and the Battle of the Alamo for social studies. Which of the following grouping patterns will be *most* effective?

   A. Students will be assigned to a group for the duration of the unit. The students will work in ability-groups. The gifted and talented students will work together and the lower performing students will work together.
   B. Students will not be placed in groups by the teacher. Each day students will be able to choose whom they want to work with for that day. Students who cannot work with peers will work alone.
   C. Each teacher will use flexible instructional groupings. Heterogeneous groups will work together some days and other days the teachers will pull together a homogeneous group for work on some specific skill or concept that these students need to learn.
   D. Students will be grouped homogeneously for English and work with the teacher for a portion of the period. In social studies, students will vote on who will be in each group.

27. To begin the unit on comparing fractions with different denominators, the fourth-grade teacher can *best* link this new knowledge with prior knowledge by saying:

   A. "Last year in third grade you learned something about fractions. Who can tell me what you learned?"
   B. "If I have one half of a bag of popcorn and you have a full bag of popcorn, who has the most? What if you eat half of your popcorn?"
   C. "I've brought in this pizza today and will be using it to help you compare fractions with different denominators. Let's look at the whole pizza first. If I cut it into two pieces what will my denominator be? What if I cut it into four pieces?"
   D. "My objective today is for you to be able to compare two fractions with different denominators. Does anyone have a question so far?"

Practice 4–8 Pedagogy and Professional Responsibilities Test III

Decision Set Begins Here

About Me Container

Purpose
The About Me Container is a vehicle for helping you to introduce yourself to your classmates. It is also a means for building community in the classroom.

Directions

1. Gather six objects that represent you as a person. One artifact must be your favorite book. See the rubric for more details.
2. Place the artifacts in a container.

Rubric

	Criteria	Self-evaluation	Teacher Evaluation
Artifacts	• Six artifacts are included. • The individual explains how the artifact represents him or her. • Artifacts are appropriate for sharing. • The container holding the artifacts is decorated.	/4	/4
Building community through sharing	• The Me Box is shared with classmates on the due date. • Students answer questions posed by peers.	/2	/2
Total		/6	/6
Comments			

GO ON TO THE NEXT PAGE

Each year the fifth-grade language arts teacher has class members introduce themselves the first few days of school through the use of an "About Me Container." The teacher uses the rubric above to grade the students' presentations.

28. What is the *best* way for the teacher to communicate the assignment to the students on the first day of school?

   A. The teacher explains each section of the rubric and discusses how to read the rubric and the points for each section.
   B. The teacher provides the students with the rubric and tells them to take it home and read it over to understand what is expected of them for the assignment.
   C. The teacher models the process by introducing himself using a tackle box with six artifacts. He explains that he is an avid fisherman and then presents six artifacts that represent his family, the book *Sounder*, and his career as a teacher. Students "grade" his presentation with a rubric.
   D. The teacher explains to the students that if he were doing an About Me Container, it would be a tackle box because he loves to fish. Inside the box he would have a picture of his family, a picture of his dog, a drawing of his favorite tree, and three of his favorite books.

29. What is the purpose of providing students with a rubric prior to an assignment or project?

   A. It provides the students with directions for doing the project so that the assignment is clear.
   B. It ensures that the assessment is congruent with the instructional objectives and communicates the assessment criteria standard to students.
   C. It is a good way to prevent parents from complaining about the grading procedures used by a classroom teacher.
   D. It is norm-referenced assessment that is much more valid than those usually used in middle school classes.

30. The teacher includes a section on the rubric entitled "Self-evaluation" for each student to self-evaluate the presentation prior to presenting it to classmates. What is the *most* likely reason for having students do a self-assessment?

   A. Students will remember to put in the correct number of artifacts.
   B. Students will have the assignment in writing so those students with a learning disability will be less likely to forget the assignment.
   C. It becomes an artifact of the school year for the teacher to use in parent–teacher conferences. By sharing the rubric, the parents will be familiar with the assignment.
   D. Students become self-directed learners. Their motivation is improved; they become more responsible and take ownership of the project.

31. As part of the student presentations, the teacher uses the digital video camera to record each student's presentation. The teacher records the first student presentation. The first student then records the second presenter, with assistance from the teacher. This procedure continues with each student recording the next student. This shows that:

    A. the teacher likes to have students learn to use technology because it makes learning fun.
    B. the teacher knows how to incorporate the effective use of technology into his teaching and to emphasize teamwork in practice activities from the Technology Applications in the TEKS.
    C. the teacher gets very tired of recording each student so he learned to share the task with students.
    D. the teacher knows how to evaluate students' technologically produced products related to the content delivery.

32. Later, the teacher edits each of the student's presentations into a collage of "All About Us" for the first Parent Night Meeting. At that time, he shows the 10-minute collage and explains in a slide presentation his curriculum plans for the year. Creating this multimedia presentation *best* illustrates:

    A. the teacher's desire to have parents understand the school year ahead.
    B. the teacher's ability to use productivity tools to communicate information in various formats.
    C. the desire to present the curriculum to parents so that there would be fewer questions later in the year.
    D. the love of technology that this teacher possesses.

33. Prior to showing the multimedia presentation, the teacher sends home notes to all parents and guardians requesting permission to include their children in the final presentation. He also has each student sign a permission form to be included in the final presentation to parents. One family refuses to allow their daughter to be a part of the presentation. The teacher should:

    A. contact the parents and ask them why they object to having the daughter participate in the recording.
    B. ask the daughter to discuss it with her parents and see if that might change their minds.
    C. remove any pictures of that student from the recording through the editing process.
    D. disregard the parents' note because not being in the recording will make the student feel that she is not part of the learning community.

Decision Set Ends Here

34. The band director at the middle school plans to work on marches for Monday's class. On Saturday, he meets a well-known country–western musician, George Strait, who offers to come to the band class on Monday. He would perform a few numbers with the band and answer questions about writing country music. What is the *best* response from the band director?

   A. "What a teachable moment! My students love country music. This is a true opportunity. I'd love to have you come Monday."
   B. "The TEKS don't really cover country music. I appreciate your offer but will have to pass. My students' learning comes first."
   C. "Great! I love your music and the principal will be out of town Monday and will never know I didn't teach my lesson plan."
   D. "Oh! Could you also do a bit of music that includes marches? That's my plan for Monday. If so, I'd love to have you come to class."

35. The seventh-grade team believes in using many types of assessment. They all use student portfolios with their classes. Students select items to place in the portfolio and teachers can also add work to the portfolio. Some items student place in the portfolio include student-selected goals, journal entries, teachers' comments, computer projects, and book reviews. The team believes the *main* value of portfolios is to:

   A. teach students organizational skills by keeping their work together in the portfolio.
   B. provide the teacher with examples of students' work to share with parents during conferences.
   C. provide a form of assessment that does not require as much preparation as traditional tests.
   D. promote self-assessment and feedback that will enhance the students' own learning.

36. The new sixth-grade teacher is not sure how to communicate with her students' parents and guardians. She talks to her mentor and gets some ideas. Which idea is *best*?

   A. You will be having parent conferences every six weeks; that is sufficient contact.
   B. Put together a monthly newsletter that you send out on a regular basis. Student work could be included and students could assist in publishing the newsletter.
   C. Send home a note asking for each family's e-mail address and provide the families with your e-mail address so they can contact you.
   D. Phone parents when students do something especially terrible or something especially wonderful.

37. During parent–teacher conferences, the science teacher shares a student's portfolio with that student's parents or guardians. What is the *best* way to make the parents feel a part of the child's learning?

   A. Remove any poor work from the portfolio because parents tend to focus on the negative and miss the positive.
   B. Suggest that the parents respond to the portfolio on a "Parents' Comments" page because parents often have valuable insights about their child.
   C. Have the parents take home any work that they believe needs additional effort. They can then work on the paper with the student.
   D. Begin the conference by welcoming the parents and thanking them for coming. Then, discuss negative information you want to share with the parents.

38. Many middle schools are not organized by disciplines. Instead they are organized into teaching teams. Language arts, science, social studies, and math teachers at the same grade level are a team and share the same student population. For teaming to work, teachers must share:

   A. information about how students perform in their class with the other teachers.
   B. common planning times in order to plan interdisciplinary units.
   C. the same philosophy of education.
   D. information with the families about how the team operates.

39. The sixth-grade social studies teacher shows a video about North American societies. A portion of the video focuses on the number of homeless families. A student runs out of the room crying. Other students explain that the student's family was evicted from their apartment and is living in the family car. The student would benefit *most* by the teacher doing which of the following?

   A. Contact the parents by sending a note, and ask them what assistance is needed.
   B. Inform the team that a student's family is having financial difficulties and suggest that they have the students do a project to raise money for the family.
   C. Arrange for the school counselor to meet with the student and ask that the school social worker contact the parents.
   D. Contact the Texas Child Protective Services and report the family for not providing sufficient food, shelter, and clothing for the student.

40. According to the copyright laws, teachers are entitled to "fair use" of certain copyrighted materials. The science teacher scans several pictures from library books to use in a multimedia presentation about tectonic plates. Which of the following is NOT "fair use"?

   A. He includes the multimedia presentation on a DVD he is publishing.
   B. He presents the multimedia presentation to the students in his classes for the next two years.
   C. He presents the multimedia presentation at the state science conference.
   D. He includes the presentation in his teaching portfolio.

41. As part of a group project, the seventh-grade English teacher has placed students into cooperative learning groups. She is teaching needed social skills, such as how to disagree with another person's ideas, to the class prior to beginning the cooperative learning groups. She believes this is important because:

   A. students at this age are just entering the concrete development stage of cognitive development and these are skills that students can easily learn.
   B. at this stage of cognitive development, students must begin to learn skills that will extend into the world beyond the school.
   C. students' behaviors will be improved if they know how to disagree.
   D. this is part of cooperative learning and will become part of each student's grade.

42. The sixth-grade teacher has instituted a plan in his classroom called, "I'm going to tell on you!" The goal of the plan is to contact all of the students' parents often to tell them things their child did well in school. The teacher believes this is important because he knows that:

   A. students at this stage of development will experience feelings of guilt rather than initiative if they are not successful.
   B. students at this age will develop a sense of industry rather than inferiority if they experience satisfaction.
   C. students like middle school teachers who are fun and who don't get them in trouble at home.
   D. students in middle school have experienced very punitive rules in elementary school and he wants them to be motivated to work for him.

GO ON TO THE NEXT PAGE

43. The health teacher does not allow students to wear any types of hats or bandannas in his classroom and requires that all tattoos be covered. A parent wants to know why he has these rules. He explains to the parents that:

   A. taking hats off inside is good manners and that he does not want to glorify tattoos because it is a form of risky behavior that can cause hepatitis C.
   B. experience teaching has taught him that if students follow rules in classrooms they will be more likely to follow rules of society.
   C. risky behaviors such as gang involvement affect learning and these requirements prevent many gang-related symbols, such as hats, tattoos, and bandannas, from being evident in his classroom.
   D. students get focused on all of these items and tend not to pay attention to the instruction.

44. Students begin the school year in the sixth grade by writing out "My goals for the day." After the first few months of school the teachers initiate "My goals for this week." These goals are word processed and stapled in the front of each student's folder that goes home each week. By the end of the year, some students are writing long-term personal and academic goals. Why do the teachers use valuable instructional time to teach students this skill?

   A. The teachers know that it is important for middle school students to learn and apply organizational and goal-setting skills.
   B. Having students set short-term goals will provide parents with information about how well the student is doing in school.
   C. This process, first thing in the morning, provides the teacher with a writing sample and helps students think of what they want to work on that day.
   D. Students who learn to set long-term goals will be the students who stay out of trouble.

45. The seventh-grade teacher has just completed a meeting with the parents of one of her students. The parents are a gay couple and want to know how the student is doing in school. They explain that they adopted the child at birth and are really proud of the student. After the conference, the teacher goes to her mentor and expresses some surprise that the child comes from a gay family. The *best* response for the mentor teacher is:

   A. "Oh no! That always makes me feel a bit uncomfortable because it is a situation I am not used to dealing with."
   B. "Just pretend that they are a heterosexual couple."
   C. "Does the student have many friends in school or is this diverse family affecting her learning?"
   D. "How wonderful that they are so involved in her education. You should be pleased whenever students have that type of support."

46. The sixth-grade teachers host a "Culture Fair" each spring. As part of the culture fair students learn about the cultures represented in their diverse school community. The grocer is from Germany. The laundry is operated by a Taiwanese family, and many other cultures are represented by shop owners. The students work in teams to interview various businesses in the community and then plan foods and activities for the "Culture Fair" that represent each culture. The students learn interviewing skills and research the various cultures for recipes and games. This has become an event the entire community and school look forward to and participate in each year. The teachers' *main* purpose in providing this experience is to:

   A. teach the students research and interviewing skills.
   B. use the diversity in the community to enrich students' learning experiences.
   C. provide the students with a reward for all of the good work they completed.
   D. provide the community with an opportunity to meet students from the sixth grade.

47. The eighth-grade team, science, social studies, math, and language arts, has a student with a hearing impairment. Each teacher is equipped with a microphone headset and the student wears a receiver that amplifies the teachers' voices. The teachers also try to adapt the instruction in ways to assist the student with the hearing impairment. Which of the following adaptations is NOT effective?

   A. Provide modifications to the process of using videos by using captioned videos in the classrooms.
   B. Provide modifications to the learning environment by arranging the desks so that the hearing-impaired student can see the face of the person speaking.
   C. Provide modifications to the learning content by using visuals to accompany teachers' instruction and discussions.
   D. Provide modifications to the product by having the student write information rather than having to discuss information.

GO ON TO THE NEXT PAGE

48. The seventh-grade math teacher understands that students' varied learning styles require a multifaceted approach to instruction for maximum learning to occur. Which of the following is NOT recommended for differentiating instruction in a mixed ability classroom?

   A. Diagnosing students' needs and designing instruction based on those diagnosed needs.
   B. Modifying goals and objectives for learners who have difficulty learning, and spending less time with the gifted learners.
   C. Removing stereotypical impressions about learners and focusing instruction on essential understandings and skills.
   D. Building a community of learners in the classroom and planning organized materials and space.

49. The fifth-grade science teacher has his students learn about animal habitats by playing a game called "Oh Deer." In this activity from the Texas Parks and Wildlife *Project Wild* Curriculum, students see how the balance of food, shelter, and water affects the deer population. The teacher should have planned the goals and objectives for this unit based on which of the following?

   A. The FOSS science curriculum that the school district adopted.
   B. The chapter in the adopted science textbook on animal habitats.
   C. The Texas Parks and Wildlife "Project Wild" Curriculum Guide.
   D. The Texas Essential Knowledge and Skills (TEKS) fifth-grade curriculum and the prerequisite TEKS.

Use the following information to answer the next three questions:

The math teacher has the following quote up on the classroom wall:

> G - grow as much academically as you can
> R - remember the big concepts and generalizations
> A - adjust your reading rate based on the purpose
> D - draw pictures of information to be learned
> E - estimate how much time you need to study
> S - study with a friend only if it helps you learn

50. When the teacher reads this sign to her class each year, she hopes to give them useful suggestions about ways to improve their grades. She also goes on to explain that "tests," or assessments, are really used to help the teacher in three ways. Which of the following is NOT one of the ways she should include?

   A. To determine which students will receive academic honor awards in math.
   B. To determine individual students' strengths and needs.
   C. To evaluate if the teacher's instruction has been effective.
   D. To plan further instruction for individuals and groups.

51. The teacher then explains to the class that she will be presenting her instructional units in ways that will assist in academic growth. Lessons will progress in a logical sequence and support the stated instructional goals. When her students ask her to explain what that means she explains it in which of the following ways?

   A. Students read the math text to learn the skill, the teacher meets with a group while the other groups begin practice activities, the teacher assesses the learning.
   B. Students are assigned homework relating to the skill. Students with poor homework grades practice the skill with the teacher and then the teacher assesses the skill.
   C. The teacher teaches the skill, students practice at home for homework, and the teacher assesses the learning.
   D. The teacher teaches the skill, students practice the skill with teacher assistance, the teacher and students check the work, the teacher reviews the skill, and students practice the skill for homework.

52. As the semester begins and the math teacher learns more about her students, she gains a better understanding of the students' readiness for learning the math concepts. She realizes that she must keep in mind the wide range of middle-level students' cognitive development. Remembering this, she plans lessons that involve the students in kinesthetic experiences. Which of the following would she select?

   A. Beginning with simple information presented on the overhead projector and moving on to the more complex information.
   B. Beginning with concrete information in the form of hands-on manipulatives and moving on to more meaningful abstract concepts.
   C. Beginning instruction slowly and moving to a quicker pace of study.
   D. Beginning instruction with a great deal of structure and assigned problems from the text and moving the structure to more open forms of learning in which students create their own problems.

Practice 4–8 Pedagogy and Professional Responsibilities Test III

Use the following information to answer the next three questions:

In a memo to the faculty, the middle school principal writes the following:

> Staff:
> Please plan to provide me with the following information by the end of the semester:
>
> 1) How are the student-teacher interactions helping learning?
> 2) How are you showing your students your love of learning?
> 3) How are you creating a safe, nurturing, and inclusive classroom?

53. The seventh-grade music teacher decides to analyze her classroom teaching and provide the principal with a self-study showing her results. She first decides to analyze how she interacts with her students. She starts a tape recorder at the beginning of the period and lets it run for the entire 50-minute period. She does this for three days and then analyzes her statements to the class. After listening to the tapes and charting her interactions, she sees that her interactions with students fall into three categories: positive, neutral, and negative. How might she use this information to improve the learning in her classroom?

    A. Let the students listen to the tapes and tell the teacher ways to improve her student–teacher interactions. Present this information to the principal.
    B. Chart the number of positive interactions and show the principal that usually she has positive teacher–student interactions.
    C. Chart the number of positive, neutral, and negative interactions. Then, examine the chart to determine the cause of the negative interactions and plan ways to correct those. Present these data to the principal
    D. Provide the principal with the data from the tapes showing positive, neutral, and negative interactions.

54. The social studies teacher is a first-year teacher and is excited about her job. She wants her principal and her students to know how much she loves learning. What is the *best* way that she might communicate her love of learning to the students?

   A. Frame her diploma from Texas State University and hang it in the classroom as a way to demonstrate that she loves to learn.
   B. Provide students with an opportunity to have lunch with her and hear about her learning in middle school
   C. Make a video of herself telling the students about her love of learning and why she wants to be their teacher.
   D. Begin each class with a brief story or explanation about why she enjoyed learning the new topic and provide a rationale about why she thinks her students will enjoy learning about the topic.

55. The language arts teacher wants to analyze his classroom environment. He knows that middle school students want to be treated like young adults, but that they also want to be nurtured. He decides to establish the following system. Each Friday all students are given a form that must be filled out anonymously. Which questions should NOT be included on the form?

   A. Do you think everyone gets the same opportunity to participate in class? If not, why?
   B. Do you know of anyone who is fearful in this class? If so, why is he or she fearful?
   C. Do you think that I am a good teacher? If so, why?
   D. Do you think that I do all I can do to make all students feel safe and cared for? If not, why not?

56. The eighth-grade math teacher grades his students each class period in some way. He may collect a homework grade, a test grade, or a participation grade. He has five different sections of math each day and must maintain grades on 150 students each day. Which method of recording grades should he use?

   A. Set up each class on a separate page in his grade book and record grades in the grade book.
   B. Use a system of note cards that he keeps in a file for each class. Grades are recorded on the note cards and then transferred to the report cards.
   C. Students record their own grades on individual grade sheets that are then given to the teacher.
   D. Create a spreadsheet for each class and record all grades on the computer.

57. The history teacher is assigned to work with students at risk of failing history before school two days each week. Three students are in the classroom and the teacher must leave the group for a few moments. He says to the group, "Do you know what to do while I am gone for a few moments?" They all nod affirmatively. On his return to the classroom, the students are running around the desks and playing. The teacher's *biggest* mistake was:

   A. not establishing the classroom rules with the group.
   B. not communicating clear expectations to the group.
   C. not having worksheets for the students to work on while he was gone.
   D. not asking one of the students to "take names" of those students who are not working.

58. The fourth-grade science teacher is planning instruction on constructing simple graphic tables to organize and evaluate information. The teacher knows that the students will benefit most if the lesson is communicated clearly. Which method would benefit students *most*?

   A. Present a video about scientific research and how important it is to present information so that others can use the data.
   B. Model the process of making a graphic table for the class prior to asking the students to do the task alone.
   C. Ask students to recall graphic tables that have helped them understand information.
   D. Present models of graphic tables to the class, such as ones depicting the number of inches of rain for the year.

Use the following information to answer the next three questions:

The seventh-grade team is working with a group of mixed-ability seventh-grade students. Some of the students have trouble learning; other students are quite capable.

59. The science teacher begins each year by doing a cloze test (a test the teacher constructs by deleting words from the text in order to assess students' abilities to comprehend the text) with each class. After the test is scored, the teacher knows students who score below a certain level will not be able to read the science textbook even with assistance. Other students scoring higher will be able to read the text with teacher assistance, and still others will be able to read the text alone. The teacher gathers this information and shares it with each student in order to:

   A. place students into one of three learning groups: low, medium, high.
   B. identify the appropriateness of the textbook for each student in the classroom and modify instruction accordingly.
   C. support his decision for not using the adopted textbook for instruction.
   D. impress upon the students that the ability to understand science is dependent on good reading comprehension.

60. After teaching a lesson, the English teacher assigns a selection of literature for students to read independently and respond to in a reader response journal before discussion. In the journals, some students write about the characters and plot and retell the story. Other students discuss what the text reminded them of from their own lives, and some write questions that they still have about the piece of literature. By having students respond in a journal first, the teacher is able to:

   A. monitor the effectiveness of her instruction by examining the students' responses and their depth of understanding.
   B. keep the behavior management problems to a minimum by keeping the students busy.
   C. provide a way for parents to see the type of literature students are reading in school.
   D. provide instruction that is designed to assist the special education students.

61. The most capable student in the social studies class is hoarse and says she is suffering from seasonal allergies. The student is not participating in the discussion of the text and continues to place her head on her desk. The teacher sends the student to the school nurse, but she returns to class with a note stating that she is not running a temperature. Based on what the teacher knows about motivation, what should be done?

   A. Try to get the student to sit up and participate by offering some type of external motivation to the class.
   B. See if peers can persuade the student to sit up and participate in the discussion.
   C. Let the students rest in class today because motivation is affected by illness and other personal problems.
   D. Offer the student the opportunity to earn extra points by sitting up and participating.

GO ON TO THE NEXT PAGE

62. One of the better students in the math class fails to pass a "Math Stars" test in order to earn a place on the Math Stars list. She says, "I don't care!" The teacher knows that the student has the math skills to achieve this. Which statement is *best* for the teacher to make?

   A. "Mary, if you work really hard at this, I will not count two errors. That way you can work on getting better and you just need to make two more points to pass."
   B. "Mary, the class cannot win the Math Stars Award if you keep failing the test. I know you can do this!"
   C. "Mary, I bet if I give you extra points in math that would help you work hard on this."
   D. "Mary, last year a student was frustrated just like I bet you are. What helped her was knowing that I was here to help her; she just kept trying and finally she passed that test."

63. The eighth-grade social studies teacher is planning on teaching her students how to do a WebQuest for social studies. She has designed a WebQuest to inquire about the early colonial period of the United States. For the WebQuest, students must go online to designated websites that the teacher has selected and look for answers to questions about the topic or to solve a problem. Often the WebQuest will involve gathering data in a chart in order to solve a problem or find a solution to a problem. Which of the following web addresses will be the *most* likely source of nonbiased, commercial-free information about the early colonies?

   A. www.theearlycolonies.com
   B. www.ushistory.org
   C. www.ushistory.com
   D. www.texasstate.edu

64. The school district keeps records about students online. The school nurse is responsible for keeping immunization information online. The classroom teachers have access to this information and can locate the correct phone numbers and addresses for students in their classes. In addition, the classroom teacher enters grades into the system every six weeks. Information about each student is stored as:

   A. presentation software.
   B. a spreadsheet.
   C. a database.
   D. a word-processing program.

65. The science teacher is planning instruction on researching famous scientists and presenting the reports through the use of presentation software for Parents' Night. The teacher knows that students' project designs, content deliveries, and relevance will be improved if he uses which of the following procedures for evaluation?

   A. Ask the parents to evaluate each presentation and select the best one, which will be awarded a prize.
   B. Prepare a rubric for students to use in the development of the presentation.
   C. Have peers evaluate the projects in a practice presentation.
   D. Make the projects worth 30% of the science grade for the six-week period.

66. Students at Mullins Middle School are regularly assessed using various methods. Some of the teachers disagree with using the Texas Assessment of Knowledge and Skills (TAKS) as a form of assessment. They think that it is a snapshot of one day and should not be used to evaluate students' learning. Other teachers believe that the TAKS test is a good test to assess schools and school district performance. Many think that it is "high stakes testing." The TAKS test is:

   A. an end-of-unit test.
   B. a norm-referenced test.
   C. a performance-based assessment.
   D. a criterion-referenced test.

67. Some of the teachers at the middle school prefer to use a form of assessment that examines student academic growth over time by collecting work selected by the student and the teacher to include in a portfolio. The science teacher, however, thinks that the best way to see if her students understand a science process is to use assessment that requires the student to demonstrate the knowledge to the teacher, for example, demonstrating correct use of the balance beam scales. This type of assessment is:

   A. performance-based assessment.
   B. norm-referenced assessment.
   C. criterion-referenced assessment.
   D. portfolio assessment.

68. The sixth-grade teacher understands the importance of family involvement in children's education. Which of the following is the *least* effective means for involving families?

   A. Prepare a monthly newsletter for parents/families that contains information about the curriculum for that month and that includes exemplary student work.
   B. Call parents/families each time a student is causing some type of disruption in the classroom.
   C. Invite parents/families to work as paraprofessionals in the classroom and at school events.
   D. Plan parent conferences at times that are convenient to parents/families and that accommodate work schedules.

69. A fifth-grade classroom has a student who is from Afghanistan. The student has been in the United States since birth and is an American citizen; both he and his parents speak English. The boy's mother wears the traditional Muslim attire including the hijab, or head scarf. The classroom teacher is planning parent conferences and is concerned about her lack of knowledge about Muslim beliefs and fears she may feel uncomfortable around the mother wearing the traditional attire. The *best* advice her mentor teacher can give to her is:

   A. Treat the family like you treat all the other families. Focus on the student and talk about the student's strengths and needs.
   B. Go online and read about the Muslim religion.
   C. Tell the parents that you have never worked with Muslims before and that you hope you are not offending them or their beliefs.
   D. Greet the parents and offer the mother a compliment on her attire.

70. Ms. Lebdo, a parent, is not able to get to get to school because she is wheelchair bound and is new to the city. When she receives the notice for the six-week parent–teacher conference, she sends the following note back to the sixth-grade homeroom teacher: "I will not be able to attend the conference because my husband works and I am wheelchair bound and cannot drive. I am sorry I cannot be there to meet you and to see how my son is doing in school." On reading the note the teacher thinks of resources that she might use. The *best* solution is:

   A. Ask the mother to have the father take a day off from work because this is a very important meeting and it is best if both parents attend.
   B. Tell the mother that maybe she needs to find someone at the church who can take her to important meetings.
   C. Contact the city transportation services and gather information about the special services available for handicapped citizens in the community. If it is helpful, call and give the information to the mother.
   D. Arrange to have someone from school volunteer to go and pick up the mother and return her to her home.

71. The middle school is working very hard to bring up the scores on the Texas Assessment of Knowledge and Skills (TAKS). The seventh-grade faculty agreed to align the curriculum to the Texas Essential Knowledge and Skills (TEKS). Everyone has looked at the TEKS for their subject and grade and is making sure that the prerequisite skills are also learned. Only one seventh-grade English teacher refuses to participate. She says, "That is teaching to the test and I will not do it." How should the other seventh-grade English teachers handle the situation?

    A. Go to their supervisor, the principal, and explain the situation and ask the principal for positive ways to address this issue.
    B. Chastise the offending English teacher for not doing what is best for the students.
    C. Send the offending English teacher a letter telling her that if she does not agree to follow the TEKS they will notify the principal.
    D. Ignore the situation and let the eighth-grade English teacher deal with the issue as it directly affects her.

72. The band director at the middle school is interested in improving his professional knowledge and skills. He is not sure of the best way to go about doing this. He talks to his mentor and decides that the *best* way to do this would be to:

    A. change his philosophy of teaching to reflect the same philosophy that his own middle school band director held.
    B. ask the members of the band to write down ways that he can improve his teaching.
    C. keep a teaching journal where he reflects on what went well and what did not go well with his instruction, and self-evaluate himself through the use of videotapes of his teaching several times each year.
    D. contact the region service center and arrange for them to videotape the best band director in the state and study that video.

73. The fifth-grade social studies teacher is getting more and more English Language Learners (ELLs) in her classroom each year. She wants to make the learning meaningful to them and is looking for ways to improve her professional knowledge and skills about teaching these students. She decides to:

    A. go to summer school at the local university to get the necessary classes to become certified as an ESL teacher.
    B. get certified as a special education teacher by taking an online class from the University of Phoenix.
    C. take a conversational Spanish class at the local community college.
    D. try some new strategies that she observes working well for the resource teacher.

74. Wanda, an eighth-grade student, recently transferred to Ajax Middle School. While registering Wanda, the mother asks about the school's Gifted and Talented (GT) program and explained that Wanda had been placed in the GT program in her previous school. What is the *least* likely answer from the school principal?

   A. Each school district has its own process for identifying gifted and talented students. Let me start the process for seeing if Wanda will qualify for our program.
   B. We love to have more gifted and talented students in the school. I will have the gifted and talented coordinator send home the paperwork with Wanda this afternoon.
   C. We have decided that all of our students are gifted and talented so we do not have a separate Gifted and Talented program.
   D. We have a process for identifying gifted and talented students for our GT program. I will ask the GT coordinator to contact you today.

75. A student in the fifth grade is a special education student. She has difficulty doing fifth-grade work and goes to a resource room for assistance in mathematics. The mathematics teacher lives next door to the student and believes that the student is capable of doing the math in the regular classroom. What should the math teacher NOT do?

   A. Request an admissions, review, and dismissal (ARD) meeting to examine the individual education plan (IEP).
   B. Meet with the resource teacher and discuss the types of problems the student has and suggest ways to work with the resource teacher.
   C. Request an admissions, review, and dismissal (ARD) meeting to examine if the student is eligible for dismissal from special education.
   D. Notify the resource teacher that the student will stay in the regular classroom for math because the teacher thinks that the student is capable of doing the work.

76. A seventh-grade student is caught in the turmoil of a family divorce. The student explains that his father moved out of the family home and is living somewhere else. This separation is very hard on the student and his grades have been much lower than usual. The father did not see the report card that went home and when he learns of the boy's failure in math from a friend he demands to see the grades. The mother refuses to show the father the report card and calls the school and tells them not to give the grades to the father. The father comes to the middle school and requests to see the math grades. The math teacher must:

   A. get a court order to allow the father to see his son's grades.
   B. provide the father with the son's grades.
   C. not allow the father access to his son's grades.
   D. provide the father with a form to request the grades. This form will be sent to juvenile court for approval.

77. A teacher is worried about her job because her sixth-grade math TAKS scores are lower than any other teacher's at the school. The principal has discussed this with her and offered her ways to bring up the students' scores. The teacher believes that she is teaching correctly. She believes that she is always given the lowest performing students because she is a good disciplinarian. This year she decides she will "look over the TAKS test guidelines" before it is given. When the tests arrive at her school she comes in after hours and uses her master key to get into the storage closet and takes a test home. The teacher could:

   A. get the guidelines for giving the test only by reading the instructions that come with the test.
   B. not improve the students' grades by doing this because there is not enough time remaining to teach them the needed skills
   C. lose her teaching certificate and have criminal charges filed against her.
   D. explain to the counselor the need to look over the test and get permission to take a copy of the test home for review.

78. The basketball coach has been told that if Francisco does not make a B or better in English this six-week period, his parents will not allow him to play basketball in the spring. The coach goes to the English teacher at the end of the semester and asks to know what grade Francisco will make in English. She refuses to tell him and explains that grades are confidential and that he has no "need to know" and must get the information from the student when grades come out the next week. The coach becomes angry and says, "If that boy gets below a B in this class you'll have to deal with me, do you understand?" The teacher has every right to report this to the principal because:

   A. the coach is guilty of sexual harassment.
   B. the coach is being rude and has no right to demand to know a student's grade.
   C. educators have an ethical responsibility to work cordially with peers.
   D. educators shall not falsify records or direct or coerce others to do so.

79. The math teacher wants to encourage all of the students in his class to perform at their highest level in mathematics. He believes that timely effective feedback will develop skills and confidence. Knowing what effective feedback sounds like, which of the following is the *least* effective statement to make to a student having problems adding fractions?

   A. "Try that next problem while I stand here. I want you to think out loud so that I can see what you are thinking and give you accurate assistance."
   B. "Think about what you did here. You must use the information that I give to you."
   C. "Good, I like the way you are drawing a picture of that fraction. That is an excellent strategy to assist you in working with fractions."
   D. "Look, don't let those fractions get to you! You've gotten 17 out of 20 problems correct; I can teach you to understand fractions too!"

80. The science teacher received his annual summative appraisal from the building principal. The district uses the Professional Development and Appraisal System (PDAS) from the Texas Education Agency. Of the eight domains assessed, his performance level was "proficient" in all except Domain 2. In Domain 2 his performance level was rated "Below Expectations."

   PDAS Domains:
   Active, Successful Student Participation in the Learning Process
   Learner-centered Instruction
   Evaluation and Feedback on Student Progress
   Management of Student Discipline, Instructional Strategies, Time/Materials
   Professional Communication
   Professional Development
   Compliance with Policies, Operating Procedures, and Requirements
   Improvement of All Students' Academic Performance

   Which of the following is NOT part of Domain 2?
   A. Goals, objectives, content, and strategies are aligned with the Texas Essential Knowledge and Skills (TEKS).
   B. Goals, objectives, content, and strategies relate to the interests of students.
   C. Goals, objectives, content, and strategies specify the behavior management program.
   D. Goals, objectives, content, and strategies engage students in critical thinking and problem solving.

CHAPTER FIFTEEN

Practice 4–8 Pedagogy and Professional Responsibilities Test Answers and Explanations

1. D

This question addresses information from PPR Competency* 011.

The teacher understands the importance of family involvement in children's education and knows how to interact and communicate effectively with families.

This is a priority-setting question. What is the *best* thing for the teacher to do? This question is about the teacher's understanding of middle-level students' development and how to plan with this in mind. Eliminate (A) as this asks the student to explain the problem. Although this is a good thing to do, it should be assumed that the student has already been asked the question by the parents. The parents are looking for a new solution. Eliminate (B) as the building principal knows little about the student and your instruction. Eliminate (C) because there is no evidence that the homework is too hard; it is a solution to stop the battle each night but does not solve the problem of why the student is not taking responsibility for his homework. Choice (D) is the correct response. By meeting with the student and parents the teacher can explain the homework policy so that both understand it. Then the student can provide input on ways to solve the problem. This provides a way for the home and school to work together and for the teacher to plan based on the meeting and input from the student and parents.

---

*Competency statements copyright © 2003 by the Texas State Board for Educator Certification and National Evaluation Systems, Inc. (NES ®). Reprinted by permission.

2. A

This question addresses information from PPR Competency 003.

The teacher understands procedures for designing effective and coherent instruction and assessment based on appropriate learning goals and objectives.

Choice (A) is the correct response because the teacher wants to be sure that the homework is a continuation of the objective taught in class and that it is not new material. Choice (B) is not congruent with the objectives. Choice (C) is not congruent with the instruction; it is harder. Choice (D) reverses the way learning occurs. The student is to do work at home before it is taught. Homework should reinforce what is taught. The goals and objectives should be congruent with all homework assignments.

3. C

This question addresses information from PPR Competency 002.

The teacher understands student diversity and knows how to plan learning experiences and design assessments that are responsive to differences among students and that promote all students' learning.

This question is about the teacher's understanding of diversity and ways to enhance that understanding. What is the *main* reason the teacher is happy to have this student in the class? Eliminate (A) because that is not a good reason to be happy about having a student from a foreign country who is fluent in English. If the teacher feels that way, it is a selfish reason for being pleased. Eliminate (B) because her job is to teach during class. This boy was not even alive during the Vietnam conflict. Eliminate (D) because this too would be a selfish type of response. We are happy to have children and we modify for all students as needed. Choice (C) is the correct response because this student can teach the teacher more about his culture. Good teachers learn more about each child's culture in order to be better teachers.

4. A

This question addresses information from PPR Competency 001.

The teacher understands human developmental processes and applies this knowledge to plan instruction and ongoing assessment that motivate students and are responsive to their developmental characteristics and needs.

This question is about understanding the importance of peer relations in middle school. Choice (B) may be true but it is not about learning in school. Choice (C) is about behavior management in the classroom and sounds like this choice prevents problems but does not address learning. Choice (D) is negative. Many parents do know what is happening at school. Choice (A) is the correct response. Having good friends and peers will improve learning. It is important for teachers to consider if a student has a circle of peers who provide positive support.

Practice 4–8 Pedagogy and Professional Responsibilities Test Answers and Explanations

5. C

This question addresses information from PPR Competency 004.

The teacher understands learning processes and factors that impact student learning and demonstrates this knowledge by planning effective, engaging instruction and appropriate assessments.

This is a priority-setting question. Eliminate (A) as the students are not learning the best thing to do. Outlining is something students often do, but it is not something the teacher does. Eliminate (B) because more reading may not improve comprehension and to summarize requires a great deal of understanding. Eliminate (D) because teachers do not change the objectives for students having trouble. They modify the instruction. Choice (C) is the correct response. The teacher is trying to find out what prior knowledge the students have so that new knowledge can be connected to previous knowledge. Good teachers preassess and structure new information so that it is linked to students' prior knowledge.

6. D

This question addresses information from PPR Competency 004.

The teacher understands learning processes and factors that impact student learning and demonstrates this knowledge by planning effective, engaging instruction and appropriate assessments.

This question is about planning instruction that asks students to think at a higher level. This involves analysis, synthesis, or evaluation, which are higher-order thinking tasks. Eliminate (A) as observing and discussing are not higher-order thinking. Eliminate (B) because making a timeline, although valuable, is not higher-order thinking. It requires putting events in order. Eliminate (C) because defining terms is a low-level task. Choice (D) is the correct response. To put on a skit about the problems, students must analyze the problems and then present them in a new form to an audience. This involves higher-order thinking. Higher-order thinking is important because that is the type of thinking that we must learn to do to be productive workers and citizens.

7. A

This question addresses information from PPR Competency 001.

The teacher understands human developmental processes and applies this knowledge to plan instruction and ongoing assessment that motivate students and are responsive to their developmental characteristics and needs.

This question is about how physical development impacts other domains, cognitive and social/emotional. Eliminate (B) because although it may be true, it is not a reason to go to the building principal. Eliminate (C) as it may be disruptive but that is not what should concern a good teacher. The picture taking is disruptive but it is a part of every school year. Eliminate (D) as it is a nice story but there is nothing in the question that tells us any of this. Choice (A) is the correct response. The teacher understands that students have different growth spurts and this procedure may damage some students' self-image if he or she is the tallest or the shortest. The teacher is concerned about the students' emotional well-being.

8. B

This question addresses information from PPR Competency 001.

The teacher understands human developmental processes and applies this knowledge to plan instruction and ongoing assessment that motivate students and are responsive to their developmental characteristics and needs.

This question is about what you know about human growth and development in middle grades. Girls are more physically mature and most will be taller and stronger. Eliminate (A) because although it may be true, it is not about human growth and it may not be true. Eliminate (C) because it does not say the eighth-grade girls are dancing with the sixth-grade boys. Eliminate (D) because we do not know that taller boys are embarrassed by their height. Choice (B) is the correct response.

9. A

This question addresses information from PPR Competency 001.

The teacher understands human developmental processes and applies this knowledge to plan instruction and ongoing assessment that motivate students and are responsive to their developmental characteristics and needs.

This question is asking you if you know the differences between the structure of a true middle school and a junior high school. Choices (B), (C), and (D) are traits of true middle schools. Choice (A), subject centered, is not part of the true middle school. So, it is the correct response. Middle schools are interdisciplinary and have teams of teachers from the major disciplines. Junior high schools are subject centered.

Practice 4–8 Pedagogy and Professional Responsibilities Test Answers and Explanations

10. D

This question addresses information from PPR Competency 001.

The teacher understands human developmental processes and applies this knowledge to plan instruction and ongoing assessment that motivate students and are responsive to their developmental characteristics and needs.

This is a priority-setting question. Which answer is *best*? This question is checking to see if you know examples of lessons that are at the concrete operational stage of development. At this stage, learning is "concrete" rather than abstract. Choice (D) is the correct response because there are abstract concepts to be learned, such as the multiplication tables. Students learn best by using "hands-on" learning because it makes the abstract very concrete. Eliminate (A) because lecture is very abstract. Eliminate (B) because reading presents abstract concepts and discussing them is difficult if the material is difficult to comprehend. Choice (C) is more concrete than lecture or reading alone, but it is not as concrete as choice (D), which involves "hands-on" learning.

11. D

This question addresses information from PPR Competency 002.

The teacher understands student diversity and knows how to plan learning experiences and design assessments that are responsive to differences among students and that promote all students' learning.

This is a priority-setting question. How can the teacher best help these students? This question is about your understanding of differences caused by socioeconomic status (SES) differences, specifically access to computers. Eliminate (A) as good teachers do not modify objectives because of SES differences. Eliminate (B) because the stem tells you these students have no home or no parents. These students will have trouble gaining access to computers. You must have an electric bill in many cities to get a library card! Eliminate (C) because the students will not be learning how to use the computer. The purpose of assignments in school should be to learn the process, not to produce a product. Choice (D) is the correct response. The teacher teaches these students the needed skills.

12. B

This question addresses information from PPR Competency 002.

The teacher understands student diversity and knows how to plan learning experiences and design assessments that are responsive to differences among students and that promote all students' learning.

This is a priority setting question. Which is the *best* differentiated or modified instruction? Eliminate (A); whole class instruction is not differentiated; everyone gets the same instruction. Eliminate (C); all teachers should have high expectations for all students. Eliminate (D) because the parents are doing the teaching, not the teacher. Choice (B) is truly modified instruction. More time may be needed for some students to learn a concept or complete an assignment.

13. D

This question addresses information from PPR Competency 003.

The teacher understands procedures for designing effective and coherent instruction and assessment based on appropriate learning goals and objectives.

This is a priority-setting question. Choice (D) is the *best* response. All integrated teaching teachers across different disciplines should examine themes and skills from their content area that overlap and are meaningful to students at this age. For example, a theme of "time" could be selected. In English, this theme would work for teaching grammar skills of future, present, and past tense. It would work for teaching about literature over different time periods or for teaching about settings in literature. In social studies, time is most important. The history of a country and the current events all relate to time. Eliminate (A) as the focus is on the content and not the interests of the students or themes that apply across disciplines. Choice (B) seems like a plausible choice but it is still more subject centered than integrated thematic teaching. Choice (C) is making the curriculum textbook-driven.

14. D

This question addresses information from PPR Competency 003.

The teacher understands procedures for designing effective and coherent instruction and assessment based on appropriate learning goals and objectives.

This is a priority-setting question. Which of the choices is *least* effective? The question is about your knowledge of available resources. Although you have focused on textbooks all your life, Choice (D) is the least effective. Choices (A), (B), and (C) all are outstanding resources that will be much more current and accurate than a textbook. A graduate student is speaking based on first-hand experiences. The World Wide Web is current and has many sites that give photographs and maps. Primary resources are always best. Textbooks are secondary resources.

Practice 4–8 Pedagogy and Professional Responsibilities Test Answers and Explanations

15. D

This question addresses information from PPR Competency 005.

The teacher knows how to establish a classroom climate that fosters learning, equity, and excellence and uses this knowledge to create a physical and emotional environment that is safe and productive.

This is a priority-setting question. Which physical setup is *least* important? This question is about classroom management of the physical space. Choice (D) is the correct response. Permanence is the least important attribute. Safety (A), accessibility to materials and supplies (B), and visibility (C), so the teacher sees students and students see the teacher, are all important. In fact, desks should be arranged based on the lesson. No classroom desk arrangement should be permanent.

16. C

This question addresses information from PPR Competency 005.

The teacher knows how to establish a classroom climate that fosters learning, equity, and excellence and uses this knowledge to create a physical and emotional environment that is safe and productive.

This is a priority-setting question. What is the *best* way to assess the classroom climate? This question is testing your knowledge of what type of climate the state wants to find in Texas classrooms. Eliminate (A), as results on the TAKS will not tell you anything about the day-to-day climate. Eliminate (B) because on-task behavior does not tell you if the climate is fair, calm, and encouraging or if it is a fearful environment. Eliminate (D) because the strategies for instruction do not tell you what the students are feeling. Choice (C) is the correct response. The state of Texas wants teachers who are nurturing and respectful of all students and students that respect teachers.

17. A

This question addresses information from PPR Competency 005.

The teacher knows how to establish a classroom climate that fosters learning, equity, and excellence and uses this knowledge to create a physical and emotional environment that is safe and productive.

This is a priority-setting question. What is the *best* way to communicate high expectation and have a classroom climate that is not threatening? Choice (A) is the correct response. The teacher states that she anticipates good work, that the topic is interesting, and that students will have choice about the types of learning activities that they will do. Choice about work is important for Texas classrooms. Choice (B) assumes the previous teacher taught certain skills or concepts. Choice (C) is threatening; Do well if you want to make a good grade. Choice (D) says you will do well because I taught so well. Although this may be the goal, it is a nonmotivating way to communicate high expectation to students.

18. B

This question addresses information from PPR Competency 006.

The teacher understands strategies for creating an organized and productive learning environment and for managing student behavior.

This is a priority-setting question. Which choice is *least* likely to help with behavior management? This question is about strategies for making students want to learn. Eliminate choices (A), (C), and (D) because these are all good ways to improve behavior problems. The least likely to help is the correct answer. Choose (B). Teachers must begin day one of school being fair, yet consistent with following the rules. If choices (A), (C), and (D) are done each year, teachers will have fewer behavior problems.

19. A

This question addresses information from PPR Competency 006.

The teacher understands strategies for creating an organized and productive learning environment and for managing student behavior.

This is a priority-setting question. How can the teacher *best* monitor her behavior plan? This question is about how you create an organized and productive learning environment and how you manage behavior. Choice (A) is the correct response. Good teachers gather data and examine the data to draw meaningful conclusions. Eliminate (B) because you may try this for specific students but it does not give you information about how the plans are working. Eliminate (C) as students want rules but will never admit that they like them. This is a biased way to monitor your plan. Eliminate (D) because this is a whole new plan (and not a very nurturing one!).

20. A

This question addresses information from PPR Competency 006.

The teacher understands strategies for creating an organized and productive learning environment and for managing student behavior.

This question is about methods for managing behavior. Choice (B) is punitive. Texas wants the climate to be positive. Choice (C) is punitive. Try again. Choice (D) is punitive. Choice (A) is the correct response. It provides the students with information about the total time available and then keeps posting the time remaining. Not everyone may like the plan but it is not punitive. You may have to be punitive at times, but do not start that way with every problem.

Practice 4–8 Pedagogy and Professional Responsibilities Test Answers and Explanations

21. B

This question addresses information from PPR Competency 006.

The teacher understands strategies for creating an organized and productive learning environment and for managing student behavior.

This is a question about behavior management. The teacher saw the student damage property. If this is the case, teachers should not offer students a way to make excuses for behavior that violates a school or class rule. Eliminate (A) because the teacher offers the student an opportunity to argue. Eliminate (C) because the teacher is the person with the power in the classroom. Do not go to the principal for problems in the classroom that have clear-cut rules and consequences. Eliminate (D) because teachers must enforce the rules or students will expect them to not be enforced. The correct response is (B). No excuses, no arguments, no anger. State the facts. Enforce the rule. Have consequences that fit the offense and quickly return to the job of teaching.

22. B

This question addresses information from PPR Competency 007.

The teacher understands and applies principles and strategies for communicating effectively in varied teaching and learning contexts.

This is a priority-setting question: which communication is *best*? Eliminate (A), as the human brain has difficulty remembering more than seven items. Covering 8 to 12 things will not help. Eliminate (C) as it sounds threatening and sarcastic. Teachers should never use threats or sarcasm with students. Eliminate (D) as it too is sarcastic and does nothing to communicate a solution. Choice (B) is positive and involves the students in creating a rubric to use for the math work. The rubric should improve the scores if students use it. Students should be involved in creating rubrics.

23. A

This question addresses information from PPR Competency 007.

The teacher understands and applies principles and strategies for communicating effectively in varied teaching and learning contexts.

This is a priority-setting question. What is the *best* question? Choice (B) is happy and positive but does not focus the question as well as the correct choice does, and it is not a question. Choice (C) is giving hints that cause students to try and read the teacher's mind rather than think about what they have learned. Choice (D) is trying to trick you. Writing a letter to the government appears to be very authentic. However, it is not a question and the "no talking" is not what the state of Texas wants of students. The idea of a community of learners is to encourage discussion of ideas in small groups or pairs. Choice (A) is the correct response. The teacher encourages the students to think and states that there is not a single correct response. She also tells them that this is a complex question, which implies that the answer takes time and thought.

24. D

This question addresses information from PPR Competency 007.

The teacher understands and applies principles and strategies for communicating effectively in varied teaching and learning contexts.

This is a priority-setting question about the best way to communicate information to the class. Communicating an assignment clearly is a very important skill. Initially, choice (A) looks like the correct response. It is what we observe every day in class and what we see teachers doing. However, a better way is available. Choice (B) is a very low-level task. Copying is not causing students to think and then demonstrate what they know about a topic. Choice (C) is temporary. An overhead projector is useful. However, when it is turned off the topic is no longer visible. Choice (D) is the correct response because the chart tablet is permanent and provides a record of the learning log assignments for students who may be absent. Also, choice (D) has the teacher read the assignment to the class and then offers students the opportunity to ask questions about the assignment.

25. C

This question addresses information from PPR Competency 008.

The teacher provides appropriate instruction that actively engages students in the learning process.

This is a priority-setting question asking you about your knowledge of instructional techniques. Choices (A), (B), and (D) are all teacher focused. The correct response (C) involves students in "hands-on learning" or active research about a topic. This would be the way to most actively engage students in the learning.

Practice 4–8 Pedagogy and Professional Responsibilities Test Answers and Explanations

26. C

This question addresses information from PPR Competency 008.

The teacher provides appropriate instruction that actively engages students in the learning process.

This is a priority setting question about your knowledge of grouping students for instruction. Choice (A) is incorrect because the state of Texas wants teachers to involve students in flexible grouping. This means the groups will change based on the tasks to be done and the skills of the students in that area. Also, choice (A) groups all of the GT (gifted and talented) students together and all of the lower performing students in another group. By using heterogeneous grouping, the more able students help the less able students learn. There will be times for homogeneous grouping, however, it is usually for reading classes. Choice (B) will be a problem. Students will choose to work with friends and no one should be working alone. There may be times that the students choose groups but not all the time. Choice (D) offers a silly idea that may sound "authentic" but it is not. Students should not vote on groups. Nor should they always be in homogeneous groups. Choice (C) is the correct answer. It is what the state of Texas expects of teachers.

27. C

This question addresses information from PPR Competency 008.

The teacher provides appropriate instruction that actively engages students in the learning process.

This is a priority-setting question. Eliminate (A) as they all came from different classes, schools, and may have very different learning about the topic. It is nice to ask what students know but it is not the best way to link new knowledge to old. Choice (B) is a trick. It mentions fractions but is not even clear. Eliminate (D) because it sounds great but it is only stating the objective and is not linking new knowledge to previous learning. Choice (C) uses what all students probably understand, pizza, and it is very "hands-on." She reviews the basics with a prop they all understand.

28. C

This question addresses information from PPR Competency 007.

The teacher understands and applies principles and strategies for communicating effectively in varied teaching and learning contexts.

This is a priority-setting question. You must go back and use the rubric to answer these questions. Eliminate (A), (B), and (D) because the *best* way to teach is to model, model, model. In choice (C), the teacher models what the students' task will look like. In all other answers the teacher is talking and telling and not modeling. Model a task for students whenever possible.

29. B

This question addresses information from PPR Competency 005.

The teacher knows how to establish a classroom climate that fosters learning, equity, and excellence and uses this knowledge to create a physical and emotional environment that is safe and productive.

This is a tricky question. Choice (A) looks correct; however, if you read all of the answers you will see that it is not the correct answer. Choice (C) assumes that teachers do things to keep parents happy. That is not why decisions are made about instruction. Choice (D) is incorrect because a norm-referenced test is not a rubric. Choice (B) is the correct response. Rubrics provide a way to make sure the assessment "matches" the instruction (congruence) and it also tells the students what will be assessed and how it will be assessed.

30. D

This question addresses information from PPR Competency 004.

The teacher understands learning processes and factors that impact student learning and demonstrates this knowledge by planning effective, engaging instruction and appropriate assessments.

This is a priority-setting question. This question is about the purpose of self-assessment. You must keep reminding yourself that assessment is not for the purpose of just giving grades. School is not just a place to keep students out of trouble Monday through Friday. The goal of education is to prepare young adults for the future. The goal is for all students to become self-directed learners and responsible for their own learning. Choices (A), (B), and (C) may all be good reasons but choice (D) is about preparing students for the future.

31. B

This question addresses information from PPR Competency 009.

The teacher incorporates the effective use of technology to plan, organize, deliver, and evaluate instruction for all students.

This question is testing your knowledge of the Technology Applications required of students at each grade level according to the TEKS and the TExES technology competencies. Choice (A) is a simple choice but there are better reasons. Choice (C) presents the teacher as being lazy. Choice (D) sounds good but one is not really sure what it means. This is not a technology project the students are presenting. Choice (B) is the correct response based on the TEKS and the TExES Technology Competencies.

Practice 4–8 Pedagogy and Professional Responsibilities Test Answers and Explanations

32. B

This question addresses information from PPR Competency 009.

The teacher incorporates the effective use of technology to plan, organize, deliver, and evaluate instruction for all students.

This is a priority-setting question. Choices (A), (C), and (D) may all be valid answers but choice (B) *best* illustrates the teacher's ability to use productivity tools such as a multimedia presentation to communicate information. Other productivity tools would include spreadsheets and databases.

33. C

This question addresses information from PPR Competency 009.

The teacher incorporates the effective use of technology to plan, organize, deliver, and evaluate instruction for all students.

This question is about your knowledge of legal and ethical use of technology. Eliminate (A) because parents do not have to justify their reasons for not wanting a child to be pictured in a visual presentation. Some children may be at risk of being abducted by an estranged parent and the parents may be in hiding. Eliminate (B); do not ask students to argue or beg parents about decisions. Eliminate (D) as this would be illegal because the child is a minor and grounds for legal action by the parents against the teacher. Choice (C) is the correct response.

34. A

This question addresses information from PPR Competency 010.

The teacher monitors student performance and achievement; provides students with timely, high-quality feedback; and responds flexibly to promote learning for all students.

This is a priority-setting question. This is a question about being flexible as a teacher. Here is a wonderful opportunity. What is the *best* response? Eliminate (B) as the TEKS have much about music and this is an opportunity for students to learn first-hand about music. Eliminate (C) because teachers do what they do for the good of students, never because the "principal will never know." Eliminate (D) because this star is a country–western star, the lesson for that day can be modified and marches can be taught another day. The curriculum must be flexible for opportunities such as this. The correct answer is (A).

35. D

This question addresses information from PPR Competency 010.

The teacher monitors student performance and achievement; provides students with timely, high-quality feedback; and responds flexibly to promote learning for all students.

This is a priority-setting question; what is the *main* value of portfolios? Eliminate (A) because the goal of portfolios is not to teach organizational skills. Choice (B) is a use of portfolios but not the goal. Choice (C) implies that teachers are lazy. Choice (D) is the correct response. The goal is to move students closer to managing their own learning by examining their work over time and setting goals for learning. This will be a life skill.

36. B

This question addresses information from PPR Competency 011.

The teacher understands the importance of family involvement in children's education and knows how to interact and communicate effectively with families.

This is a priority-setting question, which idea is *best*? Eliminate (A) as teachers talk to parents as needed, not as scheduled. Eliminate (C) as not all families will have access to e-mail. Eliminate (D) as that is not giving parents information about the curriculum. Choice (B) provides an ongoing way to communicate with parents about the curriculum and what the students are learning.

37. B

This question addresses information from PPR Competency 011.

The teacher understands the importance of family involvement in children's education and knows how to interact and communicate effectively with families.

This is a priority-setting question. How can the teacher *best* include the parents in the child's learning? Eliminate (A) because what is in the portfolio is shared with parents, good work or poor work. Choice (C) looks like a correct answer; however, parents are not teachers and if a student cannot learn from the teacher it is best not to send the work for parents to try to teach. Choice (D) may be what you have observed, however, it is not involving the parents in the learning. Choice (B) is the correct response. Parents know more about the student than the teacher. By inviting the parents to make comments, teachers will learn more about the student and the student will have the opportunity to read what the parents think.

Practice 4–8 Pedagogy and Professional Responsibilities Test Answers and Explanations

38. B

This question addresses information from PPR Competency 012.

The teacher enhances professional knowledge and skills by effectively interacting with other members of the educational community and participating in various types of professional activities.

This question is about your knowledge of the structure of a true middle school. In order for integrated, interdisciplinary, thematic teaching to occur, teachers must have a common planning time to work together. In a true middle school, teachers are grouped in interdisciplinary groups and serve as advisors to the same group of students. Eliminate (A), (C), and (D) because they are not required for the team to function successfully.

39. C

This question addresses information from PPR Competency 012.

The teacher enhances professional knowledge and skills by effectively interacting with other members of the educational community and participating in various types of professional activities.

This is a priority-setting question. It is also a question about you knowledge about the role of a teacher. Teachers are to teach. When there is a social problem the teacher should not get too involved. Choice (A) has the teacher becoming a social worker. Choice (B) may sound like a good idea, but at this age a middle school student may not want all of the students to know about family problem. Also, it takes away from instructional time. Eliminate (D) because while teachers must report abuse by law to Child Protective Services, you are given no information in this question to suggest that abuse is happening. Choice (C) presents a caring teacher who uses other school personnel to assist the child with social and emotional problems.

40. A

This question addresses information from PPR Competency 013.

The teacher understands and adheres to legal and ethical requirements for educators and is knowledgeable of the structure of education in Texas.

This question tests your understanding of the copyright laws for teachers. You will find information online about this topic. One site you might go to is: http://www.pbs.org/teachersource/copyright/copyright.shtm. Select (A) as all other choices are "fair use." Choice (A) is a violation of copyright law. The DVD he is publishing makes it a commercial publication. The word publishing is the cue that this is to be sold. Choices (B), (C), and (D) are all "fair use" for educators.

41. B

This question addresses information from PPR Competency 001.

The teacher understands human developmental processes and applies this knowledge to plan instruction and ongoing assessment that motivate students and are responsive to their developmental characteristics and needs.

This question is about the cognitive development of middle school students. Eliminate (A) because most student in seventh grade have been at the concrete development stage for some years. Eliminate (C) because although it may be a true statement, the focus is not on behavior. The focus of the teacher should be on good instruction to prepare students for life. Eliminate (D). Social skills are a part of cooperative learning, but teachers do not think instruction is important because it will become a part of students' grades. Choice (B) is the correct response.

42. B

This question addresses information from PPR Competency 001.

The teacher understands human developmental processes and applies this knowledge to plan instruction and ongoing assessment that motivate students and are responsive to their developmental characteristics and needs.

This question is asking why contacting parents with good news is important. Choice (A) is a true statement; the teacher's calling is showing that students are successful. Choice (C) implies that middle school teachers contact parents with good news in order to be liked. No action is ever warranted in order for the teacher to be popular with students. Choice (D) presents information that we do not know is true. Nowhere do we read that these students experienced punitive treatment in elementary school. Choice (B) is the better response.

43. C

This question addresses information from PPR Competency 001.

The teacher understands human developmental processes and applies this knowledge to plan instruction and ongoing assessment that motivate students and are responsive to their developmental characteristics and needs.

This question is about why a teacher has specific rules about behavior. The teacher has rules in order to make certain that students can focus on instruction and learn. Eliminate (A) because it may be a true statement but that is not a valid reason for a teacher to have a rule. Eliminate (B) because it may also be a true statement, but the teacher is not a policeman. Eliminate (D) because it too may be a true statement but choice (C), the correct response, is a more specific reason to give to parents and also tests whether you know that students in middle school may try risky behaviors.

Practice 4–8 Pedagogy and Professional Responsibilities Test Answers and Explanations

44. A

This question addresses information from PPR Competency 001.

The teacher understands human developmental processes and applies this knowledge to plan instruction and ongoing assessment that motivate students and are responsive to their developmental characteristics and needs.

This question is about helping middle-level students make decisions, have goals and have organizational skills. Choice (B) is a true statement but the goal of doing this is not just to keep parents informed. Choice (C) may also be a true statement but it is not the best reason for a teacher to do this activity. It is a short-term reason. Choice (D) may or may not be true but teachers do not teach to keep students out of trouble. Choice (A) states what the teacher knows and that this is a skill that is important. It is important because it is a life skill that all people should learn. The goal of an education is to prepare students for life decisions and skills.

45. D

This question addresses information from PPR Competency 002.

The teacher understands student diversity and knows how to plan learning experiences and design assessments that are responsive to differences among students and that promote all students' learning.

This is a priority-setting question. What is the *best* response for the mentor teacher? Choices (A), (B), and (C) are not helpful or supportive responses. Choice (D) expresses that we should appreciate parents who are involved in supporting their children in school. The fact that the parents are gay is not discussed. The fact that they are gay is not an issue. The fact that they are good parents is to be supported and praised.

46. B

This question addresses information from PPR Competency 002.

The teacher understands student diversity and knows how to plan learning experiences and design assessments that are responsive to differences among students and that promote all students' learning.

This is a priority setting question. Choices (A), (C), and (D) are all good reasons for hosting the Cultural Fair, but could be done in other ways. Research and interviewing skills could be taught within the school community. The reward for good work could be a pizza. The community could participate in the Fall Carnival. Choice (B) is the only choice that relates to learning about diversity in the community. Choice (B) is the correct response.

47. D

This question addresses information from PPR Competency 002.

The teacher understands student diversity and knows how to plan learning experiences and design assessments that are responsive to differences among students and that promote all students' learning.

This question is asking you to select which adaptation is not effective. Choices (A), (B), and (C) are all good ways to adapt (modify) instruction for a hearing-impaired student. Choice (D) is the correct answer but is not a good adaptation. There is no information that the student cannot speak. The student is hearing impaired. Therefore, there is no need to modify the task from discussion to writing.

48. B

This question addresses information from PPR Competency 002.

The teacher understands student diversity and knows how to plan learning experiences and design assessments that are responsive to differences among students and that promote all students' learning.

This question is asking you to select what is not recommended for differentiating (modifying) instruction in a mixed ability class. Choice (A) is a good way to modify instruction. Assess and modify instruction based on needs. Choice (C) is a way to focus on instruction and not stereotype some students. Choice (D) is an excellent way to modify. Students in a community of learners assist one another in learning. Choice (B) is not advisable. Choice (B) is the correct answer because teachers should not change the goals and objectives for learners who have difficulty and spend less time with the more able students. The teachers should help those learners who have difficulty by doing some of the other choices.

49. D

This question addresses information from PPR Competency 003.

The teacher understands procedures for designing effective and coherent instruction and assessment based on appropriate learning goals and objectives.

This question is asking you how teachers should select goals and objectives for a unit. While the FOSS science curriculum (A), the science book chapter (B), and the Project Wild curriculum (C) may all be correlated with the TEKS, the only way to know that the proper objectives are being covered in the fifth grade is to select objectives for science from the TEKS. Choice (D) is the correct response.

Practice 4–8 Pedagogy and Professional Responsibilities Test Answers and Explanations

50. A

This question addresses information from PPR Competency 003.

The teacher understands procedures for designing effective and coherent instruction and assessment based on appropriate learning goals and objectives.

This question is asking you to select the choice that is not a way that grades assist teachers. How students view grading and how teachers view grading may be very different. Grades are used by teachers to determine students' strengths and needs (B), to determine if the instruction was effective (C), and to plan instruction (D). The correct response is (A). Teachers do not use grades to determine academic awards. Although the school may present academic awards based on grades, that is not the purpose of grades.

51. D

This question addresses information from PPR Competency 003.

The teacher understands procedures for designing effective and coherent instruction and assessment based on appropriate learning goals and objectives.

This question is testing your understanding of designing effective instruction. Eliminate (A), as this is the teacher in the role of assigner, listener, and tester. We see this in many classrooms but the teacher is not really teaching. Eliminate (B) because this teacher assigns, tutors, and tests. Again, no teaching is taking place. Eliminate (C) because this teacher teaches and tests. Teachers must also guide and assist. Choice (D) is the correct response. This teacher teaches, guides students as they practice a new skill, assesses how well the students understand, reviews what is not understood, and then provides opportunities for more practice at home.

52. B

This question addresses information from PPR Competency 005.

The teacher knows how to establish a classroom climate that fosters learning, equity, and excellence and uses this knowledge to create a physical and emotional environment that is safe and productive.

This question is testing if you can identify what is meant by kinesthetic experiences, which is a good teaching approach for middle school students. Choice (A) is not kinesthetic. The teacher is in charge. Choice (C) is about the pace of instruction. Choice (D) is teacher-centered and students working individually. Choice (B) is the correct response. Kinesthetic learning involves students touching and manipulating objects in order to learn concepts.

53. C

This question addresses information from PPR Competency 005.

The teacher knows how to establish a classroom climate that fosters learning, equity, and excellence and uses this knowledge to create a physical and emotional environment that is safe and productive.

This question is asking you how you might study your interactions with your students and use the information to improve learning. Eliminate (A) as the students do not need to hear the same information twice and tell the teacher how to improve. Teachers should do a self-study. Eliminate (B) as the teacher is only focusing on the positive interactions. She can also learn from the other types. She is only examining one part of her interactions. Eliminate (D) because it is only part of the plan. The teacher is not planning ways to improve the classroom instruction. Choice (C) is the correct response. The teacher gathers the data, analyzes the data, plans ways to correct negative interactions and presents this to the principal.

54. D

This question addresses information from PPR Competency 005.

The teacher knows how to establish a classroom climate that fosters learning, equity, and excellence and uses this knowledge to create a physical and emotional environment that is safe and productive.

This is a priority setting question. There are many ways to communicate a love of learning. What is the *best* way for this teacher? Eliminate (A) as this is a good way to demonstrate that you did learn and that you attended an excellent school, but it does not show that you continue to love learning. Choice (B) is an excellent way to get to visit with students outside of class but the teacher only talks about loving to learn in middle school. Choice (C) is great if the teacher cannot tell the students in person. Choice (D) is the correct response. With each new lesson the teacher is positive about the new information and expresses her own interest in learning about the topic and why the learning is important. Students will have a model each day of getting excited about learning something new.

55. C

This question addresses information from PPR Competency 005.

The teacher knows how to establish a classroom climate that fosters learning, equity, and excellence and uses this knowledge to create a physical and emotional environment that is safe and productive.

This question is about evaluating the classroom environment. The question is asking you to select a way that is not advised. Choices (A), (B), and (D) are all good questions that a teacher might include on a questionnaire. Choice (D) is not about the environment. It is the correct response.

Practice 4–8 Pedagogy and Professional Responsibilities Test Answers and Explanations

56. D

This question addresses information from PPR Competency 006.

The teacher understands strategies for creating an organized and productive learning environment and for managing student behavior.

This question is about using technological tools for administrative tasks. Because computers do in seconds what may take hours to do by hand, the state wants teachers to learn to use the computer for administrative tasks. Grades must be accurate and maintained. The computer is the perfect tool. Answers (A), (B), and (C) all ignore that the computer is a better tool. Also, students should not be asked to record their own grades.

57. B

This question addresses information from PPR Competency 007.

The teacher understands and applies principles and strategies for communicating effectively in varied teaching and learning contexts.

Eliminate (A) as this is a special tutorial situation and is not the normal classroom situation. The class rules may exist but may not be used for tutoring. Eliminate (C) because "worksheet" should signal a red pepper word to you because the state wants teachers to use higher level thinking than worksheets usually deliver. Eliminate (D) because it is unlikely at the middle school level that one student would feel comfortable reporting misbehavior in a peer. Peer pressure and peer approval is very important at this age. The teacher should have been specific about what he expected. Choice (B) is the correct response.

58. B

This question addresses information from PPR Competency 007.

The teacher understands and applies principles and strategies for communicating effectively in varied teaching and learning contexts.

This is a priority setting question. Choice (A) is vague. It may be a good video but it is not specific to the lesson of constructing a simple graphic table. Choice (C) is mentioning not teaching. Choice (D) sounds good but it is showing rather than "teaching how" to do a task. Choice (B) is the correct response. Modeling is an excellent way to teach.

59. B

This question addresses information from PPR Competency 008.

The teacher provides appropriate instruction that actively engages students in the learning process.

This question is about preassessment of students in order to plan appropriate instruction. Eliminate (A) as the goal of assessment is not to place students in ability groups. Also, the state wants teachers to usually use heterogeneous grouping. Eliminate (C) because no teacher should ever have to justify a decision if it is based on assessment and best practice. Eliminate (D) because good grades in science may be the result of good reading comprehension but that is not why the teacher is gathering information about each student and sharing that information. The teacher is assessing in order to modify instruction as required. Choice (B) is the correct response.

60. A

This question addresses information from PPR Competency 008.

The teacher provides appropriate instruction that actively engages students in the learning process.

This question is about the monitoring of instruction. By asking the students to write in a response journal, the teacher is able to evaluate the effectiveness of her instruction. Choice (A) is the correct response. Eliminate choice (B) because no teacher should ever use a task for "busy work" to keep behavior under control. Eliminate choice (C) because a simple list would provide parents with the type of literature. Parents may look at this during conferences but not to see the type of literature. Eliminate (D) because responding to literature is good practice for all types of students.

61. C

This question addresses information from PPR Competency 008.

The teacher provides appropriate instruction that actively engages students in the learning process.

This question is about motivation. Eliminate (A) because a student who is a good student will learn little if feeling poorly even if given external motivation. The goal is internal motivation to learn. Eliminate (B) because peer pressure should not be used as motivation, especially if a teacher sees that a student is not feeling well. Eliminate (D) as external motivators, such as extra points, are short lived and should not be used if a good student is feeling ill. Choice (C) is the correct response. There are times that illness or personal problems may affect motivation and the teacher can discuss it with the student after class if it continues.

Practice 4–8 Pedagogy and Professional Responsibilities Test Answers and Explanations

62. D

This question addresses information from PPR Competency 008.

The teacher provides appropriate instruction that actively engages students in the learning process.

This is a priority-setting question. What is *best* to do? Choice (A), (B), and (C) all sound like forms of bribery. The good middle school teacher is understanding and supportive. The goal is to teach the student and give the students support. Choice (D) is the correct response.

63. B

This question addresses information from PPR Competency 009.

The teacher incorporates the effective use of technology to plan, organize, deliver, and evaluate instruction for all students.

This question is about your ability to evaluate electronic information. This question requires that you know about .com, .org, and .edu. Eliminate (A) and (C) because the .com indicates that these are commercial websites. Advertising by definition, is biased. Eliminate (D) because .edu is usually a school, college, or university site. This site may be unbiased but would have little information about the early colonies. Choice (B) is the correct response. Sites that are .org are organizations that are usually specific to certain types of information. In this case, www.ushistory.org indicates the site is about U.S. history, which would apply to the early colonies, and it is an organization. It is probably the most unbiased of the sites with the correct information.

64. C

This question addresses information from PPR Competency 009.

The teacher incorporates the effective use of technology to plan, organize, deliver, and evaluate instruction for all students.

This question is about your knowledge of the uses of various types of software. In this question, the school district stores a lot of different information in files about each student. Eliminate (A) as presentation software, such as PowerPoint, is used for making presentations to a group. Eliminate (B) because a spreadsheet is used for storing data such as grades. In a spreadsheet, rows and columns can be manipulated mathematically. Eliminate (D) because word processing is the ability to type letters, reports, and narrative information. Choice (C) is the correct response. A database stores all sorts of information, which can then be sorted for the specific information needed. So the nurse may store information about immunizations by student number, the teacher may store grades by student number, and the school may publish a directory that includes students' names and telephone numbers.

65. B

This question addresses information from PPR Competency 009.

The teacher incorporates the effective use of technology to plan, organize, deliver, and evaluate instruction for all students.

This question is about your knowledge of how to evaluation students' technologically produced products. Eliminate (A) as the criteria for what is good are not known. The prize is a motivator but how will students know what is expected. Eliminate (C) because peers may provide feedback but the criteria for poor, good, or excellent will be subjective. Eliminate (D) because even though it is worth 30% how will the teacher provide students with the criteria for excellence? Choice (B) is the correct response. Rubrics are given to students prior to their doing a project. The rubric specifies what is expected in each category, project design, content delivery, and relevance. A good rubric will also indicate what a poor design looks like, what a good project looks like, and what and excellent project looks like. Always provide students with a rubric before beginning a project.

66. D

This question addresses information from PPR Competency 010.

The teacher monitors student performance and achievement; provides students with timely, high-quality feedback; and responds flexibly to promote learning for all students.

This question is about your knowledge of the characteristics and uses of various types of assessment instruments, specifically the TAKS. Eliminate (A) as the TAKS are not an end-of-unit test. These are usually in textbooks. Eliminate (B) as norm-referenced tests are tests like the SATs that compare your score to a "norm group." Eliminate (C) because the TAKS are not performance-based assessment. Choice (D) is the correct response. The TAKS is a criterion-referenced test. That means that the student's score indicates how many of the criteria have been met. The criteria for the TAKS are the TEKS.

67. A

This question addresses information from PPR Competency 010.

The teacher monitors student performance and achievement; provides students with timely, high-quality feedback; and responds flexibly to promote learning for all students.

This is a question about your knowledge of the characteristics and uses of various types of assessments. Eliminate (B) and (C) as these are both "formal" tests that are used and not informal types of assessment. Eliminate (D) because portfolio assessment may include performance-based assessment but it includes more than performance on a task. Choice (A) is the correct response.

Practice 4–8 Pedagogy and Professional Responsibilities Test Answers and Explanations

68. B

This question addresses information from PPR Competency 011.

The teacher understands the importance of family involvement in children's education and knows how to interact and communicate effectively with families.

This question is a priority-setting question asking you which of four choices is the *least* effective way to involve families in students' education. Choice (A) is a very effective procedure. Choice (C) is effective because parents are welcomed and can view the classroom. Choice (D) is an excellent way to talk with parents individually. The least effective way is choice (B) because it is negative. Find positive ways to involve all families.

69. A

This question addresses information from PPR Competency 011.

The teacher understands the importance of family involvement in children's education and knows how to interact and communicate effectively with families.

This is a priority-setting question. What is the *best* way to interact with a diverse family? Eliminate (B) because the internet may give you information about Muslim beliefs, however, that is not what you are going to discuss. Eliminate (C) because your conversation should be about the student's education. Eliminate (D) because this advice does not tell the new teacher ways to discuss the child's education. Choice (A) is the correct response. The conference is about the student's education. The family attire is not important.

70. C

This question addresses information from PPR Competency 011.

The teacher understands the importance of family involvement in children's education and knows how to interact and communicate effectively with families.

This is a priority-setting question. What is the *best* solution for the teacher to choose for a resource to support the family? Eliminate (A) because no teacher should ever tell a family to take off from work. That is not a teacher's job. Eliminate (B) and (D) because teachers should not get involved in solving problems that should be handled by a social worker. Choice (C) is the correct response. The teacher has available to her a social worker at the school who could give the mother information. If that is not available, the teacher may inquire about the available resources the city provides and relay that information to the mother. If available, the school social worker should take care of such situations.

71. A

This question addresses information from PPR Competency 012.

The teacher enhances professional knowledge and skills by effectively interacting with other members of the educational community and participating in various types of professional activities.

This question is about working productively with other colleagues to address issues. Eliminate (B) as it is not productive or positive. Eliminate (C) because teachers should talk face-to-face and it tells you in the question that the teacher refuses to align the curriculum. Eliminate (D) as each teacher must align his or her curriculum to the TEKS as it is the state curriculum. Choice (A) is the correct response. The teachers have attempted to discuss this with the teacher and had no success. The next step is to go to the supervisor, the principal, for assistance.

72. C

This question addresses information from PPR Competency 012.

The teacher enhances professional knowledge and skills by effectively interacting with other members of the educational community and participating in various types of professional activities.

This is a priority-setting question. What is the best way for the band director to self-assess his teaching? Eliminate (A) as changing his philosophy will not be easy and will not help him reflect on his teaching. Eliminate (B) because students may not be objective in their suggestions. Eliminate (D) as this is observing another teacher rather than self-examination. Choice (C) is the correct response.

73. A

This question addresses information from PPR Competency 012.

The teacher enhances professional knowledge and skills by effectively interacting with other members of the educational community and participating in various types of professional activities.

This is a question about using resources and support systems. Eliminate (B) because Special Education teachers do not teach ELL students. Eliminate (C) because certification as an ELL teacher involves more than just learning one language such as Spanish. Teachers also learn strategies for working with speakers of all foreign languages. Choice (D) is a good idea to try but it will not help you become certified to teach ELL students. Choice (A) is the correct response. By getting certified, the teacher will be prepared to teach all ELL students.

Practice 4–8 Pedagogy and Professional Responsibilities Test Answers and Explanations

74. C

This question addresses information from PPR Competency 013.

The teacher understands and adheres to legal and ethical requirements for educators and is knowledgeable of the structure of education in Texas.

This question is asking about the legal requirements for placement in the gifted and talented program. Three of the choices are all good answers that the principal might give the mother. The question asks for the *least* likely. Choices (A), (B), and (D) are all good statements to say to a mother. Choice (C) is not a good choice. By law, Texas Education Code 29, schools must have a plan for identifying students who are gifted and talented and for the establishment of that program.

75. D

This question addresses information from PPR Competency 013.

The teacher understands and adheres to legal and ethical requirements for educators and is knowledgeable of the structure of education in Texas.

This question is asking you to determine which of four choices is the one that should not be done. This question is about the legal requirements for students in special education. Choices (A), (B), and (C) would be legally correct to do. Choice (D) is not legal. A teacher must follow the IEP (Individual Education Plan) unless that plan is changed in an ARD meeting in some way or the students is dismissed from Special Education placement after an ARD meeting. Even though the student lives next door to this teacher, the laws must be followed.

76. B

This question addresses information from PPR Competency 013.

The teacher understands and adheres to legal and ethical requirements for educators and is knowledgeable of the structure of education in Texas.

This question is about confidentiality of grades, interactions with others, and legal requirements. According to the Texas Education Code Section 26004, parents have access to their children's school records. The school must have on file a court order or proof that parent rights have been removed to prevent a parent from having access to their minor child's school records. Without that a school cannot prevent one parent from seeing his or her child's grades. Choice (B) is the correct response.

77. C

This question addresses information from PPR Competency 013.

The teacher understands and adheres to legal and ethical requirements for educators and is knowledgeable of the structure of education in Texas.

This question is about procedures for state mandated tests. The TAKS tests are to be kept under lock and key. This teacher was doing something illegal by gaining access to the tests. Choice (A) appears to be a correct answer but there is a better answer. Choice (B) is not correct because the way she is going about doing it is illegal. Choice (D) is incorrect because the test custodian, in this case the counselor, would not allow anyone to review the TAKS exam prior to giving the test. The correct answer is (C).

78. D

This question addresses information from PPR Competency 013.

The teacher understands and adheres to legal and ethical requirements for educators and is knowledgeable of the structure of education in Texas.

This question is about following procedures and requirements for maintaining accurate student records. Choice (A) is not correct because the coach is not harassing the teacher sexually. Choice (B) is accurate; the coach is being rude and has no right to demand to know a student's grade., This alone, however, is not a reason to report the coach to the principal. Choice (C) is also a true statement but not the best reason for reporting the incident to the principal. Choice (D) is the correct response. The coach has implied that if the teacher does not give the student a B or better, he will do something terrible. The coach is asking her to alter grades and is also threatening her.

79. B

This question addresses information from PPR Competency 010.

The teacher monitors student performance and achievement; provides students with timely, high-quality feedback; and responds flexibly to promote learning for all students.

This question is about providing feedback to students. Three of the choices are good feedback. The question is asking for the one statement that is not good feedback to give to a student. Choices (A), (C), and (D) are all good statements to make to a student. Choice (B) is the correct response because the statement does not help the student. Obviously if the student could "think about what he did here" or use information from the teacher, the students would not need assistance. The words from the teacher are not helpful or encouraging in any way.

Practice 4–8 Pedagogy and Professional Responsibilities Test Answers and Explanations

80. C

This question addresses information from PPR Competency 012.

The teacher enhances professional knowledge and skills by effectively interacting with other members of the educational community and participating in various types of professional activities.

This question is about your knowledge of the PDAS (Professional Development and Appraisal System) in Texas. Three of the choices are part of Domain 2 of the PDAS. Choices (A), (B), and (D) are all part of learner-centered instruction. Choice (C) is the correct response because it is not part of Domain 2. Behavior Management is part of Domain 4. For more information about the PDAS go to http://www.tea.state.tx.us/PDAS/

Practice Test 3 Answers, 4–8 PPR Sorted by Competency

Question	Domain	Competency	Answer	Did You Answer Correctly?	Question	Domain	Competency	Answer	Did You Answer Correctly?
4	1	001	A		28	3	007	C	
7	1	001	A		57	3	007	B	
8	1	001	B		58	3	007	B	
9	1	001	A		25	3	008	C	
10	1	001	D		26	3	008	C	
41	1	001	B		27	3	008	C	
42	1	001	B		59	3	008	B	
43	1	001	C		60	3	008	A	
44	1	001	A		61	3	008	C	
3	1	002	C		62	3	008	D	
11	1	002	D		31	3	009	B	
12	1	002	B		32	3	009	B	
45	1	002	D		33	3	009	C	
46	1	002	B		63	3	009	B	
47	1	002	D		64	3	009	C	
48	1	002	B		65	3	009	B	
2	1	003	A		29	3	010	B	
13	1	003	D		34	3	010	A	
14	1	003	D		35	3	010	D	
49	1	003	D		66	3	010	D	
50	1	003	A		67	3	010	A	
51	1	003	D		79	3	010	B	
5	1	004	C		1	4	011	D	
6	1	004	D		36	4	011	B	
30	1	004	D		37	4	011	B	
15	2	005	D		68	4	011	B	
16	2	005	C		69	4	011	A	
17	2	005	A		70	4	011	C	
52	2	005	B		38	4	012	B	
53	2	005	C		39	4	012	C	
54	2	005	D		71	4	012	A	
55	2	005	C		72	4	012	C	
18	2	006	B		73	4	012	A	
19	2	006	A		80	4	012	C	
20	2	006	A		40	4	013	A	
21	2	006	B		74	4	013	C	
56	2	006	D		75	4	013	D	
22	3	007	B		76	4	013	B	
23	3	007	A		77	4	013	C	
24	3	007	D		78	4	013	B	

What competencies did you do well in?
What competencies do you need to work on?

Practice Test Four Answer Sheet

Remove (or photocopy) this answer sheet and use it to complete the practice test.
(See answer key following the test when finished.)

1. Ⓐ Ⓑ Ⓒ Ⓓ
2. Ⓐ Ⓑ Ⓒ Ⓓ
3. Ⓐ Ⓑ Ⓒ Ⓓ
4. Ⓐ Ⓑ Ⓒ Ⓓ
5. Ⓐ Ⓑ Ⓒ Ⓓ
6. Ⓐ Ⓑ Ⓒ Ⓓ
7. Ⓐ Ⓑ Ⓒ Ⓓ
8. Ⓐ Ⓑ Ⓒ Ⓓ
9. Ⓐ Ⓑ Ⓒ Ⓓ
10. Ⓐ Ⓑ Ⓒ Ⓓ
11. Ⓐ Ⓑ Ⓒ Ⓓ
12. Ⓐ Ⓑ Ⓒ Ⓓ
13. Ⓐ Ⓑ Ⓒ Ⓓ
14. Ⓐ Ⓑ Ⓒ Ⓓ
15. Ⓐ Ⓑ Ⓒ Ⓓ
16. Ⓐ Ⓑ Ⓒ Ⓓ
17. Ⓐ Ⓑ Ⓒ Ⓓ
18. Ⓐ Ⓑ Ⓒ Ⓓ
19. Ⓐ Ⓑ Ⓒ Ⓓ
20. Ⓐ Ⓑ Ⓒ Ⓓ

21. Ⓐ Ⓑ Ⓒ Ⓓ
22. Ⓐ Ⓑ Ⓒ Ⓓ
23. Ⓐ Ⓑ Ⓒ Ⓓ
24. Ⓐ Ⓑ Ⓒ Ⓓ
25. Ⓐ Ⓑ Ⓒ Ⓓ
26. Ⓐ Ⓑ Ⓒ Ⓓ
27. Ⓐ Ⓑ Ⓒ Ⓓ
28. Ⓐ Ⓑ Ⓒ Ⓓ
29. Ⓐ Ⓑ Ⓒ Ⓓ
30. Ⓐ Ⓑ Ⓒ Ⓓ
31. Ⓐ Ⓑ Ⓒ Ⓓ
32. Ⓐ Ⓑ Ⓒ Ⓓ
33. Ⓐ Ⓑ Ⓒ Ⓓ
34. Ⓐ Ⓑ Ⓒ Ⓓ
35. Ⓐ Ⓑ Ⓒ Ⓓ
36. Ⓐ Ⓑ Ⓒ Ⓓ
37. Ⓐ Ⓑ Ⓒ Ⓓ
38. Ⓐ Ⓑ Ⓒ Ⓓ
39. Ⓐ Ⓑ Ⓒ Ⓓ
40. Ⓐ Ⓑ Ⓒ Ⓓ

41. Ⓐ Ⓑ Ⓒ Ⓓ
42. Ⓐ Ⓑ Ⓒ Ⓓ
43. Ⓐ Ⓑ Ⓒ Ⓓ
44. Ⓐ Ⓑ Ⓒ Ⓓ
45. Ⓐ Ⓑ Ⓒ Ⓓ
46. Ⓐ Ⓑ Ⓒ Ⓓ
47. Ⓐ Ⓑ Ⓒ Ⓓ
48. Ⓐ Ⓑ Ⓒ Ⓓ
49. Ⓐ Ⓑ Ⓒ Ⓓ
50. Ⓐ Ⓑ Ⓒ Ⓓ
51. Ⓐ Ⓑ Ⓒ Ⓓ
52. Ⓐ Ⓑ Ⓒ Ⓓ
53. Ⓐ Ⓑ Ⓒ Ⓓ
54. Ⓐ Ⓑ Ⓒ Ⓓ
55. Ⓐ Ⓑ Ⓒ Ⓓ
56. Ⓐ Ⓑ Ⓒ Ⓓ
57. Ⓐ Ⓑ Ⓒ Ⓓ
58. Ⓐ Ⓑ Ⓒ Ⓓ
59. Ⓐ Ⓑ Ⓒ Ⓓ
60. Ⓐ Ⓑ Ⓒ Ⓓ

61. Ⓐ Ⓑ Ⓒ Ⓓ
62. Ⓐ Ⓑ Ⓒ Ⓓ
63. Ⓐ Ⓑ Ⓒ Ⓓ
64. Ⓐ Ⓑ Ⓒ Ⓓ
65. Ⓐ Ⓑ Ⓒ Ⓓ
66. Ⓐ Ⓑ Ⓒ Ⓓ
67. Ⓐ Ⓑ Ⓒ Ⓓ
68. Ⓐ Ⓑ Ⓒ Ⓓ
69. Ⓐ Ⓑ Ⓒ Ⓓ
70. Ⓐ Ⓑ Ⓒ Ⓓ
71. Ⓐ Ⓑ Ⓒ Ⓓ
72. Ⓐ Ⓑ Ⓒ Ⓓ
73. Ⓐ Ⓑ Ⓒ Ⓓ
74. Ⓐ Ⓑ Ⓒ Ⓓ
75. Ⓐ Ⓑ Ⓒ Ⓓ
76. Ⓐ Ⓑ Ⓒ Ⓓ
77. Ⓐ Ⓑ Ⓒ Ⓓ
78. Ⓐ Ⓑ Ⓒ Ⓓ
79. Ⓐ Ⓑ Ⓒ Ⓓ
80. Ⓐ Ⓑ Ⓒ Ⓓ

CHAPTER SIXTEEN

Practice 8–12 Pedagogy and Professional Responsibilities Test IV

1. The teacher in an eleventh-grade English classroom wants students to work together in small groups for a project. She has talked to her team leader about ways to have all the students work most effectively because several students in the class are socially immature and tend to disrupt the group process. What is the *best* course of action for the classroom teacher to take in order to plan for the most effective instruction?

   A. Use cooperative learning for the project.
   B. Teach the needed social skills prior to beginning the project and stress how these same skills are needed in the workplace setting.
   C. Call the parents of the disruptive students and ask for ways to get the students to participate in a meaningful way.
   D. Modify the objectives for the project to a level that these socially immature students will find obtainable.

2. A girl in the tenth grade is physically immature. She is absent from physical education class often and has been sent to in-school suspension for refusing to "dress out" in the required P.E. shorts and shirt. The parents have asked that she be exempt from taking the class because she says she "hates it and it makes her feel sick." The school principal has directed the physical education teacher, Mr. Adler, to come up with a plan. What would be the *best* strategy for solving this problem?

   A. Tell the parents that the school district requires four years of physical education and recommend a physical exam from the family physician to see what is making her "feel sick."
   B. Allow her to participate in her school clothes as long as she can do the activities the other students do.
   C. Talk to the girl and see what she "hates" about the class and try to assure her that the exercise is not making her "feel sick."
   D. Check to be sure the girls have a private enclosure for changing clothes and request that the school counselor talk with her about what is making her "feel sick."

3. In his algebra class, the teacher uses many different methods to teach algebraic concepts. The students all do well in his classroom and say that he makes learning "fun." While teaching a unit on geometry he brought in quilts his grandmother made and had students study the angles and how geometry was critical to quilt making. Later he had students work with a partner to create a quilt square out of construction paper. Finally, each quilt square became part of the classroom quilt. The teacher has students work in pairs because he recognizes:

   A. tactile-kinesthetic learners will profit from the activity.
   B. cooperative learning is recognized as a "best practice."
   C. some students are better at algebra than others and can act as tutors.
   D. positive relations with peers are highly valued by high school students.

4. Students in an economics class are required by the classroom teacher to work on a project with a business of each student's choice. The project involves having each student spend one day as an apprentice in the business and observe the operation of the business. Then, the students must present a two-minute multimedia presentation showing what was learned related to specific concepts. The teacher plans this instructional activity because he knows:

   A. high school students are capable of relating learning to the larger community beyond the school.
   B. multimedia presentations will be an activity high school students enjoy.
   C. economics is not easy to teach in a classroom setting.
   D. students are about to enter the world of work and need to examine what economic principles are at work in various businesses.

GO ON TO THE NEXT PAGE

Practice 8–12 Pedagogy and Professional Responsibilities Test IV

5. The history teacher has an excellent textbook but knows that many of the students in the history class have trouble reading and comprehending the information. He begins each new unit by bringing in a box of books about the new topic from the elementary school library. For example, for the unit on the role of the United States in World War I, he brought in many picture books about topics such as submarines and Theodore Roosevelt. As part of his introduction of the unit, he reads aloud several of the books and encourages students to read books that they can understand and discuss in class. The teacher understands that:

   A. most students don't want to read the regular textbook.
   B. students with poor reading abilities slow down the instructional procedure for the rest of the class.
   C. adapting instruction to meet the abilities of all of the students in the classroom is the best way to ensure maximum learning.
   D. collaborating with the district librarians helps achieve the district's goals.

6. The biology teacher does many lab activities with her classes and also requires all her students to do research on the World Wide Web as part of a unit about Texas wildflowers. Students must go online and find information about specific wildflowers and import a picture of the flowers that they also collect in the field. Her team members question why she stays late in the afternoon and comes early in the morning during this unit so that students can use the classroom and library computers. This demonstrates that the teacher understands:

   A. students have different levels of skills in abstract thinking and reasoning.
   B. the need to monitor use of the World Wide Web.
   C. that not all team members must teach the same lessons.
   D. access to computers outside of school varies among her students.

7. In addition to having students work with actual wildflowers and visual images from the computer, the teacher also has a botanist from the Texas Parks and Wildlife Department talk to the students about the wildflower population in Texas and the need to continue seeding not only to beautify the roadways but also to prevent erosion. What is the teacher aware of about her students' learning?

   A. Students are capable of understanding the science TEKS.
   B. Students' varied learning styles require a multifaceted approach to instruction for maximum learning to occur.
   C. Students learn more when teachers collaborate with state and community agencies.
   D. Students should be exposed to different role models from different cultures.

8. Several members of the ninth-grade team are discussing a Limited English Proficient (LEP) student. The math teacher reports no problems with the student's ability to do the math he is covering with the other students. The English teacher, however, is concerned with the grammar of the LEP student and is considering referring her for Special Education evaluation. "Her writing is just terrible. She is always putting words in incorrect order and using Spanish terms in her work." What is the *worst* thing the English teacher is doing?

    A. Not planning instruction that is responsive to cultural differences
    B. Not planning instruction that is based on students' academic abilities
    C. Not providing the student with remedial work
    D. Not referring her to special education earlier

9. In planning to teach a math unit, the eighth-grade math teacher is deciding on objectives for the unit. She talked with her mentor and wants to make sure that the objectives can be taught in the time she has allocated for the unit. She thinks the best way to introduce the new concepts will be through direct instruction; however, her mentor teacher is trying to encourage her to use some small-group instruction and individual research. She is baffled and cannot understand how students can do research in an algebra class when studying linear equations. Her mentor realizes that one of the *most* effective methods for teaching high school students is:

    A. self-directed inquiry
    B. whole-class discussions
    C. hands-on exploration
    D. teacher lecture and practice sheets

10. The new ninth-grade algebra teacher is selecting objectives to teach. Although the students are in an algebra I class, the teacher's preassessment indicates some students are missing skills from the eighth-grade curriculum. The *most* effective teacher would do which of the following?

    A. Select all of the objectives from the Algebra I TEKS and teach them in order from simple to complex.
    B. Examine the prerequisite skills needed and review or reteach the TEKS needed.
    C. Change the course content to match the needs of the students.
    D. Recommend that students not ready for algebra be placed in a different math class.

GO ON TO THE NEXT PAGE

11. Prior to beginning a new unit on acids and bases, the chemistry teacher asks students to write what they know or think they know about the acids and bases. Based on what they write, the teacher places students in heterogeneous groups and selects the goals and objectives for the upcoming unit. The teacher is using which of the following strategies?

    A. Planning learning based on what students tell you they want to learn about acids and bases
    B. Selecting goals and objectives after beginning a unit on acids and bases
    C. Preassessing student knowledge in order to plan objectives for effective instruction
    D. Placing students in heterogeneous groups because students in each group will know about the same thing

12. The chemistry teacher has requested funds from the science department to purchase software, from the IrYdium Project. This software would simulate many different experiments such as acid–base experiments in a virtual chemistry lab. The principal is in favor of the purchase because it is safer. The other science teachers think that actual "hands-on" lab experiments are the only way to teach laboratory science. What rationale would be *best* for the chemistry teacher to use with the other science teachers?

    A. Acids and bases stronger than vinegar and baking soda can be dangerous and prevent us from doing many experiments that could be done in the virtual lab.
    B. Students must learn from all sorts of resources within and outside of the school, including technology.
    C. If we can save the money that we spend on lab equipment and supplies that would leave us more money for other things.
    D. There are many students who do not do well in the lab and complain about odors. This would provide a clean way to get them involved in "messy" lab work.

13. In planning a new lesson, the *best* approach for planning would be which of the following?
    A. Plan instructional activities, select objectives from the TEKS, make the objectives understandable to students in the form of a purpose statement, and assess learning.
    B. Determine goals and objectives from the TEKS, do a task analysis to determine the order of teaching, select instructional strategies, plan instructional activities, and assessments.
    C. Select activities, plan instructional strategies, and determine which TEKS will be covered.
    D. Prepare goals, correlate goals with the TEKS, and plan assessments.

14. The physics teacher is preparing a unit exam for her students. She has determined that the test will be worth 100 points. The test will include multiple-choice and matching questions. The teacher has an old exam from another state and decides that she will just use that test because it covers the same topic, and she does not have time to create a new test. What principle is the teacher not using?
    A. Assessment can provide teachers with information about what students know and do not know about a content area.
    B. Multiple-choice tests provide only one way to assess learning of content.
    C. Teachers should assess student learning of the content covered in the unit.
    D. Teachers should design assessment to analyze students' strengths and needs based on the selected goals and objectives.

Decision Set Begins Here

In the Edgewater High School, there is a desire by the principal for integrated, interdisciplinary, thematic teaching. A few teachers have agreed to try it for a year. To facilitate this, the faculty members are grouped into teams that cross disciplines. One team is composed of an English I teacher, an Algebra I teacher, an Integrated Physics and Chemistry teacher, and a World History Studies teacher. They all have the same students in their classes. Although these teachers have agreed to team, they are very different in their teaching styles. The theme they are using for the semester is "Systems Everywhere."

15. The Algebra I teacher, an excellent teacher, uses a didactic approach to teaching. He is excited about the theme and is teaching properties of the real number system as his first unit. Based on what you know about teaching styles, what is the *best* example of the teaching style the Algebra I teacher would use?

    A. Digressions are avoided and the teacher is the leader of the discussion, which usually involves the whole group.
    B. The teacher monitors and asks open-ended questions throughout the process.
    C. The teacher is a facilitator.
    D. Teacher is in a supportive role.

16. The Integrated Physics and Chemistry teacher, also an excellent teacher, is beginning with the system for classifying elements and compounds. She will be using an inductive method for teaching these concepts. What will her teaching *most* look like?

    A. Inspiring students
    B. Informing students
    C. Involving students
    D. Interrogating students

17. The World History teacher is new to the faculty and also a first-year teacher. He is not sure of his philosophy of teaching; however, he is a team player and decides that he will try out role-playing for the unit on city-states, empires, and barbarian systems. He wants to encourage his students to do more abstract thinking. What should he NOT plan?

    A. Students will be assigned a specific occupation from that time period to research.
    B. Students will be placed in one of three heterogeneous groups for collaborative activities.
    C. Each group will write a code of conduct for the inhabitants of a city-state, empire, or barbarian system.
    D. Each group will role-play living in a city-state, empire, or barbarian system for the other groups.

18. The English I teacher, an excellent teacher, will use writing to learn. For her writing assignments she will collaborate with the Algebra I teacher, the World History teacher, and the Integrated Physics and Chemistry teacher on the theme. After meeting with the teachers she has decided that the first paper will be: *Select a system in your life today and write about how it affects you personally. For example, you could write about the money system, the system for classifying diamonds, or any system you choose.* By doing this early in the semester, the English teacher plans to build prior knowledge about systems and also review the system of revising and editing. When designing an interdisciplinary unit, the teacher knows that effective teaching involves:

A. planning lessons in a logical sequence.
B. encouraging cooperative learning.
C. engaging in reflection and self-assessment.
D. working with other colleagues to enhance professional knowledge and skills.

19. As a group, the teachers plan to send a letter home to each family telling them about the new interdisciplinary unit and explaining the theme, "Systems Everywhere." One strand of the unit will invite parents to be a guest speaker and talk about "Systems in My Workplace." Other opportunities will be available for parents to videotape the students' presentations. What is the *best* reason for involving families?

A. Students' families should be involved in various aspects of the educational program.
B. Problems from difficult parents are avoided if they feel involved.
C. Parents see creative teaching techniques used.
D. Parents not in favor of interdisciplinary teaching will reconsider the idea.

Decision Set Ends Here

20. While researching information for a paper about World War II, the students want to use the World Wide Web and books in the school library as their only references. The teacher wants the students to include primary research in the paper if at all possible. Many of the students do not have relatives who fought in WWII. Others had relatives who are no longer alive. What might be the *best* way for students to learn more about the war?

    A. Find a retiree in the community who fought in WWII to speak to your class.
    B. Get newspaper articles about the war from the local newspaper.
    C. See a movie about World War II.
    D. Contact the Veteran's Administration and request a video about World War II.

21. After looking over your students' work on a recent test in government, you realize that they have many misconceptions about the way the judicial system works. You previously covered the information by having them work in cooperative groups and jigsaw the different court systems in the state. As time is limited and you want to present specific information about the court systems, the *best* approach would be:

    A. Plan a direct instruction lesson for the individuals who did not score well on the test.
    B. Have the students return to their textbooks and reread the chapter about the judicial system.
    C. Have the students who scored well on the test pair with another student and teach the information.
    D. Repeat the jigsaw activity with only the students who did poorly on the exam.

22. In the economics class, the students have been discussing the distribution of goods and services. One senior, Clara, remarks that the drug dealers in her neighborhood are good examples of how economics works. "They grow it, they package it, and they sell it. No middle men!" The *best* response from the teacher would be:

    A. "Clara, one more comment like that and you can count on in-school suspension!"
    B. "Clara, can you give me a different example using a legal form of commerce?"
    C. "Let's examine just how drug dealers do fit into the models we have been discussing."
    D. "That is an example of distribution of goods. Clara, that is so sad that you are even aware of drug dealing in your neighborhood. Do you see much of that going on?"

23. Students have been talking before class about how to get tickets to the rock concert that is coming to town in a month. Some were able to buy tickets when they went on sale but most were not. Some students plan to pay high prices from ticket scalpers; others are hoping to find some from Ticketmonster at a later date. The technology teacher decides to use this as a teachable moment. In class the technology teacher demonstrates how to search for tickets from Ticketmonster, how to find tickets for sale in the online classified section of the newspaper, and how to check and see if ebay has any tickets for sale. The teacher is modeling:

   A. how to surf the Web.
   B. effective strategies for locating needed information.
   C. how to modify plans for teachable moments.
   D. inappropriate use of the computer.

24. As part of his planning, the U.S. History teacher plans time each year to teach his students prereading strategies to help them comprehend their textbooks. He begins with SQ3R and then moves on to concept mapping, and other graphic organizers. The *best* reason for his doing this is that:

   A. he understands that this is a TEKS requirement.
   B. he understands that if students have an assignment, then behavior problems will be fewer.
   C. he understands the importance of teaching students to be self-directed learners.
   D. he understands that the prereading strategies he teaches will make the students feel better about themselves as learners.

GO ON TO THE NEXT PAGE

Decision Set Begins Here

The high school class is composed of many different ethnic groups and many different academic abilities. The teacher is determined to reach each student in the classroom and offer appropriate instruction to each of them. She is also insistent that the classroom is a supportive community of learners and plans to use cooperative learning groups.

25. The first day of class one of the female students arrives last and refuses to sit next to another person in the only available seat. What is the *best* teacher response?

    A. "That is the only chair that is left. If you arrive earlier you can sit next to someone else."
    B. "How would you feel if someone said they did not want to sit by you? We are here to learn, not argue."
    C. "I welcome each of you to my classroom. Please have a seat."
    D. "I welcome you to my classroom. We are all here to learn and to work. Don't make me treat you like young children and break up your arguments. Be respectful of others."

26. During the first week of school, the teacher will establish the climate of the classroom. Which of the following procedures is *best*?

    A. The teacher and students develop the classroom rules so that everyone is aware of the rules and procedures.
    B. The teacher presents her philosophy of education and how that affects her teaching.
    C. The teacher models how she expects students to enter the room and find a seat without bothering other students. She follows that with a direct teaching session on how to turn in completed work.
    D. The teacher models cooperative learning.

27. Because this high school operates with a seven-period day, the teacher wants to find ways to maximize the time that is available for instruction because one hour of each day is taken up by changing classes. Which of the following is *best*?

    A. Use prewritten notes to send home to parents where the appropriate concern is checked.
    B. Set up each class on the computer so that attendance, grades, and communications can be available and updated quickly.
    C. Use assigned seating to be able to check for absences quickly.
    D. Have students grade a peer's paper to save the teacher time for instruction.

28. The teacher prepares the first monthly newsletter to parents explaining her expectations for all of her students. A brief overview of cooperative learning is presented and parents are invited to come to the classroom and observe the cooperative groups at work at any time. The teacher includes a column: "Questions for the Teacher" in which she encourages parents/guardians to ask questions. Included in this first newsletter is a question from the previous year about cooperative learning. Several other teachers ask why she treats high school students like children by writing to their parents. Her *best* reply is:

　A. I have to schedule observations and conferences and newsletters can take the place of one of those conferences.

　B. I have a responsibility to communicate with parents/guardians and to respond to their questions or concerns about my teaching.

　C. I find that difficult parents are easier to handle if I try to send them information often.

　D. As a professional, these newsletters help me focus on the goals of my instruction.

Decision Set Ends Here

29. In his fifth-period class, the teacher has two very bright students who are dating. They always have homework done and participate in class activities; however, he has noticed that they are sending each other winks, smiles, and other socially acceptable types of body language occasionally during the class period. Another student who previously dated the male student is watching them closely and not attending to the lesson. What should the teacher do?

   A. Analyze ways to get the distracted student to return to the lesson without making an issue over what he considers typical high school behaviors.
   B. Discuss the problem with the two students who are dating and ask them to please stop.
   C. Call on the distracted female student each time she is not attending to the lesson.
   D. Inform the principal about the problem and ask how to handle the situation.

30. Students often dislike school or dislike specific classes that they feel they do not do well in. The new Integrated Physics and Chemistry teacher realizes that many students are fearful of her class and wants to present instruction in ways that demonstrate her love for science and teaching. Which of the following should she try?

   A. Planning lessons early in the year that are enjoyable and that involve hands-on learning
   B. Focusing on the product rather than the process
   C. Being very involved with her students outside of the classroom
   D. Using extrinsic rewards early in the year, such as pizza, to get the students interested in science

31. The history teacher has several handicapped students in his classes. One student is confined to a wheelchair and sometimes has trouble getting around backpacks and books that students leave on the floor. One student taunts the handicapped student by calling him, "Wheelie." How can the teacher assure all of his students that the classroom is a safe, nurturing environment that respects students' rights and dignity?

   A. Post the classroom rules where they are visible.
   B. Arrange the classroom in clusters of desks.
   C. Respond immediately to stop or redirect misbehavior.
   D. Involve parents in planning the course for the year.

32. The English IV teacher is well-liked and has taught at the school for more than 30 years. She is a very traditional teacher and all of her instruction is very teacher-centered. What seating arrangement is best for this type of teacher?

   A. Desks are arranged in rows.
   B. Desks are arranged in a large circle.
   C. Desks are arranged in group clusters.
   D. U-shaped design.

Decision Set Begins Here

The tenth-grade computer class has a diverse mixture of students. There are several students who are diagnosed with attention deficit hyperactivity disorder (ADHD), one child who has cerebral palsy and is wheelchair bound, several who have emotional problems with eating disorders, and several students with limited English speaking ability. The technology teacher rarely has behavior problems because the students love to work on the computer. Recently, several of the students have become discipline problems when he is presenting a new project using the data projector.

33. In addition, the technology teacher makes it a practice each year to communicate to families the rules and consequences of his classroom. Students take home a letter listing the rules and consequences that have been mutually agreed on the first day of class by the students and teacher. That note asks for the following information:

    How do you want me to contact you?
    - Face-to-face conference. What is the best way to reach you?
    - Telephone call. If so, number to call?
    - E-mail. If so, please provide your e-mail address.

    The students are to return the letter from their parents.
    The teacher is aware that:

    A. most poor families don't have computers so, it is best not to use only e-mail for communication.
    B. telephone calls are better than no contact, but face-to-face is better.
    C. parents will be on the side of the teacher if you reach out to them early in the year.
    D. parents want to communicate with the teacher; however, one method will not work for all parents.

34. Those parents who do not respond to the letter home are then contacted by the teacher by telephone, if a phone number is included in the student registration file. He has another employee who speaks Spanish nearby in case the families speak only Spanish. Some fellow teachers are amazed that he does all of this but he knows that good teachers:

    A. address equity issues related to the use of technology.
    B. apply theories and techniques related to managing and monitoring of student behavior.
    C. demonstrate awareness of appropriate behavior standards.
    D. interact with all families.

35. His fellow teachers jokingly call him "superman" because he is such a great teacher and because he works closely with other teachers to plan instruction that is integrated into social studies, science, and English classes. He believes that:

   A. most of the other teachers are not supporting the campus and district goals.
   B. good teachers collaborate to support students' learning and to achieve campus and district goals.
   C. lessons should be planned so that activities progress in a logical sequence and support stated campus and district goals.
   D. teachers should understand how technology can be used to assess student performance.

36. Because the technology teacher understands the legal and ethical use of technology and digital information, which of the following is NOT part of his curriculum?

   A. Students are taught to insert a QuickTime movie into a multimedia presentation.
   B. Students are taught how to exchange music files from their favorite CDs.
   C. Students are taught how to create newsletters and brochures.
   D. Students are taught how to take digital movies and save them to DVDs.

Decision Set Ends Here

GO ON TO THE NEXT PAGE

37. The government teacher begins each year with a unit on citizenship. Through group activities, the unit introduces the rights and responsibilities of consumers and businesses in the free enterprise system of the United States. One of the first lessons considers the concept of laws and the consequences for breaking laws while driving. She introduces the concepts of age requirements, traffic laws, and driving while intoxicated as all being related to citizenship rights and responsibilities. Then, she asks the groups to analyze what rights and responsibilities come with being a citizen of a high school. The teacher is:

    A. using a variety of means to convey high expectations to all of the students.
    B. demonstrating an awareness of appropriate behavior standards and expectations.
    C. applying techniques for managing student behavior.
    D. organizing groups that promote students' abilities to assume responsible roles in the classroom.

38. Which of the following is NOT a behaviorist approach to behavior management?

    A. Students are given pizza parties for doing specific behaviors.
    B. Communicating anger about behaviors in the form of "I messages."
    C. Students receive a "star" for completion of homework.
    D. Students receive immediate praise for desirable behavior.

39. The social studies teacher has one special needs student in her classroom who has difficulty staying on-task for more than a few minutes. He wants to work only at the computer. She has instigated a system that gives the student points for every 10 minutes that the student can remain on-task. After the student has earned 50 points, the student may go to the computer for a specified period of time. Her *primary* goal in setting up this reward system is to:

    A. keep this student from causing problems in the classroom.
    B. move this student from external control to self-control and self-monitoring.
    C. provide a system that the student's parents will not consider too punitive.
    D. model how to use positive reinforcement for the other students.

40. Each homeroom teacher uses a portion of the homeroom period to teach or review with students how to solve problems with peers. The procedure involves:

   - Calm down.
   - Verbalize the problem using "I" statements.
   - Discuss the problem and possible solutions.
   - Agree on a solution and shake hands on the agreement.

   What is this procedure teaching young adults?

   A. Ways to make choices
   B. Conflict resolution
   C. Team building
   D. Classroom rules

41. The first-year, ninth-grade English teacher finds that most freshmen do not understand how to budget time for in-class assignments. She writes the allotted time on the board and explains that when the time is up, groups will begin making presentations. Often when time is called, groups will say, "Wait, we're not finished. Can we have a few more minutes?" Frustrated with this pattern, the teacher has gone to her mentor for advice. The mentor suggests that the *best* remedy is:

   A. not let students use excuses as a way to have more group time with peers.
   B. insist that all groups will be graded on the product produced in the given time.
   C. set aside a class period to teach, through modeling, how to pace an activity.
   D. sit in with the slow group and serve as the time-keeper.

Decision Set Begins Here

The geometry teacher, Mr. Line, is an experienced teacher and has been asked to mentor a new first-year teacher at the school. Mr. Line uses excellent questioning as a method to obtain information from his students. He uses questioning as a way of helping his students understand the importance of logical reasoning, justification, and proof in mathematics.

42. For example, he asks, "You are able to solve math problems that use the Pythagorean Theorem, but can you prove the Pythagorean Theorem using three sheets of construction paper cut into squares? If so, show me how. If not, tell me why not?" What does this question illustrate about the geometry teacher's questioning techniques?

    A. He believes in asking questions at the knowledge level.
    B. He believes in asking low-level questions.
    C. He believes in asking higher-level questions.
    D. He knows that questions at this level produce less learning than lower-level questions.

43. Going to her mentor and asking for assistance and feedback demonstrates that the new teacher understands the importance of:

    A. reflection and self-assessment.
    B. using a support system to improve professional development needs.
    C. planning lessons that reflect student interests.
    D. adapting instruction for students who needs special assistance.

44. The new teacher asks her mentor, Mr. Line, for assistance in improving her questioning techniques. She requests that he come to her classroom and observe her teaching and then give her suggestions about ways to improve. Mr. Line observes her teaching a class of 20 students and makes the following notes about her teaching:

Teacher: "Yvette, what does parallel mean?"

Yvette: "That two lines are like a railroad track"

Teacher: "That's an interesting definition."

Teacher: "Joe, are perpendicular lines parallel?

Joe: No

Teacher: Yvette, what is the answer to problem number 4?

Yvette: Parallel

What suggestion should Mr. Line NOT give to the new teacher?

A. "It would be better to ask the question and then call on the student to answer it."
B. "Distribute your questions more equitably."
C. "Don't use wait time; too much wait time is not good."
D. "Probe answers to get more information about what students are thinking."

45. Mr. Line meets with her and suggests ways to modify her teaching so that she is teaching higher-level thinking. Weeks later Mr. Line returns to her classroom at her request. The teacher does the following activity:

On the board are the following figures:

Teacher: "The first triangle is an isosceles triangle. The second triangle is an isosceles triangle. The third triangle is not an isosceles triangle. In your groups create a definition of an isosceles triangle based on your observations."

This type of activity requires students to use what type of reasoning?

A. Deductive reasoning
B. Inductive reasoning
C. Didactic reasoning
D. Divergent reasoning

46. Mr. Line recently noticed that one student in his classroom is very talented in geometry. The student is normally considered lazy because he often falls asleep in class. Mr. Line knows that the student is bright and could someday have a promising career in math. He confers with the student after class one day and finds that the student has a job at a fast-food restaurant from 8 P.M. until 12 A.M. each night. The boy explains that his father and mother are both out of work and he must work to support the family. What is the *best* thing for Mr. Line to do?

   A. Meet with the family and the school social worker to try and find a solution to the student working such late hours.
   B. Meet with the parents and arrange for the family to get a short-term loan from the bank until summer vacation.
   C. Call the Salvation Army and see if the family can get financial assistance.
   D. Call the state employment agency and arrange for the parents to go in for a job interview.

Decision Set Ends Here

47. The biology teacher has tried to communicate the structure of DNA to his class, but the explanation does not seem adequate to him. He has pictures of the double helix strand but after the lecture and after showing the picture, he can tell from the students' body language that their understanding of a complex concept is not clear. He should:

   A. ask a fellow teacher to come in and reteach the concept.
   B. reteach the concept using a video or digital technology.
   C. ask the students to discuss it in cooperative groups.
   D. move on as there is too little time in the year to reteach.

Decision Set Begins Here

The faculty at the high school used the spring semester to do a self-study of teachers' instructional practices. They found that most of the teachers used a lecture approach all of the time. Teachers have agreed to try various types of instructional practices this year in order to improve student learning.

48. One of the new teachers is interested in determining which learning approach will keep her students most actively involved in their learning. Which approach will do that *best*?

    A. Inquiry learning
    B. Direct instruction
    C. Guided reading
    D. Lecture with questioning

49. Each teacher is free to try any method of instruction they choose, but every teacher has to select one area of their teaching to work on for the year. The history teacher has been evaluated by the principal for two years and each year she notes that he needs to examine his questioning techniques. Which of the following would NOT improve his questioning techniques?

    A. Using wait time
    B. Ordering the questions
    C. Probing for clarification
    D. Using eye contact

50. The physics teacher has selected improving assessment of her students as her goal for the year. In the past she has used lecture and end of unit exams as the way she evaluates her students. This year she plans to diagnose students' needs as well as evaluate their work. Which of the following is the *best* way to gather diagnostic information?

    A. Self-assessment
    B. Ongoing summative assessments
    C. Ongoing formative assessments
    D. Reducing the standard deviation

51. The first day of class the chemistry teacher explains to the class that she has selected a goal for her teaching for the year. Her goal is to improve how she diagnoses students' needs and how she evaluates their learning. She goes over the syllabus and notes that the first unit is on matter. She explains that the unit on matter is divided into three sections: solids, liquids, and gases. She notes that two-thirds of the instruction will be on liquids, one-sixth will be on solids, and one-sixth will be on gases. The test on matter that she prepares should:

   A. be the end of chapter test provided by the publisher.
   B. have 66 out of 100 questions about liquids.
   C. have one-third of the questions cover liquids.
   D. have equal coverage of solids, liquids, and gasses.

52. At the end of the nine-week grading period, the school offers parents the opportunity to come to school for a parent–teacher conference. The chemistry teacher sends home a note to parents notifying them of the dates and times that are available for the conferences. She explains in the note the purpose of the conference and requests parents notify her if the scheduled time is convenient or to suggest an alternative time. During one of the conferences the parents ask the teacher why their son is making a C for the nine weeks when their daughter always made As in Chemistry. She should be able to explain this by:

   A. mentioning that the student is distracted easily and that having an attention deficit often affects grades.
   B. providing the parents with a list of student needs to be worked out at the beginning of the conference.
   C. making the parents feel at ease by explaining that their son is probably less mature at this age than their daughter was.
   D. sharing with parents the student's work portfolio for the nine weeks and any teacher notes.

53. For the second nine weeks, the chemistry teacher plans to make her assessments more "authentic." Which of the following would she NOT include?

   A. Anecdotal notes
   B. Process observations in the chemistry lab
   C. End of chapter exams
   D. Student interviews

Decision Set Ends Here

54. The physics teacher will teach the concept of frequency as related to sound for the day's lesson. The *best* way to introduce the concept would be:

   A. Show how waves are formed when a pebble is dropped in a container of water.
   B. Illustrate with a computer how sound waves are visible when playing music CDs.
   C. Bring in instruments from the band department and have students discover what happens when the trombone slide is lengthened and shortened, and the strings are loosened or tightened on stringed instruments.
   D. Show the DVD *The Piano Player* and discuss why different keys on a piano sound differently.

55. The band director is aware of how much students love music, especially current music. He wants them to be motivated and interested in the music they will be playing; however, he wants to introduce them to all forms of music to enrich their knowledge. What is the *best* way to motivate the students for the major performances of the year?

   A. Each student plays a solo of a self-selected piece.
   B. Students provide ideas in writing to the band director.
   C. Students help in determining what music will be played for each performance.
   D. Students vote on music selections based on both director and student input.

56. The math teacher is trying to get her students to become self-motivated learners. Each year she has a group of students who do not do homework. She knows that many of them are good students and that their neglect of homework is causing them to have lower grades in math than they could be earning. She wants to try using reinforcement to modify their behavior and to motivate each student to do well in math. What is the *best* procedure for her to try?

   A. Use tangible rewards to motivate her students to do well in math.
   B. Begin with verbal praise early in the semester and then add extrinsic motivators for those students who are not doing well in math.
   C. Begin with intrinsic rewards early in the semester and gradually decrease the amount of reinforcement as students do well in math.
   D. Begin with extrinsic rewards early in the semester and gradually through praise increase the students' intrinsic motivation to do well in math.

GO ON TO THE NEXT PAGE

57. The principal has received several complaints about the art teacher. Students complain that he makes fun of the work students do in his classroom. The principal cannot imagine what these complaints are in reference to and has planned a meeting with the art teacher to discuss the situation. The principal informs him that several excellent students reported that, "he rolls his eyes at my artwork." The art teacher is quick to explain that he rolls his eyes when the work is excellent. The principal suggests that the *best* way to communicate with students is to:

   A. use verbal communication so that the explicit message is understood.
   B. keep up his excellent sense of humor but make sure that the body language is not misunderstood.
   C. be more serious in the classroom so that the students do not misunderstand his communication.
   D. use nonverbal communication to communicate with students who have the ability to understand the subtle meanings.

58. The government teacher is introducing her class to the judicial system in the United States. Which of the following purposes for reading is age appropriate for the teacher to communicate to the students in this class?

   A. "Please read this chapter and see if you understand what the Supreme Court is saying."
   B. "Read this chapter and then we will look up the definitions of any terms not understood."
   C. "After reading this review of the Supreme Court's decision on students' abilities to sue coaches, take one of the two sides presented and write a one-page paper that persuades others to agree with you."
   D. "After reading this review of the Supreme Court's decision on students' abilities to sue coaches, write a one-page paper that is a "How-To" paper about filing a case in the Supreme Court."

59. Which of the following is NOT a correct term for the computer screen?

   A. Input device
   B. Liquid crystal display (LCD)
   C. Monitor
   D. Output device

60. The technology teacher is installing a new virus protection program from a CD on the computers. What is the *best* way to make sure the most up-to-date virus protection is installed on the computer?

    A. Installing the antivirus on the computer is all that needs to be done.
    B. Go online to the manufacturer's website and download the latest virus patch.
    C. Purchase an update from the company.
    D. Go to Google and do a search for "antivirus update."

61. The Student Council is planning on publishing a high school student directory with students' names, addresses, phone numbers, and e-mail addresses. Students may choose not to include any of this information. What is the *best* software to use for making such a directory?

    A. Word-processing software
    B. Database software
    C. Spreadsheet software
    D. Presentation software

62. The English teacher has always used a monthly newsletter to communicate with her students' parents about the plans for the coming month. She is being asked by the school administration to limit the amount of printing that is being done due to increased costs of paper and printing supplies. She wants to continue to keep parents informed so she is examining ways to use the computer. What is *best* way to get information to parents who have computer access?

    A. E-mail to parents
    B. Class Web page
    C. Personal Web page
    D. E-mail with Word attachment

63. The history teacher requires his students to use technology applications for their research projects. Which of the following would be the *best* software to use for sharing student projects with the class?

    A. Word-processing software
    B. Database software
    C. Presentation software
    D. Spreadsheet software

64. Technology projects should be evaluated using:

   A. a rubric given to students prior to beginning the project.
   B. a rubric that is used only by the teacher for grading.
   C. a rubric that is created with the students prior to the project.
   D. the regular grading procedure used by the teacher for other grades.

65. To promote the students' abilities to use feedback and self-assessment, the math teacher finds which of the following the *least* effective?

   A. Machine-graded computer cards are used to return grades quickly.
   B. Students grade their own papers to see their errors and get feedback.
   C. Students work in groups with other students.
   D. Portfolio assessment is used.

66. The science teacher notices during an inquiry lesson that students are not engaged in the lesson and seem to be confused. He should:

   A. change his role from participant to facilitator or director.
   B. ask students to return to the textbook and read what is confusing them.
   C. stop the lesson and tell them it will be done another day when they can work.
   D. separate groups and use a different grouping arrangement.

67. The math teacher wants to encourage students to check their math problems since many of their mistakes are due to miscalculations rather than misunderstandings. What is the *best* way to monitor and assess students' process skills in math?

   A. Have students exchange papers and check the work
   B. Design a check sheet that students will use for self-assessment
   C. Grade each paper on the process as well as the product.
   D. Allow students to just work the problems and not have to check them.

68. The new English teacher has students respond to literature in a reader response journal. The students write what they liked or did not like about the text. They write about what they did not understand and about what the literature reminds them of in real life. They are free to respond as they choose. The teacher reads and replies to each entry once a week. Several of the other English teachers think that this is too much reading and have encouraged the new teacher to give tests instead. The new English teacher *most* likely does this because:

   A. students should receive constructive feedback about their thoughts and ideas in the form of a written dialogue.
   B. the journal is a way for the new teacher to grade the students' writing skills.
   C. the journal requires less time than would be required to make an objective exam.
   D. assessment should be ongoing and give students constructive feedback and inform the teacher of needed instruction.

69. The physical education teacher is a member of the Site-based Decision Committee. Several other physical education teachers express amazement that he is serving on that committee rather than something related to athletics. What is his *best* explanation?

   A. "I know it is a drag. But the principal asked me to be on it and I just couldn't turn him down."
   B. "Look I do P.E. stuff all day at school. This gives me a chance to do something new."
   C. "If no one from the physical education department participates on this committee, the P.E. department will not be represented. This is a valuable committee for our department and for us as teachers."
   D. "I came here from a school where the P.E. department was not taken seriously. All they could do was talk about sports. I'm doing this to show that we do have good ideas."

70. The French teacher is reading over his latest appraisal from the building principal. The appraisal notes that he is doing an excellent job of teaching. It suggests that he select one area of the appraisal instrument to focus on as a goal for the next semester. The principal wants this goal in one week. His *best* response is to:

   A. pick the area that he feels strongest in because it will require the least amount of change.
   B. examine the possible areas, select the one that he thinks is his weakest area, and submit that to the principal.
   C. submit no goals to the principal because the current evaluation ranked him as doing an excellent job.
   D. ask students in his class to suggest what area he needs to improve on the most and submit that area.

Practice 8–12 Pedagogy and Professional Responsibilities Test IV

71. The volleyball coach is very involved each season in volleyball or assisting other coaches. In addition to coaching, he also teaches one section of American History. He is not able to attend weekend workshops or conferences because of games and can *best* be involved in professional development by:

    A. reading the Collegiate Volleyball news.
    B. asking his students to evaluate his strength and needs and work on the needs.
    C. going to another American History teacher and asking if he can use his outline for the American History class so that the proper TEKS are covered.
    D. joining the social studies professional organization and coaching professional organization and reading those journal articles online or in print.

Decision Set Begins Here

One of the areas that teachers must understand and follow is the Texas Code of Ethics and Standard Practices for Texas Educators. After firing a teacher the previous year for giving students answers on the Texas Assessment of Knowledge and Skills (TAKS) exam, the principal of Painton High School, a large suburban school, decides to require all new teachers to pass an exam on the Texas Code of Ethics and Standard Practices for Texas Educators. She begins writing the exam the first day of classes.

72. The first question she writes is about Professional Ethical Conduct, Practices, and Performance.

    A teacher is collecting money for the yearbook. The teacher collected more than $500 the first day. Last year the book orders totaled $7000. Where is the *best* place for the teacher to keep this $500 until the sale is finished in six weeks?

    A. Keep all monies locked in a secure location in the classroom.
    B. Deposit the money in a personal account and write a single check to the school when the sales are finished.
    C. Submit monies to the school principal or designee to be deposited in the appropriate activity fund account.
    D. Take the monies to the district office and have the district office deposit the money.

73. While she is writing she overhears a teacher in the hallway say to another teacher, "I overheard the principal talking on the telephone to Ms. Lately, the biology teacher, and Ms. Lately will be fired if she does not start getting to school on time." This statement:

    A. does not violate the Code of Ethics and Standard Practices for Texas Educators.
    B. is just a conversation between two professionals and is not a violation.
    C. is in poor taste and gossip but is not a violation of the Code of Ethics and Standards.
    D. is in violation of the Ethical Conduct Toward Professional Colleagues standard.

74. While writing the test, the principal receives a phone call from a parent who is very angry. Her child is transferring into the district this year from another district and was told by a teacher that "children with autism do not qualify for Special Education." How should the principal respond?

   A. "Yes, Title VII makes your child ineligible for special education services."
   B. "I am so sorry that you got misinformation. That teacher is not a special education teacher and just made an error."
   C. "By federal law, Individuals with Disabilities Education Act (IDEA) approved the inclusion of autistic children as being eligible for special education and related services."
   D. "Welcome to the district. We will certainly work with you and see what can be done to help your child."

75. No sooner is the principal off of the phone with that parent than the superintendent of the district phones. He is also angry.

   Superintendent: "Do you know that your football coach has gone to a school board member and requested that the football program be given additional dollars?"

   Principal: "No, I certainly did not authorize him to do that, and he never talked to me about it either. The district policy states that all requests for money must be submitted to the building principal." This coach does NOT know how to:

   A. be an advocate for students.
   B. work effectively with mentors and supervisors.
   C. maintain supportive, cooperative relationships with professional colleagues to support students.
   D. to maintain relationships among campus and district offices.

GO ON TO THE NEXT PAGE

The principal is very frustrated at this point and decides that all of the teachers will take a test over the Texas Code of Ethics and Standard Practices for Texas Educators. She thinks *all* of them are excellent teachers, but too many are unaware of the laws. They need to follow all the rules to the letter!

76. The history teacher asks the principal for a few moments and shares with her a story about the student who did not make a passing grade in her class at the end of last year. The parents wanted to have the student retake the final exam and average the two grades. The history teacher refused citing the grading procedure in the class syllabus. The teacher beams and explains that the student's father just came by her classroom to thank her. He said, "That F was the best thing that ever happened to her. She has really grown up over the summer. Thank you." This *best* illustrates:

   A. relations with families are very important for student growth.
   B. students mature by having tough teachers.
   C. teachers must follow procedures and requirements for maintaining accurate student records.
   D. teachers should not ever change a grade.

Decision Set Ends Here

77. The social studies teacher wants to have students assume roles of historical characters as part of a unit about the American Revolution. The students would be required to dress in the historical attire for a presentation. Several of her peers do not think this is a good idea because:

   A. the experience would be threatening to some students, and asking them to make a presentation in period clothing may cause them to dislike social studies.
   B. the student's presentations should be done with the computer.
   C. student physical and emotional development varies and some students may find it difficult to have to dress in period clothing and make a presentation to peers.
   D. students at this age are often rebellious.

78. The teacher is expecting a new student to join his math class. When the student arrives he finds that the student is Vietnamese and speaks little or no English. The *best* way for the teacher to make this student successful is to:

   A. select objectives that are at a lower level for the new student.
   B. group the new student with other English Language Learners (ELLs) for cooperative learning so the teacher can assist this group.
   C. remember that student self-esteem and academic success are positively correlated.
   D. have the student go to the special education teacher for tutorials in math until the student is comfortable with English.

79. Before class begins, the social studies teacher overhears students in the hall laughing about the new Vietnamese student's culture. The *best* thing for the teacher to do when class begins is:

   A. conference with the offending students and make clear that no such behavior will be tolerated.
   B. teach a lesson stressing how different cultures are more alike than different.
   C. apologize to the offended student.
   D provide accurate information about cultural groups.

80. A new band director is not sure what resources she should use to guide her instruction for the year. She consults with the curriculum director who tells her the first place to begin planning is to create broad goals for the band program. Which suggestion did the curriculum director NOT make?

   A. The goals should require solo performances.
   B. The goals should be aligned to the district curriculum.
   C. The goals should be age appropriate.
   D. The goals should address current student needs.

CHAPTER SEVENTEEN

Practice 8–12 Pedagogy and Professional Responsibilities Test Answers and Explanations

1. B

This question addresses information from PPR Competency 001:

The teacher understands human developmental processes and applies this knowledge to plan instruction and ongoing assessment that motivate students and are responsive to their developmental characteristics and needs.

This is a priority-setting question. You must determine the *best* course of action for the teacher to take. Eliminate (A) because, although cooperative learning is an excellent approach, certain social skills must be pre-taught for cooperative learning groups to work effectively. Cooperative learning has three requirements: Shared responsibility, individual accountability, and social skills are taught. Begin by teaching necessary social skills. Eliminate (C) because this question is about planning instruction, not behavior management. Choice (D) is never acceptable. Teachers should modify instruction, not objectives. Doing this is often referred to as "dumbing down" the curriculum. Choice (B) is the correct response.

2. D

This question addresses information from PPR Competency 001:

The teacher understands human developmental processes and applies this knowledge to plan instruction and ongoing assessment that motivate students and are responsive to their developmental characteristics and needs.

This is a priority-setting question. Teachers should be aware that adolescent students are often very self-conscious about their appearance and this can affect performance in other domains. Eliminate (A), as this does not consider that the student may be feeling self-conscious about her physical immaturity. It places the problem on the parents rather than trying to find an immediate solution. Choice (B) would again make her appear "different" from other students. Also, it would not be logical that a girl wear a dress while participating in certain activities and breaks the established rule of dressing out. Eliminate (C) because a female student is not likely to reveal to a male physical education teacher her feelings of being physically immature. In addition, in today's society it may not be wise for a male teacher to try and discuss issues regarding sexuality with a female student. Choice (D) is the best answer because it involves the school counselor and provides privacy for changing clothes. It may not work but it is the best first choice.

3. D

This question addresses information from PPR Competency 001:

The teacher understands human developmental processes and applies this knowledge to plan instruction and ongoing assessment that motivate students and are responsive to their developmental characteristics and needs.

Choice (A) does not answer the question, "Why do the students work in pairs?" Certainly the tactile–kinesthetic learners will profit from the hands-on activity, but that is not the question. Eliminate (B) because working in pairs is not necessarily cooperative learning. It is small group activity. Cooperative learning has three requirements: Shared responsibility, individual accountability, and social skills are taught. Choice (C) is true but is not the best answer because the students are involved in a creative endeavor, not working on algebra problems. Students in high school are often highly motivated to learn when working with a peer; for that reason choice (D) is the correct answer. The state of Texas wants teachers to understand the significance of peer-related issues for teaching.

Practice 8–12 Pedagogy and Professional Responsibilities Test Answers and Explanations

4. A

This question addresses information from PPR Competency 001:

The teacher understands human developmental processes and applies this knowledge to plan instruction and ongoing assessment that motivate students and are responsive to their developmental characteristics and needs.

Choice (B) is a true statement. However, the question is broader than just the presentation. Why do the students work in the community? Eliminate (C) because the answer is simplistic, and there is a much better reason. Choice (D) is a true statement, but it is not the best answer. Ask yourself, "What does the state of Texas want me to know?" Some students are about to enter the world of work. Others are about to go on to higher education. The activity is about relating what you learned back to the class through a presentation. Choice (D) does not make that clear. Choice (A) is correct. All of the students are served by relating learning in high school to experiences in the larger community beyond the school. Students spend a day in the community connecting their school learning to the world of work and then present that learning to the class.

5. C

This question addresses information from PPR Competency 002:

The teacher understands student diversity and knows how to plan learning experiences and design assessments that are responsive to differences among students and that promote all students' learning.

Choice (A) has a "red pepper word" in "most." Some students may not like the textbook, but is that the reason the teacher brings in the books? Diverse learners may not be able to read at a high school level. Eliminate (B) as this procedure will not increase the speed of the instructional procedure. In fact, it will take more time. Eliminate (D) because this is not a question about the district's goals. Choice (C) is correct. The teacher knows that good teaching begins with connecting new knowledge to existing knowledge. The teacher adapts the instruction by using picture books to quickly build some background knowledge about World War I for students without much prior knowledge about the war, and thereby improve the students' learning.

6. D

This question addresses information from PPR Competency 002:

The teacher understands student diversity and knows how to plan learning experiences and design assessments that are responsive to differences among students and that promote all students' learning.

Eliminate (A) because access to the computer is not about reasoning skills. Eliminate (B) because students in high school do research independently at home and in the library. Choice (C) does not answer why she comes early and leaves late. Choice (D) is the correct answer. The teacher knows that access to computers outside of school varies among her students and so she arranges ways to adapt the situation to meet those students' needs.

7. B

This question addresses information from PPR Competency 002:

The teacher understands student diversity and knows how to plan learning experiences and design assessments that are responsive to differences among students and that promote all students' learning.

Eliminate (A) because it does not explain why the guest speaker is invited. Item (C) looks like a good answer, but we do not know that students learn more when teachers collaborate with state agencies. Choices (D) assumes that the speaker is from a different culture, but this is not stated in the question. Choice (B) is the correct response. Students differ in how they process information. Some students are visual, others are tactile kinesthetic. Still others are auditory, and by bringing in a speaker, the teacher is including an oral presentation that will provide a learning opportunity for these latter students.

8. A

This question addresses information from PPR Competency 002:

The teacher understands student diversity and knows how to plan learning experiences and design assessments that are responsive to differences among students and that promote all students' learning.

This is a priority-setting question. This question is about diversity. Choice (B) is incorrect because the student who is Spanish may be an excellent student when writing in Spanish. The problem is one of language, not writing skills. Choice (C) is incorrect because remedial work is used to assist a person who has been diagnosed with a problem. Choice (D) makes no sense if the student is successful in math and is a Spanish speaker. Special education is not going to be the correct placement for an Limited English Proficiency (LEP) student unless the student also has other learning difficulties that qualify him or her for admission to special education. Choice (A) is the correct response, because it is the *worst* thing the teacher is doing. Good teachers always adapt lessons to meet the needs of all learners, including English language learners.

Practice 8–12 Pedagogy and Professional Responsibilities Test Answers and Explanations

9. A

This question addresses information from PPR Competency 003:

The teacher understands procedures for designing effective and coherent instruction and assessment based on appropriate learning goals and objectives.

This is a priority-setting question about what is *most* effective. Choice (B) is incorrect because the question tells you the mentor is suggesting small-group instruction and individual research. Choice (C) sounds good, but small-group instruction is not necessarily hands-on learning. Choice (D) is very direct and traditional and is not the suggestion made. Choice (A), self-directed inquiry, is individual research. According to a constructivist approach to learning, students learn most when there is choice. The research on Writing to Learn also suggests that students learn about any subject when they must write about it. The mentor wants the students to take ownership of their learning. Students can research and write about topics in algebra just as they can in other subjects. Direct instruction has a place in teaching, but self-directed inquiry is asking students to take responsibility for their own learning.

10. B

This question addresses information from PPR Competency 003:

The teacher understands procedures for designing effective and coherent instruction and assessment based on appropriate learning goals and objectives.

This is a priority-setting question. Choice (A) is incorrect and choice (B) is correct because the TEKS are the state curriculum. However, if students lack the prerequisite skills from earlier TEKS, teachers should review or reteach these skills to build prior knowledge of the concepts. By doing this, new learning is being connected to previous learning. Choice (C) is incorrect because the course content is not changed from semester to semester. Prerequisite skills may need to be taught and although the course can be extended, it cannot be changed. Choice (D) is often done before a school year begins. Students who are not ready are placed in a lower-level math class. However, this question asks how the most effective teacher would work with students she already has in her class.

11. C

This question addresses information from PPR Competency 003:

The teacher understands procedures for designing effective and coherent instruction and assessment based on appropriate learning goals and objectives.

Eliminate (A) because he did not ask students what they wanted to learn. Choice (B) is not a strategy, and goals and objectives are planned prior to the start of a unit. Choice (D) is trying to trick you. Heterogeneous means the all of students do not know the same things. It is a mixed ability group. Choice (C) is the correct answer. Objectives are based on student needs. By using a preassessment or other assessment data, the teacher can plan better by knowing the students' level of knowledge.

12. B

This question addresses information from PPR Competency 003:

The teacher understands procedures for designing effective and coherent instruction and assessment based on appropriate learning goals and objectives.

This is a priority-setting question. Delete (A) because although the statement is true for young children, high school chemistry teachers could model stronger acids and bases and this is not a strong rationale to use. Choice (C) is simply silly as a rationale, as most labs are already equipped. Choice (D) has a negative tone that should shout "red pepper" to you. Student's complaints do not drive the curriculum. Choice (B) is the correct answer. This question is about teacher knowledge and uses of resources within and without the school, including technology. Technology allows students to experience virtual activities and prepares them for the future.

13. B

This question addresses information from PPR Competency 003:

The teacher understands procedures for designing effective and coherent instruction and assessment based on appropriate learning goals and objectives.

Teachers should not "teach to the TEKS." However, the TEKS are the state-adopted curriculum and must be followed. The TEKS represent a starting point. Through task analysis, determine the prerequisite skills. On the basis of objectives, select instructional strategies. Following all of this, teachers plan activities. The assessment is based on the objectives. Eliminate (A) because activities come before objectives. Eliminate (C) because the TEKS are examined after activities and strategies are planned. Eliminate (D) because there are no objectives, and assessment is based on objectives. Choice (B) is the correct response.

Practice 8–12 Pedagogy and Professional Responsibilities Test Answers and Explanations

14. D

This question addresses information from PPR Competency 003:

The teacher understands procedures for designing effective and coherent instruction and assessment based on appropriate learning goals and objectives.

Choices (A), (B), and (C) are all principles that the teacher is using. Choice (D) is the correct answer and is the principle that the teacher is NOT using. Assessment must be based on teacher-selected objectives. The use of a test on the same topic does not ensure that the objectives are the same. Teachers should design assessments that "match" the teaching objectives.

15. A

This question addresses information from PPR Competency 004:

The teacher understands learning processes and factors that impact student learning and demonstrates this knowledge by planning effective, engaging instruction and appropriate assessments.

This is a priority-setting question. Choices (B), (C), and (D) are all examples of an inquiry approach to teaching. Choice (A) is the correct response. A didactic approach to teaching is a direct, or traditional, approach to teaching. The teacher is the director of the learning. There is usually whole-group instruction as compared to inquiry learning, which extensively involves cooperative learning with the teacher in the role of a facilitator.

16. C

This question addresses information from PPR Competency 004:

The teacher understands learning processes and factors that impact student learning and demonstrates this knowledge by planning effective, engaging instruction and appropriate assessments.

This is a priority-setting question. What will her teaching look *most* like? Choice (A) is what all teachers should do, that is, inspire students. But this is not an exemplar of inductive teacher. Choice (B) is incorrect because a direct or didactic teacher gives information and thus informs her class. Choice (D) is hopefully only what police do to crime victims. Choice (C) is the correct answer. An inductive, or inquiry method of teaching is the opposite of a didactic/direct method of teaching. It is an indirect method of teaching that involves much student inquiry and cooperative learning groups. By definition, inquiry learning involves students in the learning, usually with "hands-on" experiences or research. The teacher will involve students in every aspect of the teaching.

17. A

This question addresses information from PPR Competency 004:

The teacher understands learning processes and factors that impact student learning and demonstrates this knowledge by planning effective, engaging instruction and appropriate assessments.

Choices (B), (C), and (D) are all things that the students should be involved in. Answer (A) is the correct answer. A teacher who is using an indirect method of instruction would NOT assign topics for students to research. Role-playing is a very indirect method of instruction. Therefore, students will have choices and involvement in their own learning.

18. D

This question addresses information from PPR Competency 012:

The teacher enhances professional knowledge and skills by effectively interacting with other members of the educational community and participating in various types of professional activities.

Choice (A) is what all teachers should do for all lessons. Choice (B) is what all teachers should encourage at various times. Choice (C) is what all teachers should do on a regular basis. Choice (D) is the correct answer because this is a question about collaborating with other professionals. As part of an interdisciplinary theme unit, teachers from different disciplines work together to integrate the theme into their specific subject area to improve student learning in all of the subject areas.

19. A

This question addresses information from PPR Competency 011:

The teacher understands the importance of family involvement in children's education and knows how to interact and communicate effectively with families.

This is a priority-setting question and a question about family involvement. Choice (B) is the incorrect answer because parents are not included as a way to control parents' behavior. Choice (C) is incorrect because families are interested in seeing what the students learn and have little knowledge of teaching techniques. Choice (D) is incorrect because it means that family involvement is motivated by something other than celebrating student learning and sharing input from families that know students best. Choice (A) is the correct response. Families should be involved in various aspects of the educational program, not just conferences or the PTA. This is the *best* reason.

Practice 8–12 Pedagogy and Professional Responsibilities Test Answers and Explanations

20. A

This question addresses information from PPR Competency 004:

The teacher understands learning processes and factors that impact student learning and demonstrates this knowledge by planning effective, engaging instruction and appropriate assessments.

This is a priority-setting question. Choices (B), (C), and (D) are not primary research. Choice (A) is the correct response. Primary research is research that yields first-hand information, such as reading news reports written during the war or interviewing someone who was in the war. A veteran of the war would have first-hand knowledge about that war.

21. A

This question addresses information from PPR Competency 004:

The teacher understands learning processes and factors that impact student learning and demonstrates this knowledge by planning effective, engaging instruction and appropriate assessments.

This is a priority-setting question. Choice (B) removes the teacher from involvement in the reteach. Choice (C) sounds like a good choice, but again, the teacher needs to quickly reteach and make certain the information is learned. The teacher previously tried groups and some did not learn. Choice (D) is incorrect. Jigsaws are a form of cooperative learning, but a great amount of time is needed to do them correctly. For this teacher, time is limited. The teacher wants students to learn specific facts quickly. Choice (A) is the correct answer. The best approach would be direct instruction to reteach. Direct instruction has a place in the curriculum.

22. B

This question addresses information from PPR Competency 006:

The teacher understands strategies for creating an organized and productive learning environment and for managing student behavior.

This is a priority-setting question and an interesting one. Choice (A) turns a discussion into a teacher threatening a student for speaking out honestly. It is incorrect. Choice (C) seems like a good answer, but because of the content, drugs, the teacher should try to acknowledge the question and keep the instruction moving. Choice (D) has the teacher departing from the instruction to offer concern to a student about her neighborhood. Then the teacher asks a question that is totally unrelated to the topic of study. Choice (B) is the correct answer. This is a question about behavior management. If possible, keep the instruction moving without interruptions. There is no need to stop the instruction and focus on a statement about the sale of illicit drugs, nor is there a need to reprimand the student for her comment.

23. B

This question addresses information from PPR Competency 004:

The teacher understands learning processes and factors that impact student learning and demonstrates this knowledge by planning effective, engaging instruction and appropriate assessments.

This question is about teaching organizational skills that are age appropriate. Students come into the class with a problem that is of interest to them. Choice (A) is incorrect because he is not teaching how to surf the Web. Choice (C) is incorrect because the teacher is modifying plans, but is not modeling this for the students. Choice (D) is incorrect because the use is not inappropriate for a computer teacher trying to connect teaching to students' interests. Choice (B) is the correct answer. The teacher uses this as a teachable moment to model for the students how to locate desired information on the computer.

24. C

This question addresses information from PPR Competency 004:

The teacher understands learning processes and factors that impact student learning and demonstrates this knowledge by planning effective, engaging instruction and appropriate assessments.

This is a priority-setting question. Choice (A) is incorrect because doing something only because it is a TEKS requirement is not a good reason. Choice (B) assumes that by using a specific type of strategy, behavior will improve. It is incorrect. There is no evidence that SQ3R prevents misbehavior. Choice (D) is incorrect because the question asks what the best reason is for using SQ3R. The best reason is related to learning, not to how students feel about themselves. Choice (C) is the correct response. This question is about teaching students to become self-directed learners. At this age students will soon be entering the workforce and must learn to be motivated and use procedures that enable them to find solutions to problems. SQ3R is a study strategy that students use to assist in learning from a text. It could be used in the workplace as well as in school.

Practice 8–12 Pedagogy and Professional Responsibilities Test Answers and Explanations

25. C

This question addresses information from PPR Competency 005:

The teacher knows how to establish a classroom climate that fosters learning, equity, and excellence and uses this knowledge to create a physical and emotional environment that is safe and productive.

This is a priority-setting question. Eliminate choice (A) because the teacher is being very negative in response to the student's negative statement. Eliminate (B) because the teacher is asking a question to which she knows the answer and that does not solve the problem. Eliminate (D) for many of the preceding reasons. The teacher is "putting down" a student on the first meeting. Choice (C) is the correct response. The question is about promoting a productive environment. The teacher did not chastise or belittle the student who arrived and refused to sit next to another student. Rather than rebuking the student, the teacher's response provided the offending student the opportunity to be welcomed and to join the class to learn. This should be your first type of response.

26. A

This question addresses information from PPR Competency 005:

The teacher knows how to establish a classroom climate that fosters learning, equity, and excellence and uses this knowledge to create a physical and emotional environment that is safe and productive.

This is a priority-setting question. Eliminate choice (B) because the teacher's philosophy is of no interest to the students. Eliminate (C) because it is not age-appropriate. This may be something you would do in kindergarten. Choice (D) does not establish any procedures for times other than during cooperative learning. Choice (A) is the correct response. The classroom rules should be planned by students and the teacher the first day of any class. Students will have direction and ownership of the rules.

27. B

This question addresses information from PPR Competency 006:

The teacher understands strategies for creating an organized and productive learning environment and for managing student behavior.

This is a priority-setting question. Eliminate (A) because this would be impersonal and not a good form of communication. Eliminate (C) because the teacher would still have to go back and enter this data into the computer. Choice (D) assumes that the teacher grades papers during class, which should not be the case. Choice (B) is the correct response. The question is about using technological tools to perform administrative tasks, and this allows the teacher more time for instruction.

28. B

This question addresses information from PPR Competency 011:

The teacher understands the importance of family involvement in children's education and knows how to interact and communicate effectively with families.

This is a priority-setting question. Eliminate (A). Conferences are set by the school district and may not be arbitrarily cancelled by a teacher. Choice (C) views the teacher as communicating with parents to keep them away from school. Eliminate (D) because it does not answer the question of why she treats students a certain way. The correct response is (B). This question is about communicating with families. Teachers should establish a way to communicate information to all parents and to provide a means of communication for answering parents' and guardians' questions.

29. A

This question addresses information from PPR Competency 005:

The teacher knows how to establish a classroom climate that fosters learning, equity, and excellence and uses this knowledge to create a physical and emotional environment that is safe and productive.

Eliminate (B) because the two students have done nothing wrong according to the information in the question. Choice (C) is a good strategy to use to get students back on task. However, this will become evident to the student if used excessively. Eliminate (D) because teachers give up their power by turning it over to the principal, who should not be the person controlling classroom problems. The principal should be involved only for major types of problems. (A) is the correct response. This question is about teacher–student interactions and student–student interactions. The teacher attempts to avoid interrupting the lesson and the positive climate in a classroom. By involving the students in the lessons, instructional time will not be lost for all of the students in the classroom.

Practice 8–12 Pedagogy and Professional Responsibilities Test Answers and Explanations

30. A

This question addresses information from PPR Competency 005:

The teacher knows how to establish a classroom climate that fosters learning, equity, and excellence and uses this knowledge to create a physical and emotional environment that is safe and productive.

This question is about the teacher's enthusiasm for learning. Eliminate (B) because students should be taught to focus on the processes of a subject and not on a final product. It also would not show that the teacher loves science, but is only focused on some end product. Choice (C) shows her love of being with her students and does not answer the question. Choice (D) suggests using extrinsic rewards to motivate students and does not answer the question about the teacher's enthusiasm. Choice (A) is the correct answer. By planning lessons that involve students early in the year, the teacher has an opportunity to showcase active learning and that physics and chemistry can be fun. The teacher will be more of a facilitator during hands-on learning and will participate with the students in the learning.

31. C

This question addresses information from PPR Competency 005:

The teacher knows how to establish a classroom climate that fosters learning, equity, and excellence and uses this knowledge to create a physical and emotional environment that is safe and productive.

This question is about establishing a classroom that is safe and one that respects others' rights and dignity. Although some may think that "Wheelie" is an acceptable nickname, the word "taunt" means "to tease." Because teasing is not positive, the teacher must stop this behavior immediately. Eliminate choices (A), (B), and (D) as these actions do not stop the action that is offensive. The dignity of the student in the wheelchair is being attacked. Although the offending student may be joking, the teacher is correct to immediately stop or redirect the comments. This could be done by simply reminding the students that this classroom is safe and nurturing for all students and no statements are allowed that are not nurturing. The correct answer is (C).

32. A

This question addresses information from PPR Competency 005:

The teacher knows how to establish a classroom climate that fosters learning, equity, and excellence and uses this knowledge to create a physical and emotional environment that is safe and productive.

This is a priority-setting question. This question is about organizing the physical environment. Because the English teacher is a traditional teacher and the instruction is teacher centered, the desks should be arranged in a way that best supports this type of instruction. Eliminate choices (B), (C), and (D) as in these arrangements some students will be facing away from the instruction at the front of the class. Teacher-centered instruction usually comes from the front of the classroom. Desk arrangements should change based on the type of instruction. The correct response is (A).

33. D

This question addresses information from PPR Competency 011:

The teacher understands the importance of family involvement in children's education and knows how to interact and communicate effectively with families.

This question is about involving families and communicating with them. Eliminate (A) as it is stereotyping the type of families who own computers. Certainly (B) is accurate, but that does not answer the question about why she sends the note. Eliminate (C) because parents do not "take sides" as a result of contact from teachers. It is a biased sounding response and words like "take sides" are red-pepper words. Choice (D) is the correct answer. Because of differences in access to technology, one method will not work for communicating with all families.

34. D

This question addresses information from PPR Competency 011:

The teacher understands the importance of family involvement in children's education and knows how to interact and communicate effectively with families.

This question is about involving families in students' learning – all types of families. Although (A), (B), and (C) are all things that teachers know, go back and ask what the question is about. Which answer is about involving families? Eliminate (A), (B), and (C) because they are not what good teachers know about involving families. Choice (D) is the correct response.

Practice 8–12 Pedagogy and Professional Responsibilities Test Answers and Explanations

35. B

This question addresses information from PPR Competency 012:

The teacher enhances professional knowledge and skills by effectively interacting with other members of the educational community and participating in various types of professional activities.

This question is about supportive, cooperative relationships with other professionals. Eliminate (A) as there is nothing in the decision set about other teachers not supporting district goals. Both (C) and (D) are true statements about teachers but not about collaborative relationships. Choice (B) is correct. Teachers who work together and plan together improve student learning.

36. B

This question addresses information from PPR Competency 013:

The teacher understands and adheres to legal and ethical requirements for educators and is knowledgeable of the structure of education in Texas.

This question is about copyright laws. As part of a good curriculum in technology, students are taught to do (A), (C), and (D). The question is, what should he NOT be teaching. Choice (B) is the correct answer. It is illegal to make copies of music from CDs and give them to others.

37. D

This question addresses information from PPR Competency 006:

The teacher understands strategies for creating an organized and productive learning environment and for managing student behavior.

This question is about using group activities to promote students' abilities to assume responsible roles that are applicable to the real world. Eliminate (A) because the teacher is not trying to convey high expectations with the activity. Eliminate (B) because the group activity is not about managing student behavior. Eliminate (C) because the teacher may be using a group activity, but the purpose of group activities is not behavior management. Choice (D) is the correct response. By connecting economics to the students' own lives (prior knowledge) and the real world, students better understand the instructional concepts.

38. B

This question addresses information from PPR Competency 006:

The teacher understands strategies for creating an organized and productive learning environment and for managing student behavior.

This question is about behavior management and is asking which of four choices is NOT behaviorist. The behaviorist approach to behavior management involves rewards and contingencies for specific behaviors. By giving some type of reward for desired behavior, choices (A), (C), and (D) are all behaviorist approaches. Choice (B) is the correct answer. Communicating "I messages" means the teacher might say, "I am angry that you are not following rule number 3. I cannot teach when there is too much noise." This is a humanistic approach to behavior management.

39. B

This question addresses information from PPR Competency 006:

The teacher understands strategies for creating an organized and productive learning environment and for managing student behavior.

This question is about behavior management. Eliminate (A) because teachers should always be setting up rules and behavior programs to move students closer to having self-control, not just to "control" the student. Eliminate (C) because teacher should follow best practices and not do things to make parents happy. Eliminate (D) because the other students are on-task. The teacher is not teaching behavior management to the rest of the class and so is not modeling for the other students. Choice (B) is the correct response. The teacher uses this reward system in the hopes that the student will begin to manage his own behavior. In the real world external control is not what is required. Most citizens use self-monitoring and self-control in their everyday lives. Students must learn to do this also. Teach in school what students will need for life.

40. B

This question addresses information from PPR Competency 006:

The teacher understands strategies for creating an organized and productive learning environment and for managing student behavior.

This question is about behavior management. Eliminate (A) as this procedure is not teaching how to make choices. Choice (C) may lead to some team building in the classroom. However, that is not what the teacher is teaching. Eliminate (D) because classroom rules are not being taught. Choice (B) is the correct response. One form of self-monitoring is the use of conflict management. Students who learn to manage conflict have a tool for avoiding confrontations. This teacher directly teaches her students the steps in conflict management. Again, this is a tool to use for life.

Practice 8–12 Pedagogy and Professional Responsibilities Test Answers and Explanations

41. C

This question addresses information from PPR Competency 006:

The teacher understands strategies for creating an organized and productive learning environment and for managing student behavior.

This is a priority-setting question. This question is about teaching and modeling classroom procedures. Don't forget, you are teaching students skills they need to know for life. Choice (A) is a good answer but not a remedy. Choice (B) is a solution but does not teach a skill for life. Eliminate (D) because the teacher is the responsible person. Students are not learning. Choice (C) is the correct answer. The good teacher knows that students must learn to budget time in group classroom activities. Those students who continue to have problems may not know how to do the task. The teacher should model how to pace an activity so that students can see what is expected. She will also be teaching a life skill.

42. C

This question addresses information from PPR Competency 007:

The teacher understands and applies principles and strategies for communicating effectively in varied teaching and learning contexts.

This question is about teacher questions. Eliminate choice (A) as knowledge-level questions are low level and his question is a higher-level thinking question. Eliminate (B) because he is asking a higher-level question. Eliminate (D) because questions such as he asked require higher-level thinking and produce more learning. Choice (C) is the correct answer. This teacher knows that higher-level questions (analysis, synthesis, and evaluation) will help students think at a higher level and comprehension will improve. This is a question about higher-order thinking (HOT), a "green pepper word."

43. B

This question addresses information from PPR Competency 012:

The teacher enhances professional knowledge and skills by effectively interacting with other members of the educational community and participating in various types of professional activities.

This question is about using resources and support systems effectively. Choice (A) does not show anything about reflection and self-assessment. Eliminate (C) and (D) because although those are good things to do, they are not about going to a mentor for advice. Choice (B) is the correct response. The new teacher is not fearful of going to her mentor and asking for assistance. The mentor provides the new teacher with help in meeting her professional development needs.

44. C

This question addresses information from PPR Competency 007:

The teacher understands and applies principles and strategies for communicating effectively in varied teaching and learning contexts.

This question is about teacher questioning. The teacher is not doing a good job of questioning. She is given good advice in choices (A), (B), and (D). She should NOT be told to not use wait time. Choice (C) is the correct response because teachers should use a wait time of 3 to 5 seconds to allow students to formulate answers.

45. B

This question addresses information from PPR Competency 007:

The teacher understands and applies principles and strategies for communicating effectively in varied teaching and learning contexts.

This question is about higher-order thinking (HOT). This is a question that requires that you memorize the meaning of inductive and deductive reasoning. Eliminate (C) and (D) because those are made-up terms. There is didactic teaching, direct instruction, and there is divergent thinking. Choice (B) is the correct answer. Students are asked to look at three triangles that the teacher identifies. Students are asked to provide a definition. This demonstrates inductive reasoning, which entails looking at examples and then drawing a conclusion. If the teacher had provided general principles about each triangle and then asked students for a conclusion, students would have used deductive reasoning, choice (A). So, general to specific is inductive. Specific to general is deductive.

46. A

This question addresses information from PPR Competency 011:

The teacher understands the importance of family involvement in children's education and knows how to interact and communicate effectively with families.

This is a priority-setting question. This question is about using family support resources. Remember, the teacher's job is to teach. Eliminate choices (B), (C), and (D) because the teacher is acting as a social worker, not a teacher. Choice (A) is the correct answer. The teacher should put the family in touch with the school social worker and the social worker will provide the family with support resources.

Practice 8–12 Pedagogy and Professional Responsibilities Test Answers and Explanations

47. B

This question addresses information from PPR Competency 007:

The teacher understands and applies principles and strategies for communicating effectively in varied teaching and learning contexts.

This question is about communication. The question tells you that the teacher taught the concept and the students did not understand. The teacher should now consider another way to communicate the information. Eliminate (A) because teachers are expected to reteach concepts students do not understand. Eliminate (C) because if students do not understand a concept, it will be of no value to try and discuss it in groups. The teacher will not know what is being taught correctly or incorrectly. Eliminate (D) as teachers must reteach critical concepts. Choice (B) is the correct response. Using a video or digital technology provides visual and auditory input and tries a different approach to the same subject matter.

48. A

This question addresses information from PPR Competency 008:

The teacher provides appropriate instruction that actively engages students in the learning process.

This is a priority-setting question. The question is about instructional approaches. You need to memorize the different approaches to teaching. The main two are direct instruction and inquiry. Eliminate choice (B) because direct instruction is teacher centered and students mostly listen. Eliminate (C) because guided reading is a procedure for guiding students through a piece of text by asking questions and/or making predictions and then reading to find the answer. Eliminate (D) because lecturing is teacher centered, as is questioning. Choice (A) is the correct response. The inquiry approach is a student-centered approach to learning. Students are the directors of their own learning. Learning is often in the form of research about a concept or science experimentation.

49. D

This question addresses information from PPR Competency 008:

The teacher provides appropriate instruction that actively engages students in the learning process.

This question is about instructional approaches. Eliminate choices (A), (B), and (C) because each of those does improve questioning. The question asks what will NOT improve questioning techniques. Although it is important for teachers to understand body language, it will NOT improve questioning techniques.

50. C

This question addresses information from PPR Competency 010:

The teacher monitors student performance and achievement; provides students with timely, high-quality feedback; and responds flexibly to promote learning for all students.

This is a priority-setting question. This question is about monitoring instruction through the use of assessment. Eliminate (A) because self-assessment, although important, does not involve the teacher gathering information. Eliminate (B) because summative assessment is assessment that is done at the end of instruction. Eliminate (D) because the standard deviation is not something that a teacher can change. The correct answer is (C). Ongoing formative assessment provides the teacher with information about students' abilities throughout the year. Summative assessment is usually a test at the end of a unit of work. For diagnostic purposes, formative assessment looks at performance over time.

51. B

This question addresses information from PPR Competency 010:

The teacher monitors student performance and achievement; provides students with timely, high-quality feedback; and responds flexibly to promote learning for all students.

This question is about instruction and assessment being congruent. Congruent means things work together or are appropriate. Eliminate (A) because teachers should construct tests that match the instructional objectives and not rely on the publisher's test. Eliminate (C) and (D) because two-thirds of the instruction was on liquids so two-thirds of the test should cover liquids, not one-third or one-half. The correct response is (B). If the teacher spends two-thirds of the instruction on liquids, then two-thirds of the test should cover liquids. This makes the instruction and the assessment congruent.

52. D

This question addresses information from PPR Competency 011:

The teacher understands the importance of family involvement in children's education and knows how to interact and communicate effectively with families.

This question is about parent conferences. Several of the choices assume that teachers are fortune-tellers. Choice (A) has the teacher making assumptions that are not given to us in the question and becoming a fortune-teller. Choice (B) begins the conference with the negative. Always begin conferences by discussing a student's strengths. Eliminate (C) as it is fortune-telling. Choice (D) is the correct response. The best way for parents to understand the grades students receive is to review the work their child did during the grading period. Teachers can show parents the work and have it available for any questions the parent may ask.

Practice 8–12 Pedagogy and Professional Responsibilities Test Answers and Explanations

53. C

This question addresses information from PPR Competency 010:

The teacher monitors student performance and achievement; provides students with timely, high-quality feedback; and responds flexibly to promote learning for all students.

This question is about authentic assessment. Authentic assessment includes using assessment formats that one might use in the real world. These include anecdotal records, observing students' work in the chemistry lab, and interviewing students about the chapter. Choices (A), (B), and (D) therefore are authentic assessment. Choice (C) is the correct response. Authentic assessment would not include an end-of-chapter test.

54. C

This question addresses information from PPR Competency 008:

The teacher provides appropriate instruction that actively engages students in the learning process.

This is a priority-setting question. This question is about presentation of subject matter. Students learn new information *best* if it can be attached to previous learning and to student interests. Because many high school students love music, the teacher is correct to introduce the concept by using musical instruments and allowing the students to explore the concept with real instruments that can be "hands-on." Although choices (A), (B), and (D) are all good ideas, choice (C) correct because it is more "hands-on" and related to student interests.

55. D

This question addresses information from PPR Competency 008:

The teacher provides appropriate instruction that actively engages students in the learning process.

This is a priority-setting question. This question is about the role of motivation. Eliminate (A) as there is not enough time at most high schools for each student to perform solo and each student would have a favorite. Although choices (B) and (C) are both good answers, neither is as good as choice (D). Both students and director have input, but students vote on the available choices. All students in the band will have favorite pieces. To be equitable the band director can gather suggestions from students. The band director may add specific pieces to the list. Students then vote on the selections for the major performances of the year.

56. D

This question addresses information from PPR Competency 008:

The teacher provides appropriate instruction that actively engages students in the learning process.

This is a priority-setting question. This question is about different types of motivation. Eliminate (A) because extrinsic rewards are being used. The goal is for students to be motivated by intrinsic (internal) motivation. This is important because if students work only for extrinsic rewards, when the reward stops the effort usually stops. However, not all students initially have internal motivation. Eliminate (B) because the teacher begins with intrinsic, verbal praise, and this may not motivate some of the students. She ends with extrinsic rewards, which is not the goal. Eliminate (C) as it also begins with intrinsic motivation. Choice (D) is the correct response. Therefore, begin with extrinsic (external) rewards and gradually move students toward intrinsic (internal) motivation because of success in school. This intrinsic motivation should carry over into life skills in the workplace. Employers do not pass out M&Ms to get workers to work.

57. A

This question addresses information from PPR Competency 007:

The teacher understands and applies principles and strategies for communicating effectively in varied teaching and learning contexts.

This is a priority-setting question. This question is about nonverbal communication. Choice (A) is the correct answer. The art teacher may mean "fantastic" when rolling his eyes. However, the students are misinterpreting the meaning. The best way for this to be avoided is to use verbal communication so that the message is understood. Eliminate (B) because although it is a good response, it is very vague. Eliminate (C) because the teacher's sense of humor is an asset and being "serious" does not guarantee understanding. Eliminate (D) because nonverbal communication is usually body language and is not used with only specified groups.

58. C

This question addresses information from PPR Competency 007:

The teacher understands and applies principles and strategies for communicating effectively in varied teaching and learning contexts.

This question is about communicating with students. Eliminate (A) as the teacher assumes some students will not understand and begins the assignment negatively. Eliminate (B) as looking up terms is a low-level skill compared to the correct answer. Eliminate (D) because a "how to" paper is an elementary school topic. Students in government class are older and should be able to write a persuasive paper about a recent topic. This is age-appropriate and a TEKS requirement. Choice (C) is the correct answer. Good teachers communicate at an appropriate level for the age, interests, and background of the students. Knowing the TEKS for your age level will assist with this type of question.

Practice 8–12 Pedagogy and Professional Responsibilities Test Answers and Explanations

59. A

This question addresses information from PPR Competency 009:

The teacher incorporates the effective use of technology to plan, organize, deliver, and evaluate instruction for all students.

This question is about technology terms. Choice (A) is the correct answer about what is NOT a correct term for the computer screen. An input device is something that sends information to the computer. Choices (B), (C), and (D) are terms for the computer screen. The screen is an output device, often a liquid crystal and usually called the monitor.

60. B

This question addresses information from PPR Competency 009:

The teacher incorporates the effective use of technology to plan, organize, deliver, and evaluate instruction for all students.

This is a priority-setting question. This question is about managing data from remote devices. Eliminate (A), as although the teacher is installing new software from a CD, the CD may not have the most current virus protection program. Eliminate (C) because on an initial installation of software there is no charge for the latest update. Eliminate (D) because this is too broad of a search. You need to go to the manufacturer's home page. The correct response is (B). The teacher should go to the software website and download the most recent virus patch at no cost after installing the software from the CD.

61. B

This question addresses information from PPR Competency 009:

The teacher incorporates the effective use of technology to plan, organize, deliver, and evaluate instruction for all students.

This is a priority-setting question. This question is about software programs. Eliminate (A). A word-processing program could create the directory, however, a database would provide much more control over the data and allow the data to be sorted by last name, phone number, or any of the entered fields. Eliminate (C) as usually a spreadsheet is used for bookkeeping and financial activities. Eliminate (D) because presentation software is used for making a presentation to a large group. Choice (B) is the correct answer. A database allows data to be stored and sorted in many ways.

62. B

This question addresses information from PPR Competency 009:

The teacher incorporates the effective use of technology to plan, organize, deliver, and evaluate instruction for all students.

This is a priority-setting question. This question is about productivity tools. Eliminate (A) and (D) because e-mail is one way to send a message, but cannot be as secure as a class Web page. Also, parents access a Web page on their time schedule. Eliminate (C) because as a professional you do not use your personal Web page. The best answer is (B), a class Web page, because the teacher can focus on the instruction and limit the access to this page to her students and their parents. It is safer and content specific to her classes.

63. C

This question addresses information from PPR Competency 009:

The teacher incorporates the effective use of technology to plan, organize, deliver, and evaluate instruction for all students.

This is a priority-setting question. This question is about incorporating technology into instructional projects. Eliminate choices (A), (B), and (D) because they cannot do the type of tasks presentation software can do. Choice (C) is the correct response. Presentation software is best for making a presentation. Students can include pictures, print, movie clips, and other graphics in the presentation. The presentation includes the main ideas that the student addresses in the presentation. It is an excellent way to share projects and other problem-solving activities.

64. C

This question addresses information from PPR Competency 009:

The teacher incorporates the effective use of technology to plan, organize, deliver, and evaluate instruction for all students.

This question is about evaluating technology products. Eliminate (A) because a rubric is best planned with the students and is always given to students before the start of a project. Eliminate (B) because the rubric is for students to use. Eliminate (D) as the use of a rubric is best for all assignments and we do not know what the "regular grading procedure" refers to. The correct choice is (C). As with other student products, a rubric that is created with students prior to the start of the project specifies how the project will be assessed.

Practice 8–12 Pedagogy and Professional Responsibilities Test Answers and Explanations

65. A

This question addresses information from PPR Competency 010:

The teacher monitors student performance and achievement; provides students with timely, high-quality feedback; and responds flexibly to promote learning for all students.

This question is about feedback and self-assessment. What is *least* effective is the question. Choices (B), (C), and (D) are all very effective ways to get feedback. Choice (A) is the correct response. A computer-graded answer sheet provides a quick return of grades but does not provide the student with information about why an answer was incorrect or which answers were answered well. In contrast, the other three procedures involve students having an opportunity to discuss the answer.

66. A

This question addresses information from PPR Competency 010:

The teacher monitors student performance and achievement; provides students with timely, high-quality feedback; and responds flexibly to promote learning for all students.

This question is about the role of the teacher. Eliminate (B) because an inquiry lesson is "hands-on" or research. Reading from the text may not give students the answer. Choice (C) puts the teacher in the role of sending negative "you messages" to the class. Choice (D) looks possible. Regrouping is a good idea if *some* of the students are not participating. Choice (A) is the correct response. In true inquiry the teacher is often a participant inquiring about a concept with the class. The lesson is student-centered. If the teacher sees that the students are not engaged and confused, the teacher becomes more of a facilitator and guides the inquiry. In the most controlled situation, the teacher becomes the director and teaches the concept directly and it is no longer an inquiry lesson. The lesson can then return to an inquiry approach.

67. B

This question addresses information from PPR Competency 010:

The teacher monitors student performance and achievement; provides students with timely, high-quality feedback; and responds flexibly to promote learning for all students.

This is a priority-setting question. This question is about assessment methods. Choice (A) will not encourage students to look at miscalculations. It will only provide feedback about the number of errors and students will be looking at another student's work. Choice (C) may cause some students to check work, but it is a type of activity that students do to avoid a penalty. Out of class, students will not be motivated to check for miscalculations. Choice (D) avoids the problem and focuses only on the product. It does not teach them anything. Choice (B) is the correct response. The teacher can focus the tasks to be completed through the use of a check sheet or rubric. This gives students the information they need to know about the tasks. Any process that will be graded is included on the check sheet. Students can self-assess using the check sheet.

68. D

This question addresses information from PPR Competency 010:

The teacher monitors student performance and achievement; provides students with timely, high-quality feedback; and responds flexibly to promote learning for all students.

This is a priority-setting question. This question is about providing students with feedback. Choice (A) looks like a good answer, but it is not the *most* likely reason. Teachers do things in order to teach concepts rather than to make students happy. Eliminate (B) as journals are not graded and eliminate (C) because teachers use journals for the value they provide in responding to literature, not because they are lazy. Choice (D) is the correct answer. Good teachers know that "assessment leads instruction." This means that by examining student work regularly, teachers can plan instruction to meet the students' needs that are observed on a regular basis. The teacher uses the assessment information to plan lessons.

69. C

This question addresses information from PPR Competency 012:

The teacher enhances professional knowledge and skills by effectively interacting with other members of the educational community and participating in various types of professional activities.

This question is about the value of participating in school activities. Choice (A) characterizes teachers as lazy and serving to please. Choice (B) does not show that the teacher is doing this for any professional reasons. Choice (D) also makes the teacher look like his reason is to prove something rather than to make the school and classes better. Choice (C) is the correct response. By serving on the Site-based Management Committee, teachers take a leadership role in studying the school curriculum and programs. Teachers are expected to serve on committees and attend staff development meetings. This is a professional activity.

70. B

This question addresses information from PPR Competency 012:

The teacher enhances professional knowledge and skills by effectively interacting with other members of the educational community and participating in various types of professional activities.

This is a priority-setting question. This is a question about teacher appraisals. Choice (A) looks for a way to do the task that is easiest, something good teachers don't do. Choice (C) has the teacher disregarding a request from the principal. Choice (D) has students making a teacher decision. The teacher should be "reflective." Choice (B) is the correct response. Even teachers who have excellent appraisals should examine ways to improve teaching through self-assessment. They should select goals for each year to work on. These goals should be based on self-assessment and previous appraisals.

Practice 8–12 Pedagogy and Professional Responsibilities Test Answers and Explanations

71. D

This question addresses information from PPR Competency 012:

The teacher enhances professional knowledge and skills by effectively interacting with other members of the educational community and participating in various types of professional activities.

This is a priority-setting question. What is the *best* way for the coach to improve teaching skills? Choice (A) would be a way to improve as a coach. Choice (B) allows students to be in charge of teacher development. Choice (C) has the teacher copying rather than thinking about the best way to teach. Choice (D) is the correct response. Professional development by reading current journal articles in your teaching fields is a good way to stay informed on a continuing basis. All teachers should join a professional organization.

72. C

This question addresses information from PPR Competency 013:

The teacher understands and adheres to legal and ethical requirements for educators and is knowledgeable of the structure of education in Texas.

This question is about legal and ethical standards for educators. Standard 1.2 of the Code of Ethics states, *the educator shall not knowingly misappropriate, divert, or use monies, personnel, property or equipment committed to his charge for personal gain or advantage.* Choice (A) leaves the money in a locked area, but in terms of safety it is not a very good and secure area. Choice (B) is a direct violation of Standard 1.2. Choice (D) is a good idea but the principal is the school leader and activity fund money is usually deposited by the local school office. Choice (C) is the correct response. By putting the money in the appropriate activity fund at the school, the teacher keeps the money safe and removes any possibilities of accusations of impropriety. The money may end up in the district offices, but it is placed there by the local school office.

73. D

This question addresses information from PPR Competency 013:

The teacher understands and adheres to legal and ethical requirements for educators and is knowledgeable of the structure of education in Texas.

This question is about legal standards for educators. Standard 2.1 of the Code of Ethics states, *The educator shall not reveal confidential health or personnel information concerning colleagues unless disclosure serves lawful professional purposes or is required by law.* Because the teacher overheard the principal talking to the teacher, the information is confidential and should not be discussed. Choice (D) is the correct response. All others violate Standard 2.1.

74. C

This question addresses information from PPR Competency 013:

The teacher understands and adheres to legal and ethical requirements for educators and is knowledgeable of the structure of education in Texas.

This question is about legal requirements for educators. The Individual with Disabilities Act (IDEA) did approve the inclusion of autistic children in Special Education and related services. Read carefully; choice (A) says ineligible. Choice (B) does not give the parent any useful information and is merely an apology. Choice (D) does not give the parent information about the child's qualification for special education. Choice (C) is the correct answer.

75. D

This question addresses information from PPR Competency 013:

The teacher understands and adheres to legal and ethical requirements for educators and is knowledgeable of the structure of education in Texas.

This question is about relationships among campus and district offices. Eliminate (A) because this is not about working with families. Eliminate (B) as nothing is mentioned about a mentor. Eliminate (C) because the problem is not with another teacher. Choice (D) is correct. The coach is not maintaining positive relationships with the campus principal or the district superintendent. If he violated district policies, he may also be violating the Code of Ethics.

76. C

This question addresses information from PPR Competency 013:

The teacher understands and adheres to legal and ethical requirements for educators and is knowledgeable of the structure of education in Texas.

This is a priority-setting question. This question is about following grading procedures to insure accurate student records. Eliminate (A) because although it looks possible, there were no relationships with parents that caused the student to grow. The father was pleased but this question is not about family relationships. Eliminate (B) because there is no evidence that this statement is true. Eliminate (D) because teachers sometimes do make errors and change grades. Choice (C) is the correct response. The teacher followed the published rules as posted in her syllabus about grading procedures. The fact that the father was happy is just additional good news.

Practice 8–12 Pedagogy and Professional Responsibilities Test Answers and Explanations

77. C

This question addresses information from PPR Competency 001:

The teacher understands human developmental processes and applies this knowledge to plan instruction and ongoing assessment that motivate students and are responsive to their developmental characteristics and needs.

This question is about students' physical changes and emotional development. Eliminate (B) because role playing is excellent for presentations too. Eliminate (D) because although students may be rebellious, that should not affect the curriculum. Choice (A) and (C) are both possible. Eliminate (A) because choice (B) relates the reason to human growth and development rather than to a vague possibility. Because of differences in physical development, some students may be embarrassed by having to wear some type of costume in front of peers.

78. C

This question addresses information from PPR Competency 002:

The teacher understands student diversity and knows how to plan learning experiences and design assessments that are responsive to differences among students and that promote all students' learning.

This is a priority-setting question. This question is about diversity. Eliminate (A) as teachers should not lower objectives. They should modify instruction. Eliminate (B) because although this may be a good idea, the students would not be exposed to English and there may not be other English Language Learners (ELLs) who speak Vietnamese. Eliminate (D) because no student ever goes to Special Education without first receiving an ARD (Admission, Review, and Dismissal) evaluation. Only students who qualify may go to Special Education. Choice (C) is the correct answer. Teachers should remember that positive self-esteem and learning go hand-in-hand. The teacher should plan lessons that build self-esteem. The teacher may work with ELL students in groups; however, it is not advisable to group all ELL students together for cooperative learning as they will not have a model of English and may all speak a different language.

79. B

This question addresses information from PPR Competency 002:

The teacher understands student diversity and knows how to plan learning experiences and design assessments that are responsive to differences among students and that promote all students' learning.

This is a priority-setting question. This question is about using diversity to enrich the learning of all students. Choice (A) may happen later but not first. It is behavior management. Choice (C) does not do anything to show the other students the positive opportunities offered by having diversity in the classroom. Eliminate (D) because we should present accurate information, but this sounds like a list the teacher will recite from. Choice (B) is the best thing for the teacher to do. Teaching a lesson about the similarities among different cultures will provide all of the students with information about many cultures and enrich each student's knowledge pool.

80. A

This question addresses information from PPR Competency 003:

The teacher understands procedures for designing effective and coherent instruction and assessment based on appropriate learning goals and objectives.

This question is about setting goals and objectives. Choices (B), (C), and (D) are all acceptable. Goals should be aligned, age-appropriate, and address current student needs. Choice (A) should not be a goal. It is the correct response.

Practice 8–12 Pedagogy and Professional Responsibilities Test Answers and Explanations

Practice Test 4 Answers, 8–12 PPR Sorted by Competency

Question	Domain	Competency	Answer	Did You Answer Correctly?	Question	Domain	Competency	Answer	Did You Answer Correctly?
1	1	1	B		45	3	7	B	
77	1	1	C		47	3	7	B	
2	1	1	D		57	3	7	A	
3	1	1	D		48	3	8	A	
4	1	1	A		15	3	8	A	
78	1	2	C		49	3	8	D	
79	1	2	B		54	3	8	C	
5	1	2	C		56	3	8	D	
8	1	2	A		55	3	8	D	
6	1	2	D		59	3	9	A	
7	1	2	B		60	3	9	B	
10	1	3	B		61	3	9	B	
80	1	3	A		62	3	9	B	
14	1	3	D		63	3	9	C	
11	1	3	C		64	3	9	C	
12	1	3	B		50	3	10	C	
13	1	3	B		67	3	10	B	
9	1	3	A		51	3	10	B	
16	1	4	C		53	3	10	C	
17	1	4	A		68	3	10	D	
23	1	4	B		65	3	10	A	
21	1	4	A		66	3	10	A	
20	1	4	A		33	4	11	D	
22	1	4	B		19	4	11	A	
24	1	4	C		34	4	11	D	
25	2	5	C		28	4	11	B	
26	2	5	A		52	4	11	D	
29	2	5	A		46	4	11	A	
30	2	5	A		35	4	12	B	
32	2	5	A		69	4	12	C	
31	2	5	C		43	4	12	B	
41	2	6	C		70	4	12	B	
37	2	6	D		18	4	12	D	
27	2	6	B		71	4	12	D	
38	2	6	B		74	4	13	C	
39	2	6	B		36	4	13	B	
40	2	6	B		72	4	13	C	
58	3	7	C		73	4	13	D	
42	3	7	C		76	4	13	C	
44	3	7	C		75	4	13	D	

What competencies did you do well in?
What competencies do you need to work on?

KAPLAN 393

GETTING STARTED: ADVICE FOR NEW TEACHERS

So you've passed the TExES with flying colors and fulfilled all the requirements for becoming a teacher in Texas. Now it's time to put all your learning into practice!

FINDING THE RIGHT POSITION

It is common knowledge that more good teachers are needed across the country. According to the National Center for Education Statistics, approximately 2 million new teachers will be needed in the United States by the 2008–2009 school year (Source: "Predicting the Need for Newly Hired Teachers in the United States to 2008–09," nces.ed.gov). But finding the right job for you can be a daunting process.

1. Do Your Research

First, determine the grade levels and/or subjects you are most interested in teaching. Make sure you have fulfilled all the qualifications to teach in Texas. The following basic requirements are necessary:

- A bachelor's degree from an accredited college or university
- Completion of an approved teacher training program
- The appropriate PPR test for the grade level(s) you wish to teach

In addition to the pedagogy test for your grade level, you will need to take one or more TExES content test, depending on the subject(s) and grade(s) you wish to teach. The list of requirements for certification in specific subjects can be found at texes.nesinc.com. This site also contains information about supplemental certificates and temporary teacher certificates.

2. Identify Where You Would Like to Work

Next, make a list of the districts and/or schools where you would most like to work. The State Board for Educator Certification has a page on which you can access job banks for each region in Texas (sbec.state.tx.us/SBECOnline/certinfo/schjobvac/sjobvaca.asp). Many school districts also have websites on which they post job openings. In addition, call the district office to find out if there are any positions open and what their application procedures are.

Use the Internet as a resource. In addition to the many general websites for job hunters, there are websites devoted solely to teaching jobs. A few websites will ask you for a subscription fee, but there are many others with free listings. A list of some of these sites is included at the end of this chapter.

Things you will want to investigate are enrollment, class size, student–teacher ratio, and special programs. The Texas Education Agency lists data on school districts on its website, tea.state.tx.us/. If you know any teachers at the school, ask them what their experience there has been.

3. Attend Job Fairs

Job fairs are a good way to learn about openings and to network with other education professionals. The Texas Association of School Personnel Administrators lists job fairs on their website (http://taspa.org/jobfairs/current-job-fairs.html). Most regions in the state host job fairs for districts throughout their region. Several of the websites for job seekers listed at the end of this chapter also have job fair listings by state.

Remember that you are assessing potential employers as much as they are assessing you. Consider asking the following:

- What is the first professional development opportunity offered to new teachers?
- What additional duties outside the classroom are expected of teachers?
- When can I expect to meet my mentor?
- What is the top school-wide priority this year?
- What kinds of materials or resources will be available in my classroom? (if applicable)
- What is your policy on lesson planning?
- What are my team members like?

You may also want to ask about the demographics of the student population and what kinds of unique challenges they present. If you feel comfortable, you might also want to ask to see the classroom you would be using.

4. Sign Up for Substitute Teaching

Substitute teaching can be another good strategy for getting your foot in the door in a particular school or district, even if there are no permanent jobs available. Think of this as an opportunity to impress principals and to learn from other teachers about possible openings. You can even submit your resume to the principals in the schools where you are substitute teaching and give them the chance to observe you in the classroom.

STARTING IN THE CLASSROOM

Don't get disillusioned if you're not immediately comfortable in your role as a teacher. Give yourself time to adjust, and don't hesitate to ask for advice from others. Be persistent about finding a mentor who can provide support during your first year and beyond. Try to find one in your subject area and determine how much experience you would like that person to have. For the sake of convenience, it's a good idea to find someone who has a similar class schedule or daily routine.

Teach Rules and Respect

With students, be friendly but firm. Establish clear routines and consistent disciplinary measures early on. This way, the students have a firm understanding of what is expected of them and when certain behaviors are appropriate. Have the principal review your disciplinary plan to make certain that he or she will support it and that there aren't any potential legal issues. Be aware of how cliques and social hierarchies impact classroom dynamics, and don't underestimate the power of your own advice.

Although disciplinary issues vary according to grade level, there are some general tips you may find helpful in setting rules in the classroom:

- Often, troublesome students misbehave merely to get your attention. Reduce this negative behavior by paying the least amount of attention when a student is acting out and giving that child your full attention when he or she is behaving.

- When it comes to establishing classroom rules, allow your students to have some input. This will increase their sense of empowerment and respect for the rules.

- Convince all of your students that they are worthwhile and capable. It is easy to assume that struggling students are lazy or beyond help–do not allow yourself to fall into this trap.

- When disciplining students, absolutely avoid embarrassing them in any way, shape, or form, especially in front of their peers.

- Double standards and favoritism will lose you the respect of all your students–always be firm, fair, and consistent. Never talk down to your students.

- Avoid becoming too chummy with your students. Young teachers often feel that they must make "friends" with students, particularly in the older grades. However, it's important to maintain some professional distance and to establish yourself as an authority figure.
- Admit your mistakes. If you wrongly accuse a student of doing something she did not do, make an inappropriate joke, or reprimand a student more harshly than necessary, be sure to apologize and explain. If a parent or administrator criticizes you for your mistake, calmly explain how you felt at that moment and why. Also, clarify how you'll handle that kind of situation in the future.

Do Your Homework

Any veteran teacher will tell you that you will spend almost as many hours working outside the classroom as you do with your students. Preparing lessons and grading homework and tests can take an enormous amount of time, so it's a good idea to be as organized as possible. You should also take some time to think about what your expectations will be: Will you grade every homework assignment or just some of them? Will you give students an opportunity to earn extra credit? What kind of system will you use for grading tests? Obviously these requirements will vary according to grade level, but there are some general suggestions that you may find helpful in preparing assignments.

Finally, you should always give yourself time to wind down and distance yourself from the classroom. This is essential to prevent burnout or resentment over a lack of free time, and will allow you to pursue other interests and personal relationships.

Design Lesson Plans Early

Before you start planning, be aware of holidays off, assemblies, and similar interruptions. Design your lessons accordingly. Similarly, be sure you know your content, your state's standards, your school's expectations, and the ins and outs of child development. Be prepared with multiple learning styles and differentiated teaching strategies.

Try to develop time-saving strategies. Saving your lesson plan outline as a template on the computer can be very helpful–instead of rewriting the whole plan everyday, you can just fill in the blanks.

Establish Rules for Grading Homework

Along with establishing a consistent disciplinary policy early on, it's important to develop grading guidelines. Some teachers set the bar high at the beginning of the year by grading a little tougher than they normally would. Just as many students will underachieve if they think you are a soft grader, they will work hard to meet your expectations if your standards are high. However, it's important to assess your students' abilities and set realistic standards.

Getting Started: Advice for New Teachers

Grading every single assignment can get overwhelming; sometimes verbally assessing comprehension is enough. Rubrics are another useful tool for outlining expectations and scoring, as well as making sure you cater to the needs of all your students. They are also effective when students grade each other.

Returning graded assignments as soon as possible sets a good example, keeps your workload manageable, and prevents students' interest from waning. However, you should never use a student's work as an example of what not to do.

Consider sending grades home on a regular basis and getting them signed by a parent in order to keep everyone aware of students' progress. This prevents students and parents from being blindsided by poor grades.

Don't confuse quietness for comprehension. Check in with all students because some may be afraid to admit that they don't understand what's going on. If you feel there is a problem, don't wait to address a student's needs. If you believe that a student may have an undiagnosed disability, let your principal know and follow your school's procedure.

Finding tangible rewards for students' achievements is a great way to keep them motivated, particularly if you focus their efforts around gradually earning the rewards. These types of incentive systems work particularly well in the elementary grades.

Deal with Parents Early On

Establish a relationship with parents from the beginning–frequent, positive communication is essential to helping the children attain the best education possible. Here are a few tips for keeping in touch with parents:

- Make phone calls, even if you're just going to leave a message. Doing so will allow you to share good news and help guardians become more familiar with you.
- Give students homework folders that frequently travel between school and home.
- Be ready to deal with breakdowns in communication: it may be necessary to send multiple messages home.
- Send home a short newsletter of things to come.

Set Up Parent–Teacher Conferences

Meeting with parents can often be intimidating for new teachers, particularly if a student is not performing well. It's a good idea to seek guidance from experienced teachers, and communicate with administrators if you encounter problems. In addition, try to follow these general guidelines when talking with parents:

- Remain professional. Don't take heated words personally, have good things to say about the student, choose your words carefully, keep examples of the student's work on hand, and document what is said during the meeting.
- Allow parents to ask the first question. This will help you understand their tone and their concerns.
- Be as thick-skinned as possible when dealing with problems: some parents want to vent a little before getting to the crux of the issue. Let them vent, try to put them at ease, and then look for a solution or compromise.
- If a parent becomes excessively confrontational, inform an administrator.
- Be confident. Listen to what the parents suggest, but also stand up for what you believe is the best course of action.

BUILD RELATIONSHIPS WITH COLLEAGUES

Meet as many teachers in the building as you can: Not only will you gain valuable insights about the inner workings of the school, but you'll also make new friends. Don't be afraid to step up and ask questions when information isn't offered. Veteran teachers are a tremendous resource for all kinds of information, ranging from labor contracts to strategies for staying sane under pressure. Also, get to know the other new teachers. These people will be valuable sounding boards and will help you feel less alone.

Earn the respect of your colleagues by stepping up to committee work, and by proving yourself to be a reliable, competent teacher. You should also be polite and friendly with the staff and custodians—you'll need their help for all sorts of reasons.

Finally, be professional, timely, and unafraid to calmly share your opinions or disagree with administrators. Your professionalism and enthusiasm will earn you their respect and ensure that your needs are met.

Dealing with Paperwork

Be aware of what kinds of paperwork you need to fill out and file, including the school Improvement Plan, special education forms relating to Individualized Education Plans, budget requests, reading and math benchmarks, and permanent record cards. Try to sit with fellow teachers when filling out forms. Their companionship will make these tedious tasks more fun.

Understanding Unions

Depending on your school district, you may be part of a teacher's union. It is important to gain a clear understanding of union requirements. Know:

- how much money will be deducted from your paycheck for union dues and
- how you can obtain a copy of the most recent union contract.

For further information, you may wish to consult the Texas State Teachers Association, tsta.org/.

ADDITIONAL RESOURCES

Books

Capel, Susan, Marilyn Leask, and Terry Turner, *Learning to Teach in the Secondary School: A Companion to School Experience.* Taylor & Francis, 2005.

Dillon, Justin. *Becoming a Teacher.* McGraw-Hill, Open University Press, 2001.

Goodnough, Abby. *Ms. Moffett's First Year: Becoming a Teacher in America.* Public Affairs, 2004.

Maloy, Robert W., and Irving Seidman. *The Essential Career Guide to Becoming a Middle and High School Teacher.* Bergin & Garvey, 1999.

Parkay, Forrest W., and Beverly Hardcastle Stanford. *Becoming a Teacher, 6th Edition.* Allyn & Bacon, 2003.

Shalaway, Linda, and Linda Beech (Editor). *Learning to Teach…Not Just For Beginners (Grades K-8).* Scholastic, 1999.

Staff of U.S. News and World Report. *U.S. News Ultimate Guide to Becoming a Teacher.* Sourcebooks, 2004.

Wong, Harry K., and Rosemary T. Wong. *The First Days of School: How to be an Effective Teacher.* Harry K. Wong Publications, 2001.

Magazines and Journals

American Educator

Harvard Educational Review

The New York Times "Education Life"

The Phi Delta Kappan

Internet Resources

teachernet.com/htm/becomingateacher.htm
Community for K-8 educators

pbs.org/firstyear/beaTeacher/
PBS: How to become a teacher

newsweekshowcase.com/teacher-training/ Newsweek
Teacher education and recruitment, teaching as a second career

eric.ed.gov/
Education Resources Information Center; large teaching and education database

aft.com
American Federation of Teachers

proudtoserveagain.com/pages/808014/index.htm
Troops to Teachers program—gives former members of the U.S. military the opportunity to become public school teachers—can help with certification, job searching, etc.

ed.gov
U.S. Department of Education

theteachersguide.com

behavioradvisor.com/

teach-nology.com
Free and easy-to-use resources for teachers

kidsource.com
Sites with tips from teachers

Getting Started: Advice for New Teachers

ncrel.org/he/tot/teach.htm
Teachers' input on teaching, learning how to teach

teachingtips.com
Tips from an experienced teacher

atozteacherstuff.com
A teacher-created site listing online resources and tips

Lesson Plan Sites

education-world.com

theteacherscorner.net

lessonplansearch.com

moteachingjobs.com/lessons/mainsearch.cfm

teachnet.com

General Teaching Job Sites

schoolspring.com

teachers-teachers.com

job-hunt.com/academia.shtml

educationjobs.com

abcteachingjobs.com

k12jobs.com

jobs2teach.doded.mil/Jobs2Teach/J2TDefault.asp
Part of the Troops to Teachers website

wanttoteach.com/newsite/jobfairs.html
National teaching job fair website

udel.edu/csc/teachers.html
MBNA Career Services Center: A list of resources for teachers

Texas Resources

texes.nesinc.com/
The TExES home page

tea.state.tx.us/
Texas education agency

sbec.state.tx.us
State Board for Educator Certification–information on how to become a teacher in Texas

tenet.edu
Texas Education Network–resources for teachers, continuing education, grants, etc.

texas.teachers.net
Texas Teachers Net–jobs, chatboards, etc.

texasteachingfellows.org/

taspa.org
Texas Association of School Personnel Administrators

deleon.tea.state.tx.us/SDL/
School district locator

APPENDICES

Glossary of Important TExES Terms

Ability grouping—placing students for instruction based on their abilities.

Abstract concepts—nonobservable concepts that are acquired only through the senses because they do not possess physical qualities.

Abstract thinking—cognitive thought that is a part or remote from any concrete reality or particular material object.

Academic learning time—the amount of time a student is actively engaged in learning academically relevant material.

Acceleration—the goal of receiving the required curriculum but at an increased level.

Accommodation—changes or modifications in the way students receive instruction to enable them to improve their learning or an experience.

Accountability—holding schools and teachers accountable for student performance.

Achievement—the act of succeeding in doing something or accomplishing a desired goal.

Achievement test—the process of measuring mastery of a given subject or specific skill.

Active listening—focusing attentively on what a student is saying.

Admission Review and Dismissal (ARD) Committee—a group of people who meet for the purpose of monitoring a student's educational process and making decisions on services that should be available for that student.

Advanced organizers—an approach to teaching that utilizes what the student already knows to relate to new material and ideas. These are often in the form of bold headings in textbooks.

Advocate for students—a professional who works with the family, the student, and the school to ensure that each student receives the appropriate education necessary to optimize his or her opportunity to achieve to the highest level of his or her potential.

Affective domain—behavior that reflects interests, attitudes, opinions, values, and emotions.

Age-appropriate—material or instruction that has been determined suitable for a student's state of development.

Aide—someone who provides assistance in the classroom.

Alignment—the lining up of standards and curriculum to meet the needs of students, school, school district, and state goals.

Allocated time—specified amount of time for learning and other school events.

Alternative assessment—a type of instruction and measurement that differs from the usual standard or paper and pencil test. Evaluation is in the form of presentations, portfolios, and projects.

Analysis—the process of separating parts and then learning the relationship of these parts.

Analyze—to look at something in detail to determine if a relationship exists.

Antivirus software—antivirus software is a type of application you install to protect your system from viruses, worms, and other malicious code.

Application—a level of learning in Bloom's Taxonomy in which students must understand information they receive and then put that information to use.

Appropriate instruction—instruction that is considered to be the best choice for a student at a given time and in a given situation.

Aptitude test—a test administered to determine how a person might perform in a certain area or activity.

Assertive discipline—classroom management techniques that are utilized in schools and that make clear statements of expectations and required behavior without employing hostile or argumentative action on the part of the teacher.

Glossary of Important TExES Terms

Assessment—a process of measuring or gathering data to discover what students know and are learning. The main purpose for assessment should be to plan appropriate instruction.

Assessment data—information received about students' abilities in subjects or areas of learning through the process of tests, observations, student work, or other measures.

Assessment methods—the way in which assessment data are measured, such as in standardized tests, criterion-referenced tests, or by alternative assessment.

Assimilation—a cognitive process in which new information is integrated into an already existing schema.

At-risk students—students who have been characterized as having a more difficult time achieving because of conditions such as poverty or physical, mental, or emotional educational problems, and who thus have a greater likelihood of dropping out of school before graduation.

Attention Deficit Hyperactivity Disorder (ADHD)—characterized by symptoms of inattention, hyperactivity, and/or impulsivity that are developmentally inappropriate and are not the result of other conditions. Symptoms must have occurred before age 7 and exist in two or more settings. Students may be classified with one of three types: predominantly inattentive, predominantly hyperactive-impulsive, or combined. This condition was previously referred to as ADD (attention deficit disorder).

Auditory learner—a student who learns best by receiving information through listening to information received rather than through visual means.

Authentic assessment—assessment that reflects the typical learning and instruction occurring in the classroom.

Basal reader—a book in a series of other books or readers and is part of a comprehensive program for teaching reading. Each book or basal increases in difficulty and is accompanied with a teacher's guide and workbooks to assist in the teaching of reading.

Basic skills—fundamental proficiencies expected of students.

Behaviorism—a hypothesis or doctrine about human behavior or learning that focuses on observable behaviors.

Behavioristic behavior modification—teacher adheres to the theory that students are more likely to repeat behaviors that have led to positive consequences and less likely to repeat behaviors that have led to negative consequences. The teacher manages the classroom so positive action is the desired outcome.

Behavior modification—a process that is employed to alter or change existing behavior by reinforcing desired behavior and ending undesirable behavior.

Behavioral objective (instructional objective)—statements or descriptions that indicate observable behaviors that students should demonstrate to make judgments that learning has occurred.

Benchmark tests—tests used to determine if a student has met a specifically described task.

Bilingual—speak two or more languages.

Bilingual education—curriculum that facilitates learning and uses a student's native language for instruction and literacy.

Bloom's Taxonomy—a hierarchy of six levels of thinking that are presented in levels of complexity from the easiest to the most difficult. (1) Knowledge (memorizing a fact); (2) Comprehension (understanding); (3) Application (applying concepts); (4) Analysis (breaking down complex information); (5) Synthesis (putting together complex ideas); and (6) Evaluation (judging or forming an opinion).

Brain-based education—educational approach that is based on the belief that learning may occur as students interact with the world. As they take in information obtained by the senses, new electrical patterns are developed between the network of neurons.

Brainstorming—an act of thinking or generating as many related possibilities or ideas about a specific problem or topic.

Bruner, Jerome—psychologist of the twentieth century whose theory of cognitive growth focuses on the environment and suggests that intellectual ability develops in stages.

Byte—the basic unit of computer storage or memory space used to store one character that is usually 8 bits.

Campus improvement team (CIT)—a representative group of campus and community people such as administrators, teachers, parents, which represents a campus and makes decisions affecting the campus and the school.

Campus-level—pertaining to activities and procedures occurring at a specific school or campus.

Campus plan—a framework stating the schools goals and objectives that are in agreement with the school district's plans.

Cause-effect relationship—a pattern showing the relationship between where one event happened as a result of another event.

Glossary of Important TExES Terms

CD-ROM—refers to Compact Disk Read-Only Memory and is a device in which large amounts of computerized read-only information and software are stored or saved.

Center for Professional Development and Technology (CPDT)—a lab that serves as a training center for pre-service teachers who are practicing in the public schools. The center helps coordinate training and use of technological equipment for the students, faculty, school, and in some cases community.

Central processing unit (CPU)—a term used to describe a processor or central unit in a computer.

Chapter I—Under the Education Consolidation and Improvement Act, Chapter I is the major source of federal aid that approves of funds to meet the needs of educationally deprived children in low-income areas.

Checking for understanding—a phase of a lesson cycle in which a teacher determines if the goals and objectives presented during the lesson have been understood and can be applied.

Choral reading—students take turns reading assigned parts of a poem or prose.

Chronological age—age measured by the time in years and months that a person has lived.

Classical conditioning—conditioning that pairs a neutral stimulus with a stimulus that evokes a reflex; the stimulus that evokes the reflex is given whether or not the conditioned response occurs until eventually the neutral stimulus comes to evoke the reflex.

Classroom climate—the atmosphere in a classroom in which the students must learn.

Classroom control—the process of creating an atmosphere in the classroom where students are expected to maintain patterns of required behavior.

Classroom management—a systematic approach to organizing a classroom so lessons can be delivered effectively and misbehaviors are redirected or prevented.

Closure—a part of a lesson cycle in which a teacher summarizes material covered in the lesson, restates objectives for the lesson, and brings an appropriate conclusion.

Coaching—assisting students in the classroom to enhance performance so they can move to greater success.

Code of Ethics and Standard Practices—standards of practice and ethical conduct toward students, professional colleagues, school officials, parents, members of the community to which the Texas educator will adhere in order to safeguard academic freedom.

Cognition—the process of thinking and reasoning.

Cognitive confusion—mental state characterized by the lack of clear and orderly thought and behavior.

Cognitive development—the process of thinking, problem solving, processing concepts, and reasoning.

Cognitive domain—the area of learning that refers to the utilization of such skills as acquisition and assimilating.

Cognitive learning style—a preferred way of perceiving and organizing information and responding to stimulation.

Compensatory education—a program designed to improve instruction for at-risk students by affecting levels of achievement thus reducing the dropout rate.

Competencies on the TExES—statements that broadly define what an entry-level educator in Texas public schools should know and be able to do. There are 13 competencies on the TExES.

Competency test—a form of measurement that tests the basic skills students should be able to acquire or master for the district or state.

Computer-assisted instruction (CAI)—software that provides assistance with instruction occurring in the classroom.

Concept map—a visual or graphic that connects ideas and shows a relationship between ideas.

Concrete concepts—basic elements of thought that reflect actual existing objects and can be achieved through one of the five senses.

Conformity to peer group—changing one's behavior to fit into a group or develop popularity.

Conservation—the ability for students in the preoperational stage of development to mentally reverse an operating or to realize that an object is the same under changing perceptual conditions.

Constructivism—a theory of learning that is based on the idea that the learner constructs knowledge.

Content area learning—material that covers a specific area of learning and for which students are ultimately responsible, such as in social studies, mathematics, English, art, or science.

Glossary of Important TExES Terms

Context for learning—to provide a situation or environment whereby students are able to process information and learn.

Cooperative learning—a way for students to work together in a group in order to help each other learn or acquire skills.

Copyright infringement—the unauthorized use of a product that has been copyrighted.

Copyright laws—a product or work is governed by federal law and is protected by copyright laws wherever the work is in a tangible or touchable form.

Core curriculum—a uniform body of knowledge that is taught to all students.

Criterion-referenced test—a formal test composing a students' test score to a list of skills (criteria). The TAKS aaand TExES are criterion-referenced tests.

Critical thinking—the intellectually disciplined process of conceptualizing, applying, analyzing, synthesizing, and/or evaluating information or situations.

Cross-age tutoring—pairing older students and younger students so the older students help the younger students with academic learning and with reaching the goal of increased performance.

Cues—stimulus that provides information about what to do or evidence that helps solve a problem, such as which behaviors will be reinforced or punished.

Culturally-biased test—tests that, in their construction, reflect the basic knowledge and interpretation of a particular cultural or subcultural group.

Deductive learning—learning that takes place from the general to the more specific ideas and generalizations.

Deductive reasoning—reasoning from the general to the particular or from cause to effect, based on laws or rules.

Diagnostic test—a means of making a proper or appropriate identification of a problem or condition.

Didactic instruction—teaching by telling with little interaction from students.

Differentiated instruction—instruction that is changed to meet the needs of students by accepting assignments or tasks in varied means.

Direct instruction—teacher-centered instruction that is based around a structured form of delivery and completion of tasks.

Director (as a role of the teacher)—an instructor who controls or supervises an action, activity, or lesson.

Discipline—the process of managing the students' behavior and actions in the classroom or school situation.

Discovery learning—learning that involves students interacting with their environments, by exploring and manipulating objects, grappling with questions and controversies, to develop an understanding of a particular idea or concept.

Divergent thinking—thinking that advances beyond an original idea.

Domains of learning (cognitive, social, emotional, physical)—categories that divide the learning process into learning and assisting teachers when selecting learning strategies.

Domains on the TExES—broad statements that form the foundation for the Texas Examination of Educator Standards (TExES). There are four domains on the exam. They are: Domain I: Designing instruction and assessment; Domain II: Creating a positive productive classroom; Domain III: Implementing effective responsive instruction and assessment; and Domain IV: Fulfilling professional roles and responsibilities.

Dyscalculia—a learning disability in the area of mathematics.

Dysgraphia—a learning disability in the area of written language, which affects the ability to formulate written letters or numbers and/or the ability to formulate a thought and express it in writing.

Dyslexia—a learning disability in reading that affects the ability to recognize and comprehend written words as a result of developmental language impairment.

8–12—Teaching certification level in the State of Texas that allows a teacher to teach a content subject to students in grades 8–12.

Early Childhood Education (ECE)—in the United States, pupils from ages birth to 8 and through grades PK–3.

EC–4—teaching certification level in the State of Texas which allows a teacher to teaching the pre-K through fourth-grade levels.

EC–12—teaching certification level in the State of Texas that allows a teacher to teach in certain specialty areas between the pre-kindergarten and twelfth grade levels.

Eclectic—the notion that a teacher selects a teaching method that incorporates the best of various teaching styles or ideas.

Glossary of Important TExES Terms

Education system—the organization of educational programs set up by the Texas Structure in Texas Education Agency.

Egocentric—one who believes that everyone sees the world as he or she does.

Elementary and Secondary Education Act (ESEA)—enacted in 1965 to provide guidance and funds to K–12 schools. The No Child Left Behind (NCLB) Act of 2001 is the latest revision of ESEA.

Emotional disturbance (ED)—an area covered by the Individuals with Disabilities Education Act (IDEA).

Emotional factors—the notion that a student's emotional health has impact on learning.

English Language Learners (ELL, formerly known as ESL—English as a Second Language)—includes the teaching of English to a non–English speaking student; includes teaching English as well as teaching cultural adjustment elements.

English as a Second Language (ESL)—an English language study program for non-native speakers. Most ESL programs have small classes so that students receive individual attention from their teachers. Students study English and also participate in the cultural and social activities of the school and community where they study.

Enrichment—the provision of richer, more varied content through strategies that supplement the standard curriculum.

Equilibrium—the restoration of balance between what is understood and what is actually experienced.

Equity in excellence for all learners—the notion that teachers must develop culturally sensitive curricula that integrates multicultural viewpoints and histories. In addition, teachers must apply instructional strategies that encourage all students to achieve and they must review school and district policies related to educational equity.

Erik Erickson—a psychosocial theorist who believes that society, history, and culture affect personality development. Erickson is best known for his concept of the identity crisis.

Essentialism—an educational philosophy that holds that a common core of knowledge and ideals should be the focus of a curriculum.

Exceptional learner—a student who deviates from the average child in any of the following ways: mental characteristics, sensory ability, neuromotor or physical characteristics, social behavior, communication ability, or in multiple handicaps.

ExCET—Examination for the Certification of Educators in Texas—former certification exam that has been replaced by the TExES (Texas Examination for Educator Standards).

Extension—a component in the lesson cycle that emphasizes the enlargement or expansion of the original learning objective.

Extrinsic motivation—motivation that is created by events or rewards outside of the individual.

4–8—teaching certification level in the State of Texas that allows a teacher to teach in the fourth- through eighth-grade levels.

Factual question—questions that require students to recall information through recognition or rote memory.

"Fair use"—guidelines for the educational use of copyrighted works.

Flash drive—a technology storage device that allows one to read, write, copy, delete and move data from a hard disk drive to the flash drive or from the flash drive to the hard disk drive.

Flexible grouping—student groupings based on a student's need for review, reteaching, practice, or enrichment.

Focus of instruction—the point in an instructional lesson where the teacher secures the students' attention and communicates the lesson objectives, thus identifying the central focus of the activity.

Formal assessment—the use of standardized test instruments to gather information regarding a student's performance in an area of educational performance.

Formative assessment—assessment that occurs before and during the learning process in order to guide the content and pace of the lessons.

Free and Appropriate Public Education (FAPE)—in accordance with the Individuals with Disabilities Education Act, Part B (34 CFR Parts 300 and 301 and Appendix C), all children with disabilities must receive a free, appropriate public education in a school district that provides special education and related services at no cost to the child or her or his parents.

Gender bias—favoring one gender over the other.

Gifted—a designation applied to students who are exceptionally creative, intelligent, and/or talented.

Goals 2000—a national approach for improving student learning through a long-term, broad-based effort to promote coherent and coordinated improvements in the system of education throughout the nation at the state and local levels.

Graphic organizers—a visual overview designed to indicate relationships among the important concepts of a lesson (types include semantic mapping, webbing, clustering and structured overviews).

Guided practice—a step in the lesson cycle where the student practices the learning under direct teacher guidance.

Hands-on—term applied to lessons which encourage students to be actively involved in learning by physically interacting with the teaching materials and/or manipulatives.

Heterogeneous grouping—classroom grouping which integrates students who have a variety of learning styles and/or abilities.

Holistic education—a philosophy of education based on the premise that each person finds identity, meaning, and purpose in life through connections to the community, to the natural world, and to spiritual values such as compassion and peace. This educational philosophy aims to engage learners in an intrinsic reverence for life and a passionate love of learning. This is done, not through an academic "curriculum" that condenses the world into instructional packages, but through direct engagement with the environment.

Homogeneous grouping—classroom grouping which places students of similar intellect, traits, and abilities for learning.

Humanism—a philosophy of education designed to achieve affective outcomes of psychological growth-oriented toward improving self-awareness and mutual understanding among people.

Humanistic behavior management—managing a student's behavior with regard to maintaining human dignity.

Hypermedia—a technology-based information retrieval system that allows a user to gain or provide access to texts, audio and video recordings, photographs, and computer graphics related to a specific subject.

Hypothesis—a possible explanation for an observation, phenomenon, or scientific problem that can be tested by further investigation.

Idealism—a philosophy of education that espouses the notion that students should develop their minds with information of lasting value. Teaching students to think is an important component of the idealist curriculum.

Imagery—the use of vivid or figurative language to represent objects, actions, or ideas.

I messages—clear messages conveyed by the teacher to let students know how the teacher feels about specific classroom situations.

Inclusion—a requirement of the Individuals with Disabilities Education Act (IDEA) that children with disabilities be educated in regular education classrooms unless "the nature and severity of the disability is such that education in the regular classes with the use of supplementary aids and services cannot be achieved satisfactorily." This means that schools have a duty to try to include students with disabilities in the regular general education classes.

Independent practice—a step in the lesson cycle that allows the student to practice the learning independent of any outside assistance.

Indirect teaching—learning that occurs incidentally from the planned objective of a lesson.

Individual accountability—in cooperative learning, the notion that each student is responsible for his or her own learning.

Individualized Educational Plan (IEP)—a written plan for a student with disabilities developed by the parents and the school's education team that specifies the academic goals and the method to obtain these goals.

Individualized instruction—a continuous progress curriculum that permits students to learn at a pace consistent with their potential and needs for building success.

Individuals with Disabilities Education Act (IDEA, formerly PL 94-142)—a federal law that requires students with disabilities to be provided with a free and appropriate education in the least restrictive environment.

Inductive reasoning—reasoning based on experience or observation that moves from the specific to the general.

Informal assessment—spontaneous, unstructured tests that occur during instruction to determine the student's level of understanding and performance.

Inquiry—an inductive teaching method that engages students in investigation and explanation of situations and is designed to promote problem-solving through critical thinking.

Inquiry learning—learning based on student-designed processes to solve a problem; requires higher-level thinking skills.

In-service training—professional development opportunities offered for practicing teachers.

Instructional grouping—the division of students into small groups for the purpose of teaching certain concepts.

Integrated thematic instruction—teaching subject matter from various areas (i.e., reading, writing, spelling, math, science, social studies) as an integrated whole.

Glossary of Important TExES Terms

Intelligence Quotient (IQ)—a measure of a person's intelligence as indicated by an intelligence test; the ratio of a person's mental age to his or her chronological age (multiplied by 100).

Interdisciplinary instruction—teaching information through themes that incorporate several subject areas.

Intermediate—defined as grades 5–8 in the State of Texas grades.

Intrinsic motivation—motivation derived from activities that are rewarding within themselves.

Invented spelling—an early writing stage characterized by spelling based on how the word sounds.

Jigsaw—a cooperative group strategy that requires each member to become an expert on one part of the whole lesson and teach it to the other students.

Junior high—an organization pattern of grades, usually 7–9, that prepares students for the rigorous academic school requirements of the upper grades in a program that focuses on the specific disciplines and the traditional six-period day.

Kinesthetic—a learning style that emphasizes the student's need to move in order to learn.

Labeling—the use of a special education category to allow a student to access special educational services.

Language Experience Approach (LEA)—a reading method that emphasizes the use of words and stories that student's dictate to a writer or write themselves. The value of Language Experience Approach is that it controls for vocabulary, as the student will only dictate words in his or her vocabulary. It can be used at all levels. An excellent method for second language learners.

Learner centered—an approach to teaching in which the teacher possesses and draws on a rich knowledge base of content, methods appropriate to the content, and knowledge technology appropriate to the content.

Learner-centered communication—the use of effective professional and interpersonal communication skills to relate to students, parents, colleagues, and other interested parties.

Learner-centered development—a philosophy about teaching that assumes that the teacher is a lifelong learner who engages in a variety of learning experiences, works with professional peers, and encourages feedback from learners for the purpose of improving practice.

Learner-centered instruction—an approach to teaching that focuses on individual learners and promotes inquiry, higher-order thinking, problem solving, high levels of literacy, and engagement.

Learning disability—a general term referring to a heterogeneous group of disorders manifested by significant difficulties in the acquisition and use of listening, speaking, reading, writing, reasoning, or mathematical skills. These disorders are intrinsic to the individual, presumed to be due to central nervous system dysfunction and may occur across the lifespan. (Taken from the LD definition created by the National Joint Committee on Learning Disabilities—NJCLD).

Learning environment—a location that promotes learning by allowing students to explore, discover, and interact with the learning task.

Learning log—a learning log is a written response to literature but may be used to respond to other texts.

Learning styles—orientations for approaching learning based on the manner of processing new information.

Learning theory—a variety of theories proposed to explain how individuals learn (Examples: constructivism, behaviorism, brain-based learning).

Least restrictive environment—required by IDEA (Individuals with Disabilities Education Act) for students with disabilities to be placed in a setting that enables him or her to function to the fullest capability.

Lesson cycle—a methodology utilized when planning and presenting a lesson.

Limited English Proficiency (LEP)—the limited use of the English language.

Local Access Network (LAN)—two or more computers connected in such a way that they can electronically share information and are all located within the same facility.

Mainstreaming—placing special needs students in the regular classroom.

Mastery learning—a teaching method that attempts to have students continue to do a task until it is learned (usually at 80% or better). Students work for mastery rather than working for a given amount of time or for a grade.

Mental retardation (MR)—students who have intelligence skills that are below average (IQ below 70). Most MR students are born with below average intelligence and may have poor social skills also.

Mentors—beginning teachers are usually assigned an experienced teacher (mentor) who is there to provide assistance and guidance for the first few years of teaching.

Glossary of Important TExES Terms

Metacognition—the ability to think about one's own thinking and to control the thinking.

Methodology—specific steps, or algorithms, for delivering instruction. Examples are direct methods of teaching and inquiry or indirect methods of instruction.

Middle school concept—a new way of organizing the middle years of school. Grades 5 through 8 or 6 through 8 have usually been junior high schools. Unlike junior high schools, the middle school concept is not subject centered. Teachers usually work in teams that cross disciplines and do integrated thematic instruction.

Modeling—the process of showing or demonstrating how to do a task or verbalizing how one does a mental task.

Multicultural education—learning about other cultures in order to foster positive relations between different cultures.

Multimedia—software, such as presentation software, that combines text, pictures, music, video, graphics, and animation.

National Evaluation Systems (NES)—the company hired by the State of Texas to produce, give, and score the TExES Exam. All registration and information about the TExES Exam comes from NES.

Negative reinforcement—a reinforcement that stops or removes an action. For example, not responding to student shouting your name is a form of negative reinforcement. The goal is to not reward the behavior so that it will stop.

Nonverbal cues/communication—often referred to as "body language," it includes eye contact, facial expressions, sighs, gestures, or physical contact that sends a message. For example, teachers often use "the look" to get students to stop talking.

Norm-referenced test—a test that has been standardized with a defined population called a norming group. The score you make on a norm-referenced test compares your performance to the norming group. A score on a standardized test of 90% means that you scored better than 90 out of 100 people in the norming group. The SAT is an example of a norm-referenced test.

Objective—what students will know or be able to do at the end of a lesson.

Overlapping—doing more than one thing at a time. The teacher who is teaching and making eye contact with a student who is off-task is overlapping.

Overlearning—practicing or learning a skill beyond mastery so that the material will remain in memory longer.

Paradigm—a philosophical or theoretical framework of any kind. In education there are various paradigms for teaching.

Paraprofessional (see Teacher aide)—a noncertified adult who works in the classroom under the supervision of a certified teacher.

Parent–Teacher Association (PTA)—a national organization composed of parents and teachers to encourage positive home–school relationships and communications.

Pedagogy—how to teach.

Peer teaching—in teacher education when pre-service teachers practice teaching a lesson to one another in order to gain practice in teaching.

Peer tutoring—students in elementary through secondary schools are often asked to assist another student with a concept.

Percentile—a score out of 100 that gives the percentage at which a certain percent of the scores fall. A score at the 90th percentile indicates that 90% of the scores were at that level or below.

Performance assessment (see Authentic assessment)—assessment that involves having students do activities that are real. For example, performance assessment would include writing a real letter to someone, doing an experiment to show the understanding of a science concept, keeping papers over time to evaluate. It is not a "snapshot" like a mid-term exam that evaluates performance with a single test.

Performance-based instruction—establishing criteria that students are expected to know or be able to do. Students are then evaluated based on how well they learned the specified objectives.

Phonics—a teaching approach that teaches the sound–symbol relationship of the letters of the alphabet. For example, the letter t makes the sound /t/.

Piaget, Jean—created a theory of cognitive development based on observations of his own children. He proposed a stage theory of cognitive development from sensorimotor to formal operational. Believed that cognitive development led to language development.

Planning—the process of selecting what will be taught (task analysis), how it will be taught (teacher strategies) and what student behaviors are expected (outcomes).

Portfolio—a collection of student work over time. Different types of portfolios are used. Some are showcase portfolios of best work; some are collections of all work over a given time. Teachers use portfolios as part of authentic assessment to look at student growth over time.

Glossary of Important TExES Terms

Portfolio assessment—using the work in a students portfolio as part of the assessment process.

Positive reinforcement—a process of rewarding behaviors that are desirable. Often students are given M&Ms or stars for good behavior. This is a form of positive reinforcement.

Practitioner—another name for a certified teacher.

Presentation software—software such as Power Point® by Microsoft that is designed for showing charts, graphs, pictures, and movie clips. It assists in presenting information to a large audience.

Probing questions—questions that are asked after a student response in an effort to get the student to give additional information or to think at a deeper level. For example, a probing question might be, "What makes you think that?"

Problem solving—the process of using analysis, synthesis and evaluation to solve a problem or find a solution. It is a form of higher-level thinking.

Professional development—often referred to as in-service education, professional development is continuing education for teachers while they are employed.

Professional Development and Appraisal System (PDAS)—The system in Texas for evaluating teacher performance. Texas Education Code 21.351.

Programmed instruction—instruction that students work through at their own pace. The instruction can be electronic or print-based.

Progressivism—an educational philosophy eschewing "learning by doing." This philosophy was popularized by John Dewey.

Prompting questions—questions that guide students to a correct answer through the use of cues or prompts, especially after an incorrect response. For example, " You say that the area is found by adding up all the sides of a table, but isn't that the same as the perimeter? Think about using the length and width, what would you do to find the area of a room for laying carpet?"

Public Law 94-142—a federal law requiring all schools receiving federal funds to provide an education in the least restrictive environment to all disabled students. This law was the beginning of special education as we know it today.

Pull-out programs—programs that remove special needs children from the regular classroom for special instruction. For example, reading recovery is a pull-out program.

Random Access Memory (RAM)—RAM is the most common type of computer memory, and it's where the computer stores system software, programs, and data you are currently using. It's formally called dynamic RAM (DRAM) because it's volatile, that is, the contents are lost when you turn off the computer (or crash). It's pronounced ram and measured in megabytes.

Read Only Memory (ROM)—basic, permanent information that tells computers specific things such as how to load up the operating system when you turn it on.

Reality therapy (Glasser)—a behavior therapy proposed by Glasser that teaches individuals to become responsible for their actions. It uses an interview procedure called a "Glasser Interview." It begins, "What is the problem? How is that helping you learn?"

Reciprocal teaching—a teaching strategy that teaches students to "think like a teacher." Teachers model asking questions about material read. Then, the student takes the role of the teacher and asks questions about the next section of the text to the teacher.

Redirecting—if a student fails to give a complete response, the teacher may ask another student, "Ben what do you think?" This is redirecting.

Reflective listening—the process of listening and summarizing a student's response to indicate it was heard and understood.

Reflective teaching—a teacher who thinks about and analyzes his or her own teaching performance in an effort to improve his or her instruction.

Regular classroom—the traditional classroom composed of regular students rather than classrooms designed for special populations.

Remediation—from the root word remedy, instruction designed to assist students who are having difficulty in school. Tutoring is one form of remediation.

Reteach—the process of teaching a lesson in a different way to students who do not master the original instructional objective.

Role playing—for a deeper understanding of a concept, students act out roles. For example, student may role play the making of a law.

Rote learning—memorizing information as opposed to learning it in way that could be discussed or explained.

Rubric—guidelines for accomplishing a task and including examples of both good and poor results.

Glossary of Important TExES Terms

Scaffolding—strategies used to bridge gaps between what students know and new content that will be taught. It involves teacher guidance and gradually giving more responsibility to the student as learning occurs.

Schema (singular); schemata (plural)—cognitive organization of information that is learned. Students build concepts and form generalizations based on the way new knowledge is stored as schemata.

Self-concept—the mental image one has of oneself.

Self-directed learning—the ability to learn something without direct instruction from a teacher. The goal of education is to prepare all students to become self-directed learners.

Self-efficacy—the belief a person has in himself or herself to be successful.

Self-fulfilling prophecy—a strong belief that becomes a fact because biased thinking. For example, when told that a group of poor learners were bright, the students scored higher because the teacher believed, incorrectly, that the students were bright. The opposite can also be true. Good learners do poorly because the teacher believes that they are poor students.

Semantic mapping—a variety of strategies designed to show how key words or concepts are related to one another through graphic representations. Clusters, webs, and concept maps are forms of semantic mapping.

Simulation—an imitative representation of a system or situation. Simulations allow students to participate in an activity without the risks. For example, students learn about the Supreme Court by presenting a simulation of the event. Often simulations involve role playing.

Site-based decision making—brings the decision making process to the school. It is often associated with terms such as: decentralization, restructuring, site-based management, school-based management, participatory decision making, school-based autonomy.

Site-based management—decisions about managing a school are determined by a committee at the school. Decisions can be made based on the students' needs at that school rather than having one rule for all schools in a district.

Skinner, B.F.—a behaviorist psychologist. His system of behaviorism was built around the concept of operant conditioning using reinforcement. If a behavior is not reinforced, it becomes extinct.

Social Science—a branch of science that deals with the institutions and functioning of human society and with the interpersonal relationships of individuals as members of society. Education is a branch of social science.

Socioeconomic status (SES)—a composite of five equally weighted, standardized components: father's education, mother's education, family income, father's occupation, and household items. The terms high, middle, and low SES refer to the upper, middle two, and lower quartiles of the weighted SES composite index distribution.

Special Education—classes for students (such as the handicapped) with special educational needs. In the 1960s, advocates sought a federal role in providing leadership and funding for efforts to provide a free appropriate public education, or FAPE, to children with disabilities. Congress took a step toward this in 1966 when it established the Bureau for Education of the Handicapped under Title VI of the Elementary and Secondary Schools Act (ESEA). For the complete history of Special Education refer to http://ericec.org/faq/spedhist.html

Spreadsheet—an accounting program for a computer; also the ledger layout modeled by such a program.

Standardized test—a test developed by a commercial publisher that compares students results to either a norming sample of individuals (norm-referenced tests) or compares results to a set of criteria (criterion-referenced tests). The SAT is a norm-referenced test and the TAKS and the TExES are criterion-referenced tests.

State Board of Educator Certification (SBEC)—the state agency responsible for the certification of Texas teachers.

State Board of Education (SBOC)—the elected group of people that approves all public school rules and regulations.

State-wide initiative—a program that is adopted for all schools in a state. The initiative is usually for remedial purposes and is funded by the state government. No Child Left Behind is a state-wide initiative and also a federal initiative.

Structuring the lesson—the framework a teacher uses to present a lesson. For direct instruction the teacher may used a Madeline Hunter Plan to structure the lesson. That would include: Objective, Rationale, Purpose, Motivating Event, Modeling, Guided Practice, Independent Practice, and Closure. For an inquiry lesson, the structure would be student directed. The framework might include Engage, Explore, Explain, Elaborate, and Evaluate.

Summative assessment—an assessment that is done after a lesson is taught. It is used to evaluate learning and to guide instruction and the curriculum.

Superintendent (TEC 11.201)—the chief executive officer of a school district.

Supervisor—in public schools, each program, such as Special Education, has a person in charge of those programs in the district. They are usually situated in the central office and report to the superintendent.

Glossary of Important TExES Terms

Synthesis—a cognitive process that is one form of higher level thinking. It involves putting ideas or pieces together to form a whole idea. For example, by putting together the legislative branch, the executive branch and the judicial branch of government, one understands the concept of a democratic system of government.

Task analysis—breaking a task into the smaller subskills. For example, prior to writing a research report, students must be able to select a topic, formulate questions, read to find information, summarize information, and create and introduction and a conclusion. These are all subtasks of library research.

Taxonomy—a system of classification. In education, a taxonomy often is used to classify educational skills.

Teachable moment—usually an unplanned event that lends itself to teaching something to students. For example, when the Twin Towers were destroyed by terrorists on 9/11/2001, many teachers used this unplanned event to discuss terrorism and threats to the American way of life.

Teacher certification—a certificate awarded to individuals after completion of specific state requirements. The certificate certifies that the individual has the knowledge and skills to be a Texas teacher. Certificates cover many different areas such as Early Childhood thorough fourth grade, fourth grade through eighth grade, and eighth grade through twelfth grade. At the upper grades the certificate is usually in a specific content area, such as language arts or science.

Teacher expectation—a teacher's belief about how successful a student will be in school. Texas teachers should have high expectations for all students in the class.

Teaching style—the manner in which a teacher presents instruction. Some teachers are very teacher-centered and use direct instruction; other teachers are very student-centered and used inquiry. Some teachers are eclectic and use a mixture of both styles.

Texas Assessment of Knowledge and Skills (TAKS)—the state mandated assessment for ensuring school accountability for student achievement. The TAKS covers the content in the Texas Curriculum, the TEKS.

Texas Education Agency (TEA)—the state agency responsible for overseeing public education in Texas. The Commissioner of Education and his or her staff follow the rules for education set forth in the Texas Education Code.

Texas Education Code (TEC)—statutes passed by the Texas Legislature in Senate Bill 1 in 1995 that governs Texas public schools.

Texas Essential Knowledge and Skills (TEKS)—the state curriculum.

Texas Examination of Educator Standards (TExES)—the state licensing examination for new teachers or new teachers to Texas. It replaced the ExCET, the previous exam.

Thematic teaching—organizing instruction around a central theme such as "Systems." Often the instruction crosses between disciplines and is "integrated thematic teaching." Often language arts, science, social studies, and math are integrated into a team of teachers that teach a central theme to a group of students.

Time-out—a form of discipline that places a child away from the other students (in time-out) for a short amount of time. The concept is that the child is misbehaving in order to get attention. Therefore by putting the child in time-out the child is not rewarded by getting attention. This is used often with young children. The time-out location can simply be a chair.

Title I (formerly Chapter I)—Title I of the Elementary and Secondary Act of 1965. This federal program is a remedial program for poor and disadvantaged students.

Title VI (Civil Rights Act)—Title VI of the Civil Rights Act of 1964. Any school receiving federal funds may not discriminate against students on the basis of race, color, or national origin.

Title VII (Bilingual Education Act)—Title VII of the Elementary and Secondary Act. Created in 1984 it provides funding for non–English-speaking students. It is better known as the Bilingual Education Act.

Title IX—a federal program established in 1972 that bars gender discrimination in schools receiving federal funds.

Unit—a group of lessons planned around a central topic.

Unit plan—the written plan for teaching a unit. The plan usually looks at broad areas to be covered over a week or longer. It usually does not contain the daily lesson plans.

Uniform Resource Locator (URL)—the global address of documents and other resources on the World Wide Web. The first part of the address indicates what protocol to use, and the second part specifies the IP address or the domain name where the resource is located.

Value-centered education—a teaching program that focuses on teaching values to students.

Verbal reinforcement—using positive comments when students are doing something well. The idea is to use positive comments to cause a response to occur more often.

Wait time—a highly recommended practice for teachers. The teacher waits 5 to 7 seconds after asking a question to allow all students to have time to think about the question and formulate an answer. The teacher then calls on a student to answer a question. Teachers who do not use wait time do not get the same level of cognitive responses.

Glossary of Important TExES Terms

Whole-class discussion—a discussion procedure that involves all students in the class discussing a topic as opposed to discussion in small groups.

Whole-language approach—a philosophical approach to teaching reading using complete texts rather than excerpts and having students respond in writing and through discussion to the text.

Wireless Fidelity (WIFI)—otherwise known as Wireless Networking.

With-it-ness—a skill that teachers should develop. It means that the teacher is aware of everything that is happening in the classroom. A teacher having with-it-ness can continue teaching a lesson while walking over to keep a child on task or hand a note to a child.

Zone of proximal development (Vygotsky)—Vygotsky proposed that rather than being too easy or too hard, instruction should be in the zone of proximal development. This zone is just a bit harder than what the child can do alone. Instruction in this zone will provide growth, but not frustration, if the child is instructed with assistance from the teacher.

Code of Ethics and Standard Practices for Texas Educators

19 TEXAS ADMINISTRATIVE CODE CHAPTER 247

Statutory Authority: The provisions of this Chapter 247 are authorized under Texas Education Code, 21.041 (b)(8), which requires the State Board for Educator Certification (SBEC) to propose rules providing for the adoption, enforcement, and amendment of an educators' code of ethics, and Section 63(1) of the conforming amendments to Senate Bill 1 (74th Legislature, 1995), which provides for a code of ethics proposed by the SBEC and adopted by the State Board of Education.

STATEMENT OF PURPOSE

The Texas educator shall comply with standard practices and ethical conduct toward students, professional colleagues, school officials, parents, and members of the community and shall safeguard academic freedom. The Texas educator, in maintaining the dignity of the profession, shall respect and obey the law, demonstrate personal integrity, and exemplify honesty. The Texas educator, in exemplifying ethical relations with colleagues, shall extend just and equitable treatment to all members of the profession. The Texas educator, in accepting a position of public trust, shall measure success by the progress of each student toward realization of his or her potential as an effective citizen. The Texas educator, in fulfilling responsibilities in the community, shall cooperate with parents and others to improve the public schools of the community.

ENFORCEABLE STANDARDS

I. Professional Ethical Conduct, Practices, and Performance

Standard 1.1. The educator shall not knowingly engage in deceptive practices regarding official policies of the school district or educational institution.

Standard 1.2. The educator shall not knowingly misappropriate, divert, or use monies, personnel, property, or equipment committed to his or her charge for personal gain or advantage.

Standard 1.3. The educator shall not submit fraudulent requests for reimbursement, expenses, or pay.

Standard 1.4. The educator shall not use institutional or professional privileges for personal or partisan advantage.

Standard 1.5. The educator shall neither accept nor offer gratuities, gifts, or favors that impair professional judgment or to obtain special advantage. This standard shall not restrict the acceptance of gifts or tokens offered and accepted openly from students, parents, or other persons or organizations in recognition or appreciation of service.

Standard 1.6. The educator shall not falsify records, or direct or coerce others to do so.

Standard 1.7. The educator shall comply with state regulations, written local school board policies, and other applicable state and federal laws.

Standard 1.8. The educator shall apply for, accept, offer, or assign a position or a responsibility on the basis of professional qualifications.

II. Ethical Conduct Toward Professional Colleagues

Standard 2.1. The educator shall not reveal confidential health or personnel information concerning colleagues unless disclosure serves lawful professional purposes or is required by law.

Standard 2.2. The educator shall not harm others by knowingly making false statements about a colleague or the school system.

Standard 2.3. The educator shall adhere to written local school board policies and state and federal laws regarding the hiring, evaluation, and dismissal of personnel.

Standard 2.4. The educator shall not interfere with a colleague's exercise of political, professional, or citizenship rights and responsibilities.

Standard 2.5. The educator shall not discriminate against or coerce a colleague on the basis of race, color, religion, national origin, age, sex, disability, or family status.

Standard 2.6. The educator shall not use coercive means or promise of special treatment in order to influence professional decisions or colleagues.

Standard 2.7. The educator shall not retaliate against any individual who has filed a complaint with the SBEC under this chapter.

III. Ethical Conduct Toward Students

Standard 3.1. The educator shall not reveal confidential information concerning students unless disclosure serves lawful professional purposes or is required by law.

Standard 3.2. The educator shall not knowingly treat a student in a manner that adversely affects the student's learning, physical health, mental health, or safety.

Standard 3.3. The educator shall not deliberately or knowingly misrepresent facts regarding a student.

Standard 3.4. The educator shall not exclude a student from participation in a program, deny benefits to a student, or grant an advantage to a student on the basis of race, color, sex, disability, national origin, religion, or family status.

Standard 3.5. The educator shall not engage in physical mistreatment of a student.

Standard 3.6. The educator shall not solicit or engage in sexual conduct or a romantic relationship with a student.

Standard 3.7. The educator shall not furnish alcohol or illegal/unauthorized drugs to any student or knowingly allow any student to consume alcohol or illegal/unauthorized drugs in the presence of the educator.

Source Note: The provisions of this §247.2 adopted to be effective March 1, 1998, 23 TexReg 1022; amended to be effective August 22, 2002, 27 TexReg 7530.

Texas Examination for Educator Standards Competencies for the Pedagogy and Professional Responsibilities Tests EC–4, 4–8, 8–12, EC–12

Competency 001—The teacher understands human developmental processes and applies this knowledge to plan instruction and ongoing assessment that motivate students and are responsive to their developmental characteristics and needs.

Competency 002—The teacher understands student diversity and knows how to plan learning experiences and design assessments that are responsive to differences among students and that promote all students' learning.

Competency 003—The teacher understands procedures for designing effective and coherent instruction and assessment based on appropriate learning goals and objectives.

Competency 004—The teacher understands learning processes and factors that impact student learning and demonstrates this knowledge by planning effective, engaging instruction and appropriate assessments.

Competency 005—The teacher knows how to establish a classroom climate that fosters learning, equity, and excellence and uses this knowledge to create a physical and emotional environment that is safe and productive.

Competency 006—The teacher understands strategies for creating an organized and productive learning environment and for managing student behavior

Competency 007—The teacher understands and applies principles and strategies for communicating effectively in varied teaching and learning contexts.

Competency 008—The teacher provides appropriate instruction that actively engages students in the learning process.

Competency 009—The teacher incorporates the effective use of technology to plan, organize, deliver, and evaluate instruction for all students.

Competency 010—The teacher monitors student performance and achievement; provides students with timely, high-quality feedback; and responds flexibly to promote learning for all students.

Competency 011—The teacher understands the importance of family involvement in children's education and knows how to interact and communicate effectively with families.

Competency 012—The teacher enhances professional knowledge and skills by effectively interacting with other members of the educational community and participating in various types of professional activities.

Competency 013—The teacher understands and adheres to legal and ethical requirements for educators and is knowledgeable of the structure of education in Texas.

Copyright © 2003 by the Texas State Board for Educator Certification and National Evaluation Systems, Inc. (NES ®). Reprinted by permission.

List of TExES Exams Currently Available

Other tests are being developed; as of this printing, these were the available tests.

064 Superintendent: Part 1 of 2
064 Superintendent District Profile Packet: Part 2 of 2
068 Principal
100 Pedagogy and Professional Responsibilities EC–4
101 Generalist EC–4
102 Bilingual Education Supplemental EC–4
103 Bilingual Generalist EC–4
104 English as a Second Language (ESL)/Generalist EC–4
110 Pedagogy and Professional Responsibilities 4–8
111 Generalist 4–8
112 Bilingual Education Supplemental 4–8
113 English Language Arts and Reading/Social Studies 4–8
114 Mathematics/Science 4–8
115 Mathematics 4–8
116 Science 4–8
117 English Language Arts and Reading 4–8
118 Social Studies 4–8
119 Bilingual Generalist 4–8
120 English as a Second Language (ESL)/Generalist 4–8
130 Pedagogy and Professional Responsibilities 8–12
131 English Language Arts and Reading 8–12

132 Social Studies 8–12
133 History 8–12
135 Mathematics 8–12
136 Science 8–12
137 Physical Science 8–12
138 Life Science 8–12
139 Technology Applications 8–12
140 Chemistry 8–12
141 Computer Science 8–12
142 Technology Applications EC–12
143 Mathematics/Physics 8–12
150 School Librarian
151 Reading Specialist
152 School Counselor
153 Educational Diagnostician
154 English as a Second Language Supplemental (ESL)
155 Speech 8–12
156 Journalism 8–12
157 Health EC–12
158 Physical Education EC–12
160 Pedagogy and Professional Responsibilities EC–12
161 Special Education EC–12
162 Gifted and Talented Supplemental
163 Special Education Supplemental
170 Pedagogy and Professional Responsibilities for Trade and Industrial Education 8–12
171 Technology Education 6–12
172 Agricultural Science and Technology 6–12
173 Health Science Technology Education 8–12
174 Mathematics/Physical Science/Engineering 8–12
175 Marketing Education 8–12
177 Music EC–12
179 Dance 8–12
180 Theatre EC–12
181 Deaf and Hard of Hearing
182/183 Visually Impaired/Braille
184 American Sign Language (ASL)